CONTRADICTION, SELF-CONTRADICTION AND COLLECTIVE CHOICE

Contradiction, Self-contradiction and Collective Choice

New directions for commodities and characteristics analysis

MICHAEL J. RYAN
University of Hull

Avebury
Aldershot · Brookfield USA · Hong Kong · Singapore · Sydney

Published by
Avebury
Ashgate Publishing Company Limited
Gower House
Croft Road
Aldershot
Hants GU11 3HR
England

Ashgate Publishing Company
Old Post Road
Brookfield
Vermont 05036
USA

A CIP catalogue record for this book is available from the British Library and the US Library of Congress.

ISBN 1 85628 380 1

Printed and Bound in Great Britain by
Athenaeum Press Ltd, Newcastle upon Tyne.

Contents

Foreword

The central purposes of this work are to provide new kinds of analysis relating to individual and to collective economic decisionmaking in ways both motivated by fundamental critiques of existing and standard approaches to such isssues, and motivating very substantially enhanced roles for linear and goal programming analyses and associated duality results.

With these perspectives, after an introductory chapter, the book continues with two chapters (2 and 4) devoted to detailed critiqes of existing and fundamentally deterministically and consistency oriented approaches to micro and macroeconomic theory in general, and to general equilibrium theory, to collective choice theory and to standard approaches to monetary theory and inflation in particular.

Complementary developments in chapters 3 and 5 will motivate new and fundamental roles respectively for standard units, prominently including standard monetary units, and for linear and goal programmming principles and processes and associated linear independence and duality results.

With these five chapters providing essential motivation and background, in Chapters 6 and 7 I will construct different kinds of essentially uncertainty based and goal oriented analyses and results. This is done in ways which extend Lancaster's characteristics approach to individual choice behaviours and provide new motivations for regulatory and self regulatory instruments, including various kinds of laws, taxes and subsidies. These analyses and results will also establish and emphasize novel and constructive roles for recognitions and exploitatiions of relative uncertainty and incompleteness principles and processes, of kinds which may be more familiar to physicists than to economists.

As well as being of interest in their own right, it will become evident that these formulations can also provide new kinds of motivation for spatial and intertemporal linear and goal programming models in general. More particularly they will provide straightforward motivations for the three interrelated classes of models focussing respectively on intertemporal and interregional planning and regulation, limited liability and corporate decisionmaking under uncertainty, and non-renewable resources, inflation and uncertainty, which constitute the subject matter of the final three chapters of the book.

Apart from its interest to researchers in these various fields, I believe that the book will be of interest, too, to teachers of advanced undergraduate courses in micro and macro economic theory, including general equilibrium theory and collective choice theory, and that it will also be useful in connection with courses devoted to advanced topics in mathematical programming theory and applications.

1 Overview

In the spring of 1971 I read a paper by Charnes, Clower and Kortanek titled "Effective Control through Coherent Decentralization with preemptive Goals" {3}. If there is a single published reference which I associate with the analytical content of what follows, it is that paper; not so much because of its content in detail, but because of the ideas which a particular part of it evoked.

As its title suggests, the paper gives a technical exposition on decentralization. Two classes of cases are considered explicitly. In the first an overall nonlinear programming problem is expressed via the speci -fication of an objective functional as a sum of strictly concave functions subject to linear constraints. The authors then demonstrate the possibility of decentralization of decision-making via prices to the problems specified as maximizations relating to each concave function separately subject to linear constraints.

The second class of cases is the maximization of linear functionals subject to linear constraints. The authors demonstrate that, in general, it will be necessary to introduce explicit preemptive goals if *decentralized* maximization problems are together to be consistent with (coherent with) a single *centralized* plan (optimization of the overall problem). This second class of cases caught my attention and, in particular, the discussion and resolution there of problems which had first arisen in connection with the "Birch Paper Case", where a decentralization procedure had yielded a net value of zero for the coefficients of the objective function of a decentralized problem.

I noticed : i) that, in the nonlinear (concave) class of cases, it was apparently straightforwardly possible to decentralize only once from a centralized problem to groups of decentralized problems associated with the individual concave functions, whereas in the linear class of cases, it would apparently be possible, by reapplying the same techniques, to decentralize again and again (decentralize from decentralized problems...) ; ii) that apparently a centralized problem could be as if composed from decentralized problems and as if decomposable to them ; iii) that apparently in general, in linear cases, a decentralization problem could itself be regarded as a problem decentralized from a higher level and, in particular, a centralized problem might be seen as a problem decentralized from a higher level. In consequence, (incomplete) information concerning the possibly otherwise unknown structure of a still higher (unknown) problem/ (unknown) problems could apparently be gained.

I was aware of the wide range and the considerable explanatory power of linear programming methods, particularly from my awareness of the work which Charnes and Charnes and Cooper had already done. In particular, I was aware that they had shown that any regularized linear programming problem could be represented as a game.[1] In this context of centralization and decentralization, the *language* of games suggested coalitions, and in particular an emphasis upon processes of formation of coalitions - of larger problems from smaller ones -and decentralization and decomposition of coalitions into players/ groups (coalitions) of players.

Depending on the sequence chosen, this would suggest emphasis upon *processes* of formation and/ or of decomposition of coalitions.

I was aware, too, that although the language of games was emotive and powerful (e.g. coalitions, players, plays, payoffs, strategies, coop -erative, non-cooperative), the empirical plausibility of the theoretical results which had been attained appeared to be slight, and in that sense disappointing – results including those developed in, and stemming from, the pioneering work of von Neumann and Morgernstern {4}. Also, the information requirements for complete specifications of games appeared typically to be implausibly great.

Here though, the context suggested games in extensive form and, informed by observation of these authors' resolution of difficulties associated with classes of cases kin to the Birch Paper Case, games of complete *and as if* incomplete information.

For me the striking feature of this resolution of the Birch Paper Case was its apparent implications for information. In context apparently a linear specification could cause circumstances to arise, *because* that specification was linear, in which a decentralized unit apparently *even when given* complete information concerning prices, costs, technologies and output quantities relevant to its part of a centralized optimum, *would not/could not* choose that optimum.

It appeared that this (logical) difficulty could be resolved by the introduction of preemptive goals interrelating centralized and decen -tralized problems. But the specification of these goals appeared to require explicitly *more than* and/or *less than* complete information, in the sense of complete information relevant to a centralized optimum.

This appeared to be quite evidently paradoxical in its implications. Apparently, as if complete consistency (coherence) could require different information than that associated with complete consistency.

Information might then appear complete,if incomplete, (more than/ less than complete?) and incomplete, if complete!

It appeared, too, that such implications had been forced (made evident) *because* the centralized, and so the consequent decentralized, problems had been given "linear" specifications.

If stated in a different way, such apparent paradoxes do not appear *logically* paradoxical. For example this observation suggested possibilities of games of incomplete information played as *as if* of complete information or, more particularly, games directed toward securing more complete information via exchanges of information. This suggested a motivation for purposive communication between individuals (players), the purpose being to secure individually and/ or mutually preferred outcomes - including the formation/ decomposition of coalitions and the determination of payoffs, where players here in context might be persons, but might more generally be persons, objects or organisations (e.g. divisions of firms, governments, government agencies, etc.).

Apparently carefully crafted "linear" specifications could *guarantee* such interpretations *because* they were linear and could thereby secure as if determinate *and* as if indeterminate outcomes over any number of levels in the game, as well as at a given level – the former apparently offering evident advantages over an a priori specification of apparently more explicitly non-linear (e.g.continuous and quasiconcave) objective functionals.

This in turn suggested that "linear" methods may be more general *and* more powerful than more overtly nonlinear ones. Also, games suggested not only players and bargaining between relatively decentralized players and a relatively centralized player or group of players, but also, for example, bargaining between players and a relatively centralized player to *create* (extinguish?) a centralized/ decentralized player (players) composed/ decomposed from or by them.

More subtly, a context of games in conjunction with linear programming formulations suggested duality and dual relations, not only between relatively decentralized players and a relatively centralized player, but between relatively decentralized players and each other. It also suggested questions pertaining to probability, its meaning and its implications. Finally, not only would "linear" programming formulations apparently offer such possibilities and interpretations, but access to a vast array of established solution algorithms and associated applicactions.

My objective here is to offer some constructive answers to questions and issues raised within the preceding remarks. It will become apparent that it is inherent in the nature of the logics which generate and govern questions and answers that those logics are themselves incomplete – that those answers will be incomplete if seeming as if complete and may be complete if seeming as if incomplete. Recognition of this has presented formidable difficulties to me as an author and will present difficulties to you in reading what I have written.

The focus of the preceding remarks is a reference to a particular case – the Birch Paper Case. It is my intention to continue to proceed from particular examples to more general analyses and principles (on occasion, I think, completely general principles of, for examples, physics, mathematics and philosophy), with the emphasis upon a search not simply for solutions, but for constructive solutions and constructive processes of solution and, within these classes, for solutions which can, at least in principle, be both logically and empirically validated.

One approach to empirical work has been to develop or to employ advanced statistical techniques in order to attempt to detect and to predict systematic stochastic relations between variables, or, as related activities, to employ established techniques to seek to replicate established results, or to adopt a technique used in one application in order to obtain further results in another.

As an example: in the late 60's there was a rash of econometric work directed toward the detection of systematic relations between the profitability of enterprises and their size. In the spring of 1970, John Tzoannos and I used a technique which had been published in a then recent issue of *Econometrica* for pooling cross-section and time series data to see whether or not significant results could be established for British shipping companies. As data we used numbers culled from their annual accounts which were then filed at Companies House. Our results were, I think, unexceptional and appeared as a Discussion Paper.[2]

At the time – and since – to me the most striking feature of this work was the fact that, throughout the period which we were studying, British shipping companies had exemption from certain provisions of the UK

Companies Act via the Shipping Companies Exemption Order (1948), exemption relating to the reporting of capital depreciation methods employed in drawing up the company accounts.

Apparently, the *purpose* of that legislation was to make it difficult or impossible for "foreign" rivals in particular to deduce any systematic information concerning their actual profitability. It seemed, then, that this law had been made explicitly as if to ensure that any exercise such as the one which we were conducting would be partially or wholly invalid, by enabling companies to vary their depreciation allowances (and so reported profit figures) in ways purposively designed by them to obscure the means whereby reported figures were attained.

Further, it appeared that it would be wholly in the spirit of that legislation if, were systematic relations between reported profit and aactual profit attained by us (or by anyone else), then the law would be changed to invalidate any predictive power imminent in that discovery.

As a related point, the existence of this legislation itself suggested that the omission of foreign shipping companies (all foreign shipping companies? all determinants of the profitabilities of all foreign shipping companies?) from our study would have been significant.

More generally, if we had found convincing (statistical) evidence that larger companies were more profitable than smaller ones, and profitability was the criterion of performance, the question would arise: why do smaller companies survive and, in particular, why is the largest company not then the only company? Conversely, if smaller companies were more profitable and profitability was the criterion, why would large companies grow? We did not find such evidence.

My purpose in citing the preceding example was to illustrate a fortiori the general point that there may be little purpose in constructing and/ or conducting statistical exercises if it is known that the participants supplying the data would see advantage in misrepresenting their position in ways unknown to the analyst, but known to them.

Indeed the preceding remarks suggest that it would not in any case be possible for any participant to represent completely and objectively the data pertaining even to its own decisions. It is significant here, too, that in this shipping context governments, companies, and an analyst/ analysts all have distinct roles according to which groups of companies may rationally cooperate in order to secure legislation designed both to condition and be conditioned by interactions with others.

The example which follows is presented here primarily because within it is an example of a statistical technique which, although arguably entirely appropriate in this application, apparently yielded implications which at first seem strictly incredible.

In 1971-72 I was associated with a project funded by the US National Institutes of Health to study the feasibility of Centralized Book Processing for Medical Libraries. There were five libraries involved in the project. The essential motivation for it was the idea that if there proved to be a significant level of duplication of acquisitions by these libraries, then there might be a significant (cost) advantage in processing these acquisitions centrally.

At an early stage it became apparent that at that time cost was not of paramount importance, since the head librarians did not then see their budgets as severely restricted; that centralized processing would introduce significant delays, and that; with the advent of cataloguing in publication (CIP), the advantages which would arise from a (necessarily standardized) centralized cataloguing and book processing facility would already be at least largely prempted. It seemed then, in these circumstances, that centralization of book processing would not be a superior alternative to the existing decentralized arrangement.

Evidently, in any serious quantitative appraisal, the actual degree of duplication could be significant. Accordingly, we selected several medical classifications and sampled four libraries' acquisitions (the fifth was a dental library). It was possible to gain information concerning the total number of books published in the preceding year in these classifications, and so it was possible to see whether or not these four libraries' acquisitions in these classifications had been consistent with an hypothesis that each library's acquisitions had been selected as if (independently) at random from that population (of titles) by reference to the number of duplicates, triplicates and quadriplicates. As it happened, these numbers appeared to be consistent with this hypothesis.

At first this result seemed incredible, for interpreting apparent randomness in selection as evidence of *lack of* skill on the part of librarians, it was apparently possible to argue that professional librarians had been acting as if unskilled.

On further reflection and further enquiry, it seemed to me that the opposite interpretation was more plausible ; that apparent randomness within designated classifications was evidence of (possibly misplaced) professional expertise, the simplest grounds for this view being that, in relation to books/ monographs as distinct from journals/ serials, librarians appeared to be primarily concerned that they provide collections for (unknown) future users, rather than exclusively or even primarily for current ones.

Apparent randomness, too, would be consistent with attempts to keep acquisitions/ book processing operations more even over the (financial year and to secure breadth in these classifications for collections, rather than, for example, acquiring all or most books from one, or a subset of publishers' lists early in the year, or acquiring by purchase only the lowest priced monographs.

In the present context, it seems significant that : i) if maximal duplication was of most significance, then apparent indifference as to particular books selected (professional impartiality?) might be used by an analyst to suggest *maximal* duplication between collections as a consequence of a policy directed toward securing maximal savings from centralized book processing! ; ii) if completeness of the collections within the selected classifications was considered to be desirable, if collectively attainable, and greater completeness if not, then apparent indifference as to books selected for individual collections might be used by an analyst to suggest a centralized and coordinated acquisitions policy directed toward securing maximal collective coverage of these classifications.

In the former case, duplications would apparently be increased and coverage reduced, whereas in the latter, apparently duplication would be reduced, but coverage increased relative to an apparently random policy.

As it happened, there appeared to be evidence that the latter policy of coordinated *acquisitions* would not be inconsistent with the individual libraries' objectives for, at the time, they were engaged in a process of establishing an interlibrary loan facility between themselves and libraries in neighbouring states (the TALON network).

The effect of such a network is to increase effective duplication via loans, most effectively if collections are as different as possible within areas of common interest until exhaustive collections are individually/ collectively attained. (I remark that each library was also linked via off-line computer terminals to the National Library of Medicine at Bethesda, Maryland).[3]

Within the context of the preceding developments, consider now four collections of numbers of "different books" x_1, x_2, x_3, x_4 and, for purposes of illustration, let $x_1 + x_2 + x_3 + x_4 = x$ and $x_1 = x_2 = x_3 = x_4$, with the collective collection being exhaustive within the chosen classifications so that there is no effective duplication. Now imagine that these four (different) collections of "different books" are arranged geometrically as in Fig.1 below.

It will be of considerable significance here that the four librarians considered above were not geometrically so arranged and that the term library generally connotes buildings and associated facilities, including storage and circulation facilities, as well as acquisitions and processing facilities, while here collections have been demonimated only relative to (different) collections of numbers related to "different books". My purpose in what immediately follows is to indicate, in a preliminary way, that implications of this constructive illustration can be discovered to be considerably richer than might at first seem apparent.

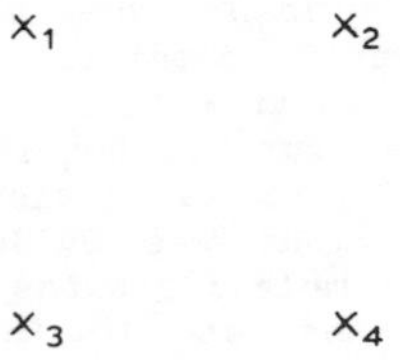

Figure 1.1

Imagine a *union catalogue* x and consider an interlibrary loan. Apparently, if a collection does not contain a book, then the *initial* specification indicates not only that another collection will have it, but *which* other collection will have it. Accordingly, let collection 3 request a book not contained in its collection of the union catalogue and let the request (question) be directed relative to the collection which does contain it (for purposes of constructive illustration, collection 1) and let the "different book" then be transmitted to collection 3 :

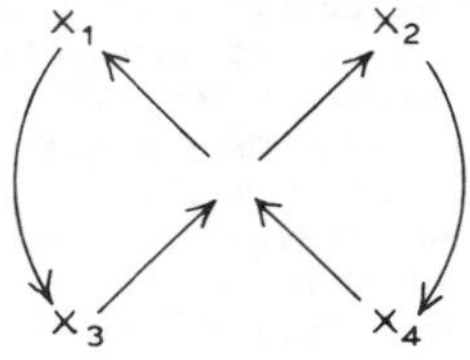

Figure 1.2

Here a request relative to a different book via the union catalogue apparently *generates* a different book. Also a consequence of the request is ultimately that collection 1 has one less book and *then* collection 3 one more "different book", an apparent difference of two ("different books"). *But*, apparently, too, relative to collection 1, the system gains *the same* book (relative to collection 1) *as* collection 1 loses and then (library) collection 3 gains, and the system loses, *the same* ("different") book as the system gained relative to collection 1. Apparently, too, a request from collection 3 for a different book not yet in its collection *predicted* the same book at the union catalogue as would be lost to collection 1 and transmitted to collection 3.

Again, for purposes of illustration, imagine a similar sequence initiated with a request from collection 4 for a "different book" which happens to be in (belong to) the collection of library 2 via the union catalogue. Apparently, then, collection 2 loses a "different book" relative to itself and collection 4 then gains that same different book (again an apparent difference of two) in a sequence apparently logically similar to , but different from, the previous case.

Evidently these sequences could be interpreted as sequences of losses or as sequences of gains and as sequences of losses *and* sequences of gains.

For example, collection 3 apparently loses relative to itself as if in order to gain communication with the union catalogue, which apparently loses relative to itself as if in order to gain communication with collection 1, which then apparently loses relative to itself as if in order that (library) collection 3 gain ...

Notice that these communications are of different orders. For example, communications (questions/ answers) relative to "different books" and communications relating and relative to different collections *of* "different books" (different libraries).

With reference to the diagrams and the preceding motivations and interpretations, it might appear that, if the above sequences were repeated, collections 1 and 2 would ultimately lose all of their books – these collections would be reduced to nothing (denominated at the order of different books), unless the "different books" were returned.

In this context reasonable conditions associated with (preconditions for) the establishment of a union catalogue and associated borrowing and lending facilities might seem to be : i) that the different books belong to different collections and ; ii) that these collections have implicitly/ explicitly agreed to lend "different books" from their collections, if available, on request.

A sustained sequence whereby one or more collections were systematically reduced and one or more systematically effectively increased by loans (to be subsequently returned?) would not conflict with this, if the agreement allowed it. But any process whereby any of the quantities x_i were reduced by an explicit or implicit process of *expropriate* by another collection would appear to do so, whereas a behaviour consistent with the appropriation of parts of/ all of collections *to* other collections as if as gifts, transmissions of and/ or exchanges of property rights would not appear to do so.

More technically, a collection with lending and borrowing facilities is sometimes termed an *open* collection and, without, a *closed* collection. In this terminology, lending and borrowing (requests to/ agreements to lend/ borrow?) can apparently open and not lending/ borrowing can close a collection at the order of "different books".

The preceding analyses and developments focus on exchanges relative to a union catalogue. Now consider processes whereby such a catalogue might be generated. Consider two possibilities as particular examples : acquisition and processing by a central facility, and acquisitions and processing by relatively decentralized libraries.

In the former case, apparently a union catalogue relative to those collections could be generated as different books were acquired and processed and individual/ union? cataloguing information and acquired different books transmitted to the libraries.

If this were the procedure from the start, all collections would apparently be as if satellite (information sources) of a central acquisition and processing unit (information source) with the central unit the initial source (relative to the satellites) of newly processed "different books". Geometrically, deliveries to the satellites from the central collection might be represented schematically as in Fig.3.

If acquisitions decisions were made centrally, the central unit would (logically?) be required to act as if deciding to which collection to send each different processed book.

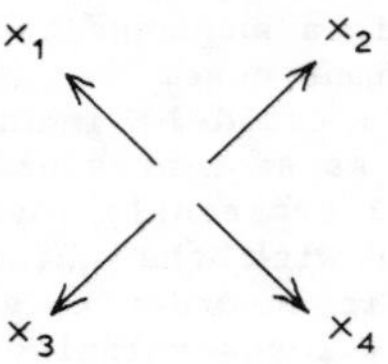

Figure 1.3

If acquisition decisions were decentralized, and acquisitions processed centrally, then apparently communication with the central unit would logically precede acquisition. Allocation of "different books", if acquired, would, in that sense, also be as if predetermined.

Decentralized acquisition and processing could apparently generate a union catalogue if books were acquired and processed at the decentralized (satellite) collections and then a centralized unit informed.

Schematically, information concerning newly acquired "different books" would be sent from an acquiring unit to the centralized unit :

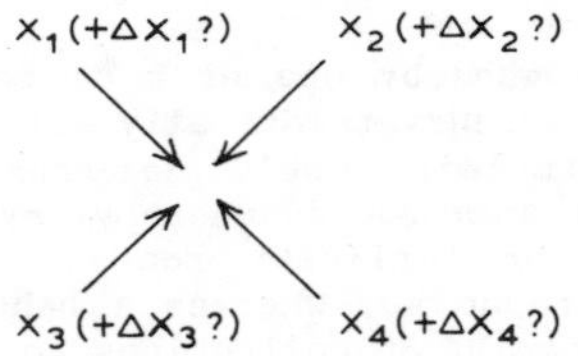

Figure 1.4

Recall now that librarians appeared to prefer decentralized processing to centralized processing on the grounds that the latter would introduce (greater) delay in the availability of acquisitions to (users of) their collections. Notice, in this regard, that the union catalogue is here formed after acquisition of new books from outside the system, establishing a (quite natural?) priority for the potential users of the acquiring collection over those of their collections via the union catalogue once formed.

Decentralization of decisions in this way apparently, in principle, enables a collection to act as if choosing *how many*, if any, different books to make available for loan to others via the union catalogue ; to decide the *degree* of openness/ closedness/ accessibility/ inaccessibility/ privateness/ publicness of (different parts of) the collection – how many, if any, different books to retain in a closed collection (not available to, and not necessarily known to other collections and their potential users) and how many to make available to (designated?) potential users via a union catalogue.

Apparently a complete union catalogue with full loan facilities would necessitate notification of all "different books" in all collections. Could a union catalogue be known to be complete or would it necessarily be incomplete (underestimated?) as long as decentralized collections were acquiring and notifying "different books"? If a union catalogue were to be composed by a centralized acquisitions and processing facility, could it be known to be complete or would it overestimate the number of different books available to the individual collections for circulation as long as different books were being acquired to be made available for circulation to the different collections?

As a further point, if a union catalogue were augmented by information from relatively decentralized collections (libraries?), then augmentation could apparently come about by changing or changes in the status of an existing "different book", groups of "different books" and/ or collections of "different books", in the collection of collections of "different books", as well as by the acquisition of additional ones.

It might seem reasonable (logical) : i) that a collection (library) would not request a different book of a union catalogue/ other collection if already available in its own and ; ii) that a collection (library) might offer another collection/ other collections use of its different books if already in its own and ; iii) putting the two preceding remarks together, that neither requests nor loans would be made between two collections if the same "different book" was available in both collections, even though offers to loan may be made.

The extent of loan activity would appear then to depend on *variety* between collections. Here there is apparently a strict sense in which loan activity could *reduce* variety, while depending upon it, both literally via the same "different book" being transmitted between otherwise varied collections,and by (consequent?) learning relative to this *same* "different book."

Seemingly processes of transmission of information by loans would ultimately lead, in some sense, to increasing *sameness* among collections, at least in part, consequent upon those processes.

It might seem logical, too, that,if there were only two collections, then a request by one would be directed to the other only if a "different book" had not been available in its own collection. But then all requests would apparently pertain to *relatively unknown* "different books" and apparently could only be met if available in the other collection, and then only if that other collection were able to act as if choosing to/ deciding to/ being required to meet that request.

If there were only two collections, and one offered the potential loan of its different book/ different books to the other, apparently the availability of a different book/ different books would become known to that other *and* the (degree of) willingness to loan them. If that offer were reciprocated by a different offer, both collections, at the order of offers, would become (more) known to the other – each would and/ or could apparently gain *knowledge* relative to the other's collection by accepting offers of a "different book"/ "different books".

Thus,if offers preceded requests,and offers were made as if to secure the other's gain, *both* could gain. If, in sequence, requests preceded offers, apparently both would/ could gain knowledge, via requests, of what the other did *not* have in its collection, but could only meet these requests if available in its collection (gain knowledge of what the other does/ did *not* have until a request is met).

Notice that a process founded upon/ initiated by certain kinds of offers might be interpreted as a process founded upon/ initiated by a principle of *altruism* - a principle whereby collections act (and so could act?) as if preferring another's (others') potential gain *via* their own loss – a principle whereby apparently collections act as if preferring another's potential gain *to* their own loss. Apparently, if this principle were reciprocated, then each could gain and so both (all?) could gain.

These remarks suggest that algorithmic processes could be possible with sequences of offer → acceptance → offer → acceptance → ... leading to consistent gain, with a process initiated by an offer (selfish or altruistic) from one, and terminated by acceptance (*of a previous offer*) by another.

But, is it inevitable that such processes, if possible, *would* lead to individual and to collective gain, if initiated by a (potential?) loss to the initiator (offer) and apparently terminated via a greater loss?/ acceptance of an offer?)

It might seem reasonable to suppose that, if two or more collections can potentially gain by association with each other and/ or with a union catalogue, then collections might act as if choosing to form unions with further collections and/ or a union catalogue/catalogues. And, if gains can be (are) imputed to individual collections via the formation of union catalogues, then it might seem reasonable to suppose that further gains might be made via further unions determined via (relative to) the union catalogue/ catalogues.

The preceding remarks and developments invite further investigation and speculation as to *how much* as well as to how collections might gain/ lose individually and/ or collectively by association – they invite (cardinal) arithmetic comparisons.

It is apparently possible for *all* collections to gain in the sense that, unless one has an exhaustive collection, each collection can act as if choosing to agree to lend/ borrow between existing collections and, if any one adds to its collection, by acting as if choosing to make these additions/ gains available for loan or as gifts to others.

It might seem here that larger collections would gain less from such associations than the smaller ones, but the converse is also possible. If smaller collections can potentially gain more by association with each other and a larger collection/ collections, then it may be in the interest of a larger collection/ collections not only to associate with, but also to *create* additional smaller collections, i.e. if a smaller collection could potentially gain more than a larger would have gained and transmit gain back to the larger, then all can potentially gain more. Evidently it may be possible for smaller collections to gain by depriving larger ones, and larger ones to gain by depriving smaller ones without recompense, but notice that, if sustained, such processes would appear to lead (logically) to the extinction of collections.

Notice that extinction of the smallest would not apparently contradict its being the smallest, whereas extinction of the largest would apparently contradict its being the largest, unless all were extinguished. And if, for example,a larger collection (larger collections) *predicted* gains by reducing smaller collections, they would apparently gain only if smaller collections were/ could be (further) reduced, whereas, apparently,if larger collections could predict gains by increasing smaller collections, they would gain if smaller collections were/could be (further) increased.

More technically you may consider what would be the *rate of gain* of a created collection *as* it is created? and ; what would be the rate of loss of an extinguished collection as it is extinguished?, anticipating in answers to these questions different yet related roles for zeros and infinities.

All gains/ losses in the above context of "different books" _ loans of "different books" requests/offers relative to "different books" are apparently potential *information* gains/ losses – gains/ losses of different books, gains/ losses generated by different books and relative to different books – and represent gains/ losses of information relative to sources of gain/ loss of information.

Evidently collections of different books, particular different books, and, indeed, *this* particular "different book" would have no purpose if their contents were already known to their potential users – and little purpose, too, if their contents were wholly unknown (and unknowable) to all of their potential users : they would apparently have little purpose unless (potential readers' and/ or "different books") information were incomplete and could be made more complete (by interaction between themselves, each other and "different books")in predictable ways.

As one way of widening the discussion and analysis which I initiated by assuming the algebraic expressions $x_1 + x_2 + x_3 + x_4 = x$, $x_1 = x_2 = x_3 = x_4$, now ask within the context of the preceding developments (how) is it possible to determine the validity of others assumptions relative to *any* collection, or to the union catalogue, without violating at least one of them?

Observe that if all collections are closed, then apparently determination of the quantities x_i is *not* possible except by contradiction (of closure), nor is the determination of x (the union catalogue). If alternatively *not* all x_i are closed, then for at least one quantity x_i, $x_i \neq x_i$.

More subtly, unless x_i communicate, x, the union catalogue, cannot be determined relative to them and, if they are communicating, apparently, at any time, *different* quantities x_i, x are being determined relative to *each* x_i and to x.

So any collection can determine other collections and the union catalogue only *relative* to itself - an individual (collection)/ observer (collection) can only determine the other collections/ union catalogue relative to himself – by principles and processes of (self) contradiction.

Now recognize libraries and a union catalogue as different information sources relative to different collections of numbers (of "different books"), and ask (how) is it possible/ (impossible?) for different numbers to determine different collections of different numbers so that those numbers become different, and/ or remain the same.In what way(s) is it possible for a different number to determine different collections of different numbers so that those collections of different numbers become different?

Also recognize an explicitly relation between (potential) readers and "different books" and ask and implicitly answer questions such as : i) (how) is it possible for a reader (readers) to determine himself (themselves?) relative to different books in such a way that different books are generated differently relative to him (them) as if in such a way (ways) that he (they) gain by that/those association(s)? Or ; ii) (how) is it possible for a reader to act as if choosing to determine himself/ herself in relation to potentially different books as if in such a way (ways) that another (other) reader(s) can gain by association with him? Or ; iii) (how) is it possible for a reader to determine a particular different book in such a way that he can determine himself in relation to (elements of) that (*this*?) particular "different book" in such a way that he (and others) can potentially gain by that association?

The preceding developments not only initially employed (apparently algebraic) *assumptions*, which those developments themselves appeared to contradict, but also a geometric structure which suggests such contradictions, and processes of interaction which can yield those contradictions.

In particular, an interpretation with "simultaeneous" requests and loans appeared to yield paths and processes not only for requests but for different books. Informally, denominating x_1, x_2, x_3, x_4 as positive (+) and denoting loss of a different book via a loan as a positive gain to the system, and a (-) loss *in the opposite direction* to the loaning collection (and conversely for a borrowed book), apparently, at the order of (different) books and relative to the system, flows could be represented as from positive to negative and, if returned, from negative to positive as in Figure 5.

Not only are relative directions and signs apparent here, but relative magnitudes. The example apparently started with an assumption of equal magnitudes for x_1, x_2, x_3 and x_4 with x_3 acting as if losing relative to itself as if in order to generate a request relative to itself as if to communicate that request relative to a union catalogue (loss to the system, gain to the catalogue) as if to generate a request from the catalogue (loss to the catalogue, gain to the system relative to the catalogue) to collection 1 (loss to the system, gain to collection 1) as if to generate a different book from collection 1(loss relative to collection 1, gain to the system relative to collection 1) as if to generate a gain to collection 3 (loss relative to system, gain relative to collection 3):

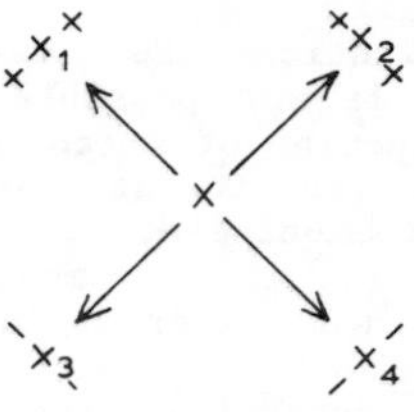

Figure 1.5

It is not only as if flows arise from positive to negative on the system, and negative to positive relative to the collections, but also as if flows *generate* changes in relative magnitudes, directions and signs, while being generated by them. Too, changes in magnitude and sign, at the order of requests relative to "different books",apparently generate changes in magnitude and sign at the order of different books (Δx_i) *and* collections of different books (x_i) *and* collections of collections of different books (x) and vice versa.

Recalling that, in relation to this example, I considered requests both from collection 4 and from collection 3, generating "different books" from collections 1 and 2 respectively, and denoting the two apparently analogous sequences of requests and loans of different books by signs relative to the system, apparently those sequences could be represented schematically via:

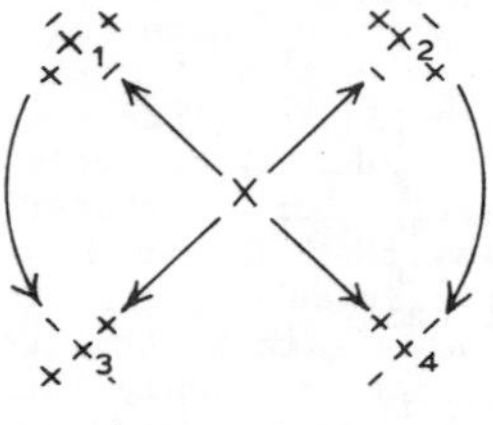

Figure 1.6

Notice now that this diagram illustrates sequences of changes *over time*. If, for example, requests via the union catalogue from borrowing collections x_3, x_4 of loaning collections x_1, x_2 are preceded by offers via the union catalogue from x_1, x_2 to loan from their collections, the diagram is apparently incomplete. Such offers relative to the union catalogue might be represented schematically, in relation to the union catalogue, via:

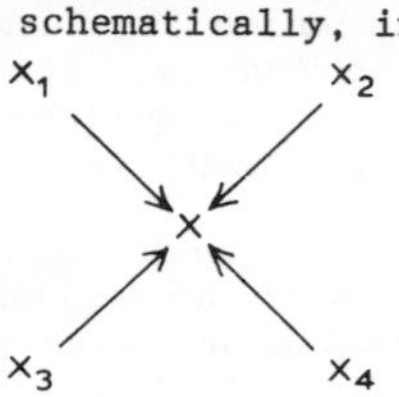

Figure 1.7

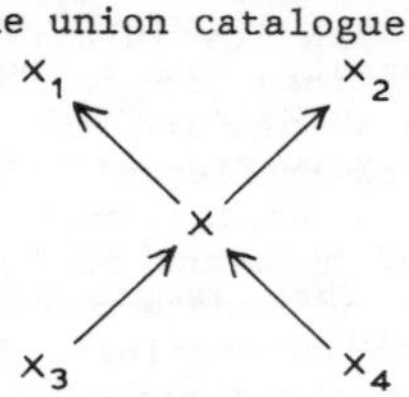

Figure 1.8

Now compare these two schema and recognize *paths* in time as if generating/ generated by sequences of gains and losses in time.

Different circulation patterns appear to be possible not only, as assumed above, loans from collections 1,2 to 3,4 (and back again?), but also of different books as one illustration - from 1 to 3 to 2 to 4 and back to 1. It seems possible to circulate a different book from collection to collection in such a way that each collection will gain – in such a way that each loaning collection loans as if in anticipation of a gain to the borrowing collection and/ or as if in anticipation of a gain to itself in consequence of its loan? Thus it seems possible to construct *cycles* of offers/ requests, loans/ borrowings such that *all* gain.

Other possibilities are : i) a case in which a loan from 1 to 3 generates a loan of a different book from 3 to 2, which generates a loan of a different book from 4 to 1.... Is seems possible for all collections to gain (knowledge?) from such a process – by generating/ sustaining such processes of borrowing/ lending.

An alternative interpretation of Figure 6 as indicates the possibility that a *collection* (of order x_i) may *move* from location 1 to 3 to 2 to 4 via a sequence of borrowings and lendings.

At first this class of cases might appear to contradict the initial conditions, at the order of requests, offers and/or of different books, *and* at the order of x_i. But it is consistent with a *consecutive* satisfaction of conditions $x_1 = x_2 = x_3 = x_4$, while sustaining $x_1 + x_2 + x_3 + x_4 = x$.

It would appear that in this case one satellite collection is in motion relative to itself *and* to a central collection (*and* a central collection in motion relative to itself and a satellite).

It seems evident to me that these examples and illustrations suggest "physical" interpretations -interpretations in relation to physics and/ or to physical (empirical) phenomena. This suggestion is strengthened by renaming collections as "bodies" and recalling that,in these examples, apparently relative magnitudes, directions and signs (polarities) and relative *changes* in magnitude, direction and sign regulate each other and regulate relative motions of collections and parts of collections relative to themselves, each other and relative to a (larger) system.

Physical analogies suggest and were suggested by the applicability of *indeterminacy* principles – at the order of atomic and/ or subatomic particles the Heisenberg Uncertainty Principle and –at astronomical orders – of indeterminancies deriving from and/ or associated with the Many Body Problem. They also suggest and were suggested by non-Euclidean geometries. In more detail the initial conditions of these examples might have suggested Euclidean geometries -projected/ mapped geometries of, for example, squares, triangles and circles, and, more primitively, lines, curves and (fixed point) orgins which these illustrations themselves appear to contradict.

Now consider if it is possible in general to *found* logically (mathematically?) consistent arguments upon contradictions of initial assumptions? Is it possible/ has it been possible to determine mathematically consistent and complete arguments *without* contradictions of initial assumptions? Is a mathematical argument necessarily incomplete if consistent with its initial assumptions and necessarily inconsistent with these assumptions, if complete? I remark that these latter questions bear directly on issues and difficulties associated with Godel's Incompleteness Theorem which implies affirmative answers.[6]

I will consider such issues, questions and answers further both directly and by means of further constructive examples but in general the preeminance of indeterminancy, uncertainty and incompleteness principles would appear to preclude the gaining of complete information/ knowledge. Nevertheless these principles can operate so that means of securing more/ less (complete) knowledge/ information are attainable in a manner consistent with them. Indeed the specification of the preceding example places no apparent restrictions upon the absolute magnitudes or scales of the (related) quantities x, x_i, Δx_i. Apparently, too, these illustrations and examples can provoke and implicitly answer further questions.

For instance, in the context of Figure 6 ask *why* circulate "different books" from 1 to 2 to 4 to 3 or, more generally *how* do collections ("different books") circulate, start/ stop circulating/ turning/ cycling relative to themselves, each other and/ or a system? More particularly, if "you" are identified (identify yourself?) with x_2 and "I" am identified (identify myself?) with x_1, what meaning, if any, attaches, for examples, to the (algebraic) expressions $x_1 + x_2 = x$, $x_1 = x - x_2$, x_1, x_2, $=$, $+$?

Can meaning attach to processes, whereby, for example, x_1 becomes different from itself/ himself/ herself (e.g.becomes less than itself/ himself/ herself relative to itself/ himself/ herself as if to determine a different (e.g. greater) value for x_2 relative to itself/ himself/ herself as if in order that x_2 can act as if choosing/ determining a greater value for himself/ itself....?

Where, when and how could x_1, x_2 be determined algebraically and/or geometrically relative to themselves,to each other, to x ? Recognize that these collections apparently necessarily act (react?) at -a -distance in space -time from one another, and relative to one another, and in motion relative to themselves, each other and x and so *cannot* be in "the same" place at "the same" time (relative to themselves, each other, a system).

Can such questions be answered without further specification of x_2 in relation to x_1? Could they be more fully answered by the introduction of "arithmetic" relationships for examples $x_1 = 2$, $x_2 = 2$, $2 + 2 = 4$, $4 - 2 = 2$? Could they be completely answered as if by x_1 and/or as if by x_2?

Still in the context of the preceding illustrations and developments, I now turn to a preliminary consideration of some issues pertaining to "probability" and randomness. (Recall here that medical books for the four libraries appeared to have been acquired as if independently and randomly from a larger population, itself determined by that analyst).

Consider the relation :

$$x_i(t) + s_i(t) = L^i(t) \qquad (1)$$

After period t (interval t?) an analyst might interpret this statement in relation to collection i as :

"numbers of different books acquired during period t = number of different books available for acquisition during period t, *less* number of different books *not* acquired during period t."

Before the beginning of period t, an acquisitions librarian might interpret the statement as :

"numbers of different books predicted to be selected during period t *plus* numbers of different books predicted *not* to be selected = number of different books predicted to become available for selection or not."

Notice that each quantity is variable here and each is a *decision* variable for and relative to the librarian.

Parenthetically, an acquisitions librarian might be represented as selecting (having selected?) via sequences of "yes", "no" :

e.g. yes, no, no, yes .....

But : i) how and when would such a sequence start/ stop relative to the librarian and/ or relative to the selection of different books and/ or relative to selected "different books" and/ or relative to a particularly selected book? ; ii) would such a sequence necessarily imply that no book was *reconsidered* for selection?

After period t an analyst might formally translate (1) into various kinds of "probability" statement. As examples, consider :

$$p_i(t) = \frac{x_i(t)}{L^i(t)} \qquad q_i(t) = \frac{s_i(t)}{L^i(t)}$$

Interpreted, respectively, as the "probability" of considering different books for collection i and : i) selecting them ; ii) not selecting them.

By means of these definitions/ assumptions/ assertions, an analyst could translate (1) into:

$$p_i(t) + q_i(t) = 1 \tag{2}$$

Going further, if each quantity in (1) was multiplied by the same quantity $\theta_i(t)$, then $p_i(t)$, $q_i(t)$ could remain as if invariant, apparently satisfying (2) as well as the following:

$$[p_i(t) + q_i(t)]\,\theta_i(t) = \theta_i(t) \tag{3}$$

As a particular class of special cases, consider those for which $\theta_i(t) = L_i(t)$. Then apparently:

$$p_i(t)[x_i(t) + s_i(t)] + q_i(t)[x_i(t) + s_i(t)] = L^i(t) \tag{4}$$

Considering (1) from a different perspective ; it is apparently possible to expand that relation by means of further assumptions/ assertions/ transformations. As a particular class of examples, consider a *partition* of $L^i(t)$ into classes (classifications)j via the relations :

$$L^i(t) = \sum_j L^i_j(t)) \;,\quad x_i(t) = \sum_j x_{ij}(t) \;,\quad s_i(t) = \sum_j s_{ij}(t)$$

and the expressions:

$$p_{ij}(t) = \frac{x_{ij}(t)}{L^i(t)} \qquad q_{ij}(t) = \frac{s_{ij}(t)}{L^i(t)}$$

Interpreted, respectively, as the "probability" of considering different books of classification j for collection i and : i) selecting them ; ii) not selecting them for collection i. And/ or the expression :

$$p^i_j(t) = \frac{L^i_j(t)}{L^i(t)}$$

Interpreted as the probability of selecting classification j relative to collection i. And/ or the expressions :

$$a_{ij}(t) = \frac{x_{ij}(t)}{L^i_j(t)} \quad , \quad b_{ij}(t) = \frac{s_{ij}(t)}{L^i_j(t)}$$

Interpreted, respectively as the probability of a particular collection of different books of classification j being considered for selection from books to be selected within classification j relative to collection i and : i) selected ; ii) not selected for collection i.

If the group of potential classifications is exhaustive of all possible (potential?) classifications j relative to collection i apparently :

$$\sum_j p_j^i(t) = \frac{\sum_j L_j^i(t)}{L^i(t)} = 1$$

and variously:

$$\sum_j p_{ij}(t) = p_i(t) = \frac{\sum_j x_{ij}(t) \quad L_j^i(t)}{L_j^i(t) \quad L^i(t)} = \sum_j a_{ij}(t)p_j{}^i(t) \qquad (5)$$

$$\sum_j q_{ij}(t) = q_i(t) = \frac{\sum_j s_{ij}(t) \quad L_j^i(t)}{L_j^i(t) \quad L^i(t)} = \sum_j b_{ij}(t)p_j{}^i(t) \qquad (6)$$

Notice that selection may be exhaustive within one or more classifications without being exhaustive within all (relevant?) classifications. If $L_j{}^i(t) = x_{ij}(t)$, then $a_{ij}(t) = 1 = p_{ij}(t)$. But if $x_{ij}(t) = 0 = p_{ij}(t)$, then $a_{ij}(t) = 0$.

Also if a "different book" is selected relative to a collection via a process of selection, then there is one less book to be selected for that collection *as* (because) one more is selected. So $x_{ij}(t)$ and $L^i(t)$ will in general be systematically (algorithmically) related.

Those familiar with linear programming methods and associated duality and complementary slackness arguments might recognize in, the immediately preceding algebraic developments and – by reference to these – in earlier developments, elements and concepts familiar in a linear programming context. If so, they will be curious to discover in what sense, if any, the component parts of linear programming problems are necessarily linear algebraically and/ or geometrically.

In that context recognize that inter alia *explicitly nonlinear* (quadratic) forms have been generated here. As a particular class of examples, consider the class of special cases generated by the assumptions $\theta_i(t) = L^i(t)$, $p_i(t) = 1/2$, $q_i(t) = 1/2$, then apparently $s_i(t) = x_i(t) = L^i(t)$, which is apparently a particular solution to the expressions:

$$2x_i{}^2(t) + 2s_i{}^2(t) = L_i{}^2(t)$$

This might be interpreted variously and/or simultaneously : i) as an algebraic expression relating to various (Euclidean) plane geometric phenomena, including triangles and circles in particular -the former, notice, apparently denoting a strictly nonlinear closed and continuous form and the latter a piecewise linear (and piecewise discontinuous) form ; ii) as only one of many possible ways of expressing the assumed set of conditions, another apparently being a particular solution to the conditions:

$$x_i{}^2\,(t) + s_i(t)x_i(t) + x_i(t)s_i(t) + s_i{}^2(t) = L_i{}^2(t)$$

iii) as embodying various kinds of numerical information and relations between various kinds of numerical information – information pertaining to (deriving from?) various kinds of numbers and relations between various kinds of numbers (fractions, integers, roots).

What part, if any, is played in these interpretations by the assumption/ assertion $\theta_i(t) = L^i(t)$?, i;e. *not* $\theta_i(t) \neq L^i(t)$, relative, as examples, to : plane geometries; simultanaeity*;* and to the apparently mutually (and logically?) contradictory character of various interpretations which are apparently possible?

In this connection it is of particular significance that if, for example:

$$x_i(t) = \sum_j x_{ij}(t)$$

$$p_i(t) = \sum_j p_{ij}(t)$$

then apparently not only :

$$p_i(t)\, x_i(t) = \sum_j p_{ij}(t)\, x_{ij}(t)$$

but, for example :

$$x_{ir}(t) = x_i(t) - \sum_{j \neq r} x_{ij}(t)$$

$$p_{ir}(t) = p_i(t) - \sum_{j \neq r} p_{ij}(t)$$

and

$$p_{ir}(t)\, x_{ir}(t) = (x_i(t) - \sum_{j \neq r} x_{ij}(t))\,(p_i(t) - \sum_{j \neq r} p_{ij}(t))$$

In particular : i) increasing (decreasing) $p_i(t)$, $x_{ij}(t)$ is apparently consistent with then decreasing (increasing) *all other* $p_{ij}(t)$, $x_{ij}(t)$ *and* $x_i(t)$, $p_i(t)$ in some combination ; ii) in principle, *each* $x_{ij}(t)$, $p_{ij}(t)$ could be expressed in terms of (as a consequence for?) the others ; iii) and, in various circumstances, for example as in the preceding definitions, $p_{ij}(t)$, $x_{ij}(t)$, $(p_i(t), x_i(t))$ might be systematically, if incompletely, related ; iv) finally these various expressions are not necessarily equivalent.

The considerations in i) can be expected to have significance in a context of algorithms . I emphasize, however, that all of the above conditions hold by definition/ assumption/ assertion and are asserted to hold simultaneously (via the script t) and in relation to a particular collection,and that each of the expressions of the form :

$$\frac{x_{ij}(t)}{L_j{}^i(t)} \quad + \quad \frac{s_{ij}(t)}{L_j{}^i(t)}$$

is of the *same* form as (2), with its associated "probability" definitions, and each could apparently be expanded and developed in ways akin to the expansion and developments, including the geometric developments in relation to (2).

Recall now that the ostensible purpose of the above definitions was to represent elements of a selection problem. But can a process of selection take place without violating/ contradicting one or all (one and so all?) of the above definitions/ assumptions/ assertions?

There are of course many ways of contradicting the above set of definitions - ways which may take the form of further kinds of mathematical relations. For example, these may yield and/ or be yielded by algebraic relations and/or Euclidean or non-Euclidean geometries in relation to the Euclidean and non-Euclidean examples considered above.

Notice that if selection does take place, then quantities and associated probabilities will necessarily change. If selection is as if purposive, for example the ostensible purpose being to select more for a particular collection, then the quantities and probabilities of selection/ non-selection will change systematically not just in relation to that collection, but to all collections in the collection of collections considered.

Thus purposive selection could determine and/ or be determined by purposive changes in probabilities. Selection of more relative to one collection decreases the number to be selected and (so) increases the probabilities of subsequent selection/rejection while decreasing the numbers to be subsequently selected/ not selected relative to the system and increasing the numbers to be selected/ rejected subsequently relative to particular (selecting) collections. But how are the numbers selected/ to be selected and whence are they to be obtained?

Recalling that four collections were considered, an analyst might assume that $L^i(t)$ had the same value for all four collections – that all four collections had selected new acquisitions as if from the same (union) catalogue of numbers of "different books" L(t), that all classified medical acquisitions as "medical" with $(p_{ij}(t))$ the same for all collections and so compute "probabilities" of duplication via the measures $x_{ij}(t)/L(t)$ for the four libraries within subject classification j on the hypothesis that acquisitions were (had been?) as if *randomly* selected within classifications j.

But are these conditions possible for the individual collection/ acquisition librarians? Recognize that,in order for these conditions to obtain, acquisitions librarians would be assumed to *predict* not only the *same* value for L(t) ; to *predict* the number of different books $L_j(t)$ in classifications j, and their distribution by classification *and* to predict $x_{ij}(t)$, *but also* to predict that the realization of these predictions would be feasible (these predictions would be realizeable).

That is, they would be assumed to predict that ; all books selected would be acquired e.g. no stockouts, and all books acquired selected e.g. no gifts ; that no book would be misclassified outside classifications j ; that all selected books be selected, ordered, acquired/ delivered and classified in such a time that the measure of duplication of classified acquisitions was the measure which would obtain in the libraries i.e. no backlogs in processing, no backorders, and that ; for example, professional and non-professional librarians' time available for acquisitions and processing and materials required for acquisitions and processing and budgest necessary for acquisitions and for staff time and for materials would be sufficient.

Even given these formidable preconditions would it be ; i) possible ; ii) desirable, for librarians to select as if randomly? Would these conditions themselves be desirable, even if attainable. In general the above conditions would appear to be (logically?) necessary.

If, exceptionally, a collection was to be exhaustive over all potential classifications (if a deposit library were to collect as if exhaustively), then apparently there would be no selection problem. If a "different book" became available, it would be acquired. Processing times and expenditure would then apparently be determined as if as *consequences* of different books being made available for acquisition.

If collections were not to be exhaustive of all potential books to be acquired for example due to budgetary reasons,or lack of resources for classification/ processing or shortage of storage/ shelf space/ circulation facilities or demand from potential readers, then apparently, as a matter of policy – if there was to be a policy – acquisitions librarians must select as if recognizing that selection would not be exhaustive within all (potential? relevant?) classifications.

Is it possible in principle to do this in a manner consistent with the preceding considerations while yet selecting as if at random? It might appear so, by *overestimating* unit processing times, unit material resources required, unit acquisition prices and *underestimating* available budgets,including salary budgets, time available for processing, and numbers to be selected in each category, while *overestimating* numbers to become available in each category,and then selecting as if at random within each category.

Apparently such an approach would be as if predictive of events. Acquisition of books would lower available processing time, resources and budgets, while reducing the numbers to be selected (by) a particular library/ collection.

Indeed this approach would apparently be consistent with the ability to process initially unknown books with longer than predicted processing times and higher than predicted material and expenditure requirements. It could also be as if the existence of unknown books had been predicted,as well as the ability to process them. Indeed these books could be of unpredicted classifications and thus, via induced change in $p_j(t)$, could reclassify the whole collection.

In general, relative to a particular prediction of the population from which selections were to be made, the probability of considering a particular book for selection would apparently increase with the numbers of books selected (or not selected), whereas, if more books became available than predicted, the probability of considering (reconsidering?) a particular book for selection would apparently decrease.

And, if a supplier of different books for consideration for selection by a particular library was able to decrease price with quantity supplied, while effectively increasing budgets available for acquisition of books, and reducing unit processing times, then apparently more "different books" could be sold than otherwise.

In relation to the preceding developments, questions concerning reasons for non-selection might be related to the quantities s and, via these, to probabilities of non-selection. In a linear programming context, the quantities s might, in turn, suggest slack variables. Although I have suggested here that the preceding issues and relations themselves suggest relationships to linear programming approaches, I will not pursue this issue in empirical detail in relation to these particular libraries. Since the investigations to which I have referred were undertaken a number of years ago, such relations would in any case necessarily be undertaken now on grounds of general principles, rather than with the possibility of re-referral to the particular libraries' operations at that time. Anyhow it is general principles which are the focus of attention here, including the elucidation of means whereby general principles may be applied to particular instances and of means whereby particular instances may be used as bases for the generation of more widely applicable general principles.

In 1972 I became associated with an interdisciplinary project entitled "The Establishment of Operational Guidelines for Coastal Zone Management". This project was funded by the US National Science Foundation and involved as principals geologists, marine biologists, environmental health engineers, and members of the Water Resources Research Institute and of the School of Public Affairs in association with Dr. A.Charnes and the Center for Cybernetic Studies at the University of Texas, as well as various state government agencies represented via the governer's office. My part in this project generated my dissertation.

The empirical nature of the project title was underlined by the fact that, at the time, Texas was being required either to enact legislation in order to establish such (environmentally oriented) guidelines or risk losing substantial quantities of US Federal funds. In this respect it seemed evident that state and federal governments had potentially conflicting objectives in the sense that it seemed that the state government (legislature) would not otherwise choose to consider the introduction of such comprehensive legislation.

At a more abstract level it seemed evident that state and federal agencies as well as state and federal governments would/ could intervene by means of regulation/ legisation. So a theoretical framework developed and/ or employed in connection with this project in order to analyze and/or predict the implications of potential or actual legislated alternatives would be fundamentally deficient (as is, for example, the economists' paradigms of pure or perfect competition) if it failed to take account of the possibility of such intervention, and associated possibilities of conflict of objectives and/ or of means of implementation in accordance with conflicting objectives between agencies/ governing bodies.

It also seemed evident that a model directed toward a comprehensive analysis of implications of legislation/ regulation and/ or potential legislation/ regulation, be those implications qualitative or quantitative, would be deficient unless it explicitly comprehended a consideration of processes of and/ or potential processes of land use *change* where, in this context, "land" might refer to water (river, sea, estuary), wetland..., and land uses to petrochemical plants, farms, houses, roads, etc.

At an early stage in the project, it was decided by the principals to concentrate on one area, namely Corpus Christi, in order to establish foci for the interdisciplinary research effort. At that time Corpus Christi was a port city with a ship channel from the Gulf of Mexico through the bay leading to an industrial area consisting largely of oil refineries and petrochemicals-related plants. It was also a significant centre for recreation directed largely via boating and fishing to the Bay and to neighbouring islands (most prominantly Padre Island). One focus of attention, then, quite naturally, was Corpus Christi Bay.

Parenthetically, it was the professional opinion of marine biologists that,in the absence of discharges from the city and refineries/ petrochemical plants, this bay would have been a relatively sterile environment for marine life. With this view such discharges were not socially undesirable "pollutants" per se, for on them depended, in large part, the fisheries in the bay and, on these, commercial and recreational activities and prosperity.

At that time the US was becoming a significant importer of oil, and oil tanker sizes were increasing. It seemed that unless monobuoys were introduced, or the ship channel widened and deepened, the refining and petrochemicals industries would decline, with deleterious consequences for local activity and employment, both in industry and recreation. Also, if effluent discharge ("pollution") standards were tightened appreciably, apparently there would be reduced incentives to continue or expand refining and petrochemicals activities, among others, in their present locations. It seemed evident that alternative sites for these could be chosen in locations possibly geographically far distant from Texas, and that a theoretical model/ models designed to comprehend the impact of such location-related factors, even phenomenologically, would apparently necessarily comprehend such potentially distant geographical alternatives and differences in factors between them.

Taking another perspective on the Corpus Christi area : Corpus Christi and its surrounding area at that time drew its fresh water for drinking as well as for irrigation largely from artesian sources which supplemented supplies from the Nueces River. Despite this, and a history of intensive drilling for oil in the area, (expert) geologists apparently did not have detailed knowledge of the relation between river flows and those of subsurface aquifers. Such knowledge would appear to be necessary if, for example, it were proposed to increase irrigation substantially or increase quality standards for river water and to meet these by drawing less water from river sources and relatively more from artesian sources.

A set of interdisciplinary relationships appeared possible in relation to the river, involving predictions of:

agricultural activity → associated irrigation requirements → discharges to surface/ river → river discharges to bay → implications, given tidal features, for marine life.

In turn these would relate and interrelate economists and economic issues re predictions of types and levels of economic activity, geologists and geological issues re artesian water/ land based effluent discharges, environmental health engineers re predictions of effluent discharges (detailed knowledge of relevant features of production processes) government agencies in relation to predicted water standards, water resources engineers in relation to predictions of e.g. suspended/ dissolved solids and dissolved oxygen distributions and solid depositions in the bay via a bay -estuarine model, and marine biologists in relation to predictions of implications of these for types, locations and (relative) populations of marine life.

These areas and associated disciplines appear clearly related, but they are also directly interrelated, for example predicted types and levels of agricultural activity may appear contingent on water availabilities/ discharge standards, but also, for example, potential water availability/ discharge standards are not in general independent of past/ predicted levels and types of agricultural activity e.g. via meteorological relationships, regulatory legislation, new types of/ expansion of irrigation, storage, exploratory drilling activities.

Fresh water, irrigation and environmental issues led to the development of an hierarchical goal programing model, the hierarchical feature relating particularly to the (potential) existence of hierarchies of levels of regulatory agencies, possibly with overlapping jurisdictions at given levels and the goal programming feature to a specification of standards via goals with associated penalties and inducements, rather than via particular (possibly individually and/ or mutually unattainable) levels.

Another early – and related – sequence which suggested itself as leading to interdisciplinary relationships could be represented schematically via :

refineries/ petrochemical plants → discharges to bay → tides → fish populations.

Such a sequence might appear to require modelling, measurement and prediction of types and levels of activity of refineries/ petrochemical plants in order to predict, model and measure compositions, timings and levels of discharges, as well as to predict, model and measure dispersion and deposition patterns and compositions and to model, measure and predict the implications of these for the composition, relative size and locations of populations of fish/ marine life.

In the context of the project, such a sequence might be seen to interrelate economists (re plant refinery activity), environmental health engineers (measurement, modelling prediction of discharges), members of the Water Resources Research Institute (re dispersion/ deposition patterns via a differential -difference equation based Bay -Estuarine transport model) and marine biologists (prediction re fish/ marine life).

Clearly such models, measurements and predictions derive from professional knowledge and/ or professional opinion (judgement/ expertise) but – given the interrelationships in relation to discharges – where would/ should boundaries, including boundaries between disciplines and between professional knowledge, opinion and judgement lie? I emphasize this by stressing that the context emphasizes regulation and potential regulation of land use and potential land use. It might seem reasonable to predict that, in general, oil refineries and/ or petrochemical activities would not be independent of regulation and potential regulation, *and* that potential regulation would not in general be independent of potential implications of oil refining/petrochemical activities (e.g. for fish populations/ fishing). Where, if at all, can a (logical?) break in these interrelationships be established? Are "logical" breaks in these interrelated sequences (potential sequences) : i) possible? ; ii) desirable?

Parenthetically, the immediately preceding developments suggest that potential as well as actual regulation would condition (cause? determine?) action/ inaction and/ or reaction/ non-reaction at-a- distance.

It might appear in this immediate context that this action/ reaction would be only a local phenomenon, but another instance to be cited very shortly will suggest otherwise.

From another perspective, in relation to Corpus Christi Bay, effluent discharges, via the river and via discharges from refineries petrochemical plants, etc., *both* bore on the Bay, and so, for example, on fish populations, and might reasonably be predicted to interact, with consequent implications for fish populations *and* for refineries/ petrochemical plants/ agricultural activities, if regulated.

In relation to oil refineries/ petrochemical plants a broader perspective would focus on prediction of other factors bearing on the levels and types of activity themselves, including further implications for the Bay. (*As* examples, widening and deepening the ship channel or not, monobuoys or not) and discharges/ potential linkages with users/ potential users of their output(s)/potential output(s). Our further investigation in this direction revealed, for example, that a large proportion of refined oil was then shipped by pipelines via Houston to the East Coast.

With the increasing use of imported crude, this promoted a query concerning the continued location of refining capacity at Corpus Christi versus alternative locations and, in particular, East Coast refineries. Also, given the increasing trend toward larger tankers at that time, queries concerning implications for shipping companies (British shipping companies? pipeline companies?) under these potential alternatives.

Significantly, at that time stringent environmental legislation was being introduced most particularly on the relatively more heavily populated and industrialized East Coast. Stringent environmental legislation was introduced in New Jersey, effectively preventing the location of new refineries in that state – and development of refining capacity in the West Indies in response to more stringent environmental legislation and potential legislation in the US.

In short "environmental" legislation might reasonably be expected to have implications not only for output but for the location of capacity, with maintenance/ establishment/ expansion/ extinction of capacity in a particular location (e.g. Corpus Christi) directly or indirectly contingent upon distant events, conditions and regulations.

These points all bear on my dissertation, which I have included here as Chapter 8. The central point in it can be related to earlier as well as to subsequent developments, by considering the relation:

$$\sum_{\ell} z^{k}_{\ell}(t) = L^{k}(t) \qquad (7)$$

Interpret $L^k(t)$ as the plan area of "land" in region k in period t and $z^k{}_\ell(t)$) as the area associated with land use of type ℓ in region k in period t and recognize :

i) that land use will in general be heterogeneous in region and might comprehend various types and configurations of "land", including water, rivers, etc ;

ii) that land uses constitute types of/ forms of production capacity with potential for output(s) ;

iii) that apparently, if (6) obtains, in order to increase any type of land use/production capacity, one or more types must be reduced and, conversely, if any type of capacity is reduced, apparently one or more types of capacity, which may be new types of capacity as well as "new" capacity will be increased ;

iv) that if more capacity is required of a particular type, then it is apparently necessary to acquire and convert elements of one or more types of (pre)existing capacity ;

v) that in general conversion or maintenance processes will be specific to the actual and/ or potential conversions to be undertaken and to capacity to be maintained;

vi) that capacity constrains (bounds) potential output and that output might be planned or scheduled to meet demand for it. This demand may be for stock, as input to production, conversion and/or maintenance processes, or for final consumption, and may be met from stocks or previous production and/or by means of barter or trade with other regions, it being recognized that stocking and shipping/ transshipping capacities, e.g. warehouses, roads, railroads, ports could also constitute land uses or potential land uses.

By considering such relations and interrelations explicitly, it becomes possible to consider regulation and potential regulation and the implications of laws, taxes, subsidies and/ or potential laws, taxes and/ or subsidies within an optimization context.

The objective function of the consequent goal programme takes the form of a maximization of "added value", where this measures the present value of final demand at specified anticipated market prices, *less* input costs, most particularly wage/ salary costs ; input costs of primary resources, *plus* the horizon value of production capacity *all* net of (potential) taxes and subsidies.

Each quantity may be subject to regulation and/ or potential regulation by means of *goals* on levels (e.g. of resources, workers employed and available by type and location, effluent discharge levels, capacity by type and location) and associated (potential) regulatory, tax,subsidy and price regimes, with all quantities susceptible to conflict and potentially to hierarchical regulation.

Using duality arguments I obtained results interpretations and optimal decision rules relating and interrelating property and commodity markets and associated issues of accounting and finance to issues of physical production and investment, spatial configurations of activities and their regulation and potential regulation. Explicit and related interpretations for laws, taxes and subsidies are also obtained, as are potentially conflicting goals, laws, taxes and subsidies and explicit treatments of issues pertaining to the aggregation/ disaggregation of micro economic and macroeconomic phenomena and the relationship between present decisions with regard to investment, output and (potential) demand, including phenomenological interrelations between resource depletion and inflation.

In related and subsequent work, using "decentralization" arguments deriving from techniques immanent in the reference with which I began this chapter, I focused on some particular issues and features more closely and more particularly than in my dissertation, and did so in ways which I recognized as being consistent with (coherent with) that overall development, in the sense of these decentralization procedures and arguments and yet (potentially) different from it,and from each other in the particular senses in which "decentralization" procedures *as* procedures may distinguish component parts of models from each other and from overall models. I was aware that, by distinguishing, component parts from each other and from an overall model, these ways might themselves become open to further exploration, investigation and understanding.

I have included two essays of this type here. They concentrate respectively on issues of corporate valuation and finance and pricing and depletion of non-renewable resources under conditions of uncertainty.

Each contains essentially the same preemptive goal programming model of an enterprise at its heart. The focus of that model is on intertemporal decisions in relation to (and relations between) types and ages of capacity. It recognizes that capacity may be acquired, relinquished and/ or maintained to supply local and/or distant markets for stocks, final demands or inter alia for processes of production, conversion and/ or maintainence.

The model also recognizes that output requires capacity (potential output is apparently logically bounded above by available capacity), that capacity acquired is apparently logically converted from a preexisting use or set of uses and that potential productivity may vary with age.

In its essentials this model is apparently quite simple and its generic relationship to the considerations above relating to "land" is perhaps evident even with these brief introductory remarks.

I have long been aware that more complicated models might be developed via further decentralization arguments applied to the developments in my dissertation. I have been aware also that the apparently "logical" structures of spatial and/ or intertemporal relationships in these models could be used to provoke questions concerning their own relationship to apparently differently motivated model types, including the "distribution" model in particular.

More generally, I have been aware that further and related models, including more complex models of enterprises could be developed from the overall models and approaches used both in my dissertation itself and via decentralization arguments in relation to it.

For example "decentralization" arguments could be used formally to secure decentralizations to regions and/ or groups of regions (e.g. "cities", "counties", "countries") thereby apparently securing further models and relations,and interrelations between these further models and the models of the enterprise which are the focus of the work presented here.

As further examples "decentralization" arguments can/ could be applied to secure models relating to statutory authorities (e.g. river authorities, regulatory boards) distinct from regions/ nations and regional/ national governments, yet again related to them via regulatory and potential regulatory powers. Indeed, such possibilities of "decentralization" and associated interrelations provided initial motivation for the hierarchical structures and inter -relationships in relation to regulations contained in my dissertation.

Although I am convinced that such developments are possible, I have not undertaken them here in direct relation to the developments of my dissertation, primarily on the grounds that, even if I were to do so in detail, the arguably more fundamental issues to which I have chosen to direct attention here would apparently remain immanent even in such developments. For example: imagine that it would be possible to secure algebraically expressed, related and interrelated models of, for examples, enterprises, government agencies and counties, countries..(I have suggested that this would be possible). Yet how, if at all, would these models be related to reality? : i) logically? ; ii) economically?, iii) algebraically?

What is the logical relationship (if any) between abstract models and real structures, between theory and experiment, between abstraction and experience? What (if any) are the relationships between governments, government agencies, enterprises and individuals and vice versa? : i) logically? ; ii) algebraically? ; iii) empirically?

More constructively, arguably more abstractly and, I think, more fundamentally, what (if any) is the relation between an organizational structure as a mathematical expression (collection of mathematical expressions?) and its realization? What is the purpose of constructing/ observing/ requiring particular relations and/ or interrelations between structures? Can organizations and/ or relations between organizations be constructed and/or reconstructed so that different (better?) organizations, different (better?) outcomes for organizations and associated individuals are attained?

As an example directed toward further directions of investigation in the context of completeness and of incompleteness theorems and results : if an organizational structure (enterprise, agency, individual?) is not completely described by abstract mathematical expressions, then apparently as an (abstract?) mathematical description of that structure, that description is (logically?) incomplete, whereas if it is asserted to be completely described by abstract mathematical (e.g. algebraic) expressions, apparently that structure is asserted to be (i.e. asserts itself to be) wholly abstract. I remark that any attempt to generate complete models of all relevant phenomena, agents and agencies and, in particular, any attempts to do so via "centralization" - "decentralization" arguments would appear to be governed by such principles.

I am aware that if I were to focus attention narrowly on particular algebraic structures, even if these structures were to take the form of a family of interrelated models, the mistaken impression might be not only conveyed, but reinforced, that I was attempting to establish groundwork from first principles in a logic of completeness and of determinancy of that family of models.

In the following Chapters I have attempted to achieve more than that. One measure of that achievement will be the indication in detail of both how and why an objective of the establishment of a self consistent, deterministic and complete family of models of that kind would necessarily be both mathematically and physically only incompletely attainable.

Another and more constructive measure of the substance of what follows will be its demonstration of how, as well as why, appropriate forms of mathematical and physical acknowledgement of the nature of that incompleteness can be productive of individual, collective and social gains. It will be apparent that in general such gains may include gains of knowledge as well as of commodities, and that such gains may be founded in systematic and fundamental ways on conditions of relative incompleteness of information and principles and processes of individual and collective self contradiction.

Footnotes

1. See Charnes and Cooper *Management Models and Industrial Applications of Linear Programming*, {2}, Vol.2 and references contained therein.

2. *Company Profitability in the U.K. Shipping Industry*. Discussion Paper 23, Graduate Centre for Management Studies, University of Birmingham, 1970.

3. Parenthetically, it seemed to me that computerization of inter-library loan operations, especially if done in coordination with that of individual libraries' own operations, might potentially offer very considerable informational advantages. As examples, records of inter-library loans by title and library, as well as titles available from other libraries, could serve to inform purchasing/ duplication decision, whereby comparisons of frequencies (relative frequencies?) of books provided for circulation via loans as opposed to acquisitions could be used to provide checks on acquisition decisions/ policies, as well as guides to their formulation. I will not pursue these matters from this perspective here. I do remark that one library was installing a computer system which would give *no* effective circulation history (due to its development for another library which had access to a machine with extremely limited core memory). It seemed evident from the

perspective of managerial information systems that this would be a retrograde rather than a progressive step, and unnecessarily so.

6. An alert analyst might look for arguments and qualitative implications supporting Godel's result, and reservations stemming from it, particularly in relation to axiomatization as a foundation for analysis and theorems (since Godel's theorem is itself a theorem) as a means of proof. (For an introduction to Godel's theorem see {1}).

References

{1} Arbib, M.A. (1965), *Brains, Machines* and *Mathematics*, McGraw Hill, New York.

{2} Charnes, A and Cooper, W.W. (1961), *Management Models and Industrial Applications of Linear Programming*, Wiley, New York.

{3} Charnes, A, Clower, R.W.and Kortanek, K.O.(1967), *Effective Control through Coherent Decentralization with Preemptive Goals*, Econometrica, 35.

{4} von Neumann, J. and Morgernstern, O.(1947), *Theory of Games and Economic Behaviour*, Princeton University Press, Princeton, New Jersey.

2 Economic theories of value and choice

To mathematical economists the term Value will evoke associations with Debreu's "Theory of Value" {8}. In that brief book Debreu made assumptions necessary for the application of Kakutani's Fixed Point Theorem [1] to prove as abstract theorems concerning an abstract economy of abstract objects and individuals[2] : i) the existence of a "competitive general equilibrium" and ; ii) that that competitive general equilibrium would be (correspond to) a Pareto Optimum -a position at which no individual could be made better off in his own estimation without at least one other individual being made worse off in his own estimation.[3] Particular assumptions are that individuals' choices are made according to abstract preference relations defined only over an individual's own (abstract?) consumption levels of consumption commodities, that choices are constrained only by (monetized) budgets, that income derives solely from work via wages and from shares in "competitive" production enterprises.

In these circumstances,and assuming known endowments of factors and known (production) relations between potential inputs and outputs, Debreu apparently shows that an equilibrium price vector exists which would clear all markets in such a way that, given those (given) prices, individuals would choose the market clearing levels of production, consumption and work.

I remark that, if individuals' preference relations were denoted by the symbols U_i, i = 1, 2 ...n, it might appear that it would then be possible to construct a relation $W = W(U_1^{*} .. U_i^{*} .. U_n^{*})$ where U_i^{*} is the value of U_i associated with the general equilibrium, itself associated with the market clearing price vector.

Even though Debreu does not prove or even require uniqueness of his result,many analysts have been tempted to represent the competitive result in words as a demonstration that individual self interest can lead to collective best interest, as if by an "Invisible Hand" (the latter term being attributable to Adam Smith {26} as, many would claim, is the competitive market clearing idea).

In 1951 Arrow's book entitled "Social Choice and Individual Values" {1} appeared in the same series of monographs as Debreu's later work. In it he uses symbolic logic (whereas Debreu used advanced algebraic topology) to demonstrate convincingly that, under apparently very weak assumptions concerning individuals' (abstract) preference relations over (social?) alternatives,it will, in general, be impossible to construct (decisive?) social preference relations without resort to dictatorship.

Arrow, perhaps unduly influenced by the selfishness assumptions central to competitive general equilibrium arguments and results, considered dictatorship per se socially undesireable.

Apparently then a decisive relation, which might be represented as $W(U_1 \ldots U_i \ldots U_n)$, cannot exist in general without dictatorship. I can illustrate this whole class of arguments and results by considering the Paradox of Voting -which antedates Arrow. (An excellent introduction to this topic as well as many others, including topics in mathematical programming is given in Baumol's book {3}).

Consider three individuals 1, 2, 3 with (abstract) preferences over three alternative A, B, C as follows:

1	A P B P C
2	B P C P A
3	C P A P B

(here P signifies "strictly preferred to")

Now adopt, for example, majority voting as a social decision rule. Then, by a majority, apparently A P B P C P A. Apparently, not only is majority voting inconclusive here but a process of decisionmaking according to these abstract ordering could/would cycle.[4] Notice, too, that if any alternative was decided,that outcome could abstractly be construed as being as if a particular individual had decided it, regardless of others' preferences (dictatorship).

Apparently there is a fundamental contradiction here between Debreu's results in his Theory of Value and Arrow's results pertaining to theories of collective choice. In the former apparently individuals would (unanimously) choose a social outcome in accordance with their independently determined (prior?) preferences, that outcome corresponding to a market clearing optimum with the Pareto property. In the latter, even under apparently weak conditions concerning individual preference relations, individuals would not (unanimously) choose *any* social alternative. (Dictatorship in the sense of an individual determining social preferences to accord with his own (selfish) preferences, and unanimity in the sense of identity of preference relations over all individualsare typically taken to be general classes of exceptions).

In fact the relationship between these two kinds of (abstract) approaches and these two kinds of (abstract) results has long remained a mystery to (mathematical) economists. For them general equilibrium theory and collective choice theory have become, and remain, largely separate areas of research and (mostly graduate) teaching. There is an extensive literature on each - in (mathematicized) general equilibrium theory going back to Walras {27} and beyond, but a typical graduate course might still centre on Debreu's book with Quirk and Saposnik {21} as glossary and guide, whereas a graduate course on collective choice might centre on Arrow's book with Sen's Collective Choice {24}, or more recent books in that vein as additional sources.

Quite evidently, as the above example suggests, collective choice theory goes well beyond the boundaries of economics, as the boundaries of that subject are usually construed, even by its practitioners, and into questions pertaining to group decisionmaking in general, including, in the present context, political decisionmaking via voting, and associated, essentially philosophical, issues pertaining to the nature of ideal political decisionmaking processes.

The economics literature on the subject of collective choice has consisted essentially of a sustained barrage of Impossibility results largely stemming from Arrow's work and founded upon varieties of collections of abstract mathematical properties for posited deterministic and abstract social decision functions/ preference relations.

These properties variously include the Pareto property (strong or weak), anonymity, non-dictatorship (sometimes strengthened as a desirable property to non-oligarchy), monotonicity, non -veto and (I emphasise) acyclicity and path independence.

I have emphasized the last two properties in particular because these, at least, suggest a context of *process* of decisionmaking wider than decisionmaking *per se* as reasons for their significance and, in practice, if binding, classes of results to the effect that process - in terms of order of decisionmaking can be crucial.

Returning now to the apparent contradiction between Debreu's and Arrow's results. Is this a contradiction : i) within mathematics? ; ii) between economists-as-mathematicians? ; iii) between mathematical economists as economic agents?

More generally : Are such (logical?) contradictions logically possible? And; Are such contradictions individually, professionally and/ or socially desirable?

Re i) I remark that Godel's theorem does not preclude the existence of contradictions within mathematics. Indeed, in one form this result as a theorem takes the form of a contradiction to the effect that (bounding) theorems may be as if true and not true.[5] Re ii) If I name two mathematicians as theorists (e.g. Arrow, Debreu) it is clear that they can contradict (indeed have contradicted) each other through mathematics by identifying themselves and/or by being identified with their theories (respectively of Social Choice and Individual Values, Theory of Value).

Emphasising this, in 1953 Arrow and Debreu as coauthors, using an approach distinct from both of those just cited, apparently established (sufficient) existence conditions for a competitive general equilibrium as being those required for a Nash Equilibrium (a game theoretic solution notion due to Nash) under these conditions.

Re iii) If two individuals act as if to agree to a particular outcome (e.g. the production of work in collaboration for publication and sale) then, if that outcome is asserted to be chosen by both, and their preferences are (were?) different, apparently a process for the resolution of that difference is logically essential - a process whereby one or both explicitly and/ or implicitly acts as if to contradict (his) prior preferences as if to secure that outcome.[6]

Consider now in more detail an assertion of an apparent contradiction between Debreu's apparent competitive possibility result and the impossibility result attained by example in relation to the Paradox of Voting. Notice in the former case, (abstract) preference relations are related to individuals' own commodities, and (non-abstract?) choices to budgets, whereas in the latter case abstract preferences might be construed as related to (abstract) social alternatives without any constraint, except implicitly via a focus on processes of (potential) collective choice founded on each individual's individual (abstract) preference orderings. In the former case "equilibrium" decisions are asserted to be attained (proved to be attainable via prices, whereas, in the latter, a decision, if asserted to be attained, can be represented to be attained as if via dictatorship.

Comparing these, an analyst might look for dictatorship in relation to Debreu's analysis and results and more particularly dictatorship as if by analysts *within* that system and/or dictatorship as if by an analyst/ analysts *relative to* that system including an analyst (Debreu?, Kakutani?)

relative to the specification of that system and/or dictatorship relative to processes, including processes of price determination relative to as well as through that system.

In relation to the voting example an analyst might find potential dictatorship in relation to each individual analyst in the system and impute dictatorship to any analyst explicitly or implicitly imposing a process of selection on that system such that any particular outcome is selected (Thus, notice, imposing a process as if such that a particular individual within the system could be abstractly construed as acting as if dictatorially).

From a different perspective an analyst might seek individual and/ or collective *purpose* in individuals' specifications of abstract preferences as individuals and/ or in individuals actions as if to secure conformability with a price-determination process. (Debreu's imposed price determination process). An analyst might seek purpose, too, in actions as if to select a benevolent/ malevolent dictator as if from a set of potential dictators via a collective decision process (and associated with that a collective decision relation/"welfare" relation).

In this context I reemphasize the assumption in Debreu's analysis, as well as in the voting paradox and Arrow's work, that individual preference relations are abstract.

An analyst seeking to resolve the apparent contradiction with reference to collective decisions between Debreu's approach and Arrow's approach might focus on (self) contradiction per se. Thus, in relation to Debreu's analysis, an analyst seeking to resolve the contradiction between Debreu's results and those of Arrow might focus on the apparent self contradiction implicit in the requirement that individuals determine abstract preference (indifference) relations and, by reference only to these abstract preferences, determine non-abstract (trading) relationships, inter -relationships and decisions in relation to non-abstract commodities.

Putting this (implicit) contradiction within Debreu's approach more starkly: apparently Debreu (implicitly) requires that individuals, by reference only to abstract preferences, act as if *contradicting* those abstract preference relations as if in order to determine "competitive" equilibrium prices and quantities.

With reference to collective choice and potential collective choice as considered either by Arrow, or via the voting paradox as above, an analyst might focus upon the relative incompleteness of explicit constraints on choice compared with Debreu's work,as well as upon a more explicit definition of classes of choice rules and processes (e.g.as if benevolent/ malevolent as if altruistic/ selfish/ indifferent).

And, given the immediate context, an analyst might notice the absence of (explicit) recognition of an initial state as non-abstract and, more generally, the absence of any explicit distinction between abstractness and non-abstractness either of states, or of relation to states.

These remarks will become clearer if I extend the previous example to include a fourth state D explicitly prescribed as being a non-abstract *initial* state via:

1	A	P	B	P	C	P	D
2	B	P	C	P	A	P	D
3	C	P	A	P	B	P	D

It might now seem that any individual might potentially determine (dictate?) a preferred state both for himself *and* for the others. But by what process? As associated questions :

i) If state D is not abstract, and A, B, C are abstract what is the relation of abstract to non-abstract (and vice versa), individually and/ or collectively? and ;

ii) If, potentially, abstractly preferred states are attainable, which, if any, of these individuals is to determine (dictate) that a particular state is (collectively) attained? and, more fundamentally ;

iii) how are individuals to determine relative to themselves and/ or relative to each other that a particular -as yet unrealized -potential state is potentially attainable, and individually and/or collectively preferred to an initial state?

I remark here that it might seem that if any individual were able to propose a state which he preferred for the others, and which the others then preferred for themselves, the outcome would be, via its very proposition, potentially attainable (at some order attainable) and, if attained, would be apparently : i) collectively preferred and ; ii) preferred as a realized (actualized non-abstract) social state to individual abstract (definitions of) preferences over individually -and so collectively -abstract social states.

In case it be thought that the above issues and questions apply only because the conjectured abstract preference relations of the three individuals over social states A, B, C, D were represented as being different, consider a different case for which it is asserted that each individual has the same abstract preference orderings over A, B, C, D. Schematically:

1	A	P	B	P	C	P	D
2	A	P	B	P	C	P	D
3	A	P	B	P	C	P	D

It might now seem that these three individuals would unanimously prefer A to B to C to D. But how are *any* of these states tobe attained, even if attainable, and *which* if any, of the three individuals is to secure its attainment? Abstractly, it might seem that *whichever* individual acted as if to realize A, B, C would secure a gain for all and, in that sense, it might seem impossible to predict which, if any, would act.

But notice that it is also apparently possible to argue that *whichever* one, if any, *did* act, *all* would gain.

Apparently, if it is required that determinacy be linked to a prediction of which one, if any, would act then the above specification is indeterminate whereas if the idea of determinacy is linked to the recognition that (abstractly) *whichever* one acted *all* would gain then, as long as any one did act, the outcome is apparently determinate -as if dictated by the action of any one (or more) of the three.

More generally I remark that the notations A, B, C, D, 1, 2, 3 do not explicitly (explicitly do not) distinguish individuality of "individual" relations to social states, nor do they explicitly comprehend interrelation or potential interrelation of individuals and/ or of social states. Going further, nor do these notations give any indication of the numbers of individuals associated or potentially associated with a (potential) social state.

I have remarked that Arrow's approach to collective choice, in common with the approach considered above, does not give explicit consideration to resource constraints on choice, whereas these are fundamental to Debreu's analysis.

Now consider resources in a context of initial conditions. In particular consider a schematic initial condition $\Sigma x_r = x$ in relation to initial endowments x_r to individuals r.

It might seem that, if an individual r were able to propose (offer) less for himself (herself/ itself) in relation to his own initial endowment as if in order that another, some others, all others might (then) gain. And, if x_r were "goods" in the sense that more would indeed be/ become preferred by that other, the members of a group of others, or all others, if made available to them, then, apparently, *any* of the individuals r might bring about an improvement for another/ others by acting as if *altruistically* -as if choosing to have less goods as if in order that others may have more.

More evocatively, any individual may act altruistically by acting as if preferring to increase goods relative to others rather than retain good(s) relative to himself (herself/ itself). If "goods" were abstractly "good" relative to such an individual an altruistic act would appear to connote (self) domination of his own (abstract) preferences as if in order to offer more to another/ others.

Other cases are evidently potentially possible. For example classes of cases in which an individual's (abstract) preferences were such that less would be *preferred*, and so such that that individual might potentially gain according to his abstract preferences, while losing a measure of his (her/ its) endowment. Within that class are cases in which others might potentially gain via that (chosen) loss of initial endowment.

More generally, if all increases in "goods" x_r however distributed, were "goods" according to each individual's preferences, each would (potentially) gain by an increase in the measure x.

I remark here that these examples : i) appear more completely applicable to gifts than to exchanges ; ii) might be straightforwardly construed as (informally) consistent with principles of individual and of collective rationality by being interpreted as illustrations of such principles ; iii) might appear to invite extension and development in various directions.

Pursuing this last remark, notice that the structure $\Sigma x_r = x$ is similar to that with which I pursued a constructive example in Chapter 1 (with r = 1, 2, 3, 4). By initially setting r = 1, 2, 3, 4 here apparently contact can be made directly with that example as well as all of the analyses and results related to and through that example. In particular relations to and results attained through Figure 1.6, p.12 -including relations to issues in algebra, geometry and calculus in general, but also including analysis of general principles of mathematical/ physical relation and/or (potential) interrelation of bodies- as -persons as objects and or as particles.

From a related perspective the examples just considered might be construed as comprehending classes of cases in which dictatorship could be considered socially *desireable*, as well as inevitable, even if individuals are asserted to have "the same" (abstract) preferences over alternatives and are, in that sense, unanimous

From these various viewpoints now reconsider whether other properties cited above as typical requirements by (economic) collective choice theorists as (desirable) properties of collective choice rules/ relations are : i) logically attainable and ; ii) either individually or socially desirable.

It seems to me evident that Chapter 1 has provided examples consistent with the inevitability and, in various senses, the desirability of path dependence and of cycling, as well as examples of individual dictatorship variously consistent with interpretation in relation to the inevitability or desirability of outcomes as secured as if by individual veto and/ or social dictatorship (e.g. via leadership in relation to a group, or more generally via opening or closure of a sequence of verbal/ mathematical/ physical exchanges).

Now consider direct analogies with these earlier developments by considering 1 : 1 correspondences as indicated schematically in Figure 2.1.

If, in the present context, A, B, C, D are understood to correspond to persons, then that correspondence apparently itself yields interpretations of persons as social states and of preference relations by persons over A, B, C, D as preference relations including (self) dominance relations, by persons over persons (including themselves) -as if to determine other-oriented preference relations. (Informally relations related to what an individual prefers for others relative to himself/ herself/ itself).

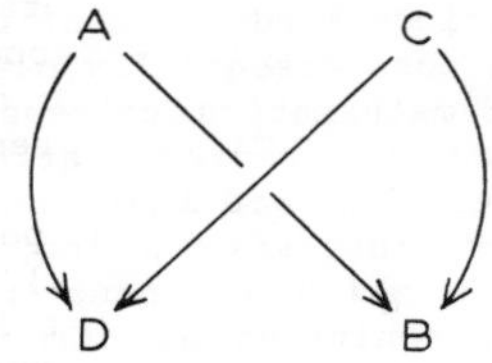

Figure 2.1

Returning now to the system $\Sigma\ x_r = x$. In the present context of collective choice it might seem that a more complete specification of choice would become available via a more complete specification of relations between abstract preference relations of individuals and relative magnitudes and relative changes in relative magnitudes of elements x_r as well as x.

In particular it might seem that, if abstract preferences over social states could be expressed in relation to distributions of endowments, it would be reasonable to represent these schematically via (individually) abstract relations, which may either take the form, or be reducible via specialization to the form, $U_i(x_1{}^i \dots x_r{}^i \dots x_n{}^i)$, with particular social states and/ or potential social states being associated with particular -and individually distinct -actual and/ or potential distributions/ redistributions.

Such a representation invites further interpretation and investigation and more particularly interpretation and investigation in relation to allocations and reallocations of property rights between persons.

For example, if abstract preference relations are related to endowments, by what process, if any, could individuals redistribute ownership of their own or others' endowments? Or, as an apparently associated question: by what processes, if any, would individuals have, or not have, the right to gain or relinquish ownership and/ or to use endowments and/ or to redistribute endowments relative to themselves, each other and/ or to and through a wider system?

From a related perspective it might appear that, given more structure, for example $x_1 < x_2 \dots$ with x_1, x_2 measured in a consistent set of units, then more meaningful statements could be generated, for example concerning transfers of endowments from smaller to larger, or conversely, and/ or from members of larger groups to (smaller) members of smaller groups. Such relations and interrelations would be of interrelating and codetermining orders of relative magnitude, change in direction, and sign .

Stressing this : If, for example $x_1 = x_2 = x_3 \dots$ with $\Sigma xr = x$ then *any* change in magnitude of *any* x_r would connote distinction of relatively smaller/larger together with related implications of change in relative magnitude change in relative direction and sign of some x_r relative to itself and to and through a wider system.

(This latter example will evoke even stronger associations with the constructive example considered in Chapter 1 with its associated determinacy/ indeterminacy issues than will the statement $\Sigma xr = x$ considered alone).

I have remarked that Arrow employed symbolic logic in relation to his investigation of Collective Choice -as I have done in relation to the Voting Paradox -whereas Debreu employed abstract algebraic topology to generate his "competitive general equilibrium" arguments and results. I have also remarked that these two references remain central to graduate courses in economic theory.

By contrast, standard intermediate microeconomics courses and associated texts rely either implicitly or explicitly on functions rather than correspondences and various kinds of continuous differential calculus. This itself : i) appears to pose essentially mathematical questions bearing on the relationship *within* mathematics between these various branches of mathematics and, in that way, to redirect attention to issues considered earlier and ; ii) emphasizes the fact that economists have employed quite different and, in that sense, inconsistent and contradictory, techniques to garner "competitive" results which are construed as "the same" or, via particular specializations, construed as directly comparable, even when these techniques are perceived as radically different.[7]

Examples of texts still widely used in the UK and in North America, in approximate order of perceived difficulty are Henderson and Quandt {9}, Leftwich {17} , Koutsoyiannis {13} and Laidler {14}.

Even a disinterested reader would gain the impression that the primary focus of these books is on competition -as -central -paradigm and that, accordingly, their principal and most essential purpose is to expound and to explain microeconomics largely, if not only, by reference to abstract (mathematicized) models of "competition".

A standard paradigmatic case is that of "two persons", "two commodities" and of "pure trade", which can be found in these and other texts treated in words and/ or illustrated by means of "Edgeworth-Bowley Boxes" and/ or via a form of continuous differential calculus. (To reinforce this, in the four sample references, cited, Edgeworth Boxes appear in association with the Pure Trade case respectively, on p.204, p.386, p.537 and p.226).

The mathematization of economics via differential calculus can be traced to Walras, Marshall and others (including Pareto) at the turn of this century, but the texts cited above more clearly trace their mathematical treatment of economics and more particularly of "competitive" economics to books by Hicks {10} and by Samuelson {23}.

Both Hicks' and Samuelson's works stressed constrained choice and optimization but, although the symbolic treatment via differential calculus is similar in each, their emphases are quite different. Hicks, in words, stresses processes of determination of equilibrium and emphasizes uncertainty and the consequently potentially temporary nature of equilibria, if attained, whereas Samuelson emphasizes stationarity and conditions for "long run" equilibrium as a stationary and stable state.

Formally, in each case, individual "competitive" decision problems are represented as being undertaken via maximization of the individual's abstract and (twice) differentiable preference/ indifference relations, $U_i = U_i(y_{i_1} \cdots y_{ij} \cdots y_{im})$ defined over own consumptions levels of "consumption commodities" subject (only) to individual budget constraints determined via (parametically) given prices and incomes. Hence, apparently necessary and/ or sufficient conditions for individual (constrained) maxima are determined by means of a form of continuous differential calculus on the assumption that budget constraints will hold with equality.

I stress here that the preference relations U_i are asserted to be determined (only) relative to own consumption levels,in distinction from the relations which I posited in the context of collective choice, where the arguments were interpreted as being related to endowments of commodities.

Both representations might be seen as different, yet not necessarily mutually inconsistent specializations of a then more general, form $U_i(y_{i_1}, \ldots y_{ij}, x_{i_1}, \ldots x_{ij})$ which can be seen as corresponding to a particular form of specialization of the characteristics and commodities structures considered in Chapters 6 and 7 below.

I have emphasized that specification via a differential calculus either explicitly or implicitly underlies standard intermediate microeconomics texts' analyses of individual choice under "competition" - as reference to the above example sources will verify. In these texts will be found not only various interpretations based on such representations, but also further "theories of consumer behaviour".

In the former class are interpretations according to which the relations U_i are, or are not, asserted to have "cardinal" significance -the former being termed a "physiocratic" interpretation and the latter an "ordinal" interpretation of a kind associated with the name of Hicks and arising from developments in the opening chapters of his book cited above.[9]

Within the cardinal class, and usually in a context of collectve social decisions, (via "cost-benefit analysis" in particular) "Marshallian" Interpretations are sometimes considered, this class of cases being attained by variously specified specializations of assumptions. (The variety of such specializations is in part due to the variety of views on the relationship of parts of Marshall's own work to economics in general and to the meaning of his writing, especially that in a footnote to Chapter VI of his Principles, on consumers' surplus in particular).[10]

Other theories which will be encountered in one or more of these texts are :

i) Samuelson's Revealed Preference Theory which, as its title suggests, emphasizes realized process rather than abstract preferences in relation to the specification of processes of decision ;

ii) von Neumann and Morgernstern's axiomatic approach, formally or informally expressed, with its focus on (potential) decisionmaking under conditions of uncertainty in general and of games (for which they developed it, see {25}) in particular. This approach is seen by mathematical economists as quasi-cardinal in character for, in distinction from an ordinal relation, a von Neumann - Morgernstern preference relation admits linear transformations but not *any* monotone transformation whereas, in distinction from a cardinal relation as usually understood, the individual is not necessarily asserted to identify with U_i ;

iii) the goods- characteristics approach intially due to Kelvin Lancaster {15}, {16}, wherein characteristics are seen as the objects of choice and a linear and, by his assumption, *objective* (in the sense of not differing between individuals) consumption technology is introduced to relate and interrelate characteristics, consumption commodities and, via the latter parametrically given prices and incomes, budget relations.

This brief review makes it apparent that it would be a mistake to believe that economists agree - even in standard treatments centred on competition-as-central-paradigm, on a single theory of consumer behaviour. A variety of approaches coexist in the established literature and these are frequently employed as if interchangeable alternatives in particular applications.

Indeed in Chapters 6 and 7 I will relate and interrelate issues pertaining to the first four approaches, stressing their distinctiveness, as well as their essentially *complementary* character - in particular the significance which can attach : to ordinality (and the associated property of monotonicity) for *abstract* preference relations ; to cardinality (and the associated property of apparent measureability for purposes of *relative* agreement/ disagreement on expressions of preferences (e.g. via trade in standard units of volume, weight and currency), and ; to "Marshallian" preferences as a measure of (potential) collective social welfare gain/loss relative to individuals.

The term "Revealed Preference" itself has incompletely specified *algorithmic* connotations. It seems natural to extend this theory to reinforce this feature. To underline this, in a context of competition, price taking behaviour is commonly stressed but, more strikingly, in a context of two-person, two-commodity trade the determination of chosen, in the sense of mutually preferred, exchange(s) carries with it the connotation of prior agreement to exchange and, deriving from that, the prior revelation, by some process(es) of *mutual preference* to exchange.

It seems to me that, in that context at least, a process of determination of preferences with a view to exchange might aptly be termed one of *Reciprocal Revealed Preference* wherein, in the first instance, one individual acts as if to dominate his own abstract preferences as if in order to reveal a preference to trade via an offer of a trade which then, conditionally accepted by the other, leads to a counter offer (reciprocal offer) as if to secure an improved position for one (or both).

The use of the term "offer" here will evoke associations with the constructive example considered re library collections in Chapter 1. For economists, with a context of trade, it will evoke associations with "offer curves" especially if trade is given geometric expression in relation to an Edgeworth Box. (I have considered such representations in some detail in connection with a geometrically based critique of competitive general equilibrium analyses. See {22}).

Specifically, insofar as the trade case is seen as corresponding to an interpretation in relation to the systems already considered in Chapter 1 these remarks in relation to offers might be seen as just one means of seeking solutions to generally and incompletely specified nonlinear programming problems. Others, including means corresponding to cases in which one or both individuals gain via gifts or via barter, will also be considered at later stages in this and subsequent Chapters.

Relation to these other developments will make it evident that essentially "physiocratic" analogues and interpretations are possible in relation to standard theoretical treatments of economic processes. But in doing so they emphasize the fundamentally restrictive and primitive nature of such standard treatments by comparison both to the inherent complexity and indeterminacy of physical processes and the inherently greater complexity of economic systems related to and generated by the choices/ decisions of persons.

I have noted that textbook approaches using a classical calculus take a budget condition as the sole constraint on individual choice, with that condition holding, by assumption, with equality. Analysts familiar with nonlinear programming might see a nonlinear programming formulation with an objective function subject to one, or more, weak inequality conditions as a more general class of cases, in the sense that a single equality condition constitutes a special case of a series of inequality conditions.

Such analysts will be familiar with the Kuhn-Tucker conditions for optimality, with various kinds of solution algorithms including Lagrange multiplier techniques, separating hyperplane methods, and supporting hyperplanes (as used by Charnes, Clower and Kortanek {5}) among others, as well as with various classes of nonlinear programming problems including, as examples, quadratic programming, integer programming, geometric programming and optimal control problems expressed via nonlinear programmes. (Those less familiar with these will find an appropriate text a convenient means of surveying these and other possibilities. For example see Zangwill's book {29}).

While apparently the Kuhn-Tucker conditions can be made applicable under quite general assumptions to each of these classes of problems, in each case their applicability is restricted by the *Constraint Qualification*.

Under this heading Zangwill states : "Unfortunately situations exist in which there are directions in (x) that are not in D(x). However such situations are generally mathematical fabrications and do not seem to arise in practice". (p.39).

The tone of the second sentence is significant here. In fact, in an Edgeworth Box context according to which strictly nonlinear representations of individual preferences are asserted to be contained by strictly linear representations in relation to commodities, it can be shown that the constraint qualification can have a central significance. Its conditions then accord with circumstances where individuals could not trade except : i) by principles and processes of self contradiction and ; ii) by associated principles and processes according to which what is relatively strictly interior to one individual's constraint set may be as if perfectly predictive of locations strictly exterior to constraints of another, or others.

In such exchange-related contexts, too, other apparently obscure phenomena, including degeneracy and "duality gaps", can play central roles for linear and nonlinear cases. Specifically, in developments which follow – and particularly in the Lancaster-like contexts of Chapters 6 and 7 – exchange requirements may be consistent with behaviours according to which individuals act as if purposively to *increase* potential differences between elements of dually interrelating subsystems.

I have noted that Arrow's and Debreu's books appeared as Cowles Foundation Monographs. Another book which appeared in that series, in 1951, was edited by T.J. Koopmans and entitled "Activity Analysis in Production and Allocation" {12}. Activity Analysis, with an emphasis on issues of economic efficiency, can be seen as an extension of the Input-Output idea developed earlier by W. Leontief (see {18}), with the primary emphasis on empirical issues for aggregated economic systems. At least in the initial stages it focused on efficiency in relation to price; on the existence, or otherwise, of "efficiency prices" in a disaggregated, linear, framework of analysis.

I have considered the input-output framework in the following chapter where I have used it both to motivate extensions to its own structure and to develop (associated) relations to linear as well as to nonlinear programming problems, *inter alia*, particular emphases upon issues of determinacy/ indeterminacy and of degeneracy.

Also in 1951, a paper appeared authored by Charnes entitled "Optimality and Degeneracy in Linear Programming" {4}. Although, as will become evident, the content of this paper is entirely theoretical, its genesis was not. The central issues arose in a context of the application of linear programming methods to the blending of aviation gasoline (the first industrial application of linear programming) where degeneracy and consequent cycling of solution algorithms were found to be serious and significant issues.

The development in this paper apparently extended duality results so that they hold over any ordered field, and fields of any order. In this way the paper made duality results entirely unexceptional in theory and, since these techniques would apparently, in principle, be computer programmable, also in practical computations, including computations relating to empirical applications and examples.

The term complete regularization in the title refers not only to the removal, in principle, of all degeneracy problems via the introduction of perturbations, but also to the resolution of (potential) infeasibility and boundedness problems in general, yielding a guarantee of bounded solutions at some order via the introduction, according to particular rules, of ordered non-Archimedean quantities.

I have emphasized the essentially empirical background to Charnes' work on degeneracy and that that work itself is essentially theoretical in character, but I have emphasized, too, that there theory and empiricism were interrelated, with an essentially empirical problem provoking a (major) theoretical advance.

An analyst consulting economics texts such as those cited here, as well as the wider literature on the economics of "pure" or "perfect" competition, will, by contrast, find the dearth of empirical evidence either to motivate the development of theory or to test theory (theories) once developed, very striking, although, I believe, not surprising on a number of grounds.

First, as I have stressed, competitive general equilibrium arguments are typically represented as if interpretations of wholly abstract mathematical systems, with the emphasis upon abstraction rather than upon empiricism. Second, as I have also stressed, economic theorists are themselves sceptical of particular mathematical expressions of competitive economic arguments.

I have noted, for example, Debreu's apparent reservations concerning the applicability of (differential) calculus vis a vis "convexity and topological properties" whereas many other economists have reservations concerning Debreu's analysis, inter alia on the grounds of its degree of abstractness, *because* in it the theory is wholly divorced from its (economic) interpretations.

In spite of – or perhaps because of, scepticism of these kinds, competitive analyses conducted via apparently radically different mathematical techniques coexist in the mainstream literature on microeconomic theory -as -theory, without empirical substantiation and/ or validation being seen as (definitive) tests of the survival, or otherwise of particular theories, or indeed of any of these theories in that literature.

Thirdly, I have stressed that Arrow's Impossibility result in relation to Collective Social Choice, together with the large body of literature stemming from it, is also familiar to economists, those results apparently conclusively demonstrating, again by means of different abstract mathematical techniques, that, in general, dictatorship is in some sense inevitable in a context of social decisions.

Such results apparently themselves provide mathematically based *theoretical* grounds for objection to *any* result and a fortiori for objection to attempts to empiricially implement any result – even if obtained by other kinds of mathematics – to the effect that many agents either could, or would, be able to independently choose the same social outcome and, in particular, (objectively) the same "competitive" outcome *without* effective dictatorship (despite claims for proofs of competitive equilibrium results to the contrary.)

More informally, students of economics typically have great difficulty with the typical assumptions and conclusions of competitive arguments. As examples :

i) an assumption to the effect that each agent has complete information concerning the range and descriptions of potential alternative (choices of) commodities and prices – in more advanced arguments this is sometimes modified to an assumption of "certainty-equivalent" information, despite the student's own awareness and experience that his own information is typically not complete in these respects ;

ii) that conditions of certainty (again in more advanced arguments conditions of certainty- equivalence) will obtain in relation to potential outcomes, despite students' everyday experience,to the contrary, of uncertainty in the senses both of incompleteness of knowledge at any given time and the related sense of incompleteness of predictability in relation to potential outcomes relative to decisions/ actions ;

iii) typical competitive assumptions and conclusions are that ultimately *the same* equilibrium price will prevail for each agent acquiring/ disposing of each scarce commodity, and that the competitive analysis abstracts from issues pertaining to distinction(s) of location and to (potential) transportation between locations.

Such assumptions and conclusions apparently ignore students' everyday experience and, more formally, ignore relations, potential relations and distinctions of time and place (logically?) dictated by relations, interrelations and distinctions of time and place between persons, between commodities and between persons and commodities *because* related yet distinct different persons and different commodities in space-time.

Typically standard intermediate textbook analyses, whether microeconomic or macroeconomic, assign no role to transportation and associated (potential) means and processes of transportation. And, with reference to the relative time aspect of space-time, standard analyses are conducted as if each period (optimally) replicates the preceding one in all respects as if via perfect prediction.

In consequence it is widely understood that, under conditions of "perfect" competition, a single, "competitively" determined equilibrium price would prevail for each commodity in a connected set of markets as if independently of time and location.

However, if distinctions of location and potential processes and means of transportation are explicitly included, then in general, even under appropriately modified "competitive" conditions for a series of markets potentially connected by trade, the equilibrium price for each commodity and/ or for any given commodity will in general *optimally* be *different* for each location in space-time.

The meaning and significance of "competitive" conditions thereby becomes radically different from the above widely understood, and widely asserted, set of conditions deriving from the omission of explicit consideration of distinctions of space and time in the underlying analysis.

For example in Chapter 8 I will refer to "competitive" price conditions on occasion in such modified senses. There, even in the simplest cases, prices might differ regionally via conditions according to which supply price = market price + transportation cost. More generally, price structures will be significantly more complex and reflect distinct elements for capacity and variable costs of production, storage and transportation, as well as various kinds of socially and environmentally oriented (and regionally specific) regulatory costs and benefits.

The contrast between that kind of development and the existing and standard mainstream literature, which omits any specific reference to space, or time, is stark. Indeed, even where transportation issues are considered, their implications for variety and complexity of interregional output and pricing mechanisms do not seem to be widely recognized.

For example, an expert familiar with Debreu's work will be aware that he indicated how his analyses might be extended in principle to comprehend explicit differences of location in space and time, as well as to comprehend elements of conditions of uncertainty.

These topics are considered together in Chapter 7 of the Theory of Value {7}, where Debreu extends his definition of (the transfer of) a commodity so that it comprehends "in addition to its physical properties, its location and its date an event on the occurrence of which the transfer is conditional" thence extending his analysis to incorporate uncertainty as well as *in principle* theoretical distinctions of place and time.

In doing this Debreu does not appear to recognize, and certainly does not stress, that in such circumstances conditions for the existence of such an equilibrium would require that at a "competitive" optimum, not only would *different* optimal prices obtain for *each* commodity distinct in space-time, but also *relative to all* other "equilibrium" locations in space-time. That is, apparently, *except abstractly*, "equilibrium price vectors" would differ not only for, but also relative to, *each* agent.

From a related perspective, a student would, I think correctly, find it confusing to see illustrations with intrinsically explicit spatial dimensions and implications associated in textbooks and advanced treatises alike with algebraic analyses explicitly asserted by their authors to abstract from spatial considerations.

Insofar as such illustrations are seen as pertaining to choice by individuals over economic commodities, a layman might be impressed by the absence from them of (representations of) collections/ aggregations/ bodies recognizable as related to/ descriptions of related, yet as if distinct, codetermining individuals and (economic) commodities.

This remark, which is developed further in the following Chapters, will evoke associations with the (related) analyses and there directly related geometric illustrations of Chapter 1. In that Chapter, and also in Chapter 4 below, principles and processes pertaining to relative space-time play central roles, as do associated principles and processes potentially interrelating elements of bodies -as -objects, bodies -as -persons, and bodies -as -particles.

Developments of these kinds can be directly related to and through particular kinds of arithmetically, algebraically and geometrically interrelated elements of underlying linear systems. This will be more evident with reference to the system III of Chapter 4 (see p.96) which I reproduce here for ease of reference:

$$\theta p_x x - \theta p_y y$$
$$x = 1$$
$$y = 1 \qquad \text{(III)}$$
$$x = y$$

Here it is particularly significant that the structure of the constraints of this underlying arithmetic-algebraic system is not only linear, but linearly dependent and so *degenerate* (as well as one which potentially, and in context *desirably*, potentiates relative *unboundedness* of elements of individual or collective resource constraints and budget conditions).

It will become increasingly evident that not only can this "same" essentially "linear" subsystem be used to develop and explore elements of potentially interrelated, and *variously* linear and nonlinear, mathematical and physical phenomenon, but it can be used to do so in ways which systematically promote and exploit elements of processes of linear dependence, degeneracy and (relative) unboundedness.

In such contexts degeneracy and the associated phenomenon of cycling will have central roles to play with reference to potential principles and processes of as if perfect mathematical/ physical *prediction*, a role which does not appear to have been recognized before.

Indeed, as I have already noted, even though degeneracy has always been recognized as both a theoretical and an empirical possibility in relation to linear programming specifications, it is nevertheless still a widely held view that degeneracy, and the associated – and, incidentally, strictly nonlinear – phenomenon of cycling would not be encountered in practice. In any case it is generally believed that for specifically algorithmic reasons of convergence non-degeneracy and acyclicity would be *desireable* features of any linear or goal programming specification or solution procedure.

This *may* be the case but, as developments in Chapter 1 have already indicated, the potential for cycling can play a crucial role in relation to *processes* of solution – processes which it will be shown can be related directly to "goal programming" extensions as if potentiating and/ or potentiated via elements of the "linear" system (III).

In such contexts potential for cycling can be thought of as potentially corresponding to *socially*, as well as mathematically and physically desireable aspects of a problem specification for they can provide a fundamental basis not just for explanations of relative motions in general but for as if perfect mathematical- physical economic predictions in particular.

Nevertheless, in relation to empirical applications of linear programming techniques it has long been asserted (and believed) that degeneracy even when feasible in theory would not occur in practice due to round-off errors of computation – despite Charnes', Cooper's and Mellon's and others' experience to the contrary at a very early date in the development of linear programming theory and applications {7}.[11]

Insofar as the preceding remarks and developments relate to standard references, they might be seen as constituting a source of standard materials for an intermediate/advanced course on microeconomic theory. At the present time a course in that area embodying significant amounts of material on "linear" programming and for example substantive reference to Baumol{3} to Koopmans{12} and/or to Charnes and Cooper {6} would be unusual and, I believe, unusually enlightened.

A student taking a (more) standard mainstream microeconomics course would be more likely to focus attention on abstract problems formulated via calculus/ algebraic topology than via linear programming methods and would be (more) likely to become primarily acquainted with (standard) competitive results by these means.

A specialist student would also become familiar with Arrow's, apparently contradictory result, as well as further well known results and analyses which he might, on reflection, see as grounds for theoretical as well as empirical objection to any proposal to take (collective/ social) action as if to implement a (wholly) "competitive" programme. Among such further (and standard) results are the Lipsey -Lancaster "Second Best" result and results in relation to the collective provision of "public goods".

Conclusion

My purpose in this Chapter has been in part to provide a survey and critique of some standard results in microeconomic theory, while, at the same time, indicating means of solution to outstanding theoretical problems posed by the apparently mutually contradictory nature of particular sets of results.

More importantly, however, I have tried to indicate how such contradictions might be used as bases for theoretical and empirical *solutions* to outstanding problems for economic theory and policy, of kinds which are developed in subsequent Chapters – and particularly in Chapters 4, 6 and 7 – all founded upon principles and processes of contradiction and self contradiction, relating to particular elements of underlying "known" subsystems.

In the following Chapter I will approach such issues and "linear" systems in related ways by considering particular kinds of potential generalizations and applications of "input-output" structures.

Footnotes

1. A theorem in relation to correspondences, generalizing Weierstrass' Theorem in relation to functions.

2. Debreu himself stresses the abstractness of his work: "The Theory Value is treated here with the standards of rigor of the contemporary formalist school of mathematics ... Allegiance to rigor dictates the axiomatic form of the analysis where the theory, in the strict sense, is logically entirely disconnected from its interpretations." {7} p.x.

3. Throughout what follows I use the term he/ his generically rather than using he/she, his/hers.

4. Many see a majority decision rule as the essential feature of democratic decisionmaking processes and might be surprised by this counterexample to a proposition that such a rule is decisive. I remark that, perhaps for reasons conditioned by his own experience, Plato in his Republic ranked oligarchy, democracy and tyranny – states which he related as transpiring by processes of degeneration in that order – all below philosopher kingship – a philosopher king having as attributes knowledge, wisdom and benevolence, (see {20}).

5. This result may itself cause any analyst, expert or laymen to have acute reservations conerning any attempt (by anyone) to assert the conclusiveness of theorems and means of proof both in general and in particular.

6. Notice that inter alia Arrow-Debreu contradicts Arrow *and* contradicts Debreu in the sense that the analysis and results of this collaborative work are not (wholly) consistent with their individual works.

7. For example, again quoting from Debreu's Preface "The effort toward rigor.. .. may also lead to a radical change of mathematical tools. In the area under discussion it has essentially been a change from the calculus to convexity and topological properties" ({8} p.x).

8. In most economics texts conditions of monopoly, of oligopoly and of monopolistic competition are established as "inefficient" market regimes, but "inefficiency" is usually *defined* as being a state inconsistent with the (abstract) conditions of "pure competition".

9. It seems to me that this explicitly "physiocratic" designation itself invites the attention of physicists, at least to this branch of the economics literature.

10. I have noted that the mathematization of economics might be traced back to Marshall who in turn expressed indebtedness to Cournot in his Preface as follows: "..it seems doubtful whether any one spends time well in reading lengthy translations of economic doctrine into mathematics, that is not his own" ... p.ix. I remark that in the absence of a (more) complete mathematical expression for his concept of consumers' surplus a considerable literature consuming a *variety of* "Marshallian" approaches has developed making not only the application of consumers' surplus but its concept a controversial matter.

11. My own experience is that essentially degenerate specifications (until the input was suitably modified) occurred with consequent break-down of the standard linear programming system at the Univervisty of Texas, Austin (1974) in work with F. Phillips running a constrained Input-Output system in a land use planning context, at the University of York, England (1975) when running a distribution problem exhibiting the More for Less Paradox and at the University of Hull, England (1981) when again running a constrained Input-Output system as the basis for R. Islam's thesis on manpower planning for Bangladesh.

References

{1} Arrow, K.J. (1951), *Social Choice and Individual Values*, Cowles Foundation Monograph 12, Yale University Press.

{2} Arrow, K.J. and Debreu, G.(1954), *Existence of an Equilibrium for a Competitive Economy*, Econometrica 22.

{3} Baumol, W.J. (1961), *Economic Theory and Operations Analysis* Prentice Hall,New York.

{4} Charnes, A. (1952), *Optimality and Degeneracy in Linear Programming*, Econometrica, No. 2.

{5} Charnes, A., Clower, R.W. and Kortanek, K.O. (1967),*Effective Control through Coherent Decentralization with Preemptive Goals*, Econometrica 35, No. 2.

{6} Charnes, A. and Cooper, W.W., (1961),*Management Models and Industrial Applications of Linear Programming,* 2 vols, Wiley, New York.

{7} Charnes, A., Cooper, W.W.and Mellon, B., (1952), *Blending Aviation Gasolines - A Study in Programming Interdependent Activities*, Econometrica, 20, No. 2.

{8} Debreu, G. (1959), *Theory of Value : An Axioimatic Analysis of Economic Equilibrium* , Cowles Foundation Monograph 17 - Yale University Press.

{9} Henderson, J.M. and Quandt, R.E.(1958), *Microeconomic Theory*, McGraw -Hill, New York.

{10}Hicks, J.R. (1946), *Value and Capital*, 2nd ed. Oxford University Press, London.

{11}Houthakker, H.S. (1950), *Revealed Preference and Utility Functions*, Economica, May.

{12}Koopmans, T.J. (ed) (1961), *Activity Analysis of Productioin and Allocation* Cowles Commission Monograph 13, Wiley, New York,

{13}Koutsoyiannis, A. (1979), *Modern Microeconomics*, Macmillan, London.

{14}Laidler, D. (1974), *Introduction to Microeconomics*, Philip Allan, Oxford.

{15}Lancaster, K. (1966), *A New Approach to Consumer Theory*, Journal of Political Economy.

{16}Lancaster, K. (1966), *Change and Innovation in the Technology of Consumption*, American Economic Review.

{17}Leftwich, R.H. (1975), *The Price System and Resource Allocation*, 5th ed Holt Dryden.

{18}Leontief, W. (1951), *The Structure of the American Economy 1919-1939* 2nd ed. Oxford University Press, New York.

{19}Marshall, A. (1920),*Principles of Economics*, 8th ed. Macmillan, London.

{20}Plato, (1955),*The Republic*, Penguin Classics, London.

{21}Quirk, J. and Saposnik, R.(1958), *Introduction to General Equilibrium Theory and Welfare Economics*, McGraw-Hill, New York.

{22}Ryan, M.J. (1980), *More on the More for Less Paradox in the Distribution Problem*, *Lecture Notes in Economics and Mathematical Systems*, 174, pp.275-303, Springer Verlag.

{23}Ryan, M.J. *Further Notes on Impossibility Results and Competitive Systems*, forthcoming.

{24}Samuelson, P.A.(1947), *The Foundations of Economic Analysis*, Harvard University Press, Cambridge, Mass.

{25}Sen, A.K. (1970), *Collective Choice and Social Welfare*, Holden-Day, San Francisco.

{26}Smith, A. (1970), *The Wealth Of Nations*, Pelican Classics, Penguin Books, London.

{27}Von Neumann, J. and Morgernstern, O. (1947), *The Theory of Games and Economic Behaviour*, 2nd ed. Princeton University Press, Princeton, New Jersey.

{28}Walras, L. (1954), *Elements of Pure Economics* (tr. by W. Joffe), Richard D. Irwin, Homewood, Ill.

{29}Zangwill, W.I.(1969), *Non-linear Programming : A Unified Approach*, Prentice-Hall, Englewood Cliffs, N.J.

3 Input output analysis, standard units, monetary units and integer arithmetic

3.1 Introduction

My main focus in this Chapter is on new kinds of motivation for standard units in general, and for standardized monetary units in particular. These follow from the recognition that principles and processes of relative indeterminacy and incompleteness are not just mathematically and physically inevitable, but may be individually and collectively economically, as well as scientifically, desireable.

Specifically, any physicist would recognize that the empirical measurement of any particular physical magnitude with absolute precision is ultimately inevitably impossible. He would recognize a fortiori that to ensure that two different physicists differently located in space-time could measure the same physical magnitude in precisely the same way would ultimately be impossible. He would recognize these points together as, in some sense implying inevitable shortcomings for any empirically based physical research.

It is argued here that empirically oriented economists, by recognizing such inevitable, and essentially subjectively determined, differences of agents' physical measurements, can potentially exploit them for their own and/ or others gain. Intuitively, in certain circumstances such potential differences of measurement may correspond to measures of opportunity for individuals to gain, either individually or collectively, from processes generating gifts, barters or trade. In such cases, not only would individuals *inevitably* measure differently from each other, but they and others may act as if *preferring* to do so by offers of gifts, barters or trades to others differently located in space-time.

In order to give more precise forms to potential developments of these various kinds, and as a preliminary to them, I will first consider some relatively more abstract developments pertaining to "linear" systems and input-output analyses.

3.2 A note on input-output systems

Consider the following algebraically expressed system of relations:

$$Ax + b = x \qquad (2.1)$$

Notice that no restrictions of magnitude or sign are placed on the elements a_{ij}, b_i, x_i of A, b, x respectively. In principle, any, some, or all, of these may be zero. However the equality sign does imply *relative* restrictions of magnitude and of sign.

Insofar as (2.1) is seen as a system of mathematical equations, a mathematician might posit many different means of determining what solutions are possible and, if possible, many means of determining those solutions. These include inspection (for a simple system) or "Gaussian elimination". Another approach is via matrix inversion. Generally a mathematician might assert that, under more or less restrictive conditions, a solution x to the above system can be expressed as:

$$(I - A)^{-1} b = x \qquad (2.1)'$$

with

$$(I - A)^{-1} (I - A) = I$$

Notice that (2.1)' implies that a valid inversion process exists, while leaving the issue of the particular process whereby $(I - A)^{-1}$ is to be determined unstated. There are many means whereby a matrix may be inverted, including means employing minors of the associated matrices, and means introducing auxilliary matrices, each with associated varieties of orders of solution.

Now, for given A, b, a solution is determinate and unique only if $(I - A)^{-1}$ is non-singular, and $(I - A)^{-1}$ is non-singular only if its elements are linearly independent.

A sufficient condition for singularity of $(I - A)^{-1}$ is that at least one row and/or at least one column of the "Leontief" matrix (I - A) contains all zero entries. Thus, if singularity/ all zero entries are allowed, or are not explicitly assumed away, the (ordered) array (I - A) may, in principle, be of arbitrarily large dimensions – its dimensions are not then bounded by assumption/ assertion.

Another sufficient condition for singularity is that a linear combination of rows and/or a linear combination of columns of (I - A) can be employed to *generate* all zero entries in at least one row and/ or at least one column.

The latter condition of singularity is different from the former and apparently stresses *processes* whereby elements of zero rows/ columns are related, interrelated and generated as well as critically located "zeroes" themselves.

Now consider an interpretation of (2.1) as follows : Let x_i be the (unknown?) output of sector i, a_{ij} be quantity of input i per unit output of sector j and b_i be the (given?) "final demand" for output from sector i.

With these interpretations, the specification (2.1) corresponds to an (open) Leontief input-output system. Emphasizing the empirical nature of these interpretations and determinacy in this Leontief context, it might seem evident that for (empirically) given named sectors i, levels of physical transactions between sectors $x_{ij}*$, levels of sector output x_i* and of final demands b_i the following relations, if exhaustive would hold by definition:

$$\sum_j x_{ij}* + b_i = x_i* \qquad (2.2)$$

Formally $x_{ij}*$ and x_j* being known, the transformation:

$$a_{ij} = \text{def} \frac{x_{ij}^*}{x_j^*} \qquad (2.3)$$

might be introduced and, with these transformations, the following system generated:

$$\sum_j a_{ij}x_j^* + b_i = x_i^* \qquad (2.4)$$

or, alternatively,

$$Ax^* + b = x^* \qquad (2.1)^*$$

With the above nomenclature and interpretations it might seem reasonable to suppose : $a_{ij} < 1$ $(x_{ij}^* < x_j^*)$, $x_j^* \geqq 0$ $b_i \geqq 0$. That is, apparently the interpretation of the system (2.1) as an input-output system itself implies further restrictions on relative magnitudes and on signs. These interpretations seem to imply no joint production, that only one process might be employed for production in each sector, while emphasizing dependence and interdependence between sectors and between output(s) and final demand(s).

In due course I will reinforce these points and introduce related issues by considering a three sector example naming the sectors as coal, steel and railways (as Baumol does in his introduction to this topic in {13}).

This interpretation emphasizes not only interdependence, but also issues bearing on aggregation (disaggregation) in time and space and, in that context, on the role of standard units of measure as means of aggregating both abstractly and empirically. Such an example also focuses attention on related issues of completeness/ incompleteness both in general and in this particular instance. Examples include incompleteness with reference to inputs to production, including labour and raw materials, incompleteness with reference to production capacity, incompleteness with reference to processes of generation of demand(s), and incompleteness with reference to process(es) of solution of the system.

Confining attention to the latter issue, consider the following, apparently abstract, extremal representation:

$$\begin{aligned} &\text{Minimize} \sum_i \overset{+}{c_i}\, \overset{+}{x_i} + \sum_i \overset{-}{c_i}\, \overset{-}{x_i} \\ \mu_i \quad &\text{subject to} \quad x_i - \sum_j a_{ij}x_j + x_i^{+} - x_i^{-} = b_i \end{aligned} \qquad (I)$$

where, in principle, the parameters a_{ij}, b_i may be the same as in (2.1).

It might seem that, if c_i^+, $c_i^- > 0$, and, if a solution with $x_i^+ = x_i^- = 0$ all i is feasible, then that solution is optimal. Such a solution would here correspond to a solution to the system (2.1) and, if that solution were unique, to an unique solution to a thereby generalized input-output system.

Evidently, therefore, if a (an unique) solution to (2.1) exists, then it can be expressed as a solution to an extremal problem. In particular if a solution were *given/ observed* it could apparently be expressed as a solution to such a problem. If a feasible solution to the generalized input-output problem did *not* exist,in the sense of $x_i^+ = x_i- = 0$ all i at the optimum, then non-zero optimal values of one, some, or all, of these values would themselves constitute evidence/ signals of infeasibility in that sense.

Now, formally, a feasible solution is *always* feasible if x_i^+, $x_i^- \geqq 0$.. I stress : i) that (I) *always* admits a feasible solution ; ii) that (I) invites optimization and ; iii) that (I) admits the system (2.1) as a particular, possibly singular, class of special cases. In particular (I) invites attention to *processes* of optimization to determine optimal solutions,whether or not "feasible" in the sense of x_i^+ , x_i^- = 0 all i, and whether or not 'the solution' is *known*.

Considering (I) from the viewpoint of linear dependence/ independence, consider quantities μ_i associated with the constraints of (I) as indicated. Then, under the usual conventions pertaining to a minimization, the dual of (I) may be written as:

$$\text{Maximize } \sum_i \mu_i b_i$$

$$\text{subject to} \qquad \mu_i(1 - a_{ii}) + \sum_{j \neq i} \mu_j a_{ji} \leqq 0$$

$$\mu_i \leqq c_i^+ \qquad\qquad (I)'$$

$$-\mu_i \leqq c_i^-$$

Here, apparently quite incidentally, I have introduced linear programming in the form of a goal programme in relation to a system which, as initially specified, took the form of a system of linear *equations* and, for which, apparently, all of the parameters a_{ij}, b_i were "known". Although here applied in an economics context, apparently, in principle, *any* given (algebraically expressed) equation system can be represented as a *solution* to a goal programming problem. With that context notice thatin the system (I)' the quantities μ_i are apparently unrestricted in sign and in (I) the quantities xi unrestricted, except via c_i^+, c_i^-, in magnitude.

Following from the usual conventions pertaining to *duality*, apparently, if at an optimum to the above dual pair of problems (I), (I)', $x_i^+=0$, $x_i^-=0$ all i, then $\Sigma\mu_i b_i = 0$.[1] In this context of input-output analysis the quantities μ_i might, at the optimum, be given interpretations corresponding to *prices*, in which case, if, for example $\Sigma\mu_i b_i = 0$ and $b_i > 0$ all i, apparently *either* $\mu_i = x_i$ all i at the optimum (all outputs and all inputs are optimally free) or μ_i, μ_j are opposite in sign for at least one pair i, j.

One interpretation of the condition $\Sigma\mu_i b_i = 0$, given the interpretation of μ_i as prices at the optimum, might seem to be as a net (demand) expenditure, but such an interpretation would itself call attention to the initial (mis)specification of all of the quantities bi as strictly positive and relating (only) to final demand rather than, for example to input resources, i.e. some relating to (potential) supply and *thence*, via μ_j, x_j to (potential) demand expenditure(s).

In turn, this calls attention to the apparent absence of explicit input resource constraints in the initial (standard) specification of the above input-output system.

Recall now that the initial input-output system (I - A)x = b was given as if with $x_i^+ = 0$, $x_i^- = 0$ and c_i^+, c_i^- unspecified. Indeed no explicit objective whatever was associated with that initial (evaluation of an) "empirical" system. But, via (I), (I)' *apparently* sufficient conditions for the initial system optimally to obtain are conditions such that apparently $x_i^+ = 0$, $x_i^- = 0$ all i. Being in principle an empirically specified system, that initial system is always feasible in that sense, even if c_i^+, $c^{i-} > 0$ all i, but apparently as if *uniquely* optimal only if c_i^+, $c_i > 0$ all i. Furthermore *optimal* conditions $x_i^+ > 0$, $x_i^- > 0$, some i, are apparently necessary for strict infeasibility in the above sense.

In this context of strict infeasibility, optimization invites *orderings* over relative magnitudes c_i^+, c_i^- ,thus directly imputing orderings over the relative sense(s) as well as the relative magnitudes of strict inequalities in (I) and, indirectly, via differences $x_i^+ - x_i^-$ over the magnitudes x_i inter alia via dominance considerations relating x_i, x_j through the input-output relations a_{ij} *and/or* a_{ji}.

If either c_i^+, c_i^- are both zero in net magnitude or, if they are equal and opposite in relative sign, then for at least one pair, a feasible solution to (I) is apparently consistent with $c_i^+x_i^+ + c_i^-x_i^- = 0$ with $x_i^+ > 0$, $x_i^- > 0$ as if $x_i^+ = 0$, i.e. as if strict inequalities in both senses *and* equality obtains at an optimum in constraint i.

Here this appears consistent with interpretation as an optimality condition wherein net supply falls short of *and* as if exceeds "final demand" for at least one commodity i, while appearing equal in magnitude to it. (Recall that a status of the magnitudes b_i as positive constraints with the interpretation "final demand" has been called in question – and remains in question).

Alternatively, an evocative interpretation of such a condition, if x_i^- were interpreted in relation to (potential) incremental "final demand", could apparently be one whereby (potentially), via x_i^+, x_i^- *realized* final demand may exceed b_i, *and realized* supply exceed an initial as if "optimal" value x_i, while appearing to equate relations in x_i via relations as if $x_i^+ = 0$, $x_i^- = 0$, i.e. apparently via (I),(I)' potential increases in output and in "final demand" may be as if generated and then realized contingent upon particular configurations of *pairs* c_i^+, c_i^-.

It seems evident to me that these and earlier considerations in relation to an, in principle, initially empirically based and, in that sense, feasible Leontief system invite further consideration of means whereby the quantities b_i might be generated, as well as consideration of associated processes of (potential) change in these and other magnitudes, inter alia via changes in and processes constraining changes in the magnitudes c_i^+, c_i, a_{ij} and both (potential) input and (potential) output related magnitudes b_i.

The initially algebraically expressed input output system here being interpreted as a representation of measurements in relation to an economic system, such considerations invite relation of b_i, a_{ij}, c_i^+, c_i-, x_{ij}, x_i, x_i^+, x_i^- not only to measurement and/ or decision(s) relative to particular persons and/or groups of persons, but also to conditions pertaining to conditions constraining potential measurement and decisions relative to persons, individually and/or collectively.

Also, the preceding considerations appear to invite the identification of conditions (potentially) *constraining* output including inter alia upper bounds on potential employment ; on production capacities and on raw material inputs, as well as ; specification of intertemporal relations and potential relation relating and interrelating potential output to (potential) final demand, and conversely ; and also to available stocks of inputs to production process, relations which themselves might be anticipated to recognize explicitly a time structure .

(Even within the standard specification of an input system wherein, for example, production anticipates realized final demand and inputs to production anticipate production and yet is as if anticipated by planned final demand).

Insofar as these and related considerations pertain to (potential) modification of a physical economic system via an algebraically expressed mathematical system they raise directly issues concerning the nature of relations, potential relations and interrelations of mathematicians individually and/or collectively to, and through, mathematics.

Such issues were considered in Chapter 1 in a context not only of standardized, and in that sense abstract, measures via the specification of the input output system itself, but a context in which agents are seeking to act collectively to *invalidate* the specification of that system via individual and/ or collective action to secure *changes* in realized values x_j,and thereby, implicitly, relative changes in magnitudes a_{ij} = def $x_{ij}*/x_j*$ for example via contradictions of x_j*.

Before turning to further consideration of these issues and, in part, to guide those further considerations, consider the following explicitly numerical examples. These will indicate that even in its simplest form an aggregated input-output analysis, though seemingly primitive,can be enlightening as well as informative:[2]

1. In a certain separable economy the leaders of the coal, steel and railway industries plan to make a joint approach to their government to stimulate final demand at constant prices $(d_c, d_s, d_c)^T$ for their products to sustain current levels of employment in their industries. If the government's proposed plan for final demand is given by the vector (10, 60, 20) ,and the levels of output which would sustain current levels of employment are given by the quantities (150, 250, 150), show how the leaders of the three industries might estimate the size of the output gap between the government plan and that of their industries if they had knowledge of the following input/output matrix:

0.6	0.1	0.1
0.1	0.6	0.1
0.1	0.1	0.6

Briefly indicate some lines of criticism which the government's economists might make of these estimates if they knew that they had been computed by this method.

2. An economic analyst has determined that in his country last year the input-output relations (expressed as units of input per unit output) between the coal steel and railway sectors were as indicated in the following matrix:

	Coal	Steel	Rail
Coal	0.5	0.1	0.1
Steel	0.1	0.5	0.1
Rail	0.1	0.1	0.5

In addition the analyst has determined that 300, 300 and 600 persons were employed respectively in each of the three industries per unit of output.

α) Given that last year's final demand vector was {40, 60, 20}T, use the preceding information to predict the implications of a 50% reduction in final demand for coal this year for output and employment in each sector.

β) Explain why your conclusion under 1) would not be reversible if capacity was cut this year in line with reductions in output.

γ) Does it follow from 2) that capacity should never be reduced?

I remark that the numerical information given in these examples is apparently sufficient to calculate $(I - A)^{-1}$ and so to compute x_i for various "final demand" conditions "b". That is, apparently numerical answers are attainable, on the (implicit?) assumption that $(I - A)^{-1}$ is invariant both to varying b and to the implications of varying b for varying x.

Notice, too, that in these cases, the relation between b and x is *explicitly asserted* to be predictive. Formally, via the mathematical approach to solution via $(I - A)^{-1}$ b, apparently changes in b can generate changes in x both directly and, indirectly, via the input-output coefficients.

More evocatively, apparently algebraically increases/ decreases in one or more elements of "final demand" can predictively *generate* increases/ decreases in output(s) not only for a given product but, via the inter-dependence explicit in the input-output coefficients, increases/ decreases in the output(s) of other products.

For that reason alone attention is (again) focused both on determinants and potential determinants of predicted (aggregated) final demand in general and upon determinants and potential determinants of particular components of predicted final demand in particular, as well as upon (potential) means of realizing final demand via production both in general and in relation to particular outputs

The numerical answers apparently attainable via the first example emphasize distinctive (predictive) planning roles for distinct agents involved, including an economist and leaders of various industries as well as workers (and potential workers) and government agents. They also emphasize issues of cooperation (non-cooperation) in a context in which explicitly cooperative action is being proposed in order to secure increase(s) in output(s).

If increased output and increased employment are regarded as "good" in general (by workers, potential workers, government agents, industry leaders and, more generally, potential suppliers of capital and resources), insofar as increased output in any, some or all of these industries predictively generates, via the input-output coefficients, increased output and employment in all three industries, increased output in any one or all is apparently *individually* (relative to workers, potential workers, managers, government and, via final demand, consumers) and *collectively* desireable and, in the absence of explicit resource constraints potentially attainable.

Conversely, apparently reductions in one sector,if predicted via the input output coefficients, would predictively reduce output and employment in *all* sectors, an outcome which, if potential *increases* were as if unanimously desireable, would seem *irrational* on prima facie grounds, if planned.

On an empirical note, substantial reduction in steel production in recent years has been reflected in the UK in the accounts of the rail and coal industries and, perhaps more dramatically, the 1984-5 coal strike was cited as a major cause of reported losses for that financial year by both British Rail and British Steel as well as the National Coal Board (and the Electricity Boards).

In both of the above questions the implication of the problems as set out is that relevant constraints on raw materials, capacity and workers are unlikely to become binding for the conditions posed. But the second question, via its attention to potential pit closures (incidentally anticipating the coal strike on that ground) calls attention to a variety of issues in relation to incompleteness of specification of such a simplified input output system in general.

First that question calls attention to potentially binding constraints and a potential difference of regime as if in consequence of the binding of constraints. Quite generally, in the absence of binding constraints, a production gain for one might appear to yield (have yielded?) a production gain for all others.

By contrast, if constraints on raw materials, on (potential) worker availabilities and/ or upon particular types of potential production capacity become binding then, insofar as (further) increases in potential output(s) become constrained or impossible due to non- availability of further elements of one or more particular types of resource, an increase in (derived) demand for input(s) and/or an increase in final demand for output of one type apparently will, in that sense, seemingly *reduce* the potential availability of that type of input for others.

In that way, apparently *increased* final demand of a (any) particular type may inter alia construe itself/ be construed as if implying *reduced* potential for (further) output(s) for one, some or all other (potential) types -and conversely.

These remarks suggest more general relations to issues and potential processes pertaining to potential principles and processes of collective choice in general.

More directly, remarks according to which as if chosen reductions in current demand(s) by one/ some potentially yield (relative) increase(s) in output(s) and thereby (relative) increase(s) in potential demand(s) invite interpretation(s) in relation to individual and collective *saving* for example as considered in Chapter 4 in relation to microeconomic and macroeconomic developments pertaining to the Paradox of Thrift.

And, potential interpretations here as if one, some, or all, may act as if to choose less relative to self as if to choose to secure more relative to another/ others differently located in space-time will invite potential interpretations in relation to principles and potential processes of individual and/or collective altruism, selfishness, barter or trade in particular (see for example related developments in the previous and subsequent Chapters —as well as potentially related developments pertaining to the More for Less and More for Nothing Paradox in {2}).

From another perspective, I have noted the apparently explicit absence of objectives as well as of resource and production capacity constraints from the simple standard input-output system (I) above. Such potential objectives and further constraints are a principal focus of developments in Chapter 6 onwards where attention becomes focussed more particularly upon potential political economic decentralization and potential economic regulation mechanisms including laws, taxes and subsidies in contexts of potentially hierarchical systems of regulatory authorities with potentially overlapping jurisdictions and potentially conflicting goals.

All of these phenomena are considered via potentially related and interrelated goal programming systems open to interpretation inter alia in relation to issues and processes pertaining to (potential) centralization/ decentralization in particular and/or to potential principles and processes of land use change in general.

Potential decentralization, regulation and control will refocus attention on issues pertaining to potential decentralization and control in contexts of potentially related goal programming systems and subsystems with which I began Chapter 1. They also anticipate attention, via the system (III) of Chapter 4, to such potential centralization decentralization issues in relation to mathematical/ physical principles in general, and to economic principles in particular.

Before considering mathematical/ physical relations and interrelations between (developments of) input-output systems and developments potentially generating and/ or potentially generated via goal programming interpretations in Chapter 4 onwards, I first consider standard units in general and potential significance for standard units as if potentially constituting collective coordinating, development and control devices in particular.

3.3 Some notes on standard units

I start by considering standardization and potential standardization generating and/or potentially generated by (standard) units of currency.

A British £5 note bears, in symbols, the statement £5 and, in words, the statement FIVE POUNDS. It also bears the statement : "I promise the bearer on demand the sum of five pounds" and a facsimile of the signature of the Chief Cashier on behalf of the Governor of the Bank of England.

In this way each £5 note axiomatizes itself relative to itself in words, to mathematical symbols in general and 5 relative to 5, 5 relative to FIVE and FIVE relative to FIVE in particular.

It might seem further that each five pounds subsumes a potentially *predictive* relation to other *different* five pounds' *each* in turn *inter alia* axiomatizing itself as if £5. Apparently, too, each five pounds and/or each potential five pounds note axiomatizes itself as if a measure potentially generating and/or generated via relation to a *relatively abstract* Governor of the Bank of England.

Focus first on the Governor's promise and its meaning. Is it to be understood literally to mean that each five pound note can potentially exchange as if *precisely* for five pounds different from itself, yet as if (identically) the same as itself? If so, the promise apparently as if perfectly predicts the existence of other five pound notes, not only as if spatially/ temporally different from itself, but apparently paradoxically, as if spatially/ temporally identically the same as itself

From a slightly different perspective, it would seem irrational for an individual to undertake a process as if to exchange a five pound note for a different as if identical five pound note. It would seem that, in that sense at least, the Governor's promise which each note bears is empty.

It might seem *rational* for an individual to choose to undertake a process of exchanging five pounds for more than five pounds but *irrational* to choose to do so for an as if identical five pounds and *irrational* a fortiori to choose to do so for less than an identical five pounds.

It is evidently possible in principle for the Governor to accede to requests to exchange five pounds for more than five pounds. One class of ways stem from his power to increase the number of pounds in circulation – by print orders if necessary. It seems evident, too, that it would be even more easily possible for the Governor to accede to requests to exchange five pounds for as if identical five pounds.(For example by returning the tendered note(s)). And/ or to accede to requests to exchange five pounds for less than five pounds. (For example by agreeing to exchange the given number of pouds for a lesser number of pounds and/or monetized fractions of pounds). More generally :

i) even with a fixed quantity of five pounds', the Governor, and/ or others for whom he may act as agent, could in principle enable himself to yield gains for some via exchanges of currency (including five pounds') relative to him, by losses for others via exchanges of currency (including five pounds') relative to him ;

ii) potential here for contracts to pay relatively more/ less/ the same amount in return for tendered five pounds' will be evocative of the idea of "change" - i.e. monetized fractions of five pounds' (including one pounds') and thence of potential processes pertaining to potential mathematically/ physically arithmetic operations;

iii) the implicit potential for contracts to pay strictly more/ less for tendered five pounds' will be evocative, too, of the idea of respectively relatively positive and negative time dependent real interest.

This, in conjunction with the observation that five pound notes yield mathematical/ physical measures on the Governor of the Bank of England, will provoke investigation of (potential) relations and interrelations inter alia between the Governor of a National Bank, potentially spatially and/or temporally distinct changes in elements of money supply and potentially spatially, and/ or temporally distinct changes in (elements of) rates of interest. Now consider these issues, even more primitively.

It has been seen that, if interpreted literally, the Governor's promise to exchange £5 notes appears empty, for it would seem *irrational* for an individual to seek to exchange a five pound note for an as if strictly identical five pounds note. But,viewed as an axiomatization, in the sense of a guarantee of relative worth such a promise might seem potentially more meaningful.

In particular such a promise seems more meaningful if viewed as a guarantee to individuals *potentially* foregoing five pounds' worth of other units of currency, of other financial instruments and/ or of other commodities in (potential) exchange(s) for five pounds' of (relative) worth of) "Five Pounds'".

Apparently for Five Pounds' (and so for other particular units of currency) such a guarantee does not appear meaningful in the sense of useful, if understood as referring strictly to 1 : 1 exchanges – for example to an exchange of a physical five pound note for an as if identical physical five pound note.

Even if the Governor's promise was understood as if a guarantee against forgery, such a class of 1 : 1 interpretations would not appear meaningful (in the sense of useful) for with them apparently a *forged* five pound note would guarantee only potential exchange with another forged five pound note.

So, if it is to be meaningful the Governor's promise would need to be applicable to circumstances when strictly 1 : 1 (physical) exchanges/ processes of exchange are *not* undertaken. That is, apparently each five pound note subsumes a guarantee of potential determinacy,*inter alia* in the sense of potential for as if 1 : 1 physical correspondence(s), which is to be useful essentially only for circumstances when a five pound note does *not* physically exchange for an identical physical five pounds note.

Thus a five pound note inter alia constitutes a measure of potential mathematical/ physical *determinacy* relative variously to itself, to the Governor of the Bank of England and/or to other five pounds' *and/ or* a measure of potential mathematical/ physical *indeterminacy* relative to (elements of) potential mathematical/ physical processes of exchange relative to other units of currency, other financial instruments and/or other commodities.

Underlining these observations, in a context of potential physical transactions pertaining to elements of currency, of financial instruments and/or of commodities, a five pounds' note may apparently yield – and so derive potential usefulness via -potential variously in relation to relative mathematical/ physical *determinacy* and/or to relative mathematical/ physical *indeterminacy*

Some implications of this will become clearer if it is noted, for example, that an individual may apparently potentially *gain* relative to himself/ herself from a (potential) transaction, if potentially choosing to exchange units of currency of overtly and as if axiomatically *precise* denomination(s) for units of (relative to him/ her potentially) a *more* highly valued commodity. Conversely, another individual may apparently *also* potentially gain relative to himself/ herself from that same potential transaction, if potentially choosing to exchange those overtly and axiomatically "same" units of currency for those "same" units of (relative to him) *less* highly valued commodity.

In this class of examples five pounds' initially "physically" determined relative to one individual and (relatively) abstract to the other, potentially, and as if perfectly predictively, becomes relatively abstractly determined to the first *because* as if relatively physically wholly *determined* relative to the second.

Here a physical five pound note is as if potentially perfectly predictive of "the same" physical five pound note *and/ or* "the same" abstract five pound note relative to *both* individuals.

Apparently the same five pound note is usefully perfectly predictive of *and/or* as if *perfectly predicted via* a five pound note potentially mathematically abstract *relative to itself* and/ or potentially relative to the two individuals, who here respectively potentially forego units of currency for units of commodities and potentially forego units of commodities for units of currency.

Clearly both individuals may potentially gain relative to themselves as if via gains relative to currency as if *because* units of currency (e.g.five pounds') axiomatize themselves as if "the same", not only relative to themselves and/ or relative to other mathematical/ physical five pounds', but as if "the same" relative to relatively mathematically/ physically *different* individuals relative to whom such integer denominated units of currency may potentially facilitate mutually beneficial exchanges (as in the class of examples just considered).

So units of currency may construe themselves and/ or may be construed as if (potentially) mathematically/ physically relatively useful because as if guaranteeing relative mathematical/ physical *determinacy* i.e. because as if potentially guaranteeing strictly precise 1:1 (relative) mathematical : mathematical, physical : physical, mathematical : physical and/ or physical : mathematical evaluations for potential *currency -currency exchanges* in relative space-time.

It now seems evident too, that units of currency may *also* construe themselves and/or be construed as potentially useful because as if potentially also guaranteeing relative mathematical/ physical *indeterminacy* i.e.because as if potentially securing strictly *non* 1 : 1 relative mathematical : mathematical, physical : physical, mathematical : physical and/or physical : mathematical evaluations for potential *currency -commodity exchanges*.

Thus, potential *guarantees* as if secured via agreements on values of currency relative to standard units of currency apparently potentially enable relative gains to be made as if via *relative disagreements* on values of commodities *relative to* standard units of currency.

Going further, standard units (here of currency) may have value because yielding potential *determinacy* (ostensible mathematical/ physical agreement(s) on value) relative to self, to others and/or relative to and through a wider system in circumstances where, fundamentally, individuals potentially gain via their essentially subjective, different and in thase senses *relatively indeterminate* evaluations relative to standard units.

For the potential exchanges just considered, apparently individuals may be understood as acting rationally when acting as if to *agree* upon a class of standard units as if *only* with the purpose of acting as if to *disagree* via them.

Notice that an exchange of commodities for currency (and vice versa) may not only take place at the *conclusion* of a single iteration bargaining process between individuals.

It may be the means of securing as if strict determinacy for an otherwise potentially indeterminate *sequence* of *potentially* mutually beneficial *processes* of disagreement each yielding potential bargains between individuals and themselves and individuals and each other as if acting relative to and through (elements of) a wider system.

Thus in contexts of potential mathematical/ physical economic exchanges, one *measure of potential gains* to (potential) exchange(s) and/ or to potential bargaining as if with a view to (a higher order of) potential exchange(s) *is the measure of disagreement between individuals* relative to a standard unit.

Apparently a seller (donor) will strictly gain on each unit only if evaluating the price of any (marginal) unit as *strictly greater than* his own *highest* (subjective) evaluation for a (marginal) unit and a buyer (receiver) will strictly gain on each unit only if evaluating the price of any (marginal) unit as *strictly less than* than his own *lowest* (subjective) evaluation for a marginal unit.[3]

The class of examples just considered makes implicit reference to potential usefulness for money as a unit of account (for example via prices), as a means of facilitating and making determinate mutually beneficial exchanges and implicit reference, too, to the potential usefulness of money as a store of value.

Why otherwise would an individual willingly act as if choosing to exchange units of a commodity for money, rather than simply acting as if, wholly altruistically, to make a gift of those commodities to the other individual?[4]

More abstractly, the *existence* - even abstractly - of a particular type of monetary unit would enable accounts to be made, and transactions and value storage to take place as if denominated in those units, whereas the physical realization of such a monetary unit would enable such monetized accounts, transactions, and value storages to be physically realized.

So, to the extent that mathematical/ physical transactions in particular monetary units are considered (potentially) individually and/ or socially desireable, the mathematical/ physical realization of those (standard) mathematical/ physical units would apparently then become (potentially) individually and/ or socially desireable.

And, to the extent that monetization (potentially) facilitates *chosen* transactions, apparently monetization and/or further monetization would become individually and/or socially (more) desireable. Monetization might be argued to be desireable inter alia because its relative flexibility as an exchange medium both in space and time potentially reduces the requirements of coincidence of needs and/or coincidence of availabilities implicit for example in (potential) commodity:commodity barter exchange mechanisms.

Conversely, if it were *required* that transactions took place relative to particular physical monetary units, then this might in general *inhibit* rather than facilitate desired exchanges if such a requirement carried with it associated requirements that those party to such (potential) exchanges command *prior* access to appropriate monetary resources.

In this regard in a highly monetized economy *reductions* in money supply might be expected in general to *reduce* realizations of (otherwise) *mutually desired* exchanges and/ or to promote the (greater) development of barter and other non-monetary transactions in that economy.

It might seem immediately to follow that, to the extent that more money promotes more desired (potential) monetary transactions then *more* money would be *desireable* both individually and socially and *less* money undesireable both individually and socially.[5]

Still in the context of monetary units as a particular class of standard units, where there is more than one type of currency, there is apparently need for mathematical and/or physical relations relating and interrelating elements of those different currencies.

This suggests not only (potential) currency -currency *exchange* rates interrelating different currencies but, thereby, a variety of (potential) exchange rates as if potentially determining and/ or as if potentially determined via (different) measures in relation to (different) Governors of Central Banks.

It is of immediate interest that, although particular currencies are determined with reference to *integers*, and potentially associated *integer* arithmetic principles and processes, the specification and determination of extranational exchange rates (including supranational as well as international exchange rates) typically employs *non-integer* magnitudes and associated *non-integer* arithmetic principles and processes.

This suggests potential for interpretation(s) of national currencies as *integer denominated* measures of relative value, potential means of securing coordinated and *determinate* opportunities for relative gain/loss between individual economic agents in each nation while *also*,via *non-integer* relative evaluations, constituting potential means of securing coordinated opportunities for continuing and in that sense *indeterminate* processes of relative bargaining/ barter/ trade/ gain/ loss between any or all individual agents in any particular nation and those of another/ others.

There is a particular kind of significance here for the potential for generation of principles and processes pertaining to integer and to non -integer arithmetics inherent in units of currency.

As far as I am aware this point has not been noticed before. I want now to stress it further in a manner which links directly to developments in Chapter 5, and thereby directly links these particular kinds of development to more fundamental principles and processes pertaining to the potential generation of mathematical/ physical principles in general, and not simply to money/ currency and/or potential mathematical/ physical monetary/ currency transactions in particular.

Notice first that each standard physical unit of currency *axiomatizes itself* as a standard unit, e.g. a five pound note as Five Pounds. In this respect units of currency constitute a special class of standard units.

Secondly physical units of currency denominate themselves and/or are potentially denominated in integer units and therefore potentially relate directly to the potential generation of principles and processes pertaining to integer arithmetic, as well as potentially relating indirectly to the potential generation of principles and processes pertaining to non-integer arithmetic. (For example via potential relation to relative gain/ loss in relation to elements of commodities and/or in relation to elements of currency, whether personally, or collectively, nationally or internationally).

The first observation (in relation to axiomatization), might be expressed abstractly as if via the relation :

$$5 = 5$$

The second observation in relation to the (potential) generation of principles and processes relative to integer and/or to non-integer arithmetic(s) might be expressed abstractly via the relation :

$$5.1 = 5.x$$

Here x might be interpreted as if having reference to a spatially and/ or temporally (relatively) different, and in that sense relatively unknown, "Pound" and/or as if having reference to spatially and/or temporally different, and in *that* sense relatively unknown, units of a different currency/ different currencies.

The algebraic statement 5.1 = 5.x may suggest associations with developments as if potentially generating and/or as if potentially (re)generated via the simpler expression :

$$x = 1$$

With this wider context both expressions anticipate developments in Chapter 5 in relation to the potential mathematical/ physical (re)generation of integers as if via measures -1 0 1 and/ or as if via relation to elements of the system (III) of that Chapter. (One means whereby the system (III) can be developed is as if via statements 1 = x, 1 = y, x = y).

Apparently, in principle, not only may *each* "Five Pounds" potentially generate *all* principles and processes pertaining to a mathematical/

physical system of arithmetic, but may generate and/or be as if generated via five "One Pounds" each in turn potentially generating all principles and processes pertaining to a mathematical/ physical system of arithmetic (including the potential for (re)generation of "Five Pounds" as if of a higher order).

In the broader context of standard units in general, apparently integer denominations for physical units of currency preclude non-integer exchanges for physical units of currency. It might seem that, to the extent that *precision* in currency transactions is desireable, axiomatically integer denominations for elements of currency would become inherently desireable .

But, as has been seen in a context of potential exchanges of other commodities, other financial instruments, and/or other currencies relative to a particular (element of) currency, apparently relative *imprecision* of measurement is arguably *also* desireable in the sense, for example, that a margin of difference between prices constituting as if potentially *objective exchange* evaluations and potentially *subjective use* evaluations, may be construed and/or may construe itself as if a measure of the margin of relative gain/ loss in a transaction.

In that way that measure of relative *imprecision* may become the relevant measure of *purpose* in undertaking and/ or facilitating the mathematical/ physical realization of principles and processes pertaining to potential bargaining and/or pertaining to potential exchange.

Underlining this latter point again: currency derives (potential) usefulness because it potentially provides an agreed and precise measure for the evaluation of (potential) exchange(s) in the context of potential processes of exchange *motivated by* relative *differences* of subjective evaluations relative to commodities – including differences in subjective preferences relative to commodities.

In this sense (relative) imprecision of measurement in relation to standard units is arguably clearly *desireable*. Stressing this still further, not only is relative imprecision of subjective measurement apparently *inevitable* , inter alia,in the Heisenberg sense, but here it is also apparently desired – and hence *desireable* _ in that sense. Here potential exchanges are, in principle, apparently in large part motivated as if to realize and/ or be as if realized via *chosen* subjective mathematical/ physical *differences* of measure(s) – *because* to that extent subjectively more personal/ less abstract mathematical/ physical differences of measures/ experiments/ experiences.

These are differences between a relatively abstract, and in that sense, relatively objective, measure of a commodity as if relative only to itself and/ or as if only relative to another individual and a relatively less abstract, as if because relatively more subjective, measure potentially physically (more) fully realized, for example via gift, barter or theft or trade, relative to a particular individual.

It seems evident that there is a significant role here not just for non-integer and/or for integer mathematics, but for principles and processes potentially generating and/or potentially generated via mathematical and/or physical principles of contradiction, including mathematical and/or physical principles and processes pertaining to potential self contradiction, between integer elements and non-integer elements of integer and non-integer mathematics/ physics, more generally.

With that perspective consider a further class of standard units in the particular context of the input-output structures of Section 2 as follows:

Interpret a quantity a_{ij} as if identically $x_{ij}^* \div x_j^*$ and thence as if defined as standard units of input of commodity i required per standard unit of output of commodity j.

Here standard units potentially serve to aggregate and/or to disaggregate (kinds of) input and/or (kinds of) output. Here, too, standard units (e.g. tonnes) apparently *necessarily* constitute *abstract* measures. For example physical tonnes (of coal, of steel ....) do not axiomatize themselves visibly as standard in the sense that each five pound note axiomatizes itself as Five Pounds.

The measures a_{ij}, x_{ij}^*, x_j^* also have potential usefulness for accounting and for planning, coordinating and/ or for control purposes, while having the general property that, in principle, abstract measures and physical measures will differ.

With reference to potential accounting interpretations, apparently total output of type i/ total potential input(s) x_i of type i might be construed as if potentially allocated to potential output(s) and final demand for examples as if variously via the relations:

$$\sum_j a_{ij}x_j + d_i = x_i$$

or as if via:

$$\sum_j \frac{x_{ij}^*}{x_j} x_j + d_i = x_i$$

In context, these relations might suggest consideration of conditions as if $x_j = x_j^*$ correspond to specific measures as if respectively : i) corresponding to *abstractly precisely realized* numbers of standard units of output and/or potential input and ; ii) corresponding to *empirically* (differently)*realized* actual numbers of units of output.

The above conditions, in conjunction with conditions as if $x_j = x_j^*$, suggest consideration of conditions as if $\Sigma x_{ij}^* = x_i^* - d_i$, in turn suggesting potential relations to the distribution problem and associated "more for less" and/or "more for nothing" paradoxes (see Chapter 5 and references in that Chapter) as well as suggesting relations corresponding to potentials for distributions/ redistributions of measures x_i^* interpreted as if total initial endowments of consumption commodities to different individuals (see for examples Chapters 1 and 2 and Chapter 5).

The potential desireability of (relatively) more for less in general and for relative error of measurement in particular will focus attention upon conditions potentially yielding/ potentially yielded via conditions as if $x_j = x_j^* - \epsilon_j$ in the context of the above relations, again directly suggesting potential relations to developments elsewhere in this and other Chapters in this book pertaining to relative mathematical/ physical error in general – the subject with which I opened Chapter 1.

Now consider measures p_j, μ_i as if, respectively, implicitly imputing distinct values to different units of potential outputs and inputs together with conditions as if:

$$\sum_i \mu_i a_{ij} = p_j$$

If, as above, the measure a_{ij} interprets itself (and/ or is interpreted) as if identically $x_{ij}^* \div x_j^*$ then apparently these latter relations correspond to conditions as if:

$$\sum_i \mu_i x_{ij}^* = p_j x_j^*$$

If measures μ_i, p_j are interpreted as if related to (standard integer) units of currency, *and* measures x_{ij}^*, x_j^* are also related to (relatively abstract) standard units, then apparently each measure in *each* of these relations relates to standard units.

Such interpretations in turn suggest potential interpretations in relation to potential empirical production plans, themselves relatively abstract to relatively abstract plans, as if denominated in standard units.

In context the relations above have (potential) interpretations as if planned revenues $p_j x_j^*$ from planned output(s) x_j^* exactly recoup planned expense(s) $\mu_i x_{ij}^*$ imputed to inputs i.

These interpretations focus attention upon (relative) desireability/ undesireability of deviation(s) from such planning magnitudes. To see this, consider a relation as if planned output x_j^* and (potentially) realized output x_j are related via:

$$x_j = x_j^* + \epsilon_j$$

so that :

$$\sum_j \mu_i x_{ij}^* = p_j(x_j - \epsilon_j)$$

This in turn appears open to interpretation *variously* as if :

Realized Income = Planned Income + Realized (relative) Profit/Loss

Realized Income = Realized (prior) Expense + Realized (relative) Profit/Loss

So, insofar as super profit/ loss is relatively desireable, relatively positive (negative) "error" might also appear relatively desireable (undesireable).

This observation and the associated economic interpretations in the context of relations as if variously $\Sigma a_{ij} x_j + d_i = x_i$ and/ or $\mu_i a_{ij} = p_j$ will evoke associations with developments with reference to analyses in Section 2 and, more generally, with reference to developments there and elsewhere in this book as if potentially embedding input-output analyses within universally applicable goal programming systems.

In the present more particular context of standard units and as if purposively potentially coordinated individual and/ or collective decisionmaking, I stress that "error" of realized measurement(s) relative to standard units is here not only arguably inevitable for an enterprise, but certain types of error are arguably *desireable*. Reinforcing this if, as above:

$$x_j = x_j^* + \epsilon_j$$

and, on the "primal" side

$$\sum_j a_{ij} x_{ij} + d_i = x_i$$

and (as above), on the "dual" side:

$$\sum_i \mu_{ij} a_{ij} = p_j$$

then apparently also (as above) on the "dual" side:

$$\sum_i \mu_i x_{ij}^* = p_j(x_j - \epsilon_j)$$

and also on the "primal" side:

$$\sum_i \frac{x_{ij}^*}{x_j^*} = p_j(x_j - \epsilon_j$$

or:

$$\sum_i \frac{x_{ij}^*}{x_j^*} x_j^* + \sum_i \frac{x_{ij}^*}{x_j^*}\epsilon_j + d_i = x_i + \epsilon i$$

Here an "error" ϵj is open to interpretation not only in potential (dual) relation to relative financial profit/ loss, but as if corresponding to an element of increased /reduced final demand for commodity i and/or : to an element of reduced/increased output of type i.

These cases by no means cover all of the possibilities. As examples consider further possibilities suggested by a relation as if:

$$\sum_j \frac{(x_{ij}^* + \epsilon^j/x_j)}{x_j^*} x_j^* + d_i = x_i^* + \epsilon_i$$

Here measures ϵ_j suggest potential interpretations in relation to potential for "error" in specification or to potential for opportunities to respecify measures corresponding to measures a_{ij} as if explicitly via measurements x_j.

More evocatively, apparently, via elements of the above interrelated relations and interpretations, increased profit appears coherent with (potential realization of) increased final demand(s), in turn apparently as if potentially (re)generating increased input(s) and/or higher prices and/ or associated potential for discovery of further elements for potential production and a fortiori potential for discovery of further potential production processes.

Such remarks pertaining to potential changes in potential supply and/ or to potential changes in potential demand in contexts of production will suggest potential opportunity, not only for individual and/or corporate gains, but also for social and collective gains both nationally and internationally, to increased understanding of potential economic processes related to principles and processes as if potentially generating and/or as if purposively and constructively (re)generated via elements of systems and subsystems corresponding to elements of appropriately specified and dually interrelated goal programming systems and potentially decentralized subsystems.

These systems all in principle explicitly incorporate potential opportunities for relative individual corporate and/ or collective gains (losses) as if via principles and processes pertaining to mathematical/ physical relativity in general and to relative "error" including as if purposively generated relative "error" in particular.

In this wider context these relations might be seen as if corresponding to as if purposive changes in relation to an initially as if optimally specified input-output system.

And "error" here might construe itself or be construed as if corresponding to potential (opportunity) for as if perfectly predictive processes of relative change as if potentially generating and/ or as if potentially (re)generated via (elements of) as if purposive goal programming interpretations in relation to elements of the above relations.

Notice for example potential interpretations for measures ϵ_i, $\Sigma\epsilon_j \div x_j^*$ as if perfect predictors of and/or as if perfectly predicted via measures x_i, x_i^- considered in the contexts of potential goal programming interpretations in relation to a simple input-output system in the preceding Section.

From a related perspective conditions as if $\Sigma a_{ij}x_j^* + d_i = x_i^*$, with conditions as if $\Sigma a_{ij}\epsilon_j = \epsilon_i$ are open to potential interpretations of an input- output system as if complete and/or as if certain and/or as if invariant, *yet* as if *potentially as if perfectly predictively* relatively incomplete (relatively indeterminate) as if because elements are as if potentially variable.

Among other things, measures ϵ_i, $\Sigma a_{ij}\epsilon_j$ might be construed as if corresponding to as if purposive errors themselves corresponding to elements of potential *change*. Further,in the above economic input output context, they might be construed as if corresponding to elements omitted from that system or to elements of potentially new processes; to elements of potential new outputs or ; to elements of potentially new kinds of final demand yet to be *discovered*, inter alia via processes apparently corresponding to the systematic (re)generation of "errors" relative to *any* determinate initial specification of that system.

By such means, an initial specification corresponding to what relatively is, might be constructed as if purposively to determine what relatively is not, where, quite evidently, too, the potential mathematical/ physical order of magnitude of elements ϵ_i, a_{ij}, ϵ_j of what relatively is/ is not as if omitted from an initial as if complete specification of such an input-output system may in principle be of larger order, lesser order, or of the same order as measures x_i*, x_j*, x_{ij}*, d_i.

Thus in principle by means of elements of goal programming interpretations, elements of an input-output system as if completely specified relative to mathematical/ physical standard units may be developed and used quite generally as if perfectly predictively to mathematically/ physically *discover* initially relatively unknown mathematical/ physical magnitudes and potential relations both of relatively higher and of relatively lower mathematical/ physical orders of magnitude relative to elements of that system.

Here physically realized errors for example as if corresponding to elements of potential increases/ decreases in final demand measures d_i may be not only desireably relatively large but may apparently in principle correspond to magnitudes, themselves potentially of order of magnitude relatively greater than and/or relatively less than elements of an initial specification.

In principle, too, relatively lower orders of change in potential final demand may regenerate and/or be as if regenerated via relatively higher orders of change in potential final demand.

On these grounds alone an economist might impute potential for the (re)generation of relations and interpretations as if potentially variously corresponding to microeconomic relations and interpretations *and/or* to potentially related and interrelated macroeconomic relations and interpretations to systems as if potentially defined as if goal programming extensions of input-output systems.

If indeed elements of microeconomic and/or macroeconomic systems and subsystems are seen as if potentially corresponding to elements of goal in general then, in any particular instance, the issue becomes one of recognition and definition of appropriate specifications as if corresponding to particular elements as if potentially generated and/or regenerated via particular goal programmes.

A context of potential exchanges as if potentially generating/ generated via orders of orders of magnitude of elements of final demand will focus attention on developments elsewhere in this book pertaining to potential processes of exchange between individuals as if potentially generating and/or generated via more for less principles and processes and interpretations in relation to elements of goal programming problems.

From this perspective, in contexts of persons, arguably even more broadly defined (potential) "more for less" principles and processes can be related very generally to potential principles and/ or processes as if potentially generating/ generated via (changes in) relative (in)determinacy of mathematical/ physical magnitudes and/or (potentially related) mathematical/ physical relative motions in general (see for example relations to Figure 5 in Chapter 5).

Such principles and processes have been related more specifically to particular kinds of potential socioeconomic exchange – for example via developments pertaining to "different books" and potential interlibrary loans/ gifts/ exchanges in Chapter 1. Developments pertaining to selfishness principles and potential exchanges and associated principles of ultimate individual and collective loss(es) as if via relative gain have also been considered in various contexts in that Chapter and in Chapters 4, 6 and 7.

More directly, with a microeconomic perspective, as if purposive reduction in final demand relative to self as if purposively to increase potential final demand relative to another/ others distinct in relative space-time will suggest principles and processes as if potentially generating gifts and/or, if reciprocated, potentially generating "barter" or "trade".

With a macroeconomic perspective, potential interpretations as if corresponding to purposive reduction of final demand relative to selves as if purposively to increase potential final demand relative to another/ others distinct in relative space-time will suggest related developments and interpretations pertaining to individual and collective saving, and/or to individual and collective taxation/ subsidisation.

More generally it might suggest potential for related developments and interpretations pertaining inter alia to the paradox of thrift, to the microfoundations of macroeconomic and to the relative individual or collective desireability – or otherwise – of demand management policies in general.

These and other issues will be considered further in the following Chapter, where input-output systems, as well as other potential systems and subsystems, including standard microeconomic and standard macroeconomic systems and subsystems, will be considered as if particular kinds of related and potentially interrelated orders of orders of mathematical/ physical example as if potentially (re)generating and/or as if purposively potentially (re)generated via goal programming interpretations in relation to elements of the system (III), p.96.

There and elsewhere in the book that system is explicitly related to potential principles and processes pertaining to the potential generation of orders of orders of mathematical/ physical systems in general.

In this Chapter I have focussed so far upon standard units as if potential coordinating devices in various planning and control contexts ostensibly pertaining most directly to mathematical economists. The following discussion widens the frame of reference and suggests potential roles for standard units as potential coordinating devices in further – yet clearly potentially related – classes of planning and control contexts.[6]

In the summer of 1966 my vacation employment was with a firm of consulting civil enginaers and, among other things, involved checking the setting out of foundations for a new gasworks in Birmingham, England. Briefly, one contractor was contracted to construct reinforced concrete foundations and another to erect a (North Sea) gas purification plant on these. The relevant point here follows from a clause in the former contract requiring that all holding down bolts (HDBs) be positioned within one eighth of an inch ($^1/_8$") of the plan levels and locations specified by the consulting engineers on behalf of the West Midlands Gas Board.

At that time this specification was unusually stringent. It had been made so in order that the second contractor could in turn be required to work to tight specifications concerning the relative locations of particular parts of the gas purification plant (much of it to be constructed from particularly expensive special steels).

Evidently standard measures pertaining to locations and levels served a coordinating role as between the various parties, including the client, the consulting engineers, the two main contractors, as well as their employees and/or their agents (e.g. subcontractors).

More subtly, if related to plans, abstract standard units of this kind – in contrast to standard units of currency – in a strict sense necessarily *remain* abstract. Empirically measured distances of these kinds not only differ from abstractly standard distances as if *because* empirically measured (i.e. not abstract), but because, unlike units of currency, empirically measured units of distance(s) of these kinds *do not* axiomatize themselves as if standard.

Indeed even if individuals act as if agreeing to agree upon measured distance(s), particular kinds of problems will be associated with measurements of relative heights and/ or distances in general, and so upon measurement of such magnitudes on construction sites in particular. Many such problems are recognized as being of standard kinds and there are recognized and standardized ways of coping with them.

In this case, the routine means of establishing and of checking plan distance was by means of standardized steel tapes with standardized corrections being made for temperature, tension and sag. Emphasizing measurement error; notice that other means of establishing and checking relative distance(s) – tellurimetry covers one class of examples – might be expected to yield different measures in general,as well as different measures to different observers/ observations.

Coordinating roles both for standard measures and for standardization of processes of measurement are evident here, and evident a fortiori when it is recalled that in this particular contract more than $^1/_8$" error, even over a distance of several hundred feet, would be unacceptable.

Yet opportunities for potential disagreement in general and potential for disagreements between engineers representing various contractors or subcontractors and those representing the client in particular, were manifold – even when all were committed to seek to use standardized methods and attain standardized and thereby agreed measurements.

The different parties had incentives, including financial incentives, as well as incentives of professional pride and of potential corporate reputation, to *cooperate* to satisfactorily complete contracts and subcontracts. Incentives to cooperate, and so to agree on measures, were evidently strong, since potentially penalties might accrue to particular kinds of disagreement. But there were also reasons, including financial reasons *purposefully* to disagree upon measurements and/or upon processes of measurement.

Consider the setting out of an octagonal base. The locations of HDBs would be agreed prior to a concrete pour. If there was disagreement between the contractor's and the consultant's representative another view might be sought but, as long as disagreement remained, the contractor would be required to remedy it – with consequent implications for the contract completion time and expense.

In fact the situation was more complicated – and more expensive – than this, since HDBs were found to move significantly when the concrete was poured into the formwork for the larger bases with the consequence that the contractor – at his expense – had to develop templates to restrain them during the pour. The significance of these remarks can be indicated more clearly if a representative octagonal base is illustrated schematically as in Figure 3.1.

In practice, setting out distances might be checked between the centres of any pairs of bolts, as well as the levels and distances checked from the datum to any particular bolt both before and after the pour. (In fact after the pour the concrete would also be checked for level and for the coverage of the bolts).

Thus the various parties had incentives to *agree* relative to measured (standard) units both abstractly and empirically including the incentives associated with completion of the contract. It will also be understood that particular parties to the contract might gain financially by *disagreement* relative to measured units, not only in particular instances of measurement (for example thereby avoiding re-setting HDBs), but also more generally. (For example by seeking a general relaxation of the $^1/_8$" tolerance clause in the contract).[7]

Figure 3.1

Remarks concerning standard units in various contexts of potential bargaining as if to (dis)agree as if in turn to measure relative gains/ losses *via* such relative (dis)agreements, will recall other classes of example – including input-output examples.

They may also cause the reader to think more widely concerning potential for as if purposive personal and/or professional (dis)agreements relative to relatively abstract standard measures concerning relative positions and potentials in relative space-time, be they with reference to relative positions and/or potentials of mathematical/ physical bodies -as -persons, bodies as if particles, or bodies as if of astronomical order in general, as well as with reference to relative positions and/or potentials in relative space time of elements of (potential) economic quantities or elements of (potential) engineering structures in particular.

So far roles for as if purposive individual and collective (dis)agreements upon, and relative to, standard units have been considered in some detail with apparently explicit reference to classes of economic and of civil engineering applications.

A related and more generally specified process of "scientific" enquiry might be characterized as one whereby individual scientists (dis)agree relative to a standard interpretation of a particular theory (*conditionally* accept a particular abstract theory), as if in order to agree upon measurements,tests and/or more general experiments relative to particular assumptions and/or predictions of that particular (abstract) theory, as if in order *thereby* to confirm, or partially or wholly to refute,those assumptions,procedures or predictions.

Collectively conditional agreements, in the sense of standardizations of theoretical expositions and/or of abstract as well as empirical principles and processes of measurement and test, apparently yield *potential* for collective gain inter alia as if *because of* the inherently conditional nature of such agreements.

Indeed, particular scientists and/ or groups of scientists may seek potential gain for all as if via loss (e.g. effort) relative to self (selves) by seeking *first* to establish *conditional* standardizations of agreements upon potential principles and processes of theoretical or empirical explanations and explorations, and *then to* seek potential gain for all via loss (e.g.effort) relative to selves by conjecturing and/or testing potential *refutations of* such conditionally standardized theoretical explanation and/ or processes of exploration and testing.

They may aim to do all of this so as to yield potential further gains in potentially constructive knowledge and understanding for self and for others – including, inter alia, knowledge and understanding of potential mathematical/ physical principles and processes. These might in turn be potentially employed, not only by themselves but by others, to yield still further potential mathematical/ physical gains both personally and socially...

These remarks are very general in character, and the prominent role in them for *potential discoveries of* principles and/ or processes of contradiction as if *purposively via* (potential) principles and (potential) processes of contradiction, including potential principles and processes as if corresponding to as if potentially individually and socially constructive principles and processes of *self* contradiction, will recall attention to roles for principles and processes as if of individual and/or of collective mathematical/ physical (self) contradiction as if potentially motivating and/ or potentially motivated via principles of relative change(s) in general.

Such principles include principles of individual and collective relative motion in general and of individual and collective (relative) economic gain (loss) in particular.

Much attention has just been given to potential coordinating roles for standardization tests in relation to potential mathematical/ physical principles and/ or processes pertaining to relativity of measurement of prices or quantities and, via a construction example, pertaining to relativity of measurement of (potential) magnitudes at -a -distance in space.

Before returning to further consideration in the following Chapters of potential mathematical/ physical developments as if potentially (re)generated via relations to goal programming and asscociated duality interpretations in relation to elements as if (potentially) generating and/or (re)generated via (elements of) the system (III) of Chapter 4, I now more briefly consider (potentially related) issues pertaining to standard mathematical/ physical units of relative *time*, including potential coordinating roles for *standard units of time* and, potentially related roles for principles and processes of contradiction and/or self-contradiction as if potentially generated via relations to standard units of relative time.

Standard measures of time, as evidenced by time zones, "summer time", "winter time", "Coordinated Universal Time" (until 1986, Greenwich Mean Time) and, more generally, for example, by standard calendar time (e.g. Gregorian calendar time) have become familiar. Here it is especially relevant that these and other kinds of standard units of time constitute further classes of potential mathematical/ physical coordinating devices between individuals and themselves, between individuals and other different individuals or other groups of individuals (potentially) operating relative to and through a wider mathematical/ physical system.

Expanding on this : various orders of orders of standard units of time and/or of relative time are considered in various mathematical/ physical contexts. Thus, nano seconds may be used with particular reference to particle physics, light years with particular reference to astronomy and centuries and millenia with particular reference to (human) history.

In these various fields, clearly standard units of time have potential coordinating roles. Among other things they yield potential for individual and/ or collective gains – including gains of knowledge as if potentially generating/ generated via mathematical/ physical principles and/ or processes of purp[osively induced "scientific" contradiction and self contradiction.

With reference to time, (self) contradictions of "scientific" kinds will be familiar – as examples : as if via potential differences with reference to billions of light years in the context of cosmology, to potential differences with reference to particular fractions of seconds in the context of particle physics ; and as if via potential differences with reference to days, months and centuries as well as millenia in the context of human history.

Contradictions with reference to time are also familiar other ways. For example via apparent potential in persons for subjectively determined potential differences between physiological, psychological and chronological units of time.

Indeed clocks and calendars operating according to accepted and standardized rules have come to be routinely used as coordinating devices for purposes of prediction, execution and/or reporting of individual and/ or collective decisions and actions.[8]

Specifically, potential principles and processes of (potential) gains and/or exchanges of knowledge and potentially related principles and processes pertaining inter alia to gifts, to barter or to trade of commodities might construe themselves as if developments with reference to (subjective) relativity of measures of time in general, and as if predictive of and/or predicted via (potential) differences between (subjectively) *relatively* past, (subjectively) *relatively* present and (subjectively) *relatively* future in particular.

Illustrating this : If an individual offers (knowledge of) a commodity to another then, as if predictively, *what was* relative to one may become as if *what is* relative to the other or; *the past* relative to one is potentially as if perfectly predictive of *the (relatively future) present* relative to the other.

Here, apparently mutually contradictory conditions prevail not only with reference to relative times in general but with reference to relative past/ present/ future in particular.

Such examples of relative time reversals emphasize potential roles for standard measurement(s) in relation to relative times as well as in relation to (relative) characteristice of mass, volume, value and locations in space.

More precisely, there is potential for each of two parties to gain by actions as if to generate gifts, barter or trade -all exchanges as if (potentially) mathematically/ physically specified not only via principles and processes of (self) contradiction as if by relation to mutually agreed numbers of standardized units of characteristics of mass, volume, location and units of currency, but also as if mathematically/ physically specified by relation to principles and processes of (self) contradiction as if in relation to mutually agreed numbers of standardized units of *time*.

Conditionally agreed quantities, locations and times, among other things immediately suggest potential relations and applications to the determination of new kinds of analyses pertaining to potential principles and processes pertaining to the generation of *contracts* in general, and not just to civil engineering contracts in particular.

Such contracts may pertain to many kinds of potential mathematical/ physical generations of gifts, exchanges and/ or trades of commodities as if potentially generated via mathematical/ physical principles and processes of contradiction between economic agents, themselves and each other, as if inter alia generating/ generated via individually and/or collectively *advantageous kinds of relations to* as if mutually agreed (standard) units of mass, volume, value, location and time -all in relation to agreed and spatially and temporally distinct commodity and/ or currency markets.

The following Chapters explore potential for the generation of private and social opportunities of these various kinds.

Footnotes

1. Notice that, by contrast with an arbitrarily specified system (I - A)x = b the system (I) always has a feasible and an optimal solution.

2. These particular examples are taken from examination papers set respectively in 1981 and 1983 for a course in which I used input-output analysis as the means of motivating and developing linear programming approaches to the modelling and analysis of economic problems.I stress that input-output systems as primitive as these would not be seriously employed by any analyst except perhaps as a means of gaining indicative predictions of aggregate magnitudes.

3. These remarks, even taken alone, will suggest a more general argument to the effect that principles and potential processes as if to secure agreement on exchange values in general, and/ or upon prices and/ or upon marginal evaluations in particular, would apparently necessarily be such as potentially to eliminate rather than to increase potential subjective gains (surplus) to individual agents via exchanges. Apparently potential (marginal) gains might (continue to) accrue to individuals as if via continuation of processes corresponding to processes as if to disagree via and/ or relative to price(s). *But* apparently, too, *no* (further potential marginal) gains would accrue to individuals if processes of relative price determination were required to be determined as if to correspond only to agreement between buyers' and sellers' *marginal* evaluations and price(s). These latter conditions correspond to some of the conditions of "pure" or "perfect" competition,in turn, suggesting a general conclusion to the effect that the specification of such conditions as *prerequisites* for exchange corresponds to a specification of conditions for a welfare *minimum* as preconditions for a competitive optimum.

4. For those familiar with introductory economics texts these remarks will recall (standard) references there to a threefold purpose for money. First as a unit of account, second as a medium of exchange and third as a store of value.

5. It might also seem to follow that policies to reduce money supply nationally and/ or internationally would be undesireable and undesireable *a fortiori* if undertaken as if with the express purpose of securing (greater) conformity with conditions of perfect competition in general, and of conformity of processes of price determination with (associated) "competitive" principles and processes in particular. (With reference to potential critiques of policies - including "monetary" policies - as if primarily directed toward the attainment of conditions of "perfect" competition also see developments in Chapters 1 and 5).

6. A construction contract among other things includes an explicitly agreed listing of prices and quantities. Perhaps more interestingly, much Civil Engineering work might be seen as related directly to principles and processes of capital formation as if potentially generating and/or generated via principles and potential processes of land use change. (On capital, potential capital formation and potential land use changes see Chapters 6 onwards).

7. In fact the conditions of the contract were accepted by both contractors - neither sought such a general relaxation of the conditions of their contract.

8. I remark in passing that standard units of time are now accepted as commonplace yet, before the advent of railways - and railway timetables - even in the UK time was not standardized nationwide. Indeed I believe that Railway Time, as distinct from local time(s) persisted in Ireland as well as in India well into this century. Perhaps, had the notion of standard time - and of standardized timetables - not become so firmly entrenched in popular imagination, Einstein's illustrations by reference to relative motions of parts of trains of the essentially location-specific nature of measurement in space-time of (relative) mass and time would have substantially less impact.

References

{1} Baumol, W.J., (1961), *Economic Theory and Operations Analysis*, Prentice Hall New York.

{2} Ryan, M.J., (1980), *More on the More for Less Paradox in the Distribution Problem*, Lecture Notes in Economics and Mathematical Systems 174, pp.275-303, Springer-Verlag.

4 Scarcity and choice

Scarcity and choice lie at the heart of economics as a subject of professional investigation and analysis. For example Oscar Lange defined economics as : "The science of administration of scarce resources." {16}.

A standard textbook way of illustrating and emphasizing fundamental interrelationships between scarcity, choice and economic value is the *diamond-water paradox*, a statement of which might run as follows :

> Water is essential to human existence and diamonds not so, yet diamonds are relatively very valuable and water relatively not so – a paradox.

The standard resolution of this paradox follows from the observation that, although water is relatively more essential, diamonds are relatively more scarce.[1]

Still with reference to this particular class of examples now consider relative scarcity further. If two persons are endowed with diamonds and/or with water then, in principle, each can potentially increase scarcity relative to themselves, and reduce scarcity relative to a wider system, by choosing to act as if to *reduce* holdings of diamonds and/or water relative to self -as if in order to increase diamonds and/or water relative to a wider system. Or, more particularly, to *reduce* holdings of diamonds and/or water relative to self as if in order to *increase* holdings of diamonds and/ or water relative to the other, as if both relative to and through a wider system.

If diamonds and water are *"goods"* for each individual then, in any of these cases, each individual is apparently choosing to act as if according to (potential) principles and processes of *self contradiction* by acting as if choosing to dominate his/ her own abstract preferences as if to reduce holdings of diamonds and/ or water relative to self.

Apparently action as if to choose less relative to self as if to generate more relative to others, is open to interpretation as if corresponding to elements of principles and processes of altruism whereby an individual acts as if to generate a preferred position relative to himself/ herself by choosing *less* relative to self as if to enable another/ others potentially to choose *more* relative to himself/ herself themselves.

Evidently an altruistic principle is consistent with chosen conditions for barter or for trade, as well as apparently more primitive (relatively more disinterested) conditions for gifts. To see this in general terms consider conditions under which actions are potentially *reciprocated*. That is, conditions as if each individual acts as if to choose to *dominate* preferences relative to self as if predictively to secure potentially greater gain relative to another/ others.

More specifically, potential sequences of this kind are apparently open to interpretation as if each individual acts as if to choose to generate potentially greater gain relative to another/ others as if *thereby* in turn to generate potentially greater gain relative to self.

Such potential actions/ reactions appear open to potential interpretation(s) as if corresponding not only to principles and processes of *Revealed Preference* _ whereby one apparently potentially reveals a preference for another/ other's gain by acting as if to choose loss relative to self, and thereby to choose others' potential gain – but a fortiori, as if corresponding to potential sequences of principles and processes which I term principles and processes of *Reciprocal Revealed Preference* whereby, potentially, *each* party may act sequentially as if to choose to dominate his/ her abstract preferences relative to self as if to generate potential relative gain (loss) relative to another/ others.

Notice that in this example, even though initially each may not know what another likes, prefers, or indeed dislikes, by means of a sequence of potential revelations of preference, each may in principle both reveal and/ or have revealed to him/ her *more of* what another likes, dislikes and/or prefers relative to him/ her.

With reference to the potential for relative starting and/or stopping of such potential sequences, in principle one may *start* by acting as if to choose *less* relative to self as if to generate (offer) potentially *more* relative to another/ others. In turn another/ others may then act as if to choose *less* relative to self (selves) as if to generate (offer) potentially *more* relative to another/others (including for example the initiator)....

Such a potential sequence of offers in principle may *stop/ be stopped* relative to a particular individual and/or (on behalf of) a particular group of individuals for example as if with the acceptance/ rejection of a particular offer – and thus the implicit rejection of subsequent offers relative to that individual/ group of individuals.

The preceding remarks can be interpreted as if referring to potential for individuals to generate more for less relative to themselves, to each other and relative to and through a wider system in turn evoking associations with developments pertaining to the More for Less and More for Nothing Paradox in contexts of spatial and/or intertemporal distribution(s) and redistributions elsewhere in the book (see Chapter 5 and also {21}).

From a related perspective, in contexts of potential developments pertaining to money, prices, incomes and expenditures in general, and relative price changes as if potentially generating or generated via "trade" in particular, consideration of such sequences will evoke associations with potential principles and processes whereby, inter alia ; i) potentially *loss* relative to self generates/ is as if generated via relative price *rise*s relative to self *and* relative price *reduction*s relative to the system and ; ii) potentially, *gain*s relative to self generates/ is as if generated via relative price *reductions*s relative to self and relative price *increases*s relative to the system.

Apparently then an *altruist* would act as if to offer less to self as if via an offer of *more* quantity at a *lower* price relative to another/ others and, if such a kind of offer were reciprocated, apparently, in turn, another/ others might act as if to choose *less* relative to self as if to generate *more* (of a different) quantity/ quantities and a *lower* price/ lower prices relative to the system, in that way apparently potentiating potential gain(s) relative to another/ others.

Thus far emphasis has been placed upon (potential) principles and processes as if corresponding to sequences of choices to exchange as if universally motivated by principles of altruism (selflessness). But it is quite evident – particularly in the context of the diamond-water example – that, both in principle and in practice, individuals might act as if being motivated primarily by principles of selfishness.

For example, in principle as well as in practice, either or both individuals may act as if to dominate his/ her own (abstract) preferences relative to self as if in order to choose to *deprive* the other of some or all of his/ her endowment by direct or indirect use of unwanted force/ duress and in that way seek to gain by the other's (others') loss.

Selfish behaviour with reference to elements of others' endowments and/ or potential endowments of property rights is evident. Stark examples of types of behaviour as if purposively selected to yield gain to self as if via imposition (by duress) of loss upon another/ others include verbal or physical threats or intimidations, as well as simple theft.

Other kinds of potential principles or processes for (relative) individual and/or collective deprivation founded upon principles of selfish behaviour may be mathematically and physically considerably more subtle. One such is that associated with theories of "perfect" competition explicitly founded by its advocates upon principles of self interest interpreted as if selfishness.

In this context attempts to secure conditions either theoretically or empirically as if potentially ultimately to secure universal *loss*(es) because as if motivated by principles *as if purposively designed to* secure other *less well endowed individuals' loss*(es) might seem not only perverse but, if conducted knowingly, to be both academically and socially damnable.

Emphasizing this : attempts to secure "pure" competitive conditions either theoretically or empirically would apparently *necessarily* be designed to yield the operation of price and associated exchange mechanisms as if founded upon principles of individual selfishness *and* upon associated attempts to obtain "competitively" determined exchange values and quantities.

These correspond inter alia to conditions under which relative prices and quantities are to be attained via *loss*(es) relative to *smaller* as if in order to secure *gain*(s) relative to *larger*.

Clearly such principles and processes are consistent with conditions for ultimate annihilation – both individually and socially and both theoretically and empirically – since consistent with successive loss(es) *of* as well as successive losses *relative to* relatively smaller as if to secure relative gain(s) to relatively larger.

It might seem that, transiently at least, the relatively larger would become relatively still larger but notice that, since founded upon loss relative to and so, ultimately, loss *of* relatively smaller, such principles and processes would (if sustained) apparently ultimately lead to the annihilation of all bar one – and, even for that one, ultimately to *loss* relative to self since, at each stage gain would be *anticipated* relative to self and so, ultimately, with the incidence of no (further) gain, realized loss would be *inevitable* relative to self.

In the context of such apparently specifically microeconomic arguments relative to potentially agreed "market clearing" prices, attention here has just been focussed quite generally upon mathematical/ physical principles and processes as if potentially securing and/or secured via potential mathematical/ physical economic principles and processes which I have termed *Reciprocal Revealed Preference*. These approaches, among other things, contrast with standard mathematical economic approaches to individual economic decisionmaking by specifically interrelating different theories of individual behaviour.

Standard mathematical economic analyses typically impute nonlinear and ordinal abstract preference/ indifference relations to individuals, and make much of (potential) distinctions between such classes of abstract ordinal relations – as for example developed by Hicks {12} and, for example, pre-existing "cardinal utility" approaches generally, and "Marshallian" cardinal utility approaches particularly, as well as subsequent weak and strong theories of revealed preference, respectively associated with the names of Samuelson {22} and of Houthakker {13}.

In contrast developments here not only naturally impute distinct, *yet related*, roles to each of these kinds of potentially abstract and/or potentially empirical expressions of preference/ indifference relations, but *found* potential for principles and processes pertaining abstractly and empirically to individual and collective choice(s) *upon* (potential) mathematical/ physical economic principles or processes whereby individuals may act as if *purposively* to secure individual and/or collective gains/ losses as if *purposively via* principles and/or processes of (self) contradiction.

These include principles and processes pertaining to potential mathematical/ physical (self) contradiction(s) generating/ generated via contradictions between abstract and non-abstract preference/ indifference relations in general. Important cases will be those generating/ generated via contradictions between as if abstract and *nonlinear* preference/ indifference measures and as if empirically chosen *"linear"* preference/ indifference measures.

One particularly evocative class of cases is that for which potentially mathematical/ physical preference/ indifference relations may differ from and/or as if via as if agreed measures denominated relative to standard units in general, and may differ from and/or as if via agreed integer measures when denominated relative to standard units in particular.

Potential mathematical/ physical principles and processes of contradiction, including potential mathematical/ physical principles of self contradiction, are of fundamental significance. They provide potential for mathematical/ physical / economic developments in general, as well as in particular.

From this perspective contradictions might be considered as if *purposively* potentiating and/or as if *purposively* potentiated via mathematical/ physical "errors" of measurement in general and, for example, as if via mathematical/physical differences between subjectively determined "marginal" evaluations of elements of commodities, and evaluations as if generating generated via elements of commodities in relation to standard units in particular.

Notice here apparently natural interpretations for as if purposive differences between spatially/ temporally distinct (subjective) *use* values and (as if objectively agreed) spatially/ temporally distinct *exchange* values for elements of commodities and, more directly, potential interpretations as if *purposively* generating/ generated via potential differences (potentially) generating/ generated via such distinctions.

There are bases here for interpretations corresponding to as if objectively agreed spatially and temporally distinct unit costs/ expenses for elements of commodities, as well as for as if purposive *differences betweem* (subjective) evaluations of costs/ opportunity costs for elements of commodities and their as if objectively agreed costs/ expenses.

Thus potential gifts/ exchanges may in part be understood as if generating/ generated via potential differences between (subjective) cost/

opportunity cost/ preference/ indifference evaluations of elements of commodities relative to self, relative to another/ others and/ or relative to and through elements of (wider) mathematical/ physical systems.

Going further, given the potential for subjectively determined cost/ opportunity cost measures and interpretations in the previous paragraph it is apparent that, in general, subjectively evaluated opportunity cost(s) would *inevitably* be relatively mathematically/ physically *unknown* as between individuals.

It is apparent, too, that, according to related interpretations, potential for mutually advantageous gifts/ exchanges may construe itself/ be construed as if, in a fundamental sense, springing from potential differences themselves deriving *fundamentally from relatively unknown* differences between *different* (subjective) cost/ opportunity cost evaluations relative to self to another/ others and/ or relative to as if objectively agreed cost/ opportunity cost measures relative to a (wider) mathematical/ physical system.

These latter remarks emphasize not just the essentially subjective and potentially (self) contradictory nature of different cost/ opportunity cost evaluations, but also potential for relative gain(s)/ loss(es) to individuals via potential differences stemming essentially from subjective and potentially (self) contradictory evaluations relative to self, to another/ others and/or relative to a wider mathematical/ physical system.

Since in general *untaken* alternatives necessarily remain (relatively) *unknown* to individuals, evidently, in particular, ex ante (subjective) cost/ opportunity cost evaluations of those potential outcomes must necessarily constitute contingent evaluations of costs/ opportunity costs relative to relatively *unknown* contingent alternatives. But experience of mathematical/ physical actions/ interactions relative to self, another/ others and/ or relative to and through a wider system, necessarily generates potential for ex post subjective cost/ opportunity cost *reevaluations* relative to empirical realizations of contingent alternatives.[2] More technically:

i) here principles and processes pertaining to the potential generation of relative individual and/or collective gain(s)/ loss(es) can be seen as potentially open to interpretation(s) as if potentially *not only* stemming essentially from potential mathematical/ physical principles and processes of (self) contradiction in general, *but* from potential mathematical/ physical principles of contradiction as if generating/ generated via "errors" of measurement relative to "economic" commodities as if (potentially) evaluated in relation to standard units of spatial temporal and/ or intertemporal characteristics in particular. And/ or ;

ii) with a context of potential choices relative to potential gift/ exchange opportunities, apparently an individual would not rationally act as if willingly to choose to forego an element of a commodity *unless* at least indifferent between evaluations of the mathematical/ physical economic alternatives potentially generated via its relinquishment and those potentially generated by its retention.

Thus as if agreed transaction values (e.g. prices) would constitute as if chosen *upper bounds* relative to thereby (foregone) opportunity cost(s) for a seller/ donor and *lower bounds* relative to potential opportunities for a buyer/ recipient.

Together these remarks suggest significant roles in formal analyses of potential market price determination processes for inequalities as well as for equalities and – potentially related – roles, too, for the determination of relative price/ cost/ opportunity cost evaluations as if, inter alia, generating/ generated via *potential differences*, themselves potentially generating/ generated via potentially (self) contradictory relations and/ or interrelations between nonlinear and linear and/or abstract and empirical and/or subjective and as if objective individual and collective mathematical/ physical indifference/ preference measures.

Even with a context of developments as if applying specifically to mathematical/ physical economics and mathematical/ physical economists, these remarks nevertheless suggest explanations and explorations pertaining to mathematical/ physical phenomena in general – and to such principles and potential processes as if potentially generating/ generated via appropriate mathematical/ physical specification(s) and solutions of (elements of) goal programming systems and associated duals in particular.

A wider mathematical/ physical context of this kind would emphasize not just potential for mathematical/ physical principles and processes of (self)contradiction as if potentially generating/ generated via potential differences in general, but potential differences potentially generating/ generated via principles and processes pertaining to relativity of measurement and relative "error" of measurement in contexts of systems as if potentially constituting (particular elements of) mathematical/ physical goal programming models and of their duals in particular.

It would also again emphasize principles and processes of contradiction, including potential mathematical/ physical principles and processes potentially (re)generating/ (re)generated via differences in relative sign as if themselves potentially (re)generating/ (re)generated via (all) potential mathematical/ physical principles and processes in general -and pertaining to relativity (e.g.subjectivity) of measurement and relative "errors" (e.g. via subjective/ as -if -agreed -as -objective differences) in particular.

From a more restricted perspective these remarks apparently impute potentially fundamental significance to (potential) principles and processes of relative certainty/ uncertainty, as well as potentially fundamental significance to (related) ex ante/ ex post distinctions in relative space-time, all ostensibly with reference to particular varieties of microeconomic analysis in general and microeconomic analysis pertaining to the diamond-water paradox in particular.

In standard *macroeconomic* (as opposed to microeconomic) contexts, foci upon uncertainty and upon ex ante/ ex post decisions might evoke associations with "Keynesian" ideas in general and with the work of Clower {5} and of Leijonhufvud {17} in particular. More directly, the above remarks pertaining to standard microeconomic arguments were introduced and developed with reference to a standard microeconomic paradox. Now consider standard macroeconomic – and more particularly standard "Keynesian" and standard "monetarist" macroeconomic systems with reference to a standard macroeconomic paradox known as the Paradox of Thrift. A statement of this might run as follows:

> While *individual* saving can be seen as individually *desireable* _ because seen as consistent with thrift, itself perceived as a virtue – *collective* saving can be seen as socially *undesireable* _ because seen as potentially consistent with insufficiency of aggregate demand and thence output and employment.

As one means of indicating a basis for the Paradox just stated I set out briefly a "Simple Common Model" taken from a highly influential paper by Milton Friedman entitled "A Theoretical Framework for Monetary Analysis" {9 }.[3]

$$\frac{C}{P} = f(\frac{Y}{P}, r)$$

$$\frac{I}{P} = g(r)$$

$$\frac{Y}{P} = \frac{C}{P} + \frac{I}{P} \text{ (or, alternatively, } \frac{S}{P} = \frac{Y-C}{P}\text{)}$$

$$M^D = P \times \ell\,(\frac{Y}{P}, r)$$

$$M^S = h(r)$$

$$M^D = M^S$$

Together the first three equations of this simple system are understood as describing (aggregate) "goods market" relations. The latter three in turn, are understood as describing "money market" relations corresponding respectively to a money demand relation, a money supply relation and a money market equilibrium condition.

Friedman states that (at the time of writing) these six relations at this level of generality would be accepted by "Keynesians" and by "Monetarists" alike. He goes on immediately to make the observation that :

> Although there are six equations here, there are seven unknowns. There is a missing equation ({9}, p.219)

With this remark as background he then notes that a simple income-expenditure analysis would append a condition :

$$p = p_o$$

and a simple "monetarist" analysis would append the (different) condition :

$$y = y_o$$

With reference to these conditions Friedman remarks that :

> ... Both fill in the missing equation by an assumption that is not part of the basic theoretical analysis. This is less blatant, in one sense, for the quantity theory, since at least there is a well developed economic theory, summarized in the Walrasian equations of general equilibrium, that explains what determines the level of output, so that the equations chosen for analysis can be regarded as a subset of a complete system. That is why ... essentially all economic theorists, whatever model they prefer for short run analysis accept the quantity theory model, completed by the Walrasian equations, as valid for long run equilibrium.The rigid price assumption of Keynes is, in this sense much more arbitrary It is entirely a deus ex machina with no underpinning in economic theory.... ({9},p.222).

These remarks are particularly revealing because, with them, Friedman apparently *founds* the preceding simple "monetarist" macroeconomic system on an *assumption* of Walraisian competitive general equilibrium. Notice immediately, that, in context, it might appear that Friedman is suggesting that conditions of competitive general equilibrium are not only potentially theoretically and empirically attainable, but also potentially and empirically individually and collectively *desireable*, even if only in order to underpin the above "monetarist" macroeconomic system.

Readers and potential readers of his work, whether experts or laymen would do well to be extremely wary of any such claims, however plausibly they may be made by Friedman, by monetarists, by neo-Keynesians, or by anybody else. In this context, with reference to conditions of "perfect" competition as an asserted underpinning for a monetarist system, readers might for example notice :

i) that standard competitive general equilibrium proofs are typically posed in strictly theoretical (as opposed to empirical) terms ;[4]

ii) that even though the theoretical assumptions apparently theoretically establishing existence for a competitive general equilibrium are typically extremely stringent, typically no claim is made of uniqueness for such equilibria, and a fortiori no claim is made, either for the empirical inevitability, or the empirical desireability of any particular process of equilibration ;

iii) that, with reference to potential collective choice(s), standard impossibility results (including Arrow's results) will be familiar to anyone familiar with an intermediate economics course.

A claim to the effect that a particular competitive equilibrium choice is desireable apparently implies not only potential attainability and potential (uniquely specified) desireability for such an equilibrium,but also potential for the (collective) choice of that social outcome according to some uniquely decisive social choice rule.

This in turn points directly to apparent contradiction with established "impossibility" results in the collective choice literature to the effect that, under apparently weak conditions decisiveness of collective rule choice would follow in general only from conditions of dictatorship or from unanimity of preferences.

It has been noted that, in the context of such results, it is a standard assumption that dictatorship is socially undesireable, and that unanimity of preferences – commonly understood as if corresponding to identity of relevant preference (pre)orderings – is highly unlikely.

With reference to potential decisions of the kinds under consideration here, it might seem, too, that, according to standard analyses and interpretations, a "perfectly" competitive solution would in general be socially *undesireable*, even if attainable by means consistent with a social decision rule/ social welfare function. (Because standard assumptions and developments impute conditions of implicit or explicit *dictatorship* to decisiveness of social decision rules – and consider dictatorship socially undesirable).

In due course still further attention will be concentrated upon potential resolutions of apparent (potential) paradoxes and contradictions of this kind – resolutions in part stemming from conditional rejection on the one hand of standard assumptions pertaining to the (un)desireability of principles and processes of "perfect" competition and, on the other hand, conditional rejection of standard assumptions pertaining to desireable properties for collective decision rules – including inter alia conditional rejection not only of non-dictatorship, but also conditional rejection for examples of the social desireability of properties of acyclicity and path independences.

Before proceeding further in these directions I draw attention to another class of standard objections to "perfectly" competitive conditions – objections which stem from a different direction to those indicated by a perspective of (standard) developments pertaining to the apparent impossibility of developing conditions consistent with the establishment of decisive collective decision rules in general. (And as pertaining to the apparent impossibility of developing conditions consistent with conditions of "pure"/"perfect" competition in particular).

These further, and different, classes of objection can be seen via considerations of "Second Best" and associated types of analysis and results deriving from the work of Lipsey and Lancaster {18} (and qualified by McManus {19}). In words the Second Best idea might be summarized thus:

If for any reason it is not possible to meet *all* of the marginal conditions of optimality associated with a general competitive equilibrium then, in general, it is not desireable – in the sense of a social welfare function - to meet *any* of the marginal conditions of general competitive equilibrium.

The logic of this result is evident. If all processes are recognized as interdependent then variation in *any* one – including in principle variation (for whatever reason) from any condition of "competitive" equilibrium – will in general necessarily connote variation(s) for *all* others.

Interested readers are referred to the references just cited for more detailed developments pertaining to marginal conditions of general competitive equilibrium. Here it is significant that any student familiar with the content of a moderately rigorous introductory microeconomics course would be familiar with this latter class of standard Second Best result as well with the essence of Arrow' Impossibility result and of simple (and highly restrictive) classes of Competitive Equilibrium <=> Pareto optimality result.

Conditions as if potentially generating "Second Best" results might for example include the recognition of technological and/or social phenomena demonstrably empirically at variance with standard competitive assumptions including the technological phenomenon of increasing returns to scale at an optimum for at least one (potential) product[5] and/or the phenomenon of abstract and/or empirical interdependence of preference relations for at least one class of potential consumer.[6]

Given these classes of counter example to standard competitive assumptions alone, it might seem that "Second Best" analyses and "Second Best" solutions to social issues could be intrinsically *superior* to "Competitive" ones, both on theoretical and on empirical grounds, even if only in the sense that "Second Best" formulations apparently offer potential for yielding results both theoretically and empirically more consistent with everyday observation than the conditions of individualism and selfishness associated with "pure" or "perfect" competition.

Attention has just been focussed on apparent potential for contradictions, both theoretical and empirical, between general competitive equilibrium results centred upon individuality and selfish decisionmaking by economic agents, impossibility results pertaining to collective social choice(s), and second-best results, including results which might in principle recognize theoretical and/or empirical implications of *any* deviation – whether individually or collectively theoretically/ empirically *inevitable* and/or (potentially) individually or collectively theoretically/ empirically *dsireable* _ from marginal conditions of optimal choice associated with constrained preference/ profit maximization for persons/ firms under conditions of "pure"/"perfect" competition.

I now stress that, in the wider contexts provided by other developments in this chapter, as well as by developments in other chapters in this book, it has been seen that contradiction(s), including apparent self contradiction(s) is (are) not necessarily pathological in their implication(s) for an element of a theory, or for the force of an argument.

Indeed, by means of these wider developments, principles and potential processes of contradiction, including principles and potential processes of self contradiction have been seen not only to be significant with reference to (the determination of) potential mathematical/ physical principles and/or processes of mathematical/ physical change in general, but with reference to (the determination of) potential mathematical/ physical economic principles and/ or processes of mathematical/ physical economic change in particular.

It might seem, for example, that conditions *consistent with* competition might in principle emerge as if *via* potential principles and processes of contradiction including potential principles and/or processes of self contradiction with reference to a potential collective decision rule.

Issues pertaining to choice between theories might then seem to become much more subtle. For example, with reference to potential conditions of "perfect" competition, consider whether standard conditions of "perfect" competition could be individually *and* collectively *desireable* in general – even if attainable in particular ;

i) via principles and/or processes of contradiction in relation to individual and collective decision rules/ social welfare functionals as if themselves *optimally* corresponding to selfish and individualistic price taking behaviours for each and all economic agents ;

ii) as if optimally corresponding, too, to the *absence of* explicit roles for taxes, subsidies, and ;

iii) more generally, *absence of* explicit roles for (levels of) government action and/ or government agency including actions securing and/ or secured via *choices of* governments including for example choice(s) of (levels of) governments' incomes and governments' expenditures.

Preceding as well as subsequent developments and remarks argue to the contrary – as, indeed, from a different perspective do Second Best results.

With reference to potential conditions for decisive collective social choice(s), consider whether (standard) conditions for collective choice rules which, for example, impose conditions of non-dictatorship, acyclicity, path independence.. would be individually *and* collectively desireable, either in general or in particular. Again preceding as well as subsequent developments and results argue to the contrary.

With these remarks and associated warnings with reference to any assumption to the effect that a condition $y = y_0$ (as above) is potentially theoretically, empirically and/or *desireably* underpinned by conditions of competitive general equilibrium, notice that, given the conditions $y = y_0$ (however it is motivated), apparently the three "goods market" conditions might be manipulated to yield two equations determining the interest rate.

Apparently that interest rate might be used in turn as if to interpret the three "money market" conditions as if then yielding a 1:1 relation between money supply and price level.

This is known as the Classical Dichotomy and, more generally, this kind of thinking might be used as a foundation for "monetarist" statements such as : "Inflation is solely a monetary phenomenon" or ; "In order to control inflation it is necessary and sufficient to control the money supply."

By contrast, with an assumption as if $p = p_0$, apparently no such dichotomy between goods and money market conditions is attainable. That is; apparently in principle, under the conditions $p = p_0$, the above goods and money market conditions may be seen as if *necessarily* solved together.[7]

Those familiar with macroeconomics might see these latter considerations in turn as consistent with representations as if, under a condition as if $p = p_0$, the first three goods market relations may be used to generate a single (conditional) $IS(P_0)$ relation between y and r, and the latter used to generate a *different* (conditional) $LM(P_0)$ relation between y and r,with an overall "equilibrium" solution of the system then apparently corresponding to conditions as if consistent with simultaneous solution of both of these conditions (and so simultaneous solution of all market relations).[8]

Still in the context of the above "Simple Common Model" Friedman notes – as would any standard textbook course – that, following the appearance in 1958 of Phillips' work in {20} demonstrating apparently statistically significant *empirical* relationships of a particular form between rates of change of money wages and rates of unemployment in the UK over the period 1861-1958, even a simple macroeconomic model would draw a seventh equation from a relation derived from that work.

Briefly, Phillips regressed rate of change of money wages against unemployment for various intervals during the period 1861-1958 to obtain statistical relations which apparently had a remarkably stable form, and which have come to be known as (simple) "Phillips Curves". The standard textbook representation of one of these is similar to that sketched as follows:

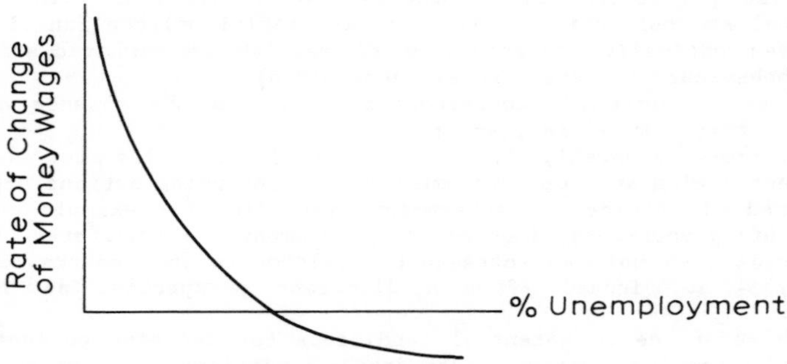

Figure 4.1

For purposes of comparison and contrast two of Phillips' own estimated "Phillips Curves" with his associated data are reproduced from his paper in the Appendix. There, also, UK data for the rate of change of money wages and unemployment are given for some more recent years.

Two points are of great significance. First, according to current interpretations of Phillips' Phillips Curve, the intercept on the Unemployment axis corresponds to the "natural rate of unemployment". For the period of Phillips' studies magnitudes for this appeared to be remarkably stable in the range of 5.5% - 7.5%, a range of values which is significantly smaller than UK unemployment rates thus far in the 1980/90s. Secondly, both Phillips' data and more recent data exhibit characteristic "Phillips Loops", which are ignored in (standard) simple representations of Phillips curves. In due course further attention will be given both to this point and to the 'natural rate of unemployment' interpretation.

It is of substantial interest here that, especially in the United Kingdom, macroeconomic models were used with increasing mathematical, economic, and associated econometric sophistication as mathematical economic and econometric specification and estimation methods and associated computation facilities and techniques themselves become increasingly more sophisticated during the 1950s, 1960s and 1970s.

In this context simple Phillips curves were generally understood as if offering potential *tradeoffs* to societies between (increased/ reduced) rates of inflation and (respectively reduced/ increased) rates of unemployment in general and between (relatively) reduced unemployment at the expense of (relatively) increased inflation in particular.

In the United Kingdom the apparent potential for such trade-offs was argued to provide both theoretical and empirical bases for post Second World War "Keynesian Demand Management" policies designed to attain and then to sustain full employment -policies consistent with the ambitions and promises accompanying acceptance of recommendations of the Beveridge Report of 1944 entitled "Full Employment in a Free Society" which argued powerfully for policies to be designed by post war governments to prevent a return to prewar levels of unemployment.[10]

I have stressed that Phillips' work was itself seen as essentially empirical in character, and that Phillips Curves, which were thus essentially founded upon empirical relations, were subsequently used to close up macroeconomic models – models which were then developed both for theoretical and for empirical policy making purposes. In the late 1960s the phenomenon known as "stagflation" emerged in the United Kingdom as well as in most developed countries in the West. In this period apparently *increasing* rates of inflation coexisted with *increasing* rates of unemployment (see the graph in the Appendix).

This apparently systematic and widespread empirical break-down in (empirically based) simple Phillips' relations immediately precipitated crises both for the development of macroeconomic models and for the macroeconomic policymaking which had become increasingly based upon macroeconomic models in general, and macroeconomic models incorporating simple Phillips Curves and associated apparent potential for inflation-unemployment tradeoffs in particular.

This was a crisis, then, for macroeconomic theory as well as for macroeconomic policymaking.

From the perspective of theory : with no simple Phillips relation apparently a simple macroeconomic model would revert to six equations in seven unknowns. From the perspective of policies based on macroeconomic/ econometric models ;in the absence of viable models of this kind preexisting kinds of model-based policy information and prediction became unattainable.

In more general terms, apparently if there were no inflation-unemployment tradeoff there would be no room for policies directed toward the empirical realization of particular kinds of tradeoff.

I have noted that the empirical breakdown of the simple Phillips curve in the late 1960s precipitated a crisis for macro-economic theory and for policy. From a related perspective, this breakdown could be seen as providing opportunities for the development and assimilation of *new* theories, as well as for the critical reevaluation of existing ones.

From that perspective, for example, "neo-Keynesian" theorists sought to found their theories on microeconomic principles – sought microfoundations for macroeconomics – and by that route have come to stress roles for expectations and for uncertainty as constituting the essence of Keynes' contribution to economic theory, thereby downplaying central roles for governments, as well as associated roles for government expenditures and for fiscal and monetary policies,except insofar as these latter are construed as providing responses to conditions of market uncertainty/ indeterminacy.

Incidentally, despite this change in emphasis by the majority of macroeconomists, many economists (including myself) and most laymen would continue to understand Keynes' major contribution as having been to legitimize government intervention not just as if to stabilize fluctuations in existing markets in the face of uncertainty but, among other things, as if to generate (new kinds of) social objectives and, with these, new kinds of output, income and employment opportunities – for example by undertaking new kinds of government expenditure as if in order to attain and/ or to sustain (new kinds of) reductions in levels of involuntary unemployment.

Milton Friedman, too, (as well as other quantity theorists) formulated a response to the breakdown of the simple Phillips relation. In most respects Friedman's response was apparently even less subtle than that of the neo-Keynesians. For example in his influential paper entitled "Unemployment Versus Inflation : An Evaluation of the Phillips Curve" {10}[11] he apparently takes the view that not only did the breakdown of the simple Phillips relation signal that trade-offs between inflation and unemployment, as if via a simple Phillips relation, could no longer be attained, but that attempts to attain and/ or to sustain such trade-offs would *necessarily* be (and had necessarily been) founded upon actions as if designed by governments to mislead peoples into conformity with governments' designs by means of "money illusion".

Briefly, in his paper Friedman seeks to rehabilitate the simple Phillips curve while at the same time critiquing Phillips' presentation on the grounds of naivete with respect to expectations formations, by considering it as if corresponding to a special class of cases in the context of developments pertaining to a "Long-Run" Phillips Curve.

Friedman founds his analysis on particular kinds of assumptions with reference to approaches to price and wage determination(s), respectively in product and in labour markets. For both classes of cases his analyses rest essentially on "competitive" market clearing assumptions and a focus upon (differences) in expectations in labour markets as indicated in the following diagram:

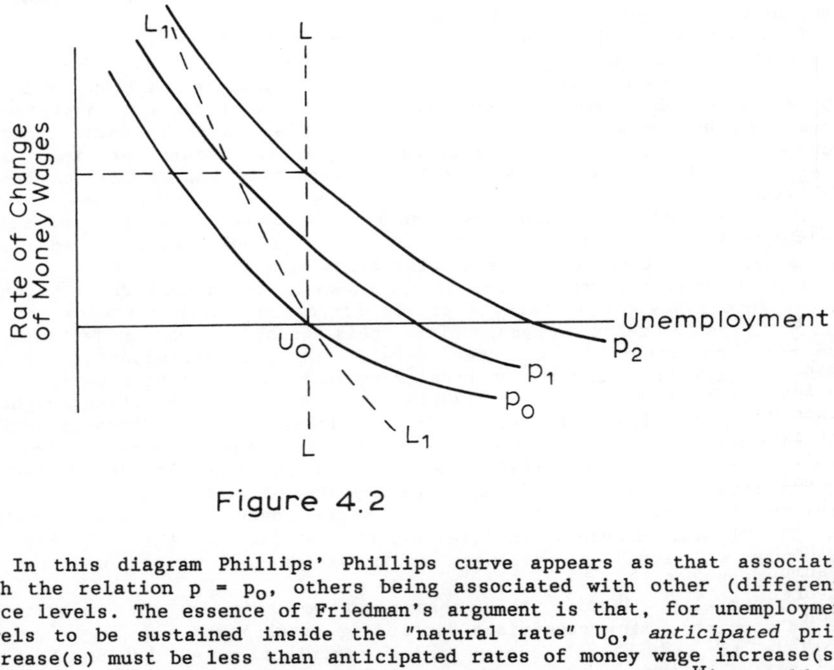

Figure 4.2

In this diagram Phillips' Phillips curve appears as that associated with the relation $p = p_o$, others being associated with other (different) price levels. The essence of Friedman's argument is that, for unemployment levels to be sustained inside the "natural rate" U_o, *anticipated* price increase(s) must be less than anticipated rates of money wage increase(s), so that anticipated ("real" outputs and) "real" wages $^W/_p$ would be perceived as if increasing and, in the "short run", *more than* "market clearing" levels of unemployment thus obtained, as indicated schematically in Figures 3and 4 below.

In this context Friedman rests his analysis upon an inflation transmission mechanism suggested by Irving Fisher in a 1925 paper {8}, distinguishing this mechanism from that invoked by Phillips to motivate his work – asserting indeed that Fisher's work was essentially true and Phillips' essentially erroneous.[12]

Briefly, according to Fisher/ Friedman interpretations, increases in nominal demand for products (for example increases in *nominal* demand generated by an increase in money supply) are interpreted as if perceived by individual enterprises as corresponding to increases in *real* demand for products (generating d_1d_1 in the first diagram), in turn generating increases in demand for workers ($d_1'd_1'$) in the second diagram.

The role of money illusion in realizing increases in output(s) and in employment in this argument is evident and Friedman goes further to assert that, in the long run, governments would find it impossible to sustain money illusion and so impossible to induce workers by such means to sustain unemployment inside the natural rate U_o, so motivating LL in Fig. 2.

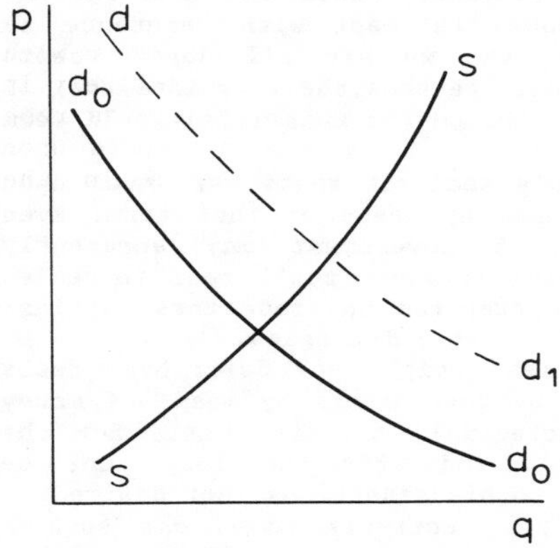

A Representative Product Market

Figure 4.3

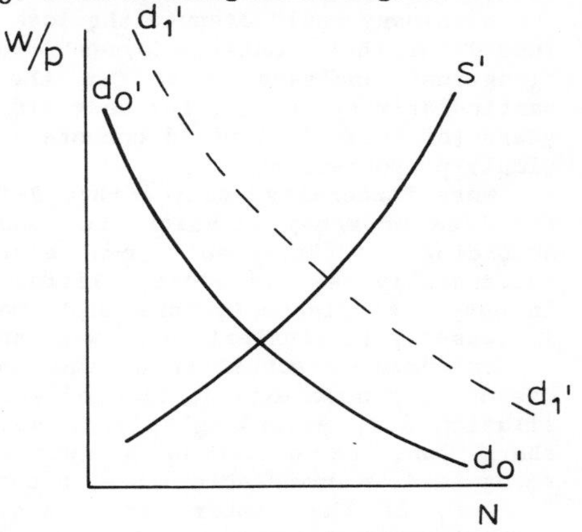

Labour Market

Figure 4.4

From these developments Friedman draws the policy conclusions that, in the long run, it would be neither possible nor desireable for a society to seek, by means of demand management policies, to sustain unemployment inside the natural rate of unemployment, i.e. that in the long run (in the absence of money illusion) the Phillips Curve would become a vertical straight line at the natural rate of unemployment and that, in the "short run", attempts to keep unemployment inside the natural rate would (predictively) constitute a recipe for accelerating inflation (motivating L_1L_1 in Fig. 2).

In many ways this influential work by Friedman marked a watershed in thinking. The (simple) analysis in this paper is based on competitive assumptions and has been used not only to motivate particular kinds of theoretical approaches to macroeconomic policy, including a primary focus upon labour market wage expectation formation and transmission mechanisms in general, but also to motivate condemnations both of Phillips' results and models based directly upon them in particular,[13] and of Keynesian Demand Management policies and associated (higher) inflation, (lower) unemployment tradeoffs in general.

I again stress that competitive models in general, and the above simple common model, as well as the labour and product market analyses in Friedman's Unemployment Versus Inflation paper in particular, explicitly do not incorporate roles for government expenditure or taxes/ subsidies.

Going further, it is evident that those accepting or promoting such essentially "competitively" based models and interpretations as if (the only) desireable kinds of model for macroeconomic policymaking purposes, would seek not only to *reduce* increase(s) in money supply and rates of money wage increase(s) as if in order to reduce rates of increase in inflation but, more generally, to *reduce* roles for government via *reductions* in levels and kinds of government expenditure(s) and taxes/

subsidies and, by those means among others seek to *impose* "competitive" conditions upon their own and/ or upon other societies.

In the context of Friedman's - and others' – criticisms of "Keynesian" macroeconomic analyses and policies, many would see a 31 year-long period of less than 5% unemployment – and, incidentally, a 31 year period of unemployment inside any natural rate found in Phillips' work – as a success and a cause for congratulation rather than condemnation.

Also many would dispute the idea that 31 years constitutes a short run. Indeed in that context Keynes' well-known statement with reference to "long-run" analyses, viz: "In the long run we are all dead", seems particularly apt since, for most (if not all) persons,the very idea that 31 years (of this life) would connote a short period (of this life) would seem simply preposterous.

More forcefully, notice that Friedman's analysis rests very much upon the idea of money illusion and condemnation by means of that term. Even according to Friedman's own analysis, a government may apparently successfully seek to adopt policies to yield ("short run") *real* increases in output(s), income(s) and employment,if prepared to trade these against increase(s) in (inflationary) wage and price level increases.

Friedman asserts that the mechanism which he describes rests essentially upon *exploitation* of workers by governments by means of money illusion and, accordingly, that such (potential) policies must, for the short run, be condemned as undesireable and, for the long run, be recognized as unworkable since, according to his assertions, not desired.

But, if the members of a society were actively to *choose* such a mechanism as if a desired means of achieving desired ends of higher output(s)/ employment/income(s), then no illusion would be involved. I believe that in the UK at least such trade-offs were indeed chosen by the members of that society in awareness inter alia of inflationary implications.

On an empirical note, too, while there *is* evidence, I believe, including that in the diagrams in the Appendix, for levels of unemployment *less* than the "natural rate" of 5% - 6% (interpreted in relation to Phillips' Phillips curves) being successfully chosen for the UK by government and people alike over a long sequence of "short runs" in the interval 1945 - 1970, there is no evidence of any kind in that data to support Friedman's contention that in the long run the Phillips curve will necessarily be (or become) a vertical straight line at the natural rate of unemployment – wherever he, or anyone else, may elect to choose to set their particular interpretation for the natural rate. (Subsequent to 1975 some economists have attempted to argue that the natural rate has become systematically greater than it had been for the preceding century).

Underlining this latter point Friedman himself has volunteered that his contention that the Phillips curve necessarily becomes vertical in the long run is at best only weakly supported by empirical evidence.(On this point see {10} p.44).

Now return specifically to the Simple Common Model and consider the three goods market relations in it in even more detail with a view first to consideration of the Paradox of Thrift and then to consideration, more generally, of potential significance for phenomena, including production, trade, taxes, subsidies, government expenditure (foreign) trade and, more primitively, (economic) resource constraints variously simply and/ or commonly omitted and/ or ignored in that overall Simple Common Model.

With these aims in view first consider a (standard) linear representation for the three goods market relations as follows:

$$C = C_0 + b.Y$$

$$I = I_0 - e.r$$

$$Y = C + I$$

Apparently these three relations may be used to generate an IS relation variously via the expression:

$$Y = C_0 + b.Y + I_0 - e.r$$

or, more commonly, via an expression of the following form:

$$Y = \frac{1}{1-b}(C_0 + I_0 - e.r)$$

These relations are of a standard form and, in them, the magnitude b is known as the "marginal propensity to consume" disposable income (since apparently dC/dy = b in the first relation).

Now notice that apparently, for $b \leq 1$, the larger is b, the larger is the value of the measure 1/(1-b)in the latter income-expenditure relation. Terming C_0 and I_0 elements of autonomous expenditure, apparently the measure 1/(1-b) corresponds to a simple multiplier of income(s) as if potentially *generated* via changes in demand/ expenditure. In this context apparently the higher the marginal propensity to save from income the lower the value of the multiplier at the margin.

Even with such a naive representation for a "Keynesian" system as the one considered above, this remark immediately suggests potential relations to the Paradox of Thrift.

That these three goods market relations do indeed correspond only to a naive representation is evident if it is noted, for example, that no potential for taxes/ subsidies or other government expenditure(s) appear in them. More directly, given the context of potential saving relations, notice that the consumption relation – and so implicitly the saving relation – is naive in not explicitly incorporating any interest rate. Both of these kinds of criticisms can be accommodated – at least schematically – without undue difficulty. For example a modification to incorporate interest in the consumption relation might be made schematically via the term d.r as follows :

$$C = C_0 + bY - d.r$$

so that:

$$S = Y - C = (1-b)Y + d.r - C_0$$

and, the appropriately modified IS relation becomes:

$$Y = \frac{1}{1-b}(C_0 + I_0 - d.r - e.r)$$

With this (simple) modification the multiplier, 1/(1-b) remains as before and both the saving-related term d.r and the investment-related term e.r apparently operate in the same direction. Apparently, a fortiori relative reductions in interest rates and/or relative increases in autonomous expenditures and/or in the marginal propensity to consume all potentially (relatively) increase the measure Y. More constructively, it might seem that policies directed toward potential increases in income Y might fruitfully be selected as if potentially to secure actions/ reactions/ interactions as if in turn potentially to *regenerate* relative increases in autonomous expenditures and/or in "marginal propensity to consume" and/or reductions in interest rates.

Now consider potential relations to the Paradox of Thrift in this context. Clearly increases in autonomous consumption C_0 and *increases* in marginal propensity to consume b are associated here *both* with *reductions* in levels and rates of saving and *increases* in potential income. And, conversely, apparently *decreases* in autonomous consumption and decreases in MPC are associated *both* with *increases* in levels and rates of saving and *decreases* in potential income.

As before, therefore, links between simple goods market relations, a simple IS relation and a statement of the Paradox of Thrift seem readily attainable.

As a class of examples, apparently *sufficient* (microeconomic) conditions for the generation of a macroeconomic phenomenon corresponding to the Paradox of Thrift are that *each* and *all* potential savers act as if to choose to consume and/or invest *less* relative to self, as if in (therefore mistaken) anticipation of actions as if to consume/ invest *more* by another/ others.

More generally, and more constructively, apparently one class of cases potentially resolving the Paradox can be based on the observation that, inter alia, net gains are attainable if *some* act as if to choose *less* relative to self as if predictively to secure *more* relative to another/ others, as if in turn thereby potentially to gain *more* relative to self.

In a microeconomic context the latter kind of case will suggest links to principles and processes relating to potential principles and processes of gain from potential gifts/ barter/ trade spatially and/ or inter-temporally whereas, in both micro and a fortiori in macroeconomic contexts, it will immediately suggest roles for principles and processes pertaining to (differential) taxation/ subsidies in particular and constructive roles for governments and for government interventions more generally.

Now consider graphical representations of the linearized goods market consumption and investment relations as in Figures 5 and 6 and all three goods market relations represented schematically as in Figure 7 as follows:

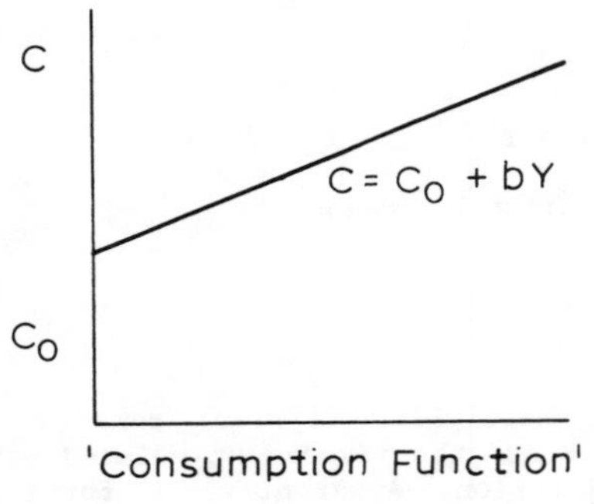

Figure 4.5

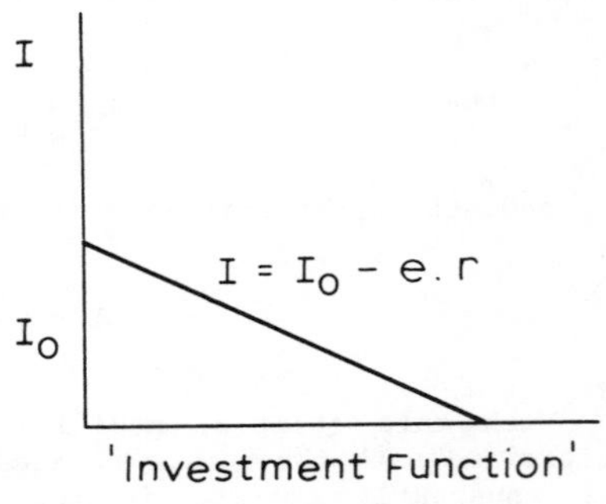

Figure 4.6

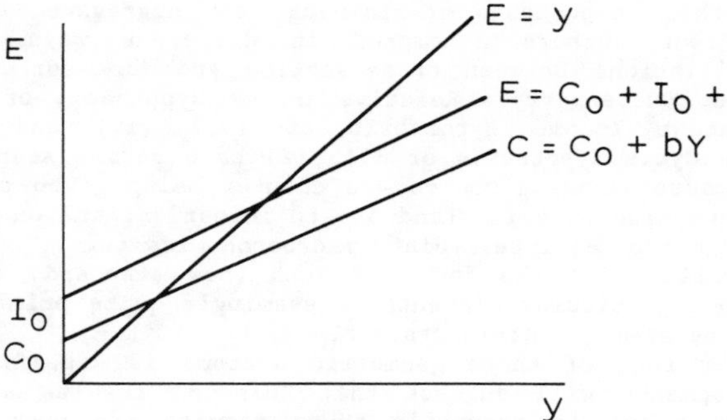

Figure 4.7

Each of these diagrams will be familiar to anyone familiar with standard treatments of Simple Linear Keynesian Income-Expenditure systems.[14]

In a standard development, diagrams and underlying algebraic systems such as those just considered are typically used respectively to introduce slightly more discursive treatments pertaining respectively to Consumption Functions, to Investment, and so to goods market equilibrium.

For example, focussing on the consumption function, the relation $C = C_0 + b.Y$ in the first diagram might initially be interpreted as if corresponding to a (naive interpretation of) an Absolute Income Hypothesis which is commonly imputed to Keynes (see {3} p.95). Then Kuznets' empirical work entitled "National Product since 1869",({15}), published in 1946 which used consumption-income data for the USA, might be introduced. Kuznets found empirically quite distinct income-consumption relations for cross-section and time-series data as indicated schematically in Figure 4.8:

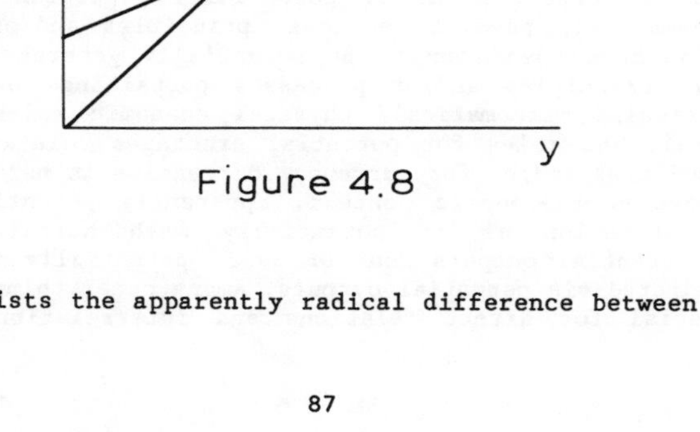

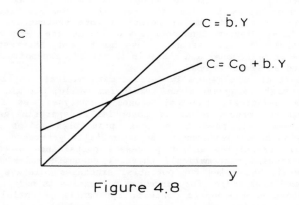

Figure 4.8

For economists the apparently radical difference between cross-section and time-series results not only made a naive representation of an Absolute Income hypothesis seem evidently inadequate, but led to the development of numbers of further hypotheses pertaining to aggregate consumption behaviour. Different authors attempted in different ways to secure empirical reconciliations between cross-section and time-series results. Thus, as examples, Duesenberry's Relative Income Hypothesis of 1949 {7}, Friedman's Permanent Income Hypothesis of 1957 {11} and Ando and Modigliani's Life Cycle Hypothesis of 1963 {2} have become standard parts of any standard macroeconomics course – a chapter being given over to the topic of the consumption function (and one to investment and one to market equilibrium)[15] in a typical intermediate macroeconomics text.

The reader will notice the focus of such (now standard) econometric investigations upon particular elements of seemingly quite primitive kinds of algebraic and *related* geometric systems.

The particular form of these geometric systems is significant since subsequent developments will suggest that Kuznets' results and others' efforts to motivate and to reconcile these results are open to interpretation as if only focussing attention selectively *and variously* upon particular elements of more comprehensive arithmetic/ algebraic/ geometric structures themselves open to interpretation in relation to the relative (in)determinacy of potential mathematical/ physical principles and processes of mathematical/ physical systems in general, and mathematical/ physical economic systems in particular.

With a view to such further developments and implicit criticisms I now emphasize first the essentially *geometrical* focus of developments and interpretations ostensibly pertaining to consumption and to investment relations via the diagrams just considered and, second, the essentially *empirical* focus of attention for these developments and interpretations.

This refocusses attention upon issues considered more widely in other chapters – issues pertaining to potential relations and interrelations between theoretical and empirical mathematical/ physical systems, and subsystems in general, and pertaining to potential relations and/or interrelations between theoretical and empirical mathematical/ physical economic systems and subsystems as if generating/ generated via particular kinds of arithmetic/ algebraic/ geometric principles and processes pertaining to potential mathematical/ physical principles and/ or processes of as if perfect prediction in particular.

With potential relations to wider and more generally applicable contexts of these kinds in mind, now reconsider the graphical representations of the three goods market relations more abstractly, by noticing that in the first diagram Consumption and Income are represented as if *orthogonal*, that in the second, Investment and Interest Rate are represented as if *orthogonal* and that, in the third, Expenditure and Income are represented as if *orthogonal*.

In a context of more generally defined mathematical/ physical systems, orthogonality might suggest *mutual exclusion* while, in the context of (potential) mathematical/ physical economic analyses, as if purposive principles and/ or processes as if potentially generating/generated via potential mathematical/ physical economic principles and/or processes of mutual exclusion have been seen to be potentially generated, inter alia, via (potential) principles and/or processes pertaining to the (re)generation of particular mathematical/ physical economic roles for standard units in general, and roles for potential exchanges relative to standard units for commodities and/or for currency/ currencies in particular.

In the above macroeconomic context, apparently potential *inputs* are open to interpretation as if potentially mathematically/ physically predictive of potential *outputs and/ or* as if potentially mathematically/ physically predicted via potential outputs. Among other things this suggests potential for direct relations and interrelations to analyses incorporating simple multipliers.

Considering these points together : As if *variously* via elements of the above goods market relations *first* : apparently standard mathematical/ physical units (including standardized monetary units) of *income* are apparently potentially mathematically/ physically *predictive of* and/ or as if potentially mathematically *predicted via* (relatively abstract) standard mathematical/ physical units (including standardized monetary units) of *expenditure* and, *second* ; apparently potentially mathematical/physical *inputs* are as if potentially mathematically/ physically predictive of and/ or as if potentially mathematically/ physically predicted via mathematical/ physical *outputs*.

With these perspectives an analyst might schematically relate potential income(s), expenditure(s), input(s) and output(s) schematically as follows:

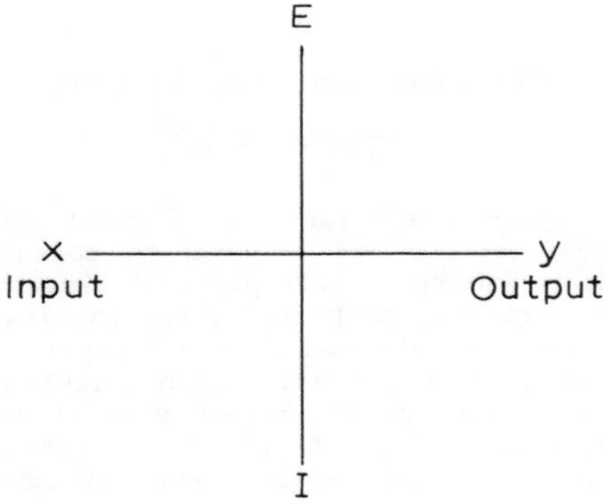

Figure 4.9

With reference to this schema there are evidently potential input-output and income-expenditure links across it. More generally reference here to potential input-output relations and/or interrelations will recall developments in Chapter 3 pertaining specifically to input-output systems and will thereby direct attention to the apparent absence from the above diagram of measures corresponding for example to deviations from input/ output *goals* or to a system Ax as if intervening between measures x, interpreted in relation to potential output, and y interpreted in relation to potential "final demands" for output(s).

From another perspective, apparently the above schema is open to inte pretation as if *predictively* : i) expenditures potentially *generate* income(s) and ; ii) inputs potentially *generate* outputs.

It is also open to interpretation as if inputs potentially *exchange* for *nominal* income(s) and outputs potentially *exchange* for *nominal* expenditure(s).

Together these conditions apparently may mathematically and physically construe themselves/ be construed as if potentially generating *and/ or* as if potentially (re)generated via a "circular flow" of inputs, incomes, outputs and expenditures in relative space-time corresponding to that indicated schematically in the following diagram:

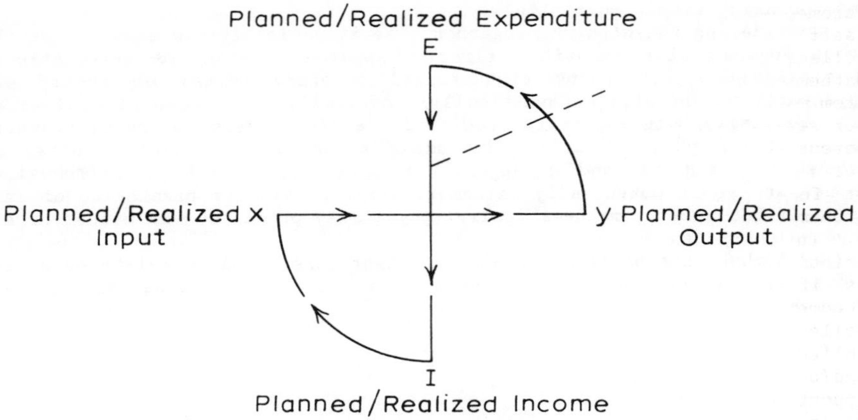

Figure 4.10

In contrast to Figure 4.9, Figure 4.10 makes explicit distinctions between *plans* and *realizations* and is open to potential interpretations among other things as if (mathematical/ physical elements of) mathematical/ physical *plans* as if perfectly mathematically/ physically *predict* and/ or are as if perfectly *predicted via* mathematical/ physical *realizations*.

Expanding on this : Here planned output might construe itself/ be construed as if (potentially) predictive of planned expenditure, in turn, as if (potentially) predictive of planned income, in turn, as if potentially predictive of planned resource used, in turn, as if potentially predictive of planned output .....

The context of previous mathematical/ physical developments pertaining more generally to as if perfect prediction will prompt a search here for evidence of (potential) mathematical/physical (economic) principles and processes of *(self) contradiction*.

And there appears to be a potentially *desireable* role here for principles and/ or processes pertaining to *cycling* in relation to potential processes as if potentially generating/ (re)generated via *individual and/or collective* microeconomic and/ or macroeconomic *choice*.

With reference to (self) contradiction an analyst/ reader might focus not only on apparent potential for *oppositions* in the preceding diagram between potential physical and potential monetary/ financial flows but apparent potential, too, for the *generation/ regeneration* of physical and/ or monetary/ financial flows inter alia as if *purposively* by means of potential principles and processes of contradiction potentially generating elements of physical flows as if potentially via *opposed* monetary/ financial flows, and vice versa.

Reference here to potential desireability for cycling in relation to potential choice by individuals and/or groups will recall developments and associated remarks in relation to so-called Impossibility Results pertaining to (potential) Social Choice(s)/ Collective Choice(s) in Chapter 2 – as well as in Chapters 1 and 7 – Impossibility Results which commonly rest, among other things, upon an assumption by an analyst to the effect that *acyclicity* for (potential) individual/ collective (revealed) pref- rence relations is necessarily individually and/or collectively *desireable* and potential *cyclicity* individually and/or collectively necessarily *undesireable*

More generally reference to potentially *predictive* roles for planned incomes and expenditures and to potential principles and processes of (self) contradiction pertaining to potential for individually and/ or collectively *advantageous* reallocations and/or redistributions of mathematical/ physical units of economic commodities deriving, inter alia from monetary/ financial units, will again underline potential significance for *standard units*, and for target prices and quantities relative to as if potentially agreed monetary/ standard units and, *by such means*, potential for formation of (potential) mathematical/ physical (economic) plans and/ or for (potential) realization(s) of potential mathematical/ physical economic plans.

In the context of potential economic interpretations pertaining to principles and/or processes of mathematical/ physical economic prediction as if potentially generating/ (re)generated via a "circular flow of income", notice that outcomes *nominally or physically exceeding* individual/ collective planned target values might seem potentially individually/ collectively *desireable* (undesireable) if corresponding to individually and/or collectively relatively *desireable* (undesireable) commodities/ opportunities. Here are potentially individually and/ or collectively *desireable* roles for appropriately defined kinds of relatively *imperfect prediction*.

This remark will recall attention to developments elsewhere in this Chapter as well as elsewhere in this book pertaining to potentially individually and/or collectively *desireable* mathematical/ physical economic *opportunities* in general and, in particular, to potential classes of opportunity potentially (re)generated *by* and/ or *for* individuals/ societies by means of mathematical/ physical economic principles and/ or processes as if potentially generating/ (re)generated via mathematical/ physical economic principles and processes of contradiction between mathematical/ physical economic measures relative to self, mathematical/ physical economic measures relative to each other and/ or, mathematical/ physical economic measures relative to and through wider mathematical/ physical systems.

In summary, there appear to be potentially constructive roles here not only for as if *perfect* prediction as if relative to mathematically/ physically *perfect* prediction and for *imperfect* prediction as if relative to mathematically/ physically *imperfect* prediction, but potential for principles and/or processes potentially generating/ (re)generated via mathematical/ physical economic principles and processes of contradiction *between* as if *perfect* mathematical/ physical economic predictors/ prediction relative to self, to others and/or to and through a wider mathematical/ physical economic system and as if *imperfect* mathematical/ physical economic predictors/prediction relative to self, to others and/or to and through a wider mathematical/ physical economic system.

These remarks again suggests potential for interpretations pertaining to the generation of microeconomic as well as of macroeconomic phenomena in general and pertaining to apparent potential for generation of micro-economic phenomena as if via macroeconomic phenomena, and conversely, in particular. But now they do this in wider mathematical/ physical contexts of geometric representations and interpretations which potentially relate – via developments in Chapter 1 and elsewhere – to the elucidation and explanation of *all kinds* of mathematical/ physical principles and/ or processes of relative change and/ or of relative motion in relative space-time

It has been noted that Figure 4.10 emphasises potential – and as if potentially predictive – *macroeconomic* relations, between Input X and Output(s) Y, and between Income I and Expenditure E, across it. It has been seen, too, that the former measures X, Y may suggest potential arithmetic/ algebraic/ geometric relations to developments pertaining to goal programming interpretations as if potentially generating and/or generated via developments in relation to input-output analyses.

Now notice that the measures X, Y can also suggest (thereby apparently related) potential interpretations respectively in relation to "endowments" (of potential inputs to "consumption" commodities) and to consumption levels for "consumption" commodities considered in the context of critiques, in Chapters 1, and 2, as well as this one, of fundamentally *microeconomic* structures ostensibly developed by economic analysts for the purpose of elucidating, analyzing and/or realizing potential for individuals and collective gains as if via principles and/ or processes pertaining to two commodities, to "pure trade" and to trade as if potentially generating/ generated via principles and processes of "perfect" competition between two individuals (and/or groups of individuals/ nations/ states).

An analyst/ observer, seeing the above schematic algebraic/ geometric system in this way, might thereby immediately see potential in it for specific kinds of *microeconomic* interpretations *as well as* for, ostensibly, *macroeconomic* interpretations.

More fundamentally, an analyst/ observer would note, first : potential implicit in that system for the discovery of principles and/or processes *not only* potentially generating/ regenerating elements of microeconomic and/or macroeconomic *interpretations and/or* potentially generating/ regenerating potential *relations* and *interrelations* between elements of mathematically/ physically/ economically relatively aggregated macro economic systems and mathematically/ physically/ economically relatively disaggregated macroeconomic systems/ subsystems *but*, apparently too, potential for the mathematical/physical/ economic *generation/ regeneration/ growth/ decline* of elements of relatively *larger* mathematical/ physical/ economic systems as if *via* the mathematical/ physical intermediation of *smaller* ones, and for the mathematical/ physical/ economic *generation/ regeneration/growth/ decline* of (elements of) relatively *smaller* mathematical/ physical/ economic (sub)systems as if *via* the mathematical/ physical/ economic intermediation of (elements of) relatively *larger* ones.

More directly, an analyst/ observer, by comparing the above diagram with algebraic/ geometric interpretations variously in relation to potential trade/ pure trade/ perfect competition in Chapters 1 and 2 would note that, whereas here reference is apparently explicitly made only to a *single* measure X, and a *single* measure Y, in those other places at least *two* algebraically and geometrically distinct measures appear for each, algebraically via: x_1, x_2, y_1, y_2 and geometrically for example via:

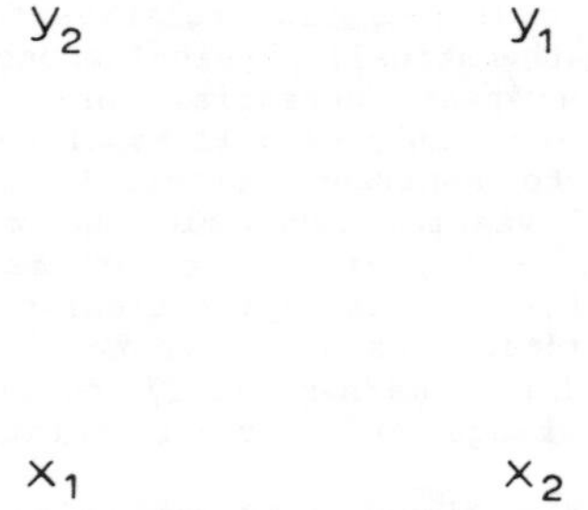

Figure 4.11

From these perspectives the previously considered macroeconomic income -expenditure interpretations might seem *more primitive* than microeconomic interpretations – while evidently being potentially algebraically/ geometrically related to them – not only because measures x, y in a macroeconomic context might seem more highly aggregated, but also because, by contrast with microeconomic systems and interpretations of the kind just considered, in macroeconomic interpretations there is apparently no specific reference to potential gifts/ barters/ exchanges/ trade(s) as between (potential owners of) distinct elements of inputs and distinct elements of outputs of (potential) consumption commodities.

But from another perspective the essentially microeconomic interpretations for example ostensibly considered in relation to "pure trade" in other Chapters might seem *primitive* by contrast with the above "circular flow" macroeconomic interpretation since, by contrast with this latter context, in the former there is explicitly no reference to money and/ or to monetized units.

Thus two ostensibly quite different kinds of points have been related to different interpretations in relation to algebraic/ geometric structures which are thus evidently potentially *common both* to macroeconomic and to macroeconomic analyses and interpretations. This suggests consideration of the "circular flow" diagram as if potentially yielding explicitly microeconomic as well as macroeconomic interpretations. From this many observations immediately follow. Consider the following classes as examples.

If x_1 is identified with X and y_1 with Y, quantities which are not specifically monetized in a microeconomic "pure trade" diagram are inter alia (potentially) as if specifically monetized via relation to a macroeconomic "circular flow" interpretation. This suggests several related points.

First : with a context of microeconomics, it might seem that potential for identification of (all) commodities in relation to standard/ monetary units would potentially provide means of defining/ determining macroeconomic *aggregates* as if in relation to otherwise essentially *disaggregated* and disparate elements of commodities.

Second : with a context of macroeconomics, identification of commodities as if in *potential* relation to monetized units provides one kind of circumstance appropriate to the determination of principles and processes of relative *gain* (loss) as if *via* principles and/or processes of (self) contradiction *between :* as if *subjective* measures, including preference/ indifference measures, relative to self, to another/ others and relative to and through a wider system *and* ; as if *objective* measures/ measurement(s) relative to self, to another/ others and relative to and through a wider mathematical/ physical/ economic system.

This again suggests a role for *relative* increases/ decreases in monetization as if potentially predictive of, and/ or as if potentially predicted via, relative increases/decreases in "trade(s)" *both* in microeconomic and in macroeconomic contexts. (Respectively directing attention to relative influences of relative increases/ decreases in monetary transfers for the generation of increases/ decreases in *individual* expenditure and/ or in *collective* levels of income and/ or expenditure).

In turn this reemphasizes potential roles for standard units in general and for standard units in relation to monetary measures and/ or for monetary policies in particular in potentially securing conditions of as if perfect mathematical/ physical prediction -conditions under which individually and/ or collectively relatively advantageous (or disadvantageous) transfers or exchanges might take place as if relative to microeconomic and/or to macroeconomic conditions of as if perfect mathematical/ physical economic prediction in relative space -time.

In general – for example by relation to developments in Chapters 1 and 2 – as well as in relation to particular classes of interpretation, including specifically the macroeconomic circular flow and microeconomic pure trade interpretations just considered – the above geometric structures variously related to measures x_1, x_1, y_1, y_2 and X, E, Y, I, will suggest considerations pertaining to *relativity of motion*(s) in general and relative motion(s) *not only* as if potentially generating/ generated via relative motions by each mathematical/ physical element of those systems as if relative to self and/or to each other, *but also* as if potentially generating/ generated via relative motions for (all) mathematical/ physical elements of those mathematical/ physical economic systems and subsystems relative to and through (other) elements of those mathematical/ physical systems –*all* according to generally applicable principles and/ or processes generating/ generated via (potential) mathematical/ physical (self) contradictions in relative space time.

When seen as if pertaining to relative motion in relative space-time in general – and interpreted accordingly – the above circular flow diagram can also, yield interpretations as if corresponding to motions as if (relatively) *back*, *down* and *to one side* as if purposively to secure motions as if (relatively) *forward*, *up* and *to the other side*.

This in turn suggests potential developments of other kinds relating to potential mathematical/ physical principles and processes pertaining to motion in general and to potential mathematically/ physically related/ interrelated motions by bodies- as -stars/ planets (e.g. relative motions of earth/sun/moon), bodies -as -persons (e.g. walking, climbing, looking, seeing as well as buying/ selling/ giving/ receiving) and/ or by bodies -as -particles/atoms/electrons (e.g. relative motions of electrons/ protons/ neutrons ....)

Also a focus on as if perfect prediction will, among other things, suggest potential interpretations corresponding to elements of orders of orders of mathematical/ physical phenomena as if themselves corresponding to as if perfect *predictors*. Thus in the apparently mathematically/ physically *interrelated* contexts just considered, at different orders *electrons* might variously be considered as if potentially constituting *predictors* in relation to *nuclei* or conversely, *earth's moon* as if a mathematical/physical predictor in relation to *earth*, or conversely and/or *persons* as if mathematical/ physical economic predictors in relation to different mathematical/ physical economic *commodities*, or conversely.

More directly, the dotted line ....in the circular flow diagram in an *astronomical* context might focus attention upon as if perfect mathematical/ physical predictors of relative motions of earth/ earth's moon and/or earth/ earth's *sun*. In the here related context of *particle physics* such a potential interrelation might focus attention upon as if perfect predictors for examples of relative motions of elements of atomic nucleii and/or (*orbiting*) particles/ electrons.

In the context of mathematical/ physical *economics* a focus upon as if perfect predictors as if in relation inter alia to a particular (potential) measure y_1 will focus attention upon the potential in man to generate potentially *enhanced* macroeconomic as well as microeconomic *opportunities* for others by generating standard units of measure in general - *and* standard units of measure in relation to commodities and to currency as if *purposefully for* the generation of enhanced mathematical/ physical economic opportunities relative to himself and/or relative to another/ others in particular.

In a specifically "Keynesian" macroeconomic context the dotted line is associated with a measure of aggregate *expenditure* in general and as if a predictor of effects of relative *increases/ decreases* in levels of individual and/ or collective taxation/ subsidy/ monetization in particular. In such a Keynesian framework, for example, it was for many years routinely argued that, in the absence of "full" employment, relative reductions in tax rates/ revenues and/ or relative increases in government expenditures, by increasing aggregate demand, would in turn as if *predictively* increase output, income and employment.

Recalling that here measures X, Y have been related to input-output interpretations, the immediately preceding remarks pertaining to as if individually and/or collectively agreed measures/ measurements for mathematical/ physical economic commodities in relation to standard units, apparently *themselves* suggest that, in general, individuals/ societies could be mathematically/ physically represented as if choosing by relation, not only to as if agreed *target* inputs and outputs, but also by relation to *as if agreed* temporally and locationally dependent (potential) input prices, taxes and subsidies (including contingent wage rates and other contingent input and resource prices, valuations, taxes and/or subsidies) and (potential) output prices and capital valuations.

In turn this suggests relations as if potentially generating/ generated via particular kinds of goal programming models and analyses,including analyses pertaining to (potentially) decentralized corporate decisionmaking models such as are contained in Chapters 8, 9 and 10. It also emphasizes potentially more general roles for goal programming models and methods, as well as potentially constructive roles for individual and/or for collective mathematical/ physical "errors" of measurement *both* in the context of potentially centralized/decentralized decisionmaking processes *and* in potentially related contexts as if potentially mathematically/ physically predictive of and/or as if potentially mathematically/ physically predicted via *otherwise* individually and/or collectively relatively *unknown* mathematical/ physical economic *opportunities* and so among other things returns attention to the opening remarks of Chapter 1.

Recalling that in different contexts Figures 4.10 and 4.11 could be considered in relation *both* to as if perfect *and* to imperfect prediction, now reconsider potential for as if perfect prediction in general in relation to the first of these diagrams by considering the following conditions:

$$\theta U = \theta p_x . x$$

interpreted in relation to elements of the circular flow diagram as follows:

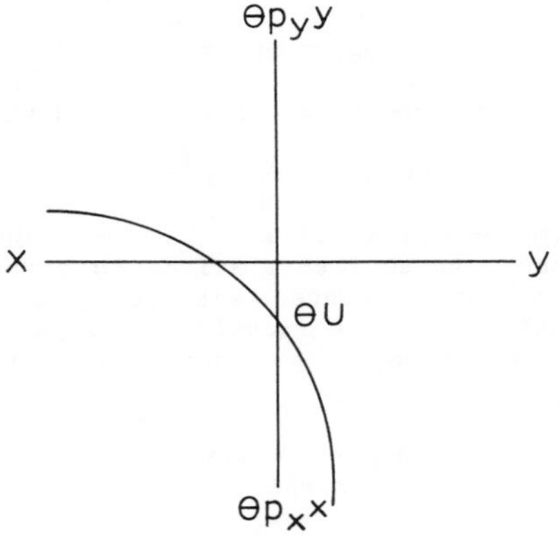

Figure 4.12

If the relation between U and $p_x x$ is understood as if 1 : 1, then the relation $\theta U = \theta p_x . x$ suggests potential interpretations in relation to a theory of explicitly nonlinear *functions* in general and, if understood as if 1 : many, then this relation suggests potential interpretations in relation to a theory of *correspondences*.

With a context of potentially specific *macroeconomic* interpretations for the above diagram, the relation $\Theta U = \Theta p_x.x$ suggests a potential class of Phillips-like interpretations for elements of the measure $\Theta p_x.x$ as if corresponding to (potential changes in) *money wage rates*, and thence for interpretations for (elements of) the measure x in relation inter alia to potential (un)*employment*.

Such a class of empirical interpretations would in turn immediately also suggest potential relations to standard classes of macroeconomic interpretations as if relating to price -conditional individual and/ or collective wage-hours, work -leisure decisions.

More directly, in a context of standard *microeconomic* analyses, a relation as if $\Theta U = \Theta p_x.x$ will suggest interpretations relating to individual utility functions/ preference relations/ indifference relations in general, and to "Marshallian" utility functions/ preference relations/ indifference relations as if potentially generating/ generated via 1 : 1 relations between elements of utility functions/ preference relations/ indifference relations and elements of income(s)/ potential expenditure(s) in particular.

In turn a class of interpretations of a measure ΘU in Figure 4.12 as if *conditionally* related to individual preferences/ indifferences will suggest an interpretation for ΘU in relation to a *particular* indifference relation (possibly either ordinal or cardinal).

Now go further and consider a potential relation as if not only a condition obtains as if :

$$\Theta U = \Theta p_x.x$$

but *also* condition obtains as if identically :

$$\Theta U = \Theta p_y y$$

Then, together, these conditions become as if equivalent to conditions potentially generating and/ or as if potentially (re)generated via conditions as if :

$$\Theta p_y y = \Theta p_x.x$$

Or, as if potentially generating/ (re)generated via conditions as if :

$$\Theta p_x.x - \Theta p_y.y = 0$$

If conditions also obtain as if x = 1, y = 1 then not only does the latter condition suggest potential relations to systems as if themselves potentially generating or generated via integers but, more directly, conditions then obtain as if variously contingently corresponding to arithmetic and algebraic conditions together constituting the following system (III) :

$$\begin{array}{c} \Theta p_x.x - \Theta p_y.y \\ x = 1 \\ y = 1 \\ x = y \end{array} \qquad \text{(III)}$$

since arithmetic/ algebraic conditions (then) obtain variously as if :

$$\begin{array}{c} \Theta p_x.x - \Theta p_y.y = 0 \\ \Theta U = \Theta p_x.x \\ \Theta U = \Theta p_y.y \\ \Theta p_x = \Theta p_y \end{array}$$

as well as contingently corresponding interpretations as if :

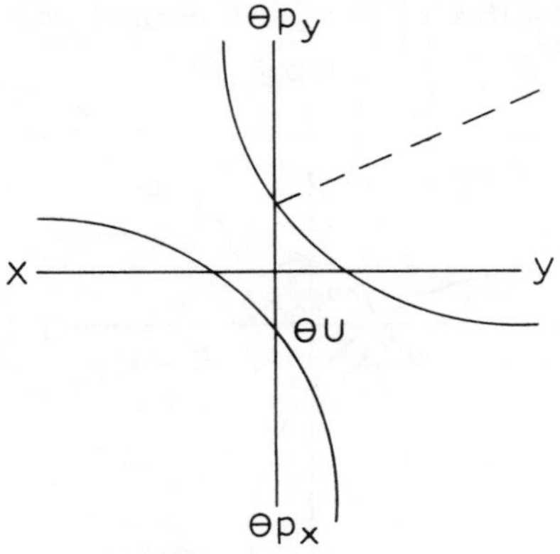

Figure 4.12a

Figure 4.12a clearly yields potential interpretations in relation to *microeconomic* price-quantity relations and interrelations. Clearly, too, this diagram yields contingent interpretations in relation to *macroeconomic* relations and interrelations. For example, contingent relations to the preceding diagram interpreted in relation to potential mathematical/ physical *flows* of incomes and expenditures are self -evident. Consider these remarks together and the potential here for macro-micro and/or micro-macro economic relations and interrelations becomes self -evident too.

From perspectives which can also be seen to be relevant to the potential discovery of and to the potential analysis of *orders of orders of* mathematical/ physical phenomena in general,[16] as well as to the mathematical/ physical generation of micro/ macro economic phenomena in particular, notice that this latter diagram incorporates potentially *mutually exclusive* linear/ nonlinear interpretations *each* as if potentially generating and/or as if potentially predictively (re)generated via elements of the arithmetic – algebraic system (III).

The apparent potential here for particular classes of apparently mutually exclusive interpretations in relation to "the same" elements in (III) will, in turn, refocus attention, very generally upon potential principles and processes of (self) contradiction as if potentially mathematically/ physically generating and/or as if mathematically/ physically potentially (re)generated via elements of that system and, in particular, upon measures Θ, Δx, Δy, Δp_x, Δp_y and *as if perfectly predictive of* mathematical/ physical/ economic changes in general and relative mathematical/ physical motions in particular – all with a context of potential principles and/ or processes of (self) contradiction.

Renewed attention to measures Θ, Δx, Δy, Δp_x, Δp_y in the context of preceding diagrams might suggest potential relations, interrelations and interpretations such as those illustrated in Figure 4.13 below.

From a narrowly macroeconomic perspective an analyst seeking a Phillips relation between unemployment and the rate of change in the price of labour services (money wages) might see it here in the bottom left quadrant of this diagram, *first* interpreting Δx as if corresponding to a measure of unemployment of potential resources/ potential inputs in general and, *conditionally* corresponding to a measure in relation to unemployment of potential labour services as if potential inputs to production in particular and, *second*, interpreting the measure Δp_x as if a measure of (relative) change in prices of inputs/ resources in general, and as if *conditionally* corresponding to change in *nominal* wages of potential labour services in particular.

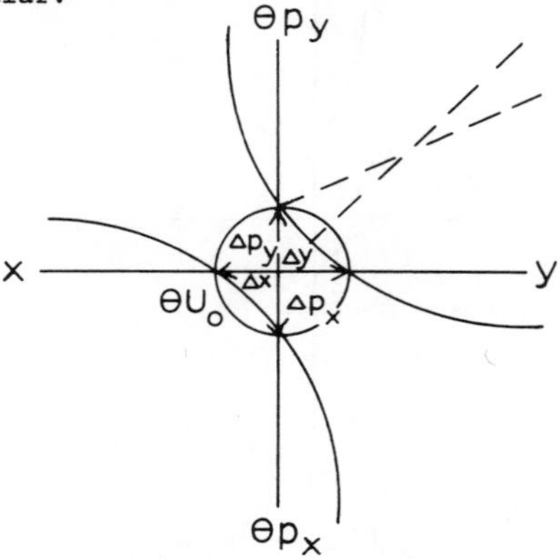

Figure 4.13

With these kinds of *conditionally* Phillips-like interpretations in view, an analyst might go on to interpret the indicated measure ΘU_o as if *conditionally* corresponding to a mathematical/ statistical/ econometric *estimate of* a "natural rate of unemployment".

Interpretations of Δx as if *conditionally* corresponding to (un)employment, and of Δp_x as if *conditionally* corresponding to money wages/ rates of change of money wages, would draw attention to a wider class of interpretations of those measures, for example *respectively* to other primary inputs and/or to intermediate inputs, including elements of capital and/or of capital services *and* to prices/unit valuations for other primary inputs and/or for intermediate inputs, including elements of capital and of capital services.

Then Δx might be interpreted as if corresponding to unemployment of labour services and Δp_x to rate of change of money wages ceteris paribus i.e. conditional upon implicit assumptions of relative *invariance* with reference *both* to other potentially related quantities *and* to other potentially related prices.

With this context, a mathematician (and a fortiori a mathematical economist) might see potential interpretations for measures Δp_x, Δx in relation to *partial derivatives*. More specifically, macroeconomists and/ or microeconomists might consider such potential classes of interpretations as if consistent with assumptions (whether implicit or explicit) of "short run" conditions as if corresponding to *fixity both* for prices/ valuations *and* for other potential inputs, including elements of production capacity/ potential services of elements of production capacity.

Those familiar with standard analyses of micro/ macroeconomic systems will immediately see potential for relations between these remarks (and associated arithmetic/ algebraic/ geometric structures) and standard assumptions to the effect that :

i) "labour", N, and "capital", K, are the *only* (potential) inputs to production and :

ii) in the "short run" the quantitiy of capital $\bar{K}$ and an interest rate r (considered as if a proxy for the price of capital services) are considered as if *fixed* and/ or ;

iii) with a context of Phillips-like interpretations in relation to a measure ΘU_o, asumptions to the effect that prices more generally are considered as if fixed.

In conjunction with conditions as if potentially generating/ generated via conditions of as if perfect prediction, the preceding diagram might be interpreted as if *conditionally* indicating, for example, that, *as if perfectly predictively* :

i) relatively *less* (potential labour) inputs/ resources relative to *self* is potentially as if perfectly predictive of relatively *more* (potential labour) outputs/products relative to the *system* and/ or ;

ii) relatively *higher* prices for particular (potential labour) inputs/ resources relative to *self* is potentially as if perfectly predictive of and/ or as if perfectly predicted via relatively *more* (potential labour) inputs/ resources relative to the *system* and/ or ;

iii) relatively *less* labour/ resource income relative to *self* is apparently potentially as if perfectly predictive of/ predicted via relatively more (potential) income relative to the *system* and/ or as if perfectly predictive of/predicted via relatively *more* (potential) income relative to *another/ others relative to* the system.

The classes of (potential) interpretations just considered suggest potential relative *directions* as well as potential relative *magnitudes* for the measures Δx, Δp_x and/ or for Δy, Δp_y, x, y, p_x, p_y. They also suggest potential mathematical/ physical *relations* and/ or *interrelations* between these measures *all* under conditions as if potentially generating/ generated via mathematical/ physical conditions of as if perfect mathematical/ physical prediction.

Emphasizing this, notice that elements of Figure 13, as well as these particular remarks pertaining to specific kinds of qualitative mathematical/ physical economic interpretation(s) are apparently consistent with conditions as if *variously* :

$$\Theta p_x = \Delta p_x,\ \Theta p_y = \Delta p_y,\ \Delta p_y = \Delta y,\ \Delta y = \Delta x$$

$$x = \Delta x, \quad y = \Delta_y, \quad \Delta p_x = \Delta x, \quad \Theta = 1$$

These conditions, even if considered in isolation, would evoke associations with developments elsewhere pertaining to conditions of as if perfect mathematical/ physical prediction in general, and conditions as if perfectly predicting/ predicted via potential mathematical/ physical relations and/or potential mathematical/ physical inter relations themselves as if potentially generating/(re)generated via (any or all) orders of orders of mathematical/ physical economic predictorsin particular.

Such perspectives would provoke a search in relation to the preceding diagram for interpretations as if potentially corresponding to relations and interrelations, themselves as if potentially generating/ (re)generated via (the discovery of) *other* orders of orders of mathematical/ physical phenomena in general, *and* as if potentially corresponding to relations as if potentially generating/ (re)generated via orders of orders of phenomena as if (potentially) mathematically/ physically *related to*, yet as if (potentially) mathematically/ physically *different from* mathematical/ physical measures Θ, p_x, p_y, x, y, Δp_x, Δp_y, Δx, Δy in particular.

Recall here preceding developments, giving prominent roles to standard units in general – and prominent roles to standard units of money/ currency in particular – in contexts of potential micro/macroeconomic decision making by individual economic agents, by groups of economic agents (e.g. persons, corporations, nations, societies) and/or by groups of groups of individuals (e.g. groups of corporations, persons, societies, nations).

More directly – and more technically – in an explicily "mathematical" context, these remarks will redirect attention to the apparent potential for classes of interpretations in relation to mathematical principles and/ or processes as if potentially variously generating/ generated via differential/ integral calculi in general, and by potential mathematical/ physical principles as if pertaining to conditions for partial differentiation and for integration/ integrability more specifically.

An analyst/ observer seeking evidence in the preceding diagram for potential mathematical/ physical relations as if potentially generating/ generated via different orders of orders of mathematical/ physical phenomena, might focus attention upon potential mathematical/ physical *boundaries* apparently *not only* potentially generating/ generated via conditions of as if perfect prediction themselves as if corresponding to as if perfectly predictive mathematical/physical *equations between* conditions of different orders Θ, p_x, p_y, x, y, Δp_x, Δp_y, Δx, Δy , *but* upon potential for such equations in a wider context of consideration of different orders of orders of mathematical/ physical principles as if pertaining to the generation of relative mathematical/ physical changes/ motions in general, and thence pertaining to the generation of *particular kinds of* mathematical/ physical equivalences,or boundaries, as if corresponding to appropriate and particular classes of special cases.

In either of these kinds of mathematical/ physical contexts a mathematician/ physicist, seeking evidence potentially pertaining to differential/ integral calculi in general, and/ or pertaining to potential principles and/ or processes of relative maximization/ minimization in particular, would notice the apparently explicit *absence* from the immediately preceding diagram of mathematical/ physical symbols as if directly corresponding to *predictors* of relative mathematical/ physical change/ invariance in general and of relative mathematical/ physical changes in magnitudes and/or of directions of relative motions in particular.

Emphasizing this : by contrast with the "circular flow" diagram from which it is derived, Figure 13 contains no explicit symbolism even potentially pertaining to process(es) of relative macroeconomic change in general, and pertaining to process(es) as if predictive of and/or as if predicted via relative macroeconomic changes in potential inputs, outputs, incomes and/or expenditures in particular.

More narrowly, absence of symbolism here is open to interpretation(s) as if corresponding to absence of symbols corresponding to as if purposive loss of (potential) income relative to self as if purposively to generate potential gains of outputs, incomes and/or expenditures relative to another/ others and/or relative to and through a wider microeconomic system.

These latter remarks will evoke associations with many different kinds of developments elsewhere in the book but, most fundamentally, will evoke associations with a principle of *altruism*. And, with the explicitly macroeconomic context of Phillips-like macroeconomic relations, and associated considerations pertaining to potential for successful (or otherwise) individual and/ or collective Demand Management principles and policies, such remarks might also suggest consideration of the particular (kinds of nonlinear indifference) measures ΘU_o as if corresponding to particular kinds of *social indifference curves*. If so, they will refocus attention upon considerations pertaining to Social Welfare Functions.[17]

More directly the remarks pertaining to (potential) *process*(es) in the preceding paragraph will draw attention a fortiori to the apparently explicit *absence* from the preceding diagram of measures as if corresponding to potential mathematical/ physical processes potentially generating/ (re)generated via, individually and/ or collectively preferred relative to, a measure ΘU_o.

With these various remarks pertaining to potential mathematical/ physical process(es) as background, now consider the preceding diagram in explicit conjunction with the preceding "circular flow" notations as follows:

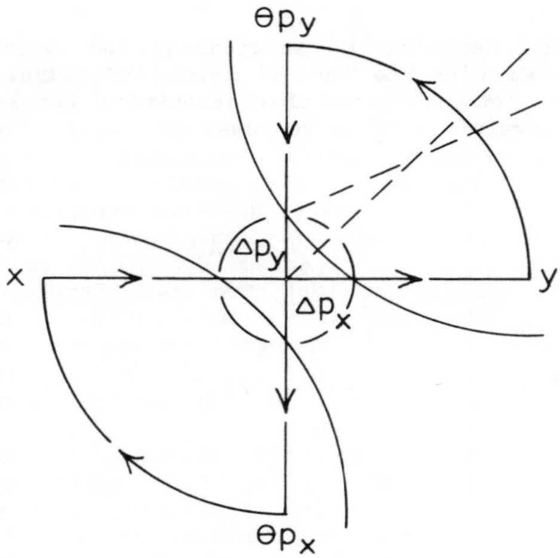

Figure 4.14

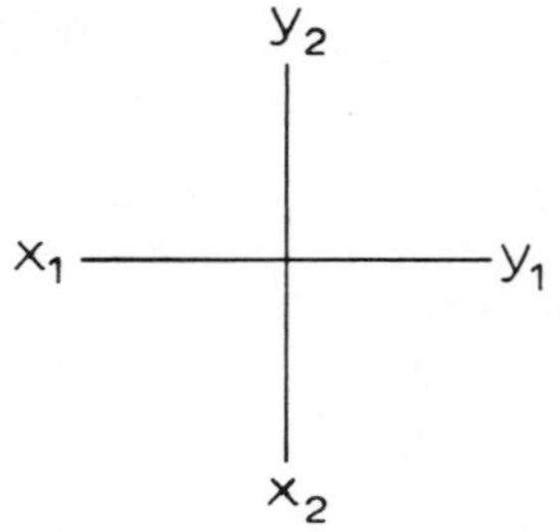

Figure 4.15

Notice immediately that although the *genesis* of Figure 14 was explicitly *macroeconomic* in character,with emphasis upon aggregate (potential) inputs, outputs, incomes, expenditures and potential Phillips -like interpretations, this diagram nevertheless most directly suggests *microeconomic* interpretations.

Primitively, it appears open to interpretation as if suggesting that (potentially) *change in* output demand generates *change in* output prices, in turn generating *change in* (potential) input prices, in turn potentially generating *increased* supplies of inputs to production and thence potentially *realizing* increases in outputs as if inter alia *via* changes in relative input and output prices.

Described in this way, such sequences emphasize potential roles for suppliers/ demanders. More evocatively, if the diagram is seen as potentially generating/ generated via a context of as if perfect prediction then, apparently, not only does (change in) input price as if *predictively* generate (change in) input quantity,and (change in) output price as if *predictively* generate (change in) output quantity, but also, as if *predictively*, (changes in) *realized* expenditures potentially generate/are potentially generated via (changes in) *nominal* expenditure(s), in turn as if *predictively* generating/generated via (changes in) nominal incomes *and/or* changes in (potential) input resource availabilities.

In a microeconomic context such potential *sequences* of processes of relative change evoke associations with potential mathematical/ physical economic *exchange/ trade* as if relative to and/ or as if mediated via potential principles and processes of (self) contradiction in relation to standard units, including standard monetary units.

But, if seen in contexts both of microeconomics and of potential trade(s), apparently the preceding diagram is *incomplete*. Among other things, only *one* (relatively aggregated?) input price and only *one* (relatively aggregated?) input quantity, and only *one* (relatively aggregated?) output price and only *one* (relatively aggregated?) output quantity are given explicit representation in it.

Going further, if Individual 1 is understood as if potentially related to an endowment x_1 and a potential consumption level y_1 of Commodity 1, with prices respectively represented via measures $\Theta_1 px_1$, $\Theta_1 py_1$, then the preceding diagram apparently gives explicit representations to elements (potentially) pertaining only to *one* such relatively abstract individual.

With such perspectives an analyst/ observer might seek relations to developments as if potentially relating to endowments and potential consumptions of *more than one* commodity and *more than one* individual, for example via schematic representations of (potential) endowment levels x_1, x_2 and (potential) consumption levels y_1, y_2 as follows.

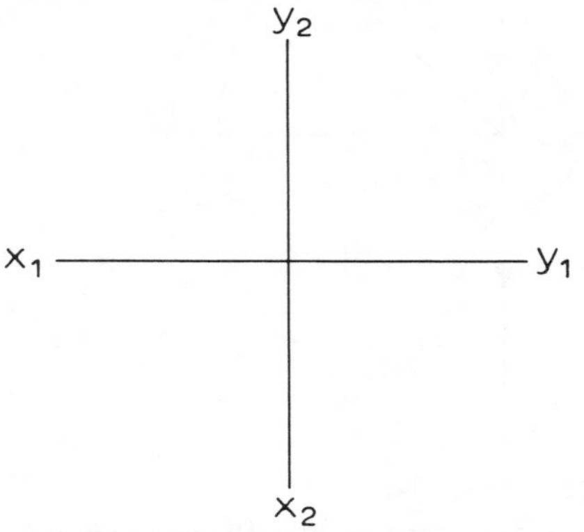

Figure 4.16

Now comparison of elements of Figure 16 with elements of Figure 14 suggests, interpretations according to which (changes in) $\theta_1 p x_1$, $\theta_1 p y_1$ are as if *explicitly* perfectly predictive of/ perfectly predicted via (changes in) quantity measures x_2 , y_2 in turn suggesting *implicit* correspondences according to which *implicitly* (changes in) quantity measures x_1, y_1 may be/ become (potentially) as if perfectly predictive of/ as if perfectly predicted via (changes in) relative price measures $\theta_2 p x_2$, $\theta_2 p y_2$....

The wider context within which these remarks have been made immediately suggests classes of interpretation in relation to potential principles and/ or processes of Reciprocal Revealed Preference[18] by individuals for elements of relatively micro/macro economically (self) *contradictory* change/ exchange/ barter/ trade relative to self/ selves/ another/ others

Primitively individuals may act as if purposively to determine *less* relative to self/ selves as if purposively to potentiate/ reveal preferences for *more* relative to self/ selves/ another/ others differently located in space time relative to self/ selves.

In more detail, individuals/ groups may act as if implicitly to contradict/ *dominate* elements of relatively abstract individual/ collective preferences for elements of consumptions/ endowments y_1, y_2 (resp. x_1, x_2) relative to self/ selves as if thereby to potentiate (revelations of preferences for) *more* relative to another/ others differently/ distantly located in space-time.

More subtly, elements of Figures 15, 16 are open to representations as if actions as if purposively relatively abstractly to determine *less* consumptions/ endowments y_1, y_2, x_1, x_2 relative to relatively abstract preference/ indifference relations relative to self/ selves thereby potentiate *higher* prices $\theta_1 p_{yi}$, $\theta_1 p_{xi}$ relative to self/ selves, by potentiating offers of gifts/ barters/ trades of relatively *more* quantities y_i, x_i, and relatively *lower* prices relative to a system relative to self/selves -and thence relative to another/ others potentially differently/ distantly located in space-time.

All of these actions and interactions, if relative to "goods", are open to interpretation as if purposively to potentiate (revelations of) *relatively preferred gain*(s) relative to self/ selves, *whether accepted*, *reciprocated or declined* relative to another/ others.

Clearly such classes of actions/ reactions/ interactions focus attention not just upon potential *principles*, but upon potential *processes* of relatively *decentralized* mathematical/ physical (self) contradiction according to which individuals/ groups might act/ react/ interact as if purposively sequentially/ cyclically to potentiate (revelations of) relatively *more* of what *might be/ become* knowledge/ endowments/ consump -tions relative to another/others via the determination of relatively *less* knowledge/ endowments/ consumptions of what *might otherwise be/ become* relatively *more* known relative (only) to self/ selves.

This again emphasizes potentially individually/ collectively *desireable* roles for individual/ collective exploitations not just *of* but *via* essentially relatively mathematically/ physically *sequential/ cyclic* mathematical/ physical/ economic (in)determinacy/ (in)completeness/ (un)certainty principles as if themselves potentiating/ potentiated via *elments of relatively* mathematically/ physically/ economically determinate/ complete/ certain *predictors* relative to self/ selves/another/ others.

Especially with the wider contexts of developments in Chapters 1 and 2 these remarks will suggest reconsideration of orders of orders of *generally applicable* mathematical/ physical/ astronomical/ geographical/ geological/ statistical/ political/economic....principles, processes and/ or phenomena as if themselves potentially (re)generating/ (re)generated via elements of the following schematic representation in Figure 17.

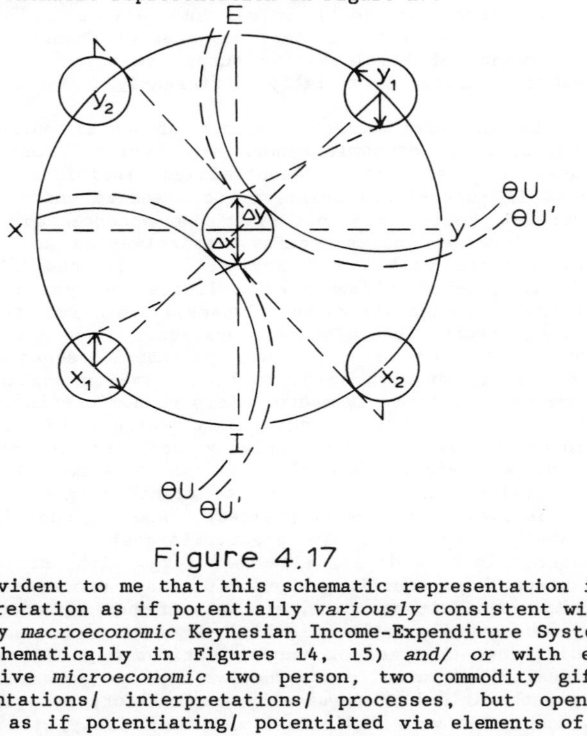

Figure 4.17

It seems evident to me that this schematic representation is not just open to interpretation as if potentially *variously* consistent with elements of a relatively *macroeconomic* Keynesian Income-Expenditure System (e.g. as represented schematically in Figures 14, 15) *and/ or* with elements of standard relative *microeconomic* two person, two commodity gift/ barter/ trade representations/ interpretations/ processes, but open ,too ,to interpretation as if potentiating/ potentiated via elements of relatively abstract (e.g. money, price, tax, subsidy...) *standard units* as if themselves potentiating/ potentiated via relatively individually/ collectively *desireable* principles/ processes of essentially *relatively* individually/ collectively (self)contradictory interrelations between (elements of) *relatively* macroeconomic and *relatively* microeconomic relations/ interrelations/ processes.

Appreciated from another perspective, Figure 17 might suggest elements of relatively *abstract and collective* mathematical/ physical economic *welfare* measures on consumption levels/ endowments Θ_1U_1, Θ_2U_2 relative to a relatively central/ centralized location as if potentially isomorphic with elements of relatively *non-abstract and individual* mathematical/ physical economic *preference/ indifference* measures Θ_1U_1, Θ_2U_2, e.g. relative to relatively decentralized measures/ locations y_1, y_2 and interpretations as if inter alia potentiating/ potentiated via identifications between changes/ exchanges between elements of measures x_1 and y_2... .

Not only are relatively central/ centralized measures Θ_1U_1, Θ_2U_2 open to relatively abstract interpretations as if potentiating/ potentiated via changes in welfare measures relative to a relatively central/ centralized measure/ location, but comparison, for example, with elements of Figure 9 above will suggest consideration of elements of such relations as if potentiating/ potentiated via both Phillips-like *output* price/ quantity changes/ exchanges *and* Phillips-like *input* price/ quantity changes/ exchanges.

More constructively such comparisons will suggest consideration of as if *purposively induced* principles and/ or processes of *contradiction* according to which, among other things, as if *purposively* individually/ collectively induced measures of relative change/ exchange/ error relative to elements of Phillips-like input relations relative to relatively centralized/ decentralized self/ selves may act as if *purposively* to potentiate relatively *greater* (lesser) measures of change/ exchange/ *error* relative to elements of Phillips-like output relations relative to self/ selves/ another/ others potentially differently/ distantly located in space-time.

Such remarks in turn suggest elements of as if purposively induced *relatively* macro/ micro economic *sequenbces/ cycles/ loops*[19] according to which measures of relatively decentralized individual gains/ losses relative to as if purposively relativistic standard units (e.g. physical, fiscal, financial units) may not just be *potentiated via* relatively centralized collective losses (gains) relative to as if purposively relativistic standard units, but may act as if *themselves relatively* (im)*perfectly to predict* elements of relative net gains (losses) (e.g. physical, fiscal, financial gains (losses)) relative to a relatively abstract central/ centralized measure/ location.

It seems evident to me that such potential sequences/ cycles, if generated and exploited with care, might be used among other things to *motivate* elements of relatively macro/ micro economic principles/ processes according to which particular individuals/ groups of individuals .... nations/ groups of nations may *actively seek to generate* individual/ collective/ social gain(s) *via* elements of relative physical/ fiscal/ financial changes/ exchanges of claims to/ rights to goods *from* relatively larger *to* relatively smaller....smallest, and thence *from* relatively smaller.... smallest *to* relatively larger...largest.

As has argued in more detail elsewhere (e.g. with particular reference to standard competitive equilibrium principles and processes in Chapter 2), if used selfishly and without care, elements of such classes of potentially individually and mutually mathematically/ physically/ economically *creative* self contradictions/ changes/ exchanges/ motions may be used in fundamentally individually and mutually *destructive* ways to potentiate individually and mutually mathematically/ physically annihilatory principles/ processes in general, and relatively individually/ collectively/ socially annihilatory mathematical/ physical/ economic principles/ processes in particular.

With a focus on potential principles and processes of (self) contradictory changes/ exchanges/ motions as if potentially (re)generating elements of mathematically/ physically....relatively smaller....smallest via elements of mathematically/ physically....relatively larger....largest, now consider Figure 18, which may evidently be appreciated as if directly developing/ developed via elements of Figure 17.

With an *astronomical* context elements of Figure 18 suggest elements of mathematical/ physical principles and processes as if potentiating or potentiated via relative motions of earth/ earth's moon and, more generally, as if for example potentiating/ potentiated via essentially mathematically/ physically ....*electromagnetic* sequences of as if perfectly (self)predictive (self) contradictions/ changes/ exchanges/ motions from relatively abstractly *larger* (and *positive*) to relatively *smaller* (and *negative*), and thence from relatively *smaller* (and *negative*) to relatively *larger* (and *positive*).... .

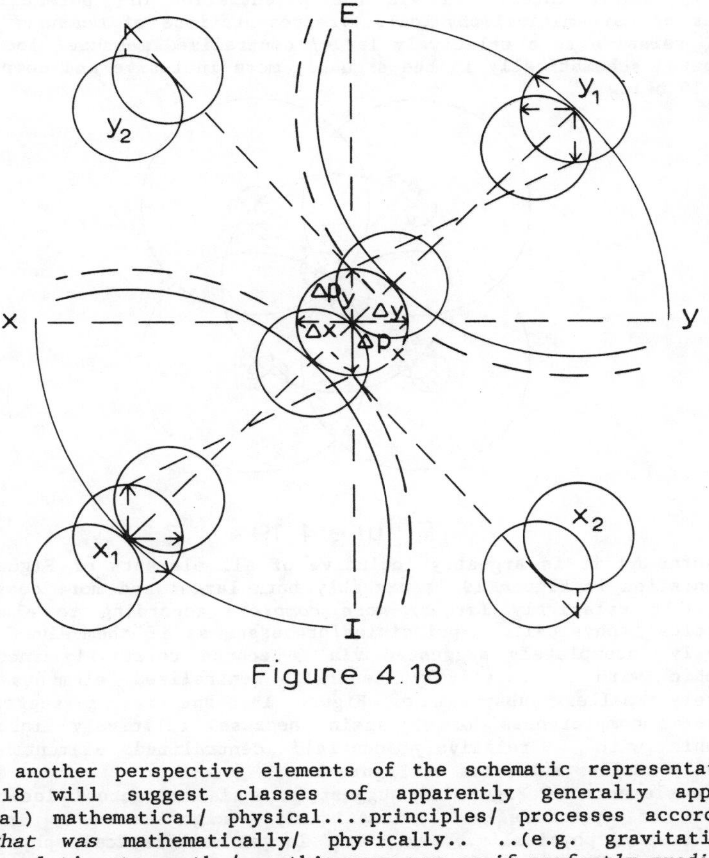

Figure 4.18

From another perspective elements of the schematic representation in Figure 18 will suggest classes of apparently generally applicable (potential) mathematical/ physical...principles/ processes according to which *what was* mathematically/ physically.. ..(e.g. gravitationally) *interior* relative to earth / earth's moon may *as if perfectly predict* and/ or *be as if perfectly predicted* via *what will be* relatively mathematically/ physically (e.g. gravitationally) *exterior* relative to earth's moon (earth).

Among other things then, apparently relatively *incomplete* mathematical/ physical....representations/ interpretations/ processes relative to earth may be as if relatively (in)completely perfectly predictive of and/ or as if relatively (in)completely perfectly predicted via (elements of) mathematical/ physical ....representations/ interpretations/ processes relative to earth's moon....

More abstractly – and more subtly– with contexts of as if *pandemically* (and indeed cosmologically) *purposive* relative *incompleteness* of mathematical/ physical....representations/ interpretations processes, notice that relatively *decentralized* elements y_1, y_2, x_1, x_2 of Figure 18 might interpret themselves/ be interpreted as if *themselves* relatively incompletely mathematically/ physically....variously potentiating/ potentiated via mathematically/ physically....isomorphic elements relatively *equal to* self/ selves, relatively *larger than* self/ selves (e.g. via circles/ spheres centred on self/selves), and/ or as if relatively *smaller than* self/ selves. E.g. via implications of measures Δy_1, Δp_{y_1}, Δx_1, Δp_{x_1} relative to self/ selves as if themselves perfect predictors of/as if perfectly predicted via measures Δy_2, Δpy_2, Δx_2, Δpx_2 relative to another/ others, inter alia via the potentiation of/ potentiation via elements of mathematical/physical....representations of measures Δy, Δp_y, Δx, Δp_x relative to a relatively large/ centralized measure/ location, as represented schematically in the arguably more inclusive and comprehensive Figure 19 below :

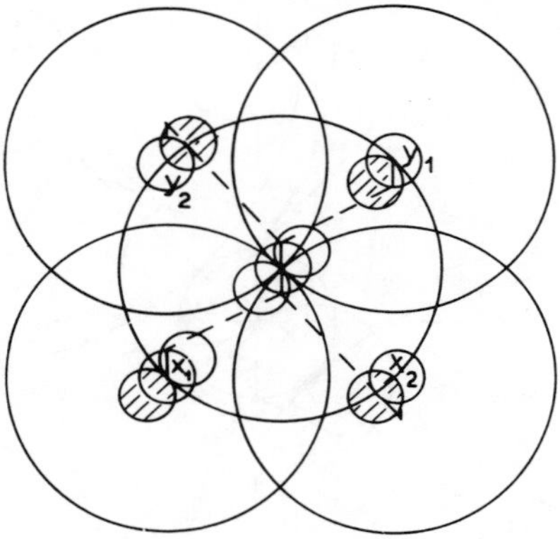

Figure 4.19

Insofar as it is arguably inclusive of all elements of Figure 18,the representation in Figure 19 is arguably both larger and more complete. It is arguably relatively *larger/ more complete* according to elements of mathematical/ physical.... principles/processes as if themselves *not just* relatively incompletely suggested *via* _ because relatively incompletely isomorphic with – relatively central/ centralized elements of the relatively smaller subsystem of Figure 18, but itself suggestive *of* relative incompleteness *of* _ again because relatively incompletely isomorphic with – relatively central/ centralized elements of the relatively smaller subsystem of Figure 18.

Thus elements of Figure 19 suggest potential measures/ locations for elements of potentially systematically/ algorithmically relatively mathematically/ physically....*exterior/ larger* mathematical/ physical .... *predictors/ predictions* relative to elements of Figure 18.

Elements of Figure 19 *also* suggest potential measures/ locations for elements of potentially systematically/ algorithmically relatively mathematically/ physically.. ..*smaller/ interior* mathematical/ physical. ..*predictors/ predictions* relative to elements of Figure 18 – and thence potential for the relatively incomplete (re)generation of orders of orders of mathematical/ physical....relations/ interpretations/processes via (elements of) principles/processes of (self) contradiction variously relative to elements of Figure 18.

This recalls developments in Chapters 1 and 2, pertaining to the *general* applicability of elements of mathematical/physical principles/

processes immanent in elements of *representations similar to* Figure 19 to *all* potential orders of orders of mathematical/ physical phenomena and, more subtly, to appreciation that, according to particular kinds of mathematical/ physical interpretations, *any* or *all* orders of *any* or *all* kinds of mathematical/ physical phenomena which may pertain to *elements of* (e.g.*persons* as if elements of) earth/ earth's moon,might be relatively abstractly represented as if potentially systematically interrelated.

With such perspectives it is again apparent that attempts by particular kinds of economists to *impose* essentially individualistic, selfishly oriented and deterministic "competitive", "long-run", "stationary equilibrium" paradigms, on individuals and societies are open to interpretation as *fundamentally ill-founded* on the grounds of evidence immanent in elements of Figures 18, 19, and, through them, in elements of the space-worlds which those representations relatively abstractly both model and predict – for the *absence* of elements of "competitive" conditions in general, and of determinacy and complete information conditions of individualistic "long run", "stationary competitive equilibrium" conditions in particular.

More positively these representations *do* include evidence, verifiable in worlds which they relatively abstractly represent, for the potential individual and collective scientific, moral *and* social *desireability* both of particular kinds of individual/ collective *recognitions of* and of particular kinds of mathematical/ physical/ economic *exploitations via* mathematical/ physical principles/ processes open to interpretation as if potentiating/potentiated via as if *purposively* individually/ collectively mathematically/ physically/ fiscally/ financially relatively *incomplete*, relatively *indeterminate*, relatively *nonconservative non-standard* mathematical/ physical (re)generation of elements of represen tations of, essentially and fundamentally, *interrelated* income- expenditure principles, processes and phenomena.

A focus on potentially socially *constructive* and *purposive* exploitations *of* mathematical/ physical/economic *"errors"*, and/ or *via* mathematical/ physical/ economic *"errors"* will again suggest socially constructive roles for individually and collectively conditionally (relatively) standardizing/ standardized measures as well as for associated principles and processes of individually/collectively *essentially* self contradictory measurement.

Further, a focus on as if purposive exploitations of "errors" with reference to elements of Figures 16, 17, now considered as only *contingently* relatively individually/ collectively standardized elements of relatively abstract individual/ collective mathematical/ physical/economic (sub)systems, can suggest potentially individually and collectively *advantageous* roles for such elements *per se*. Examples include elements of relatively abstract representations of input and/ or output related simple Phillips curves, relatively abstract representations of potentially individually/ collectively non-abstract preference/ indifference/welfare measures $\Theta_1 U_1$, $\Theta_2 U_2$ and, more directly, for elements of relatively abstract physical/ fiscal/ financial "budget" relations.

They may *also* suggest potentially advantageous roles for such elements as if *because* themselves potentiating relatively individually/ collectively *more advantageous* changes/exchanges/ motions open to interpretations as if mathematically/ physically/ economically potentiating/ potentiated via principles and processes of as if purposive (self) *contradiction and error relative to* elements of such relatively abstract and standardized mathematical/ physical representations.

I remark here that apparently empirically robust simple Phillips-like relationships are frequently found by econometricians, and their very robustness used to argue fundamental significance for them. *But* the immediately preceding context suggests that discoveries of apparently naive Phillips-like relations may be fundamentally traceable simply to the fundamental place of such relations in *any* and *all* mathematical/ physical.. .. principles, processes and phenomena!

More constructively the present context suggests potential individual/ social gains *not* to determinations *of* (standard) simple Phillips-like relations per se but, among other things to as if purposive individual/ collective relative micro/ macro econometric determinations *via* "errors" relative to them.

While these remarks focus attention narrowly on simple Phillips-like relations, similar remarks might for example be applied to (also essentially naive) estimates of "consumption functions" such as those considered variously by Kuznets, Friedman, Duesenberry and Ando and Modigliani (see p.88).

From another direction the algebraic notations and the geometric orientations of elements of Figures 17 and 18 will, among other things, recall attention to the (sub)system (III) of Chapter 2 (see p. above) and potentially associated linear dependence/ duality principles and processes in general -and principles and processes as if themselves potentiating/ potentiated via elements of relatively decentralized linear/ nonlinear, integer/ noninteger goal programming principles, processes and interpretations in particular.

Before proceeding to developments of these kinds in the next Chapter the reader should notice that the essentially *geometric* Figure 19 is also open to interpretation as if giving geometric expression to elements of the following essentially *algebraic* (sub)system (III), which, clearly, can potentially generate, or be as if purposively generated via, the system (III) of Chapter 2 :

$$\begin{array}{lllll} \Theta p_x(x - \Delta x) - \Theta p_y(y + \Delta y) + \Psi_1\mu + \Psi_2\mu & & & & \\ x - \Delta x & & + \Psi_1 & = 1 & \\ & y + \Delta y & - \Psi_2 & = 1 & (III)' \\ x - \Delta x \; - & y - \Delta y & & = 0 & \end{array}$$

More abstractly this system may appear as if potentially also consistent with principles/ processes as if themselves mathematically/ physically potentiating/ potentiated via elements of relatively abstract arithmetic/ algebraic/ geometric representations +, - as in Figure 20 below.

The immediately preceding remarks suggest particular kinds of developments relative to Figure 20, for example to generate elements of Figure 21 as if via the generation of elements of relative *motions from* relatively negative *to* relatively positive *and* thence *from* relatively positive *to* relatively negative, such as have been considered via the system (III) and associated arithmetic, algebraic and geometric developments in this and other Chapters.

In these and other ways elements of Figure 19 might suggest self contradictions/ motions *variously* relatively down, back and to one side as if purposively to potentiate motions relatively forward up and to the other....as well as self contradictions/ motions as if purposively mathematically/ physically... *inside* relative to self/ selves as if purposively to potentiate motion mathematically/ physically....*outside* relative to another/ others relatively differently/ distantly located in space-time :

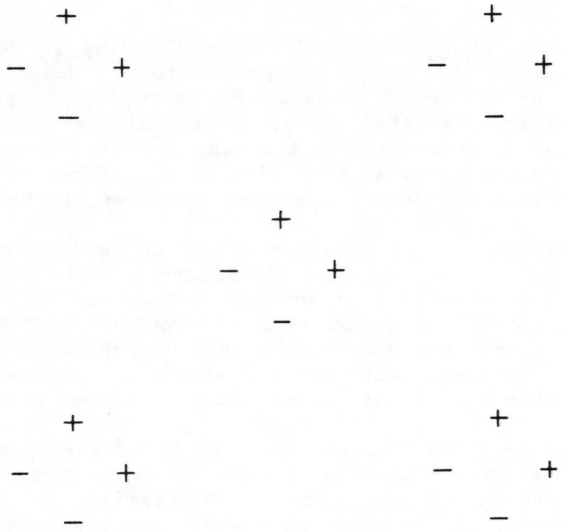

Figure 4.20

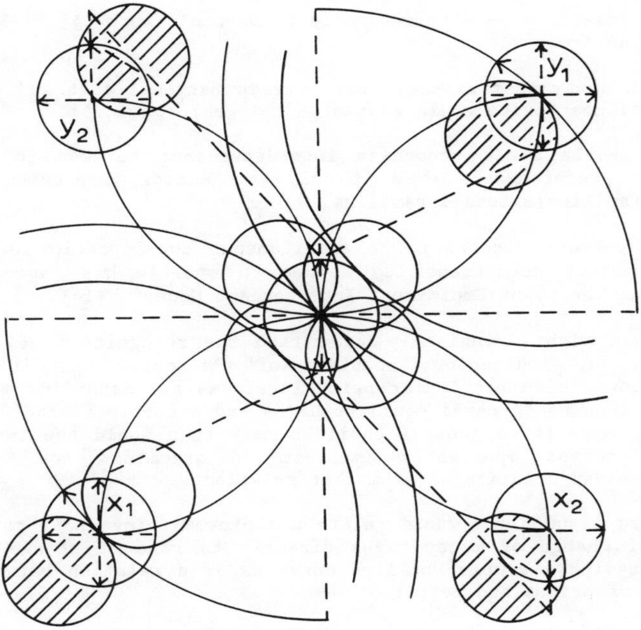

Figure 4.21

Footnotes

1. A certain amount of professional preconditioning is necessary if this standard resolution is to be accepted without qualification, for its truth is not at all self evident. For example, in parts of Namibia where diamonds are plentiful, water is typically extremely scarce.It is worth noting that economists-in-training may expect to be conditioned in such ways to accept *as if true* without qualification statements such as the above which are demonstrably *not* true, unless qualified.

2. While the opportunity cost idea has long been recognized as fundamental to (micro)economic analyses, the significance of relative *ignorance* in that context has usually been neither recognized nor stressed. There are exceptions however as for example provided by Buchanan who uses hypothetical cases to generate a discursive treatment of issues pertaining to the essentially subject nature of personal evaluations of cost/ opportunity cost in his short and provocative book {4}.

3. I have cited this paper not just because it is a standard reference in an intermediate macroeconomics course but also because Friedman has been recognized as an authority on Monetarism and was undoubtedly highly influential in the shift in the 70s and 80s to avowedly Monetary if not Monetarist policies.In this connection it is well known that Keynesian economic policies were highly influential in many countries through the late 40s, the 50s and the 60s.The date of this paper - as well as its focus on monetary analysis -is significant insofar as it approximately coincided with the end (at least temporarily) of these strong Keynesian influences both on theory and on policy.

4. Recall remarks made with reference to Debreu's work {6} in Section 1 of this Chapter.

5. In such a way that average cost exceeds marginal cost and such that a marginal cost price would guarantee loss(es).

6. Most people would recognize interdependence between their own and others' preferences - even if only recognizing interdepenence within their families/extended families.

7. This apparent necessity for simultaneous consideration of goods and money market conditions led Keynes to entitle his famous book the "General Theory of Employment Interest and Money", {14}.

8. A layman might immediately understand the recognition of a necessity for as if simultaneous solution of all market conditions as if conditional upon particular price levels as corresponding more closely to his idea of "general equilibrium" - and a fortiori his idea of price taking competitive general equilibrium - than would the two (or more) stage process apparently implicit in arguments for "Classically Dichotomous" solution(s) of market relations.

9. Standard assumptions would relate unemployment inversely to output and rate of change of money wages directly to rate of change of prices, thus arguing a simple Phillips curve *as if* a relation between rate of change of prices and output.

10. Notice that by this measure economic policies seem to have been *successful*, at least for the period 1941-1971 when unemployment was consistently below - and most of the time very substantially below - 4%.

11. At the time of writing this would be a standard reference for an intermediate macroeconomics course.

12 Quoting from the opening sentences of Friedman's paper on the point: "The discussion of the Phillips curve started with truth in 1926, proceeded through error some 30 years later and by now has returned back to 1926 and to the original truth". Looking at the output and unemployment data for 1925-1940 and/or for 1975 - and contrasting those with typical figures for intermediate years, laymen might be forgiven for preferring "error" to "truth" and accordingly easily forgiven for being - or becoming - sceptical of economists' advice in this instance -or in general.

13. Friedman's specific criticisms of Phillips' work may be summarized briefly as, *first* : that apparently Phillips implicitly assumes price *invariance* and thereby implicitly assumes that workers would perceive (potential) nominal wage increases as if (potentially) constituting real wage increases. *Secondly*, and less subtly, Friedman asserts that Phillips' motivation for inflation is *erroneous* in general - and erroneous in asserting relative levels of unemployment levels as if generating rates of money wage changes rather than *vice versa*,in particular. In this context the reader may wish to contrast the sense of the following sentences, which open Phillips' paper, with the Fisher/Friedman motivation for an inflation mechanism given above:

> When the demand for a commodity rises relative to the supply of it we expect the price to rise, the rate of rise being greater than the excess demand. Conversely when the demand is low relative to the supply we expect the price to fall, the rate of fall being greater the greater the deficiency of demand.

The reader is referred to the two papers for more detailed motivations of these two - apparently quite distinct - kinds of inflation mechanisms. Here I remark that disinterested readers might find *both* kinds plausible.

14. For examples see Ackley's book {1}, which was influential in the 1960s, and Beare's more recent book {3} which gives an excellent treatment of standard topics in macroeconomics,specifically incorporating more recent developments including most particularly "neo-Keynesian" arguments.

15. I stress here – as standard presentations typically have not – that the third of these diagrams explicitly incorporates an otherwise implicit assumption of an exogenously fixed value for r*. (Notice that in a fully specified Keynesian system r* would be fixed only in conjunction with money market relations).

16. Including for example *orders of orders of* mathematical/ physical x's and/ or *orders of orders of* mathematical/ physical 1's in particular.

17. See also Chapters 1, 2 and 7 for developments pertaining to welfare functions and welfare potentials.

18. My term. See also p.36 above.

19. e.g. Phillips Loops see p.80 and the Appendix.

References

{1} Ackley, G. (1961),*Macroeconomic Theory*, Macmillan, New York.

{2} Ando, A. and Modigliani, F. (1963), *The Life Cycle Hypothesis of Saving: Aggregate Implications and Tests*, American Economic Review, March.

{3} Beare, J.B. (1978),*Macroeconomics: Cycles, Growth and Policy in a Monetary Economy*, Macmillan, New York.

{4} Buchanan, J.M. (1969), *Cost and Choice*, Markham, Chicago, Ill.

{5} Clower, R.W. (1965), *The Keynesian Counter Revolution: A Theoretical Appraisal* in F.H. Hahn and F. Brechling, the Theory of Interest Rates, Macmillan, London.

{6} Debreu, G. (1959), *Theory of Value: An Axiomatic Analysis of Economic Equilibrium*, Cowles Foundation Monograph 17 - Yale University Press.

{7} Duesenberry, J. (1949),*Income, Saving and the Theory of Consumer Behaviour*, Harvard University Press, Cambridge.

{8} Fisher, I. (1926), *A Statistical Relation between Unemployment and Price Changes*, International Labour Review. (And Journal of Political Economy 1973).

{9} Friedman, M. (1970), *A Theoretical Framework for Monetary Analysis*, Journal of Political Economy, 78.

{10}Friedman, M. (1975), *Unemployment versus Inflation: An Evaluation of the Phillips Curve* (UK) Institute of Economic Affairs Occasional Paper 44.

{11}Friedman, M. (1957) *A Theory of the Consumption Function*, Princeton University Press, Princeton, New Jersey.

{12}Hicks, J.R. (1946),*Value and Capital*, 2nd ed. Oxford University Press London.

{13}Houthakker, H.S. (1950), *Revealed Preference and Utility Functions*, Economica, May.

{14}Keynes, J.M. (1936), *The General Theory of Employment, Interest and Money*, Macmillan, London.

{15}Kuznets, A. (1946), *National Product Since 1869*, National Bureau of Economic Research, New York.

{16}Lange, O. (1946), *The Scope and Method of Economics*, Review of Economic Studies, 13.

{17}Leijonhufvud, A. (1968), *On Keynesian Economics and the Economics of Keynes* Oxford University Press, New York.

{18}Lipsey, R.G. and Lancaster K. (1956), *The General Theory of the Second Best*, Review of Economic Studies, 24.

{19}McManus, M. (1959), *Comments on the General Theory of Second Best*, Review of Economic Studies, 26.

{20}Phillips, A.W. (1958), *The Relation between Unemployment and the Rate of Change of Money Wage Rates in the United Kingdom 1861-1957*, Economica.

{21}Ryan, M.J. (1980), *More on the More for Less Paradox in the Distribution Problem*, Lecture Notes In Economics and Mathematical Systems, 174, pp. 275-303, Springer Verlag.

{22}Samuelson, P.A. (1947), *The Foundations of Economic Analysis*, Harvard University Press, Cambridge, Mass.

Appendix : Inflation versus unemployment*

Econometrica

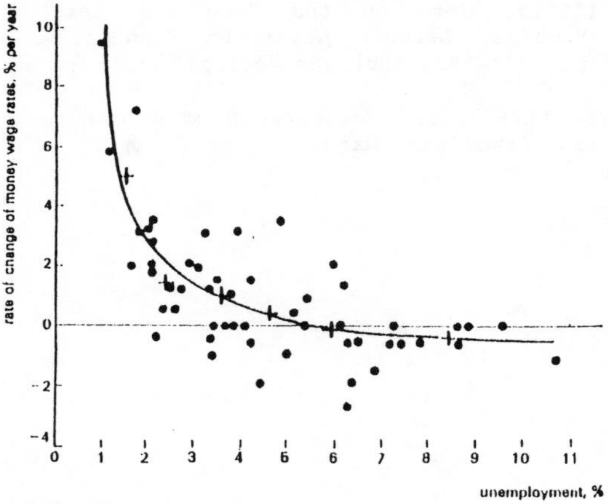

Figure 1 1861–1913

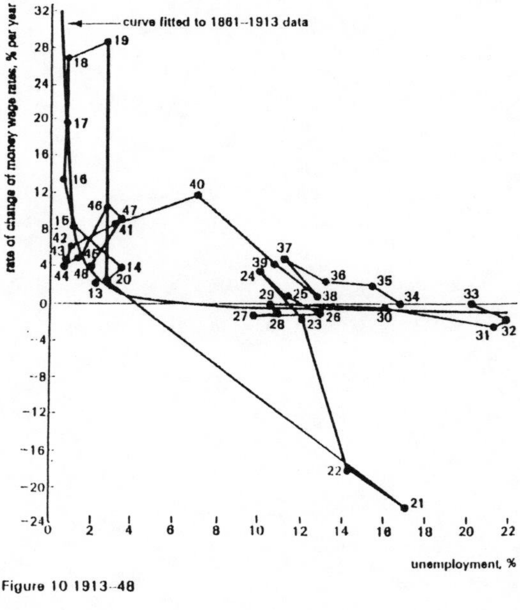

Figure 10 1913–48

*These two figures are reproduced from Phillips' highly influential paper on inflation and unemployment in the United Kingdom. See {20}.

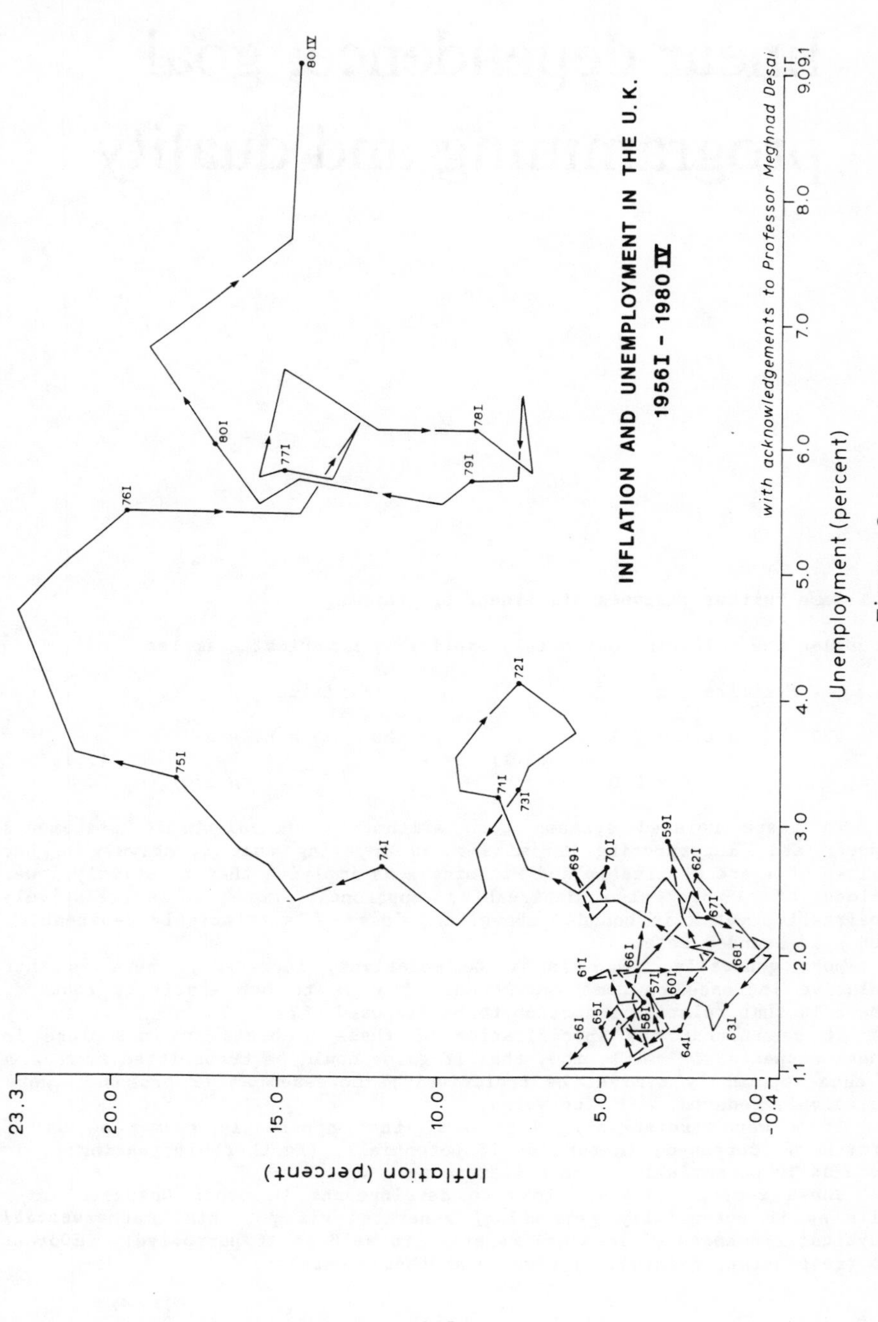

INFLATION AND UNEMPLOYMENT IN THE U.K.
1956I - 1980IV

Figure 3

5 Linear programming, linear dependence, goal programming and duality

5.1 Some further analyses via linear programming

Consider the following ostensibly explicitly numerical examples :

$$\begin{array}{llll} & \textit{Maximize} & x & \\ \mu\geqq 0 & \text{s.t.} & x \leqq 1 & \\ & & & (5.1) \\ & & x \geqq 0 & \end{array} \qquad \begin{array}{llll} & \textit{Minimize} & \mu & \\ x\geqq 0 & \text{s.t.} & \mu \geqq 1 & \\ & & & (5.1)' \\ & & \mu \geqq 0 & \end{array}$$

In these related systems both arithmetic and algebraic statements appear and, interpreting Maximize x as implying that relatively higher values of x are desireable and Minimize μ as implying that relatively lower values of μ are also desireable, apparently *more* x is relatively desireable, yet x is bounded above, and *less* „ is relatively desireable, yet μ is bounded below.

More generally, if x is to be relatively increased, where is that relative increase to come from? And, if μ is to be relatively reduced, where is that relative reduction to be disposed of?

It seems that the specification of these problems is incomplete in these respects. It seems, too, that if gains could be transmitted *from* „ *to* x then apparently x might be (relatively) increased as if *because* „ were relatively reduced, and vice versa.

If μ were (relatively) increased, then apparently x may be as if (further) increased, in turn as if potentially (further) increasing μ, in turn as if potentially further increasing x...

These remarks suggest links to developments in other Chapters inter alia as if potentially generating/ generated via potential mathematical/ physical *sequences* of loss(es) relative to self as if purposively in order to (re)generate gain(s) relative to another/others).

Now consider another pair of systems :

	Maximize	x			*Minimize*	μ	
μ	s.t.	$x = 1$	(5.2)	x	s.t.	$\mu = 1$	(5.2)'
		$x \geqq 0$				$\mu \geqq 0$	

Together, these systems constitute both feasible and optimal solutions to (5.1), (5.1)', being optimal in senses as if *variously* corresponding to conditions as if $x^* = 1$, $\mu^* = 1$ *and* :

$$\text{Maximize} \quad x = x^* = 1 = \mu^* = \text{Minimize} \quad \mu$$

$$\text{s.t.} \quad x \leqq 1 \qquad\qquad \text{s.t.} \quad \mu \geqq 1$$

Apparently problems (5.2), (5.2)', in distinction from (5.1), (5.1)', *also* constitute optimal solutions to the following pair of systems :

	Minimize	x			*Maximize*	μ	
μ	s.t	$x \geqq 1$	(5.3)	x	s.t.	$\mu \leqq 1$	(5.3)'
		$x \geqq 0$				$\mu \geqq 0$	

More generally these three apparently quite distinct pairs of problems might be interpreted as if constituting particular classes of solutions to:

	Maximize	$cx - c^+x^+ - c^-x^-$		Minimize	μ	
μ	s.t.	$x + x^+ - x^- = 1$	(5.4)	s.t.	$-c^+ \leqq \mu \leqq c^-$	(5.4)'
		$x \geqq 0$			$\mu \geqq c$	

With reference to (5.4), (5.4)',notice :

i) Conditions as if *identically* $c = 1$, $x^+ = 0$, $x^- = 0$, $c^- \geqq 1$, $c^+ = 0$, (5.4), (5.4)', *appear* consistent with (5.2),(5.2)';

ii) Conditions as if *identically* $x^- = 0$, $c^- \geqq 1$, $-c^+ = 0$, (5.4),(5.4)' *appear* consistent with (5.1), (5.1)' and;

iii) Conditions as if *identically* $c = 0$, $x^+ = 0$, $c^- = 1$, $-c^+ \leqq 1$, (5.4),(5.4)' *appear* consistent with (5.3), (5.3).'

In these various ways the *goal programming* system (5.4) and the related system (5.4)' are open to interpretation as if potentially corresponding *variously* to (5.1), (5.1)', to (5.2), (5.2)' and to (5.3), (5.3)'.

More directly, via conditions *as if* identically;

$$x^+ - x^- = 0, \qquad\qquad c^+ - c^- = 0$$

elements of (5.4) are open to interpretation as if *variously* in relation to strict equality *and/or* in relation to strict inequalities of either sense.

In this way the system (5.4) is open to interpretation as if potentially *complete* (e.g. as if via $x = 1$) while *incomplete* (e.g. as if via $x^+ = x^- \neq 0$) and/ or, conversely, as if potentially *incomplete* (e.g. as if via $x^+ = x^-$) while as if *complete* (e.g. as if via $x = 1$).

Similarly it is open to interpretation as if *determinate* (e.g. as if via $x = 1$) while *indeterminate* (e.g. via $x^+ = x^- \neq 0$, $c^+ = c^- \neq 0$ with x^+, x^- and/or c^+, c^- indeterminate) *and/or* as if *indeterminate* (e.g. via $x^+ = x^- \neq 0$, $c^+ = c^- \neq 0$) while *determinate* (e.g. as if via $x = 1$).

Further it is open to interpretation as if *bounded* (e.g. via $x = 1$)

while as if potentially *unbounded* (e.g. via x^+, x^- relative to $x = 1$).

These remarks will suggest relations to preceding developments as if via (III) of Chapters 2 and 4. This will be clearer if it is noticed that the conditions just considered might be expressed as corresponding to conditions as if:

$$-c^+x^+ - c^-x^-$$

$$x^+ = 1$$
$$x^- = 1$$
$$x^+ = x^-$$

with 1, c^+, c^- open to potential interpretations variously in relation to relative *determinacy* and/ or to relative *indeterminacy*. One kind of relationship between this system and (III) is evident if conditions obtain as if identically:

$$x^+ = x, \quad x^- = y, \quad -c^+ = \theta p_x, \quad c^- = \theta p_y y$$

With these translations/transformations (5.4) becomes :

$$\textit{Maximize} \quad cx + \theta p_x x - \theta p_y y$$

$$\text{s.t.} \quad x + x - y = 1$$

$$x \geqq 0$$

One class of solutions is that for which $x = 1$, $y = 1$, $x = y$, with $\theta p_x = \theta p_y$, $c = 0$. The potential for more restrictive conditions as if *identically* $p_x = 1$, $p_y = 1$, $\theta = 1$ serves to emphasize the potential which is apparent in these conditions for relations between the goal programming system (5.4) and further developments in relation to (III) of Chapters 2, 4.

Rather than proceed directly in that way I now proceed *indirectly* by considering the following algebraically expressed linear programming problem:

$$\begin{array}{lll} & \textit{Maximize} & \sum_j \theta_j p_j x_j \\ \mu_i \geqq 0 & \text{s.t.} & \sum_j a_{ij} x_j \leqq b_i \\ & & x_j \geqq 0 \end{array} \qquad (5.5)$$

System (5.5) can be used to generate the following "dual" problem (5.5)' by associating the indicated dual variables μ_i with its constraints:

$$\begin{array}{lll} & \textit{Minimize} & \sum_i \mu_i b_i \\ \mu_j \geqq 0 & \text{s.t.} & \sum_i \mu_i a_{ij} \geqq \theta_j p_j \\ & & \mu_i \geqq 0 \end{array} \qquad (5.5)'$$

The related systems (5.5), (5.5)' are strictly algebraic in character.

No particular meanings attach to particular variables of these systems as they stand. Nor is it appropriate to assert that elements of these systems are identical to particular arithmetic (numerical) magnitudes in the absence of applications, explicitly or implicitly, of arithmetic principles or processes as if (potentially) *generating* and/or as if potentially (re)*generated via* elements of this algebraically expressed system.

However, one class of potential interpretations is as follows: $\theta_j p_j$ represents the potential unit price associated with a commodity potentially produced in amount(s) x_j via a process j, a_{ij} is the potential input of type i required per unit output by process j, with b_i corresponding to the total available amount(s) of that type of input.

The objective of (5.5) is then open to interpretation as if corresponding to the choice of a production plan such as to *maximize the return* to given, and in that sense fixed, endowments of inputs.

Now interpret the measures μ_i as if potentially corresponding at an optimum *variously* to marginal opportunity costs and/or to unit rentals of units of production capacity.

Then the objective of the (dual) system (5.5)' corresponds to the *minimization of the opportunity costs/rentals* imputed to (relatively) "fixed" quantities of inputs.

Together, these objectives are open to interpretations as if corresponding to an overall objective of planning production as if to maximize the return to fixed inputs, while minimizing the opportunity costs imputed to those inputs.

Introducing measures S_i into the constraints of (5.5), and K_j into the constraints of (5.5)', apparently conditions *always* obtain as follows:

$$\mu_i \qquad \sum_j a_{ij}x_j + S_i = b_i$$

and thence

$$\sum_{ij}\sum \mu_i a_{ij}x_j + \sum_i \mu_i S_i = \sum \mu_i b_i$$

$$x_j \qquad \sum_i \mu_i a_{ij} - K_j = \theta_j p_j$$

and thence

$$\sum_{ij}\sum \mu_i a_{ij}x_j - \sum_j K_j x_j = \sum_j \theta_j p_j x_j$$

In context, the first class of relations is open to interpretation(s) as if available input of type i is employed for output(s) j, *or* retained (unemployed) for other types of potential output(s) via S_i. The second class of relations then appears open to *accounting* interpretations as if value of output(s) *plus* value of retained/unused input(s) *equals* value imputed to inputs b_i.

Via potential *interrelations between* elements of (5.5), (5.5)',the third class of relations appears open to interpretation as if, for potential output of type j, unit contingent price equals opportunity cost(s) imputed to its production via measures μ_i, *less* a unit opportunity *loss* (if K_j positive) or unit opportunity *profit* (if K_j negative) contribution K_j.

With these interpretations, the fourth class of relations yields a potential (accounting) interpretation *as if*(time adjusted) contingent potential revenue(s) for output(s) equal opportunity costs imputed to output(s) *plus or minus* net measures of "profit" or "loss" $K_j x_j$. Considering the second and the fourth of these relations together, apparently, algebraically:

$$\sum_i \mu_i b_i - \sum_i \mu_i S_i = \sum_{ij}\sum \mu_i a_{ij} x_j = \sum_j \theta_j p_j x_j + \sum_j K_j x_j \qquad (5.6)$$

Here conditions as if identically $S_i = 0$, $K_j = 0$ *all* i, j are open to interpretation, respectively, *as if* ; all inputs of type i are used for output(s) of types j (i.e. all inputs are *relatively scarce* in the sense that no input is relatively unused/ unemployed) and ; *as if*, for each type of output, anticipated revenue exactly equates to imputed (opportunity) cost(s).

The objectives of (5.5), (5.5)' are apparently equated as if *via* their constraints so that the above relations (5.6) appear consistent with a contingent duality result as if maximum anticipated revenue equates to minimum opportunity cost under conditions as if *minimizing* potential (opportunity) surpluses imputed to inputs via S_i, while also *minimizing* relative opportunity losses potentially generated via K_j in relation to potential output(s).

If measures S_i are constrained to be non-negative, then apparently a motivation as if to maximize $\Sigma\theta_j p_j x_j$ while minimizing S_i, might be interpreted as if implicitly corresponding to a more comprehensive objective as if to maximize $\Sigma\theta_j p_j x_j - \Sigma c_i^+ S_i$ where $c_i^+ > 0$.

With such an interpretation, the *specification* of (5.5) appears explicitly incomplete. And the specification of the objective of that system is *implicitly* then open to interpretation as if corresponding to maximize $\Sigma\theta_j p_x x_j - \Sigma c_i^+ S_i$ with conditions as if identically $c_i^+ = 0$.

In context interpretations as if identically $c_i^+ > 0$ ($c_i^+ = 0$) might appear open to interpretation as if relating to relative preference(s) indifference(s) in relation to measures S_i as if potentially corresponding to relatively more/less (availabilities of) relatively unused / planned availabilities of input(s) b_i.

Analogously, if measures K_j are constrained to be non-negative, then apparently a motivation as if to minimize $\Sigma\mu_i b_i$ while minimizing K_j might be interpreted as if corresponding to a more comprehensive objective as if to minimize $\Sigma\mu_i b_i + \Sigma\tilde{c}_j^- K_j$ where $\tilde{c}_j^- > 0$.

Again notice that, with such an interpretation, the specification of (5.5)' appears explicitly incomplete. Notice, too, that the objective of that system is *implicitly* (then) open to interpretation as if corresponding to minimize $\Sigma\mu_i b_i + \Sigma\tilde{c}_j^- K_j$ with conditions as if identically $\tilde{c}_j^- = 0$.

In context interpretations as if identically $\tilde{c}_j^- > 0$ ($\tilde{c}_j^- = 0$) might appear open to interpretation as if corresponding to measures of relative *preference/ indifference* in relation to measures K_j as if themselves corresponding to relatively *more/less*, *higher/lower* in relation to relative prices.

By way of further preliminaries to the consideration, via (5.7), (5.7)', of systems explicitly incorporating apparently (potentially) more comprehensive objectives, notice that conditions as if generated via measures R_i, K_j and the *constraints* of (5.5), (5.5)' are such that, if $R_i \geq 0$, $K_j \geq 0$, the objective of (5.5) is bounded *above* by the objective of (5.5)' or, via (5.6)), for all μ_i, x_j, S_i, K_j :

$$\sum_j \theta_j p_j x_j = \sum_i \mu_i b_i - \sum_i \mu_i S_i - \sum_j K_j x_j \qquad (5.7)$$

thus yielding apparent equality of the objectives of (5.5), (5.5)' under conditions *as if*, for all i, j : $S_i = 0$, $K_j = 0$.

By contrast with (5.7), for systems such as the systems (5.9), (5.9)', to be considered shortly, dual equality of relations as if, respectively, to maximize $\Sigma\theta_j p_j x_j - \Sigma c_i{}^+ S_i$ and to minimize $\Sigma\mu_i b_i + \tilde{c}_j{}^- K_j$ apparently implies, among other things, a condition as if:

$$\sum_j \theta_j p_j x_j = \sum_i \mu_i b_i + \sum_i c_i{}^+ S_i + \sum_j \tilde{c}_j{}^- K_j \qquad (5.8)$$

Evidently (5.7), (5.8) are (potentially) *mutually contradictory* in their implications for the measures S_i, K_j - unless conditions obtain as if $S_i = 0$, $K_j = 0$ all S_i, K_j.

These relations are open to interpretations as if not only potentially generating generated via (elements of) potential principles and/ or processes of *contradiction* between elements of relatively abstract mathematical/ physical objectives and different elements of relatively different mathematical/ physical constraints.

These remarks will recall attention to potential significance for the *rationality* of potential principles and processes of mathematical/ physical contradiction in general - and so for principles and processes of contradiction in potential relation to mathematical/ physical economics and/or in potential relation to mathematical/ physical economists in particular.

Here conditions as if relatively *minimizing* measures S_i correspond *both* to conditions as if, via (5.5), *maximizing* economic agents may relatively *prefer* produced output(s) x_j *to* retention of inputs via S_i *and/ or* to conditions as if economic agents act as if *empirically* to *prefer* relatively *feasible* solutions to (5.5) to relatively infeasible solutions, even though *abstractly* preferring relatively *infeasible* output/ potential consumption plans as if corresponding to solutions associated with potential input requirements (abstractly) *exceeding* one, or all, of the (empirically) planned availability measures b_i.

From the wider perspective of developments pertaining to fundamental significance for potential principles and processes of mathematical/ physical contradiction in potentially generating/ regenerating principles and/ or processes of relative mathematical/ physical *change* in general, it is evident that, according to one class of interpretations, measures S_i, K_j can interpret themselves as if corresponding to measures of *potentials for change*(s) in relation to production plans in general, (and potential for the mathematical/ physical realization of relatively mathematically/ physically economically *more* as if via mathematicaly/ physically economically *less* in particular).

I stress that here measures S_i, K_j are potentially interpreted in relation to potential for individually/ collectively *preferred* mathematical economic change(s) in general, and in relation to potentials as if potentially generating (relations to) classes of *otherwise relatively unknown*, yet potentially individually and/ or collectively mathematically/ physically abstractly/ empirically *prefered*, mathematical/ physical economic opportunities in particular.

According to these observations, classes of solutions associated with *inequalities* between the objectives of (5.5), (5.5)' can be individually/ collectively *preferred* to solutions associated with equality between them. More generally if K_j, S_i are understood to connote measures as if potentially corresponding to potentials for individual/ collective mathematical/ physical *change*, then conditions of equality between the objectives of (5.5), (5.5)' *as if via* $S_i = 0$, $K_j = 0$ all S_i, K_j might appear to connote *incompleteness* of specification, since apparently connoting relative *absence* of potential for relative mathematical/ physical economic changes in general -as well as absence of potentials as if potentially generating individually and/ or collectively mathematically/

physically relatively (more) *desireable/ desired* specifications and/ or solutions in particular.

Here are further reasons for the consideration of measures S_i, K_j as if corresponding to elements of potentially interrelated goal programming problems, because in a goal programming context issues of relative mathematical/ physical feasibility/ infeasibility, boundedness/ unboundedness, certainty/ uncertainty *and/or* individual/ collective desireability/ undesireability, become endogenous.

As a move in the direction of consideration of (5.5),(5.5)' as if corresponding to elements of a pair of goal programmes consider the following pair of systems:

$$\begin{array}{lll} & \textit{Maximize} & \sum_j \theta_j p_j x_j - \sum_i c_i^+ S_i \\ \mu_i & \text{s.t.} & \sum_j a_{ij} x_j + S_i = b_i \\ K_j & & x_j = ?\tilde{c}_j^- \end{array} \quad (5.9)$$

$$\begin{array}{lll} & \textit{Minimize} & \sum_i \mu_i b_i + \sum_j \tilde{c}_j^- K_j \\ x_j & & \sum_i a_{ij}\mu_i - K_j = p_j \\ S_i & & \mu_i = ?c_i^+ \end{array} \quad (5.9)'$$

The systems (5.9), (5.9)' might be construed as if corresponding to (5.5), (5.5)' with the explicit introduction respectively of "slack" variables S_i, K_j in the constraints, and of measures c_i^+, $\tilde{c}_j^-$ associated with those (potentially) "slack" elements in the objectives of those systems.

In the sense that measures S_i, K_j, c_i^+, $\tilde{c}_j^-$ might be construed as if "missing" (omitted) from (5.5), (5.5)', those systems appear relatively *incomplete* by comparison with (5.9), (5.9)' and, conversely, apparently (5.9), (5.9)' relatively (more) complete by comparison with (5.5), (5.5)'.

Apparently measures c_i^+, $\tilde{c}_j^-$ not only potentially relate (via S_i, K_j) to potential *changes* in elements of the primal (resp. dual) problems but *also*, via conditions $x_j = ?\tilde{c}_j^-$, $\mu_i = ?c_i^+$, apparently potentially *interrelate changes in* "primal" and "dual" measures.

As one evocative class of examples, apparently in (5.9) a (potential) *change in demand* for available inputs might be construed *as if generating/* generated via a *change in* S_i, in turn *as if* potentially *generating/* generated via a *change in* input price in (5.9)', in turn as if (potentially) *generating/* generated via *change*(s) *in* potential output(s) in (5.9).In turn this is open inter alia to interpretation as if potentially *generating/* generated via potential *change*(s) *in* demands for available inputs ....

Such potential sequences of interpretations will suggest mathematical/ physical economic processes in general, and in relation to potential mathematical/ physical *economic* processes of production, altruism, barter, trade in particular.

In general (5.9), (5.9)' might be construed as if potentially yielding, via the constraints (as above):

$$\sum_{ij}\sum \mu_i a_{ij} x_j + \sum_i \mu_i S_i = \sum_i \mu_i b_i$$

$$\sum_{ij}\sum \mu_i a_{ij} x_j - \sum_j K_j x_j = \sum_j \theta_j p_j x_j$$

so that, if $\mu_i S_i = 0$ *all* i, *and* $K_j x_j = 0$ all j then:

$$\sum_j \theta_j p_j x_j = \sum_{ij}\sum \mu_i a_{ij} x_j = \sum_i \mu_i b_i \quad (5.10)$$

Under conditions as if *also* $c_i^+ S_i = 0$ *all* i and $\tilde{c}_j^- K_j = 0$ *all* j apparently:

$$\text{Maximize } \sum_j \theta_j p_j x_j - \sum_i c_i^+ S_i = \sum_j \theta_j p_j x_j = \sum_{ij}\sum \mu_i a_{ij} x_j = \sum_i \mu_i b_i$$

$$= \text{Minimize } \sum_i \mu_i b_i + \sum_j \tilde{c}_j^- K_j \quad (5.11)$$

In the context of (5.9),(5.9)'conditions (5.10), (5.11) appear consistent with a duality result with conditions, $\mu_i{}^* S_i{}^* = 0$, $K_j{}^* x_j{}^* = 0$ interpreted as if *Complementary Slackness* conditions, and conditions $c_i + S_i{}^* = 0$, $\tilde{c}_j{}^- K_j{}^* = 0$ interpreted as if *specified* as if identically $c_i^+ = 0$, $\tilde{c}_j^- = 0$.

Such interpretations, via measures as if identically $c_i^+ = 0$, $\tilde{c}_j^- = 0$ would apparently imply *indifference* with respect to deviations *below* primal (resp. above dual) bounds *and*, via assumptions of non-negativity for measures a_{ij}, x_j, S_i, μ_i, θ_j, p_j, would assume *feasibility* for chosen production plans.

A goal programming farmulation would be more general in both of these senses. Such a formulation would allow deviations *either* above *or* below such bounds, and would associate zero weights with such deviations only as a class of special cases.*And*, by allowing potential deviations in *either* direction from (potential) bounds, such a formulation would render (potential) relative feasibility/ infeasibility and/ or relative boundedness/ unboundedness issues *strictly endogenous*.

As another way of providing motivation for such generally specified systems notice that, if measures a_{ij} are interpreted/ interpret themselves as if corresponding to "input-output" coefficients, and, if x_j correspond to outputs, then in a context of standard input-output analysis (see Chapter 3), the constraints of (5.9) might be interpreted as if *identically* $x_i = b_i$ and $S_i = d_i$,*where* b_i is total output and d_i "final demand" of type i.

In such a context apparently positive "slack" S_i is desireable because as if corresponding not only *indirectly* to *more* potential output(s) but also *directly* to *more* potential final demand. And if, *via* $c_i^+ > 0$, "slack" appeared with positive weight in the objective of (5.9) it would seem desireable. Conditions would then obtain as if a standard input-output structure $Ax + d = x$ was associated with an optimizing relation *Maximize* $\sum \theta_j p_j x_j - \sum c_i^+ S_i$ with the measure c_i^+ apparently having a potential relation to (potential) final demand price.

Still in the context of (standard) input-output structures, it might seem that such a structure for the constraints of (5.9) is *contingently* attainable under conditions as if *identically* $a_{ij} x_j = y_i$ for some j. Such conditions are consistent with conditions as if $x_{ij} = x_j = y_i$. These in turn implicitly identify some of the measures $\theta_j p_j$ in the objective of (5.9) as if corresponding to *contingent* demand prices (then implicitly *opposite* in sign to supply prices).

Now look for these and other possibilities with the context of the following developments *via* (5.9), (5.9)' :

$$\begin{aligned} \text{Maximize} \quad & \sum_j \theta_j p_{x_j} x_j - \sum_i \theta_i p_{y_i} y_i - \sum_i c_i^+ S_i \\ \text{s.t.} \quad & \sum_j a_{ij} x_j + y_i + S_i = x_i \\ & x_j \qquad = ?\tilde{c}_j^- \\ & y_i \qquad = ?\tilde{c}_i^- \end{aligned} \tag{5.12}$$

Via interpretations as if $S_i = 0$, $y_i^* = d_i$ the system (5.12) yields conditions contingently consistent with a standard input-output structure $Ax + d = x_i$ for elements of its constraints. More evocatively, (5.12) potentially yields *or* is as if potentially yielded via (potential) principles and processes of *contradiction* - including (potential) principles and processes of self contradiction -in relation to a standard input-output structure.

While conditions as if $S_i = 0$, $y_i^* = d_i$ might appear *contingently* consistent with an "initial" input-output specification, conditions as if *identically* $S_i = \Delta y_i$, $c_i^+ = \Delta p_y$ would appear open to interpretation as if relating to as if *purposive process* in relation to potential change as if *via* potential principles and processes of *optimization* in relation to the potential specification or potential for (optimal) *re*specification(s) of such an "initial" input-output system.

While suggesting potential generalizations of these kinds as if potentially generating/ generated via relations themselves potentially yielding or yielded via potential processes of generalization of standard input-output systems, the structure of the system (5.12) more immediately suggests a *goal programming* framework with the measures c_i^-, c_j^- construed as if corresponding to *goals*. Now consider the following structure in which potential deviations x_j^+, x_j^-, y_i^+, y_i^- above and/ or below goals x_j^*, y_i^* are *explicitly* incorporated both in the objective and the constraints:

$$\begin{aligned} \text{Maximize} \quad & \sum_j \theta_j p_{x_j} x_j - \sum_i \theta_i p_{y_i} y_i - \sum_i c_i^+ S_i - \sum_j c_{x_j}^+ x_j^+ - \sum_j c_{x_j}^- x_j^- \\ & - \sum_i c_{y_i}^+ y_i^+ - \sum_i c_{y_i}^- y_i^- \\ \mu_i \qquad \text{s.t} \quad & \sum_j a_{ij} x_j - y_i + S_i = x_i \\ \theta_j \psi_j \qquad & x_j + x_j^+ - x_j^+ = x_j^* \ (\equiv \tilde{c}_j) \\ \theta_i b_i \qquad & y_i + y_i^+ - y_i^- = y_i^* \ (\equiv \tilde{c}_i) \\ & S_i = ? \end{aligned} \tag{5.13}$$

With interpretations as above, apparently measures $\theta_i px$ and $\theta_j p_y$ are open to interpretations corresponding to initial or potential *target* prices/ unit valuations, respectively for potential inputs x_j of type j and potential final demands y_i of type i, with c_{xi}^+, c_{xi}^-, c_{yj}^+, c_{yj}^- potentially corresponding, respectively,to potential deviations *above and below* output and demand goals.

The remaining conditions of (5.13) then correspond to conditions that total contingent outputs x_i be at least sufficient to meet potential final demands y_i *plus* potential intermediate demands $\Sigma a_{ij}x_j$ for inputs i to subsequent output.

Such interpretations implicitly impose a relative *time* structure on elements of the system (5.13). For example, produced outputs x_i apparently here rationally *antedate* realized final demands y_i. And/or planned final demands y_i^* apparently rationally *antedate* production and/or realized final demands.

Apparently *planned* demands y_i^* are not only open to potential interpretations as if *antedating* production (and so *realized* demands), but also to interpretations as if *motivating* production as if *to differently realize* planned final demands.

The measures S_i now also appear open to a variety of interpretations. As one class, measures S_i yield potentials for optimizations as if *relative to* a standard input-output system $Ax + d = x$.

As a related class, measures c_i^+ associated with measures S_i are open to interpretation as if measures of *relative preference/ indifference* over *relative "errors"* S_i in relation to a standard input-output structure.

Clearly there are senses here in which (relative) mathematical/ physical "error" is relatively more/less *desireable* - as well as potential senses in which relative mathematical/physical error is relatively more/ less *inevitable*.

If, for example an input- output system $Ax + d = x$ is understood to correspond as if identically to conditions as if $x_i = x_i^*$, $d_{ij} = x_{ij}^*/x_j^*$, $y_i^* = d$ then, in the context of (5.13), these conditions apparently correspond to conditions as if x_j^+, x_j^-, y_i^+, y_i^-, S_i *each and all* mathematically/ physically/ economically potentially correspond to relative measures of potential mathematical/ physical "errors".

To emphasize that, in principle, such "errors" may not only correspond to economic *desireabilities* in relation to potential principles and processes of (relative) mathematical/ physical economic measurement but also, more generally, potentially correspond to economic *inevitabilities* in relation to principles and processes of relative mathematical/ physical measurement in general, notice that (5.13) may be interpreted as if potentially corresponding to (III) of Chapter 3 under conditions for example as if $x = y$ and as if identically $x^* = 1$, $y^* = 1$, $a_{ij} = 0$, $S_i = 0$, in turn, as if potentially consistent with conditions as if *identically* $x_j^+ = 0$, $y_i^+ = 0$, $y_i^- = 0$.

These latter conditions are consistent with interpretations as if corresponding to *no* (relative) *errors* of measurement; they are also variously consistent with interpretations as if corresponding to *absence* of relative error(s) as if *in consequence of* absence of process(es) of change in relation to mathematical physical measurements in general and *absence of processes* as if corresponding to the generation of (changes of) outputs and/or as if corresponding to the generation of (changes of) final demand in particular.

Conditions contingently consistent with interpretations in relation to *invariance*,of the kinds just considered yet *also as if explicitly* yielding contingent potential for interpretations as if corresponding to *change*(s) (*variations*) are immanent in (5.13)-for example via conditions as if :

$$\theta p_{yi} = \theta p_{xi}\ ,\ y_i^+ - y_i^- = 0,\ x_j^+ - x_j^- = 0,$$

c_{yi}^+, c_{yi}^- (resp. c_{xj}^+, c_{xj}^-) opposite in relative sign, with conditions as if x_j^+, x_j^- potentially as if perfectly predictive *of* and/or as if perfectly predicted *via* y_i^+, y_i^-, either directly or indirectly.

(Consider classes of supply-demand examples as if identically $y_i = y_i^*$, $x_j = x_j^*$, $x_i = y_i$, yet as if perfectly predictively $S_i + \Sigma a_{ij} x_j = 0$, with S_i a measure of potential increase in *potential* final demand).

With a view to these and other kinds of developments in relation to principles and processes of mathematical/ physical relativity in general as well as to relative *desireability* and/or to relative *inevitability* for (relative) mathematical/ physical errors/ indeterminacy / incompleteness, and/or certainty/ uncertainty in particular, now associate the indicated variables with the conditions of (5.13) and use *linear dependence* arguments to generate the following system:

$$(\textit{Minimize})\ \sum_j \theta_j \psi_j x_j^* + \sum_i \theta_i \lambda_i y_i^*$$

$$\begin{array}{lll}
x_j \quad \text{s.t.} & \sum_i a_{ij}\mu_i - \mu_j + \theta_j\psi_j = \ ?\!-\theta_j p x_j & \\
y_i & \mu_i + \theta_i\lambda_i = \ ?\ \theta_i p_{y_i} & \\
x_j^+ & \theta_j\psi_j = \ ?\ C_{x_j}^+ & \\
x_i^- & -\theta_j\psi_j = \ ?\ C_{x_j}^- & (5.13)' \\
y_i^+ & \theta_i\lambda_i = \ ?\ C_{y_i}^+ & \\
y_i^- & -\theta_i\lambda_i = \ ?\ C_{y_i}^- & \\
S_i & \mu_i = \ ?\ \tilde{C}_i &
\end{array}$$

Observing (5.13)' an analyst might proceed to include further variables R_i, K_j (implicitly unrestricted in sign) in order to resolve the apparent ambiguities in the first two relations. Going further, an analyst might also introduce the *pairs* of measures $(\psi_j^{++}, \psi_j^{+-})$, $(\psi_j^{-+}, \psi_j^{--})$, $(\lambda_i^{++}, \lambda_i^{+-})$, $(\lambda_i^{-+}, \lambda_i^{--})$, again implicitly unrestricted in sign, into the next four relations of (5.13)' to obtain the following system (5.13)'' :

$$(\textit{Minimize})\ \sum_j \theta_j \psi_j x_j^* + \sum_i \theta_i \lambda_i y_i^*$$

$$\begin{array}{lll}
x_i & \sum_i a_{ij}\mu_i - \mu_j + \theta_j\psi_j + K_j = -\theta_j p_{x_j} & \\
y_i & \mu_i + \theta_i\lambda_i + R_i = \theta_i p_{y_i} & \\
x_j^+ & \theta_j\psi_j + \psi_j^{++} - \psi_j^{+-} = C_{x_j}^+ & (5.13)'' \\
x_j^- & -\theta_j\psi_i + \psi_j^{+-} - \psi_j^{--} = C_{x_j}^- &
\end{array}$$

y_i^+ $\qquad \theta_i\lambda_i + \lambda_i^{++} - \lambda_i^{+-} = C_{y_i^+}$

y_i^- $\qquad -\theta_i\lambda_i + \lambda_i^{-+} - \lambda_i^{--} = C_{y_i^-}$

S_i $\qquad \mu_i = ?\ \tilde{C}_i$

Comparing (5.13)'' with (5.13)', the former is open to interpretation as if (relatively) *incomplete* and the latter (5.13)'' correspondingly as if (relatively) *more* complete.

Considering (5.13)'' as if potentially (re)generating (5.13) via linear dependence arguments, (5.13)'' apparently potentially contingently (re)generates *not only* the relations of (5.13) but *also* further conditions, as if (via K_j) corresponding to $x_j = ?\ 0$ *or* as if (via R_i) corresponding to $y_i = ?\ 0$. In that sense (5.13) might be construed as if relatively incomplete and/ or as if *potentially* (relatively) more complete.

Apparently (5.13)'' is open to interpretation as if *omitting* relations inter alia pertaining to measures R_i, K_j, ψ_j^{++}, ψ_j^{+-}, ψ_j^{-+}, ψ_J^{--}, λ_i^{++}, λ_i^{+-}, λ_i^{-+}, λ_i^{--} from its objective, thereby potentially implicitly omitting magnitudes from systems potentially generated from it via linear dependence arguments (including systems as if potentially corresponding to augmentations of the system (5.13)).

If, for example, $C_{yi^+} = C_{yi^-}$, the sixth and seventh relations of (5.13)'' might *appear* equivalent. With reference to (5.8) such conditions might be interpreted as if corresponding (via the objective of (5.8)) to *relative indifference* between deviations above and below a target y_i^*.

Also if $C_{yi^+} = C_{yi^-}$, then apparently *either* the sixth or the seventh relation of (5.13)'' might be *omitted* on the grounds of linear dependence. Such a class of cases would associate *mutual exclusion* in (5.13)'' with conditions of *linear dependence* in (5.13)'' and conditions as if of *indifference* in (5.13).

So conditions of (5.13)'' might be rendered implicit via the *implicit* assumption that "dual" variables y_i^+, y_i^- (resp. x_i^+, x_i^-) associated with it, and thence within the objective of (5.13),are unrestricted in relative signs.

With this observation, and considering particular measures $C_{\psi i^+}\psi_i^+$, $C_{\psi j^-}\psi_j^-$, $C_{\lambda i^+}\lambda_i^+$, $C_{\mu i^-}\lambda_i^-$ as if implicit in its objective, (5.13)''might be expressed as if *conditionally* equivalent to the following system:

$$(\mathit{Minimize})\ \sum_j \theta_j\psi_j x_j^* x + \sum_i \theta_i\lambda_i y_i^* + \sum_i C_{\psi_j^+}\psi_j^+ + \sum_i C_{\psi_j^-}\psi_j^- + \sum_i C_{\lambda_i^+}\lambda_i^+ + \sum_i C_{\lambda_i^-}\lambda_i^-$$

x_j $\qquad \sum_i a_{ij}\mu_i - \mu_j + \theta_j\psi_j + K_j = \theta_j p_{x_j}$

y_i $\qquad \mu_i + \theta_i\lambda_i + R_i = \theta_i p_{y_i}$ $\qquad$ (5.13)'''

Δx_j $\qquad \theta_j\psi_j + \psi_j^+ - \psi_j = C_{x_j^+}$

Δy_i $\qquad \theta_i\lambda_i + \lambda_i - \lambda_i = C_{y_i^+}$

S_i $\qquad \mu_i = ?\ \tilde{C}_i$

Now associate measures Δx_j, Δy_i as if unrestricted in relative sign with the fifth and sixth conditions of (5.13)'' as indicated. In the context of (5.13)' this will suggest conditions as if identically $\Delta x_j = x_j^-$, $-\Delta x_j = x_j^+$, $\Delta y_i = y_i$, $-\Delta y_i = y_i^+$. In that sense (5.13)'' can be seen as if corresponding to a special class of interpretations in relation to (5.13)'

From another perspective, the association of interpretations corresponding to measures x_j, y_i, Δx_j, Δy_i with constraints of (5.13)'' will evoke associations with preceding developments with reference to potential principles and processes of as if perfect prediction in general *and* with macro/ microeconomic principles and processes as if potentially generating changes in relative prices via changes in relative quantities - and vice versa - in particular.

These broader perspectives refocus attention on (5.13)'' with a view to the identification of magnitudes in that system with measures Δp_{xj} , Δpy_i , corresponding to (potential) changes in input (output) price(s).

Clearly the measures ψ_j (resp. λ_i) might be identified in these ways. Then as if *via elements of* the potentially related and interrelated systems (5.13), (5.13)''', relative *changess in* input (output) price(s) may (potentially) *generate* relative *changes in* input (output) quantities, and conversely.

And, if Δx_j, Δy_i, Δp_{xj} , Δp_{yi} refer to (relatively) different *orders* of magnitude than measures x_j, y_i, p_x , py then such magnitudes may potentially generate/ be as if (re)generated via relations and inter -relations between *different orders of magnitude*, including for example relations as if corresponding to *loss* relative to relatively *larger* as if to generate *gain* relative to (relatively) *smaller* as if, in turn, to generate *gain* to relatively *larger*.

These classes of process in turn suggest potential relations to *cycling* in general and/or, especially with the context here of potential inter -relations between measures Δx_j, Δy_i, Δp_{xj} , Δp_{yi} , x_j, y_i, p_{xj} , p_{yi} , pertaining to potential cycling in contexts of potential principles and/or processes of *as if perfect prediction* in particular.

More primitively, with the preceding classes of potential interpretations, the conditions:

$$\sum_i a_{ij}\mu_i - \mu_j + \theta_j\psi_j + K_j = \theta_j p_{x_j}$$

$$\mu_i + \theta_i\lambda_i + R_i = \theta_i p_{y_i}$$

might be interpreted respectively as if corresponding to:

(*Change in*) input cost(s) + Kj = (*Change in*) contingent output price

$$= \theta_j(p_{x_j} - \psi_j)$$

(*Change in*) output cost(s) + Ri = (*Change in*) contingent market price

$$= \theta_i(p_{y_i} - \lambda_i)$$

In context R_i, K_j suggest interpretations in relation to (contingent) unit production and to unit consumption *taxes/ subsidies*, inviting further developments not only as if in relation to (5.13)'' per se, but as if in relation to (5.13)'' as if potentially generating/ generated via elements of (5.13). This will suggest links to the goal programming models in

Chapter 6 onwards with contexts of microeconomic and/ or of macroeconomic planning and regulation in general, and of hierarchical planning and regulation in contexts of potentially overlapping agencies with potentially conflicting goals in particular[1]

More directly, if seen as potentially generating/ generated via relations kin to those apparently potentially generating/ generated via (5.13)'', such interpretations will suggest potential relations *between* such potentially interrelated classes of relatively micro and macro economic interpretations and relations potentially mathematically/ physically generating and/ or regenerated via goal programming specifications.

From such a perspective an analyst might interpret measures x_j^+, x_j^-, y_i^+, y_i^- as if potentially corresponding to measures of potential relative mathematical/ physical *change* in general and, more evocatively, as if potentially mathematically/ physically corresponding to potential mathematical/ physical....elements themselves potentially generating/ generated via (all) particular classes of mathematical/physical *processes* of mathematical/ physical change in particular.

If seen in the context of potential mathematical/physical....process, attention would focus inter alia upon issues pertaining to relative mathematical/physical *feasibility/ infeasibility*. For example, if measures x_j^*, interpreted themselves in relation to *plans/ endowments* and x_j in relation to potential *realizations*, then measures x_j^+ appear open to interpretation as if measures of relative mathematical/ physical *feasibility* (in the sense of potentially corresponding to realizations relatively *inside* plans/ endowments), and x_j^- as if measures of relative mathematical/ physical *infeasibility* (in the sense of apparently potentially corresponding to realizations relatively *outside* plans/ endowments).

Then x_j^+, x_j^- might interpret themselves as if *variously* potentiating *or* potentiated via relative *possibilities* (impossibilities), relatively *inside* (outside), relatively *boundedness* (unboundedness), relatively *known* (unknown)... .

With contexts not just of changes, but of potential mathematical/ physical/ economic *exchanges*, such interpretations might appear as if *variously:* to potentiate *realizations of* relative *impossibilities* relative to self/ selves as if *via* the potentiation realization of relative *possibilities* relative to self/ selves/ another/ others.

And to potentiate realizations of elements of sequences of *what might be/ become* mathematically/ physically *outside* relative to self/ selves/ another/ others as if purposively via elements of *whatis/ was* mathematically/ physically *inside* relative to self/ selves/ another/ others.

And/or more simply, to potentiate elements of mathematically/ physically relatively *unknown/ infeasible* and/ or *unbounded* mathematical/ physical opportunities relative to self/ selves/ another/ others as if *via* elements of mathematically/ physically relatively *known/ feasible/ bounded* mathematical/ physical opportunities/ experiences relative to a relatively abstract mathematical/ physical "self".

Not only are measures x_j^+, x_j^- open to interpretations as if *variously* potentiating/ potentiated via relatively mathematically/ physically *inevitable* error/ uncertainty/ incompleteness/ indeterminacy relative to self/ selves/ another/ others ; they are open to interpretations as if potentiating/ potentiated via elements of relatively mathematically/ physically *desireable* error(s)/ uncertainty/ incompleteness/ indeterminacy relative to self/ selves/ another/ others, according to principles/ processes as if individuals might act as if to determine *less* relative to self/ selves as if to potentiate *more* relative to another/ others as if thereby purposively *perfectly predictively* to potentiate relatively *more* unknown, relatively *more* (in)feasible, relatively *more* unbounded mathematical/ physical opportunities relative to self/ selves/ another/ others relatively abstractly located at -a -distance in space time *relative to* self/ selves/ another/ others.... .

Such remarks, especially if seen in contexts of potential linear dependence/ duality principles/ processes/ phenomena in general suggest potential for (extended) *duality* of relative mathematical/ physical (in)*feasibility* principles/ processes and of relative (un)*boundedness* principles/ processes.

They also suggest associated reasons to expect that not only may relatively individually/ collectively mathematically/ physically *unknown*, *infeasible* and relatively *unbounded* principles/ processes and phenomena be as if individually/ collectively *purposively related* but as if individually/ collectively/ socially systematically/ algorithmically *purposively (re)generated* via correspondence to elements themselves potentiating/ potentiated via appropriately specified and potentially *dually related goal programming systems*, as considered for example via the (sub)system (III) of Chapter 4 or more technically in Section 2 of this Chapter.

As if purposive determinations of conditions of relative unboundedness here suggest as if systematic/ algorithmic mathematical/ physical.. ..determinations of orders of orders of *relatively infinite* (non-Archimedean) mathematical/ physical measures.

This in turn suggests links to non-Archimedean principles/ processes/ interpretations developed by Charnes {1} to ensure acyclicity ,feasibility and boundeness of solutions tolinear programming problems and/or by Charnes, Clower and Kortanek {2} to ensure potentially individually/ collectively *coherently decentralizable* outcomes. It also suggests a role for an essentially *opposite* emphasis upon as if individually/ collectively/ socially *purposive* determinations of relatively *infeasible/ indeterminate/ unbounded sequences/ cycles* of, among other things, potentially informationally *distinct* and in that sense *incoherently* decentralized individual/ collective/ social outcomes[2].

With the context of developments in Chapter 3, measures as if (relatively) identically ∞, -∞ will directly suggest elements of essentially algebraic interpretations as if potentially (relatively) "next", "previous" and thence interpretations as if themselves potentiating/ potentiated via *relativity* of mathematical/ physical. ...*futurity* in general and mathematical/ physical.. ..principles/ processes according to which *what was* relatively mathematically/ physically -ve relative to self might as if relatively (im)perfectly predict *what will be* relatively mathematically/ physically +ve relative to another/ others -and thence classes of as if relatively mathematically/ physically (im)perfectly predictive mathematical/ physical principles/ processes open to interpretations as if variously sequentially/ cyclically *from* relatively *larger* (+ve) → relatively *smaller* (-ve) → relatively *larger* (+ve).., in turn again suggesting classes of relatively arithmetically/ algebraically/ geometrically (im)perfectly predictively related interpretations as schematically represented as follows (see also Chapter 1, p.6 and Chapter 2, p.33) :

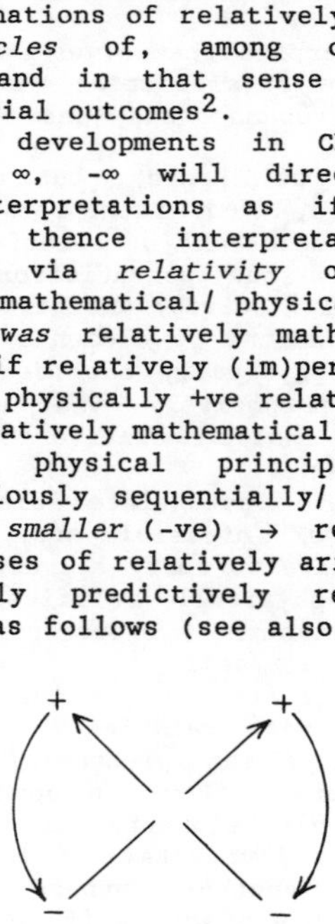

Figure 5.1

Such considerations suggest classes of potentially associated *pairs* of apparently explicitly mathematically/ physically.. ..*electromagnetic* relations/ interpretations/ processes as if themselves systematically/ algorithmically potentiating/ potentiated via elements of *pairs* of sequences of *purposively relatively self contradictory* changes/ exchanges/ motions *from* relatively ++ *to* relatively -- ..*to* relatively ++ .... and/or *from* relatively NN *to* relatively SS, *from* relatively SS *to* relatively NN.... .

If looking at such interpretations as if themselves potentially systematically/ algorithmically potentiated via elements of mathematical *or physical* linear (in)dependence and/ or extended duality principles/ processes/ interpretations, an analyst/observer would notice apparent potentials here for as if *purposive* mathematical/ physical *correspondences between* elements of mathematical/ physical linear (in)dependence, extended duality and as if purposively relatively mathematical/physical (in)determinately *cyclic* principles/ processes/ interpretations.

Extending this; there are opportunities here for potentiations of as if relatively individually/ collectively/ socially mathematically/ physically/ economically *more purposive* and *more desireable* changes/ exchanges/ developments via appropriate *exploitations* of *appropriately* (re)*specified* individual/ collective/ social correspondences *(e.g.appropriately (re)specified preference relations)* as if themselves relatively (im)perfectly predictively potentiating/ potentiated via relatively individually/ collectively/ socially desireable (undesireable) *errors/ perturbations relative to* relatively (de)centralized elements of linear dependence, duality and cycling principles/ processes/ interpretations.

With such perspectives now reconsider measures x_j^+, x_j^-, y_i^+, y_i^- as if potentiating elements of mathematical/ physical "errors" in more detail. In the context of the system (5.13),elements x_j^+, x_j^-, y_i^+, y_i^- may appear open to interpretations as if potentiating/ potentiated via changes/ exchanges/ motions relative to elements of relations :

$$x_j = x_j^* \ , \ y_j = y_j^*$$

by potentiating conditions as if :

$$x_j + x_j^+ - x_j^- = x_j^*$$

$$y_i + y_i^+ - y_i^- = y_i^*$$

according to which measures x_j^+, x_j^- , y_i^+, y_i^-, $x_j^+ - x_j^-$, $y_i^+ - y_i^-$ ... ..may appear as if not just variously potentiating/ potentiated via elements of as if purposively determining/ determined changes/ exchanges, but as if potentially determining/ determined via as if purposive mathematical/ physical *indeterminacies/ errors* relative to measures x_j, x_j^*, y_i, y_i^*.

It has already been seen that, according to conditions as if identically $a_{ij} = x_{ij}^*/x_j^*$, conditions as if purposively potentiating/ potentiated via "errors" variously relative to measures x_i^*, x_j^* are open to interpretations as if purposively systematically/ algorithmically potentiating/ potentiated via elements of potentially relatively individually/ collectively/socially *decisive respecifications* of as if purposively in such ways (only) *relatively* standardized "input-output" systems (such as have been considered in Chapter 3). And, more generally, open to interpretation as if *purposively* systematically/ algorithmically potentiating/ potentiated via elements of relatively individually/ collectively/ socially *decisive respecifications* of as if purposively (only) *transiently* standardized linear and goal programming (sub)systems. (See for example now clearly potentially interrelated developments on Limited Liability and Corporate Control Under Uncertainty in Chapter 9).

Summarizing : elements x_j^+, x_j^-, y_i^+, y_i^-, especially if considered with connotations of potentiation of "errors" relative to self/ selves/ another/ others might be interpreted as if, for example, potentiating elements of what is relatively (more) *unknown* relative to self/ selves *via* as if purposively determined inducement(s) of what is relatively (more) *unknown* relative to another/ others differently/ distantly located in space-time relative to self/ selves.

Such remarks suggest links to classes of interpretations as if themselves potentiating essentially mathematically/ physically "probabilistic" interpretations according to which, for example, offers of changes/ exchanges may potentiate relatively *higher* (mathematical) "probabilities" of physically *less* relative to self/ selves via relatively higher (physical) "probabilities" of physically *more* relative to another/ others..

And *relatively* probabilistic interpretations for relatively indeterminate/ indeterminacy measures x_j^+, x_j^-, y_i^+, y_i^- among other things as if themselves potentiating/ potentiated via changes/ exchanges relative to relatively *more* certain/ *less* indeterminate measures x_j, x_j^*, yi, y_i^*, in turn suggest consideration of potential classes of mathematical/ physical distinctions between relative *subjective/ objective* (in)determinacy classes for "probability" measures according to which such measures might *variously* construe themselves/ be construed as if potentiating/ potentiated via relative mathematical/ physical *certainties*, relative mathematical/ physical *risks* and relatively mathematical/ physical *uncertainties* relative to self/ selves/ another/ others.... .

With a context of linear programming, characterizations of elements x_j of the (sub)system (5.13) as if potentiating/ potentiated via elements of mathematical/physical "probability" measures suggests interpretations of elements of that (sub)system as if potentiating/ potentiated via elements of essentially "game theoretic" relations/ interpretations/ processes, according to which measures x_j would (probabilistically) potentiate *various* mathematical/ physical *strategies* j, and/or measures a_{ij} , as if (conditionally) perfectly predictively potentiating elements of *payoffs* to probabilistically relatively known/ unknown *joint* strategies j,i.

Apart from suggesting interpretations according to which elements of mathematically/ physically contingent probability measures might be/ become as if mathematically/ physically *identical with* elements of contingent *outcomes* - in that way suggesting links to issues considered in the context of *constrained games* in {4} - these remarks with reference to elements of the (sub)system (5.13) will, via the now essentially contingently relatively "probabilistic" conditions:

$$x_j + x_j^+ - x_j^- = x_j^*$$

$$y_i + y_i^+ - y_i^- = y_i^*$$

suggest interpretations of such a system as if not simply potentiating/ potentiated via *constrained game* theoretic mathematical/ physical relations/interpretations, but, more subtly, as if *through* (potential) measures x_j^+, x_j^-, y_i^+, y_i^- potentiating/ potentiated via essentially constrained game theoretic mathematical/ physical *processes*.

They suggest interpretations potentiating elements of as if *purposively* (relatively) *bounded* mathematical/ physical *risks* via elements of as if *purposively* (relatively) *unbounded uncertainties*, or according to which individuals or groups may act as if systematically/ algorithmically to potentiate relatively *more* (un)*known* opportunities/ strategies/ outcomes relative to self/ selves via the potentiation of potentials for relatively *more* (un)*known* opportunities/ strategies/ outcomes relative to another/ others and/ or relative to elements of a wider mathematical/ physical....(sub)system.[3]

More simply, contexts of constrained games, in conjunction with potentially related mathematically/ physically *relatively* probabilistic and mathematically/ physically relatively *dichotomous* relations/ inter -pretations/ processes suggest straightforward interpretations for a class of cases encountered in the paper on constrained games just cited, according to which subjective probability rankings for adversely interrelating individuals apparently *must be mutually opposed* in order from relatively largest to relatively smallest, if they are to accord with conditions of as if perfect mathematical/ physical prediction, and/ or of as if complete information for such individuals relative to self/ selves and/or relative to each other.

Such circumstances, which seem very remarkable there, might seem quite *un*remarkable here, if understood as potentially mathematically/ physically corresponding to classes of cases according to which (elements of) what physically *is* (*is not*) relative to self/ selves may be/ become as if contingently *variously* perfectly predictive *of* and/ or as if perfectly predicted *via* (elements of) what mathematically *is* (*is not*) relative to self/ selves, what mathematically *is* (*is not*) relative to another/others *and/ or* what physically *is* (*is not*) relative to self/ selves.

It has been seen here how such processes may be as if purposively potentiated via elements of *as if purposively induced* individual *and/ or* collective mathematical/ physical contradictions/ changes/ exchanges/ motions relative to self/ selves/ another/ others, themselves corresponding to (elements of) *relatively* individually/ collectively mathematically/ physically/ economically (in)determinate physical/ fiscal/ financial principles and/ or processes pertaining to (potential)*knowledge* of/ *characteristics* of/ *experience* of *gifts/ thefts/ barters/ trades*.

Interpretations of these kinds suggest (re)consideration of potentially interrelated elements of the (sub)system (5.13) from a perspective of elements of change(s)/ exchange(s)/ motion(s) as if among other things potentiating/ potentiated via (changes in) elements of relatively decentralized *microeconomic* and/ or relatively centralized *macroeconomic* mathematical/ physical...physical/ fiscal/ financial supply- demand determined (self) contradictions/ changes/ exchanges.

With a relatively naive perspective of narrowly input-output relations/interpretations/processes, they might return attention to measures S_i in the following relations of (5.13) as if potentially (re)generating/(re)generated via elements of supply-demand relations/ interrelations/processes via interpretations as follows (see also Chapter 3):

$\sum_j a_{ij}x_j$	+	y_i	+	S_i	=	x_i
Intermediate		Final		Net		Output
Input		Output		Excess		Supply
Demand		Demand		Demand		

This suggests interpretations for the measures S_i variously in relation to net *excess supply* (if +ve) and net *excess demand* (if -ve) in turn suggesting classes of potentially interrelated interpretations for elements of the measure S_i *respectively* : i) in relation to potentiations of/ potentiations via relative transmissions *to other* relatively different and/ or distant locations in relative space-time (e.g. via disposal/storage and/ or out-shipment) *and* ; ii) in relation to potentiations of/ potentiations via relative transmissions *from other* relatively different and/ or distant locations in space-time (e.g. via retrievals from storage and/ or inshipment).

These remarks, even if considered alone, suggest potential goal programming -like interpretations -and, as specializations of these, potential linear programming -like interpretations, for elements of (5.13) via recognition of the relatively *unrestricted* magnitudes and sign(s) of (elements of) the net excess supply-demand measures S_i by means of translations/ transformations as if identically:

$$S_i = S_i^+ - S_i^-$$

with relatively disaggregated elements of such a relationship potentiating/ potentiated via inshipments ΣS_{ik} and outshipments to relatively *accessible*[4] regions/ states/ locations k* according to conditions as if together:

$$S_i = \sum_k S_{ik} - \sum_k S_{ki}$$

For those familiar with them, such conditions will suggest *generalized network* structures as if potentiating/ potentiated via elements of two-way changes/ exchanges/ trades, and as specializations of these, will recall elements of apparently more primitive *distribution* -like structures, in such contexts apparently open to interpretations as if purposively potentiating/ potentiated via relatively individual/ collective gains to one-way trade(s).

More subtly the wider context provided by further constraints of (5.13) as if variously:

$$y_i + y_i^+ - y_i^- = y_i^*$$

$$x_i + x_i^+ - x_i^- = x_i^*$$

suggests elements of goal programming -like structures and interpretations according to which relatively (dis)aggregated individuals/ groups/ societies might act as if purposively to generate greater/ lesser measures of relative difference between *planned* and *realized* production levels, (e.g. output levels, production capacity levels, investment levels, retention levels) and/ or *planned* and *realized* consumption levels (e.g. consumption levels, savings levels, capital consumption goods levels...).

They also suggest interpretations according to which relatively (dis)*aggregated* elements of measures S_i might as if *purposively* potentiate and/ or be as if *purposively* potentiated via relatively individually/ collectively determined *differences between* relatively (de)*centralized planned* and *realized* (potential) production levels x_i, x_i* and (potential) consumption levels according to conditions as if:

$$\sum_j a_{ij}x_j^* + \sum_j a_{ij}x_j^+ - \sum_j a_{ij}x_j^- + y_i^* + y_i^- - y_i^- = x_i^*$$

Narrowly construed, via the measures x_j^+, x_j^-, y_i^+, y_i^-, these relations will recall developments on p.61 above and appear open to interpretations as if potentiating/ potentiated via "errors" relative to a more narrowly defined "input-output" specification.

By potentiating principles and processes of (self) contradiction relative to elements of measures x_j^*, y_i^*, x_j^+, x_j^-, y_i^+, y_i^-, such relations appear open to interpretations as if potentially systematically/ algorithmically purposively potentiating elements of relatively individual/ collective. ..gains/ losses via the specification of potentials for relatively individually/ collectively *purposive* errors relative to elements of, therefore only *relatively*, individually/ collectively standardized mathematical/ physical/ fiscal/ financial input -output structures/ principles/ processes.

By means of such potential measures, elements of the goal programming -like constraints of (5.13) may be seen to be explicitly open to inter -pretations according to which individuals/ groups might act as if purposively systematically and algorithmically sequentially and/or cyclically to potentiate relatively *more/ greater* uncertainty/ incompleteness/ indeterminacy relative to self/ selves as if thereby purposively to potentiate more/greater *opportunities* relative to self/ selves/ another/ others potentially differently located in relative space-time.

And/ or, interpreting measures a_{ij}, x_j* as if respectively corresponding to elements of as if contingently optimal *payoffs* and contingently optimal *strategies* within then contingently game-like structures, measures x_j^+, x_j^-, y_i^+, y_i^-, y_i* (y_i, S_i) may appear open to interpretations as if potentially corresponding to elements of *further* and relatively *unknown* contingent payoffs and contingent strategies.

Such measures then appear open to interpretations as if potentiating elements of relatively *more* mathematically/ physically *knowable* strategies/ outcomes/ payoffs relative to self/selves/ another/ others potentially differently located in relative space-time *via* as if (currently) systematically/ algorithmically, sequentially/ cyclically *purposive* (re)generation(s) of relatively *less knowable* (relatively incomplete/ indeterminate/ uncertain) strategies/ outcomes/ payoffs relative to self/ selves.

Apart from relations to elements of relatively individual/ collective supply -demand interpretations, and/ or elements of potential principles and processes open to interpretations as if themselves potentiating/ potentiated via elements of more *for* less, more *from* less and/ or more *for* nothing or more *from* (relatively) *nothing* principles and processes, such remarks can focus attention more primitively upon classes of more narrowly *algorithmic* interpretations with reference to elements of (5.13) on p.122

They might suggest classes of interpretation of measures x_i^+, x_i^- as if identically $x_j^+ = \infty$, $-xj^- = -\infty$ in turn suggesting interpretations variously corresponding respectively to relatively sequentially/ cyclically "next", relatively sequentially/ cyclically "preceding" and/ or to *orders of orders* relatively sequentially/ cyclically bounded/ unbounded evaluations of elements variously of the constraints and/ or of the objective of the (sub)system (5.13).

This suggests *semi-infinite programming* interpretations for elements of *both of* the related systems (5.13), (5.13)' as if potentiating/ potentiated via elements of the constraints of (5.13) and/ or elements of *preemptive goal programming* interpretations for elements of the objective of (5.13) as if themselves perfectly predictively potentiating/ potentiated via conditions as if identically $C_{xj}^+ > 0$, $C_{xj}^- > 0$.

More subtly, interpretations as if identically $x_j^+ = \infty$, $x_j^- = -\infty$, particularly if viewed with contexts of potentially systematic/ algorithmic mathematical/ physical principles/ processes of change/ exchange/ motion relative to elements of the (sub)system (5.13), suggest consideration of potential sequences of changes/ exchanges/ motions as if themselves potentiating/ potentiated via *orders of orders of infinities* -orders open to interpretation as if variously potentiating/ potentiated via (elements of) *earlier/ later*, *larger/ smaller* relative to individuals/ groups potentially differently located in space -time relative to self/ selves/ another/ others.

Such considerations suggest related perspectives according to which (elements of) these systems may be interpreted as if potentiating/ potentiated via principles/ processes of as if individually/ collectively purposively *contingently* individually/ collectively *(un)bounded rationality*.

More directly they suggest relations to principles and processes of relatively individual/ collective mathematical/ physical (self) contradiction according to which, individuals/ groups may act as if purposively to determine relatively *more abstract* relatively *further inside* relative to self/ selves as if thereby to potentiate opportunities relatively *further outside* relative to (elements of)self/ selves/ another/ others potentially differently located in relative space-time.

More precisely elements of the objective and of the constraints of the (sub)system (5.13) appear open to relatively linear/ nonlinear, integer/ noninteger principles and/or processes of (self) contradiction according to which individuals might act as if purposively to determine relatively *less* relative to a relatively abstract preference/ indifference/ welfare measure relative to self/selves as if thereby systematically/ algorithmically/ sequentially/ cyclically to potentiate relatively *more* relative to a relatively abstract preference/ indifference/ welfare measure relative to self/ selves/ another/ others potentially differently/ distantly located in relative space-time.

Especially when viewed with the context of the preceding developments, these remarks suggest roles for individually/ collectively/ socially/ professionally systematic *exploitations* relative to relatively standardized mathematical/ physical/ fiscal/ financial units.[5] With a context of (5.13) they suggest roles, too, for as if individually/ collectively/ socially/ professionally systematic *gains via exploitations* of elements of principles and processes of relatively individual/ collective mathematical/ physical contradictions/changes/ exchanges/ motions as if potentially *purposively* (re)*generating/* (re)*generated* via elements of linear (in)dependence and duality principles as if themselves relatively (im)perfectly predictive of/predicted via elements of that system.

5.2 Linear dependence, goal programming and duality

Consider the following relations:

$$\mu_i \qquad \sum_j a_{ij}x_j = ?\ 0$$

Now employ the magnitudes μ_i and a conditional linear dependence argument to generate the following relations as if themselves conditionally expressive of linear dependence/ independence:

$$x_j \qquad \sum_i a_{ij}\mu_i = ?\ 0$$

Each of these related and isomorphic systems of relations is open to interpretations *variously* in relation to relative completeness/ incompleteness, to relative linearity/ nonlinearity, to relative certainty/ uncertainty *and* in relation to equality, inequality, identity.

More deeply such relations may be used not just to give prominence (as in Chapter 1) to questions and to potential answers in general but to give prominence to questions as if *themslves potentiating* means of conditionally generating answers *and/ or* of conditionally generating further classes of potential mathematical/ physical questions.

In context such questions may pertain to relative mathematical/ physical completeness/ incompleteness, to relative mathematical/ physical linearity/ nonlinearity, to relative mathematical/ physical certainty/ uncertainty and/ or relative equality, inequality, identity.

More primitively, if, for example, a relation as if $\Sigma a_{ij}x_j = 0$ is interpreted as if *complete* then, apparently, at least *two* statements $a_{ir}x_r$, $a_{is}x_s$ must be of relatively *opposite signs* (recalling developments in other Chapters as if potentially mathematically/ physically generating/ generated via relative opposition of relative signs).

If such an opposition obtains, and if (restrictively) the quantities $|a_{ir}x_r|$, $|a_{is}x_s|$, are as if equivalent in absolute magnitude then, according to one class of interpretations, conditions obtain as if these two magnitudes net to "zero".

Potential for interpretations of this latter kind will be clearer if the above questions are considered as if explicitly related respectively as follows :

$$\mu_i \qquad \sum_j a_{ij}x_j + x_i^+ - x_i^- = \theta_i b_i$$

$$x_i \qquad \sum_j a_{ij}\mu_j + \mu_j^+ - \mu_j^- = \theta_j c_j$$

Underlining the potential for correspondences between these statements and the above questions, notice that interpretations as if potentially variously $b_i = 0$, $b_i \neq 0$ (respectively variously $c_j = 0$, $c_j \neq 0$), apparently correspond to one class of specialized interpretations of the statements $\Sigma a_{ij}x_j = ?\ 0$ and/or statements as if variously $x_i^+ - x_i^- > 0$, < 0, $= 0$ to others (with the last again emphasizing potential for incompleteness as if completeness/ completeness as if incompleteness).

Recalling now that linear *dependence* arguments were used to relate statements $\Sigma a_{ij}x_j = ?\ 0$, $\Sigma a_{ij}\mu_i = ?\ 0$, now use such arguments also with reference to the immediately preceding statements to generate :

$$\sum_j \theta_j c_j x_j = ? \qquad\qquad \sum_i \theta_i \mu_i b_i = ?$$

$$\sum_j a_{ij}x_j + x_i^+ - x_i^- = \theta_i b_i \qquad\qquad \sum_i a_{ij}\mu_i + \mu_i^+ - \mu_i^- = \theta_j c_j$$

$$x_j^+ = ?\ 0 \quad (5.14) \qquad\qquad \mu_i^+ = ?\ 0 \quad (5.14)'$$

$$-x_j^- = ?\ 0 \qquad\qquad -\mu_i^- = ?\ 0$$

The latter statements (e.g. $x_j^+ = ?\ 0$), $\mu_i^+ = ?\ 0$) are similar in kind to those with which I began this Section (e.g. $\Sigma a_{ij}x_j = ?\ 0$, $\Sigma a_{ij}\mu_i = ?\ 0$) except that, in them, the analogues of measures "a_{ij}" are as if identical to "1"s. This remark suggests connections to issues pertaining to the potential (re)generation of relations and /or interrelations between orders of orders of different arithmetic magnitudes *in general*, while focussing attention upon potential relations and interrelations and/ or potential differences between (orders of) measures x_j^+, x_j^-, x_j and 1, 0, -1 in particular.

Now incorporate measures c_i^+, c_i^- (resp. $\tilde{c}_j^+$, $\tilde{c}_j^-$) into the objectives of (5.14), (5.14)' and reconsider them as if potentially generating/ potentially generated via the following relations and interrelations:

$$\sum_j \theta_j c_j x_j - \sum_i c_i^+ x_i^- - \sum_i c_i^- x_i^- \qquad\qquad \sum_i \theta_i \mu_i b_i - \sum_j \tilde{c}_j^+ \mu_j^+ - \sum_j \tilde{c}_j^- \mu_j^-$$

$$\sum_j a_{ij}x_j + x_i^+ - x_i^- = \theta_i b_i \qquad\qquad \sum_i a_{ij}\mu_i + \mu_j^+ - \mu_j^- = \theta_j c_j$$

$$x_j + x_j^+ = ?\ -\tilde{c}_j^+ \quad (5.15) \qquad\qquad \mu_i + \mu_i^+ = ?\ -c_i^+ \quad (5.15)'$$

$$-x_j - x_j^- = ?\ -\tilde{c}_j^- \qquad\qquad -\mu_i - \mu_i^- = ?\ -c_i^-$$

The form of these systems suggests the potential for the generation of goal programming models, methods and interpretations in general as if via linear dependence arguments in particular.

With a context of goal programming consider the first relation in (5.15) as if potentially corresponding to an objective as if purposively to *maximize* the measure $\Sigma\theta_j c_j x_j$ while also acting as if purposively to *minimize* measures $\Sigma c_i^+ x_i^+$, $\Sigma c_i^- x_i^-$.

The preceding paragraph suggests *game-like* interpretations according to which, via relatively individual/ collective orderings over measures x_j, x_i^+, x_i^- individuals and groups may construe themselves/be construed as if purposively systematically acting/ reacting/ interacting to determine an as if agreed relative *maximum* (minimum) relative to self/ selves as if via the *potentiation* of an as if agreed relative *minimum* (maximum) relative to another/ others.

This may be achieved via sequences of mathematical/ physical principles/ processes as if, for example, *systematically* measures x_i^+ (resp. x_i^-) relatively *exterior* to self/ selves might potentiate *less* (more) relative to self/ selves as if thereby to potentiate *more* (less) relative to a system relative to self/ selves, as if in turn among other things *via* that system, to potentiate *more* (less) relative to relatively *unknown* selves/ others relatively differently/ distantly located in space-time.

From such a perspective measures x_i^+, x_i^- will appear open to interpretations not just as if together potentiating/ potentiated via relative "slack", but as if potentially systematically algorithmically potentiating *more* relative to relatively differently/ distantly located selves/ others via the potentiation of *less* relative to self/ selves - in turn again directly suggesting potential classes of potential mathematical/ physical structures as if themselves contingently perfectly predictive of relatively integer/ non-integer "distribution" or "generalized network" principles and processes via classes of relations and interpretations for example as if identically $x_i^+ = \Sigma x_{ij} = \theta_i b_i$, $x_i^- = \Sigma x_{ij} = \Sigma a_{ij} x_j$.

For example via consideration of measures x_i^+, x_i^- in contexts of relations as if :

$$\sum_j a_{ij} x_j + x_i^+ - x_i^- = \theta_i b_i$$

components of the (sub)system (5.15) might suggest potential classes of interpretations pertaining to relative mathematical/ physical change(s)/ exchange(s) according to which not only might *what is less* (more) relative to an individual/ group construe itself/ be construed as if purposively to potentiate/ be as if purposively potentiated via *what was more*(less) relative to another/ others differently located in space-time, but related classes of relations/ interpretations/ processes according to which :

i) what is relatively *feasible* relative to an individual/ group might construe itself/ be construed as potentially systematically/ algorith -mically potentiating/ potentiated via what had become *infeasible* relative to another/ others ;

ii) what is relatively *known* relative to an individual/ group might construe itself/ be construed as if potentially systematically/ algorithmically potentiating/potentiated via what *has become relatively unknown* to another/ others;

iii) what is relatively *negative* relative to an individual/ group might construe itself/be construed as if potentially systematically/ algorithmically potentiating/ potentiated via what *becomes* relatively *positive* relative to a system, in turn potentiating/ potentiated via what *will be* relatively *positive* relative to another/ others (and relatively *negative* relative to a system). *And/or*:

iv) what *is* relatively *smaller* relative to self/ selves might potentiate what *will be* be relatively *larger* relative to another/ others differently/ distantly located in relative space-time.... .

Notice that conditions as if $x_j^+ = ? -\tilde{c}_j^+$, $x_j^- = ? \tilde{c}_j^-$ are not only open to interpretations as if themselves potentiating/potentiated via elements of classes of related interpretations, such as those just considered, but, via associated measures μ_j^+, μ_j^- and linear dependence arguments, as if potentially systematically generating/ generated via *otherwise relatively infeasible* solutions to elements of the system of relations :

$$\sum_j a_{ij}\mu_i + \mu_j^+ - \mu_j^- = \theta_j c_j$$

in turn, among other things, as if via measures μ_i, potentiating/ potentiated via (changes in) other elements of relatively *infeasible* solutions, to conditions of a relatively "primal" system (5.15).

These remarks will not just draw attention to potential classes of mathematical/ physical principles/ processes as if themselves potentiating/potentiated elements of "price"/ "quantity" changes/ exchanges relative to self/ selves/ another/ others, but here, will return attention to classes of potentially systematic/ algorithmic principles/processes open to interpretation as if themselves systematically/ algorithmically potentiating *any and all* elements of *any and all* orders of potentially relatively (de)centralized mathematical/ physical (sub)systems according to relatively individual/ collective uncertainty/ indeterminacy/ incompleteness principles/ processes whereby what is relatively (un)*known* relative to an individual/ group might as if *systematically potentiate* or be as if *systematically potentiated via* what might be/ become potentially *knowable* relative to another/ others.

The isomorphism between the immediately preceding remarks in relation to the (sub)systems (5.15), (5.15)' with remarks made in relation to the (sub)systems (5.13), (5.13)' in Section 1 will suggest consideration of particular classes of as if perfectly predictive relations/ interpret -ations/ processes according to which elements of the (sub)system (5.13) of the previous Section may be construed as if variously perfectly predictive of and/or as if identical to elements of the (sub)system (5.15)in this Section.

From that perspective it might seem that the system (5.13) is arguably *more* generally applicable than (5.15), insofar as measures x_j, y_i are open to interpretations as if potentially explicitly distinguishing between (elements of) production commodities and of consumption commodities.

Once it is recognized that the system (5.15) may potentially admit *partitions* of the measures x_j to comprehend classes of interpretations as if potentially implicitly comprehending elements *both* of (potential) production commodities and of (potential) consumption commodities, it becomes apparent that the system (5.15) is not just arguably more *simple* than (5.13), but arguably more *generally applicable* - and in that sense more fundamental - than (5.13).

Focusing on just one facet of this, interpretations as if (potential) measures of (elements of) consumption commodities relative to individuals potentially stem directly from (relatively incomplete predictions of) measures x_j in (5.15), suggest *contingently objective* goods -characteristic interpretations as if relative to an individual/ group of individuals i, potential commodities-characteristics technologies may obtain as if identically $x_{ij} = y_{ij}$ for some i, j and

$$c_{ik} = \sum_{j}^{k} a_{ij} x_{ij}$$

Such conditions anticipate further extensions to Lancaster- like goods-characteristics analyses and interpretations in the next two Chapters.

5.3 Conclusion

Developments here have suggested ways in which individuals/ groups might act as if purposively systematically/ algorithmically to generate and to exploit relative mathematical/ physical indeterminacy/ incompleteness/ uncertainty principles and processes relative to self/ selves/another/ others as if thereby to potentiate relative gains/ losses (including gains/ losses of knowledge, of information, of individuals and/ or of commodities) *all* as if themselves potentially systematically/ algorithmically (re)generating/ (re)generated via elements of individually/ collectively purposive relatively linear/ nonlinear, integer/ noninteger (self) *contradiction* and elements of potentially associated relative linear (in)dependence/ *duality* principles and processes relative to self/ selves/ another/ others potentially differently located in relative space-time.

Footnotes

1. In such a context potential classes of as if optimally non-regulated *and/or* fully decentralized cases might correspond to classes of cases for which conditions obtain as if *contingently* relative tax/ subsidy measures R_i, K_j equate to zero. Notice that in an hierarchical context,potential output/ consumption measures x_i, y_i and/or regulatory measures R_i, K_j might in general relate to *more than one* private and/ or social objectve. Going further, different and in general potentially mutually *inconsistent* (e.g. production, consumption, construction, storage....) objectives may be associated with different levels of relative social/ geographical (dis)aggregation (e.g. international, national, state, city, personal) in relative space-time.

2. See the opening sentences of Chapter 1.

3. Notice that *more* as in the context *more* (un)known opportunities is essentially ambiguous and apparently open to interpretations *variously* : i) in relation to *degrees* of uncertainty/ risk/ certainty ; ii) in relation to more *different kinds* of relatively (un)known opportunities/ strategies/ outcomes *and/or* ; iii) in relation to more, in quantity/ magnitude of *particular* kinds of, nevertheless *relatively* mathematically/ physically....(un)known mathematical/ physical.. ..opportunities/ strategies/ outcomes.

4. In general states are *not* directly accessible to each other — (potential) accessibility in general will connote elements of potential *processes* of translations/ transformations in space-time. On this point with particular reference to potential principles and processes of potential capital formation see developments early in Chapter 8.

5. See also Section 3 of Chapter 3.

References

{1} Charnes, A. (1952), *Optimality and Degeneracy in Linear Programming*, Econometrica 20, No 2.

{2} Charnes,A., Clower, R.W. and Kortanek K.O. (1967), *Effective Control through Coherent Decentralization with Preemptive Goals*, Econometrica 35, No 2.

{3} Charnes, A.,Duffuaa, S. and Ryan, M.J. (1987), *The More for Less Paradox in Linear Programming*, European Journalof Operational Research 31, pp.194-197.

{4} Ryan M.J. (1992), *Constrained Gaming Approaches to Decisionmaking Under Uncertainty*, European Journal of Operational Research (Forthcoming).

6 Lancaster-like characteristics and bases for regulation and self regulation in first best economies: The Crusoe case

6.1 Introduction

The primary purpose of this Chapter is to show how Lancaster's approach to consumer theory can be adapted and developed in ways which establish positive roles for self regulation – and ultimately for taxation, subsidies and other forms of government regulation – in determinations of "first best" allocations and (re)distributions of resources and products, even in a world of (suitably modified) "pure" competition.

This central point is established in stages. In this Part attention is confined to a single individual, it being shown that his optimal consumption plan can be both represented and found by means of particular kinds of nonlinear programming problems, which are related to particular kinds of goal programming problems with associated duality and decentralization properties and processes, as well as to particular kinds of essentially process-oriented Lancaster-like commodities- characteristics analyses.

In the next two Sections such representations and analyses are developed in ways which can be related, respectively, to consumption and to production oriented microeconomic analyses of conventional types.

Particular emphasis will be put on intertemporal consistency issues. But by contrast with approaches such as those of Blackorby and others {2} attention here will focus not so much upon consistency properties, for example on consistency properties of axiomatically continuous and differentiable preference/ indifference relations, but upon processes of mathematical, physical and economic decision making in general, and of purposively induced mathematical, physical and economic processes of self *inconsistency* and self *contradiction* in particular.

Prominent among developments of the latter kind will be cases open to interpretation as themselves potentiated via mathematical, physical and economic distinctions between preferences and characteristics relative to a relatively abstract self, and measures on such preferences and characteristics generated via transactions relative to elements of a wider system.

With this context the considerably enhanced role for Lancaster-like characteristics analysis which is the central focus of Sections 3 and 4 will already be evident. There the principal focus of attention will be upon new kinds of exploitations of distinctions (and self contradictions) already immanent in such analyses, between individuals' characteristics based, and relatively *abstractly* personal (i.e. relatively *theoretical*) potentiations of preference/ indifference relations relative to self, and individuals' commodity related, and relatively *non-abstractly* personal (i.e. *empirical*) *realizations* relative to characteristics based preference/ indifference relations relative to a wider system.

In Sections 3 and 4 the mathematical, physical and economic inevitability of distinctions and contradictions between elements of relatively abstract measures relative to self, and relatively non abstract measures relative to elements of a wider subsystem, are shown to provide natural motivations :

i) for standard physical, fiscal and financial measures in general, and for elements of measures isomorphic with elements of tax and subsidy in particular and, more subtly ;

ii) for potentials to generate relative mathematical, physical and economic *gains* (*losses*) relative to self, another and/or relative to a wider system deriving from the *inevitability* of processes of mathematical/ physical contradiction and inconsistency relative to a relatively abstract self, if that self is to interact in an essentially non abstract manner relative to elements of a wider system.

Those familiar with goal programming principles[1] may already intuit their central role in all that follows. Goal programming principles and processes are in any case open to interpretation *as if purposively* potentiating/ potentiated via relative mathematical/ physical *infeasibilities* and *impossibilities* and essentially related principles and processes of mathematical/ physical (self) contradiction.

But here goal programming -like principles and processes are recognized as open to interpretation as if potentiating mathematically physically and economically fundamental distinctions between relatively *abstract*, "nonlinear" and *personal* preference/ indifference measures relative to self, and relatively *non-abstract*, "linear" and *standardized* physical, fiscal and financial regulatory measures relative to a wider system relative to self.

In this Part attention focuses on single individual "Crusoe" economies and, with that context, on appropriate determinations of relatively abstract preference/ indifference relations relative to self as if purposively thereby to potentiate particular kinds of intertemporally optimal interactions with a wider system, *all* with the objective of *gain* relative to a relatively abstract self relatively differently and distantly located in space-time.

In Part II, with the relaxation of the single individual assumption, more subtle and complex classes of analyses and interpretations emerge. Among these are new perspectives on classes of cases which in general terms will be familiar. These include cases according to which two or more individuals may act as if purposively to potentiate less relative to self/ selves as if thereby, by variously altruistically or selfishly oriented principles and processes of giving/ taking, bartering or trading, to potentiate relatively more/ less relative to another/ others potentially differently/ distantly located in space-time.

In such more generally specified n person cases relatively standardized physical, fiscal or financial units have potentials for more purpose and meaning in general than in the single person case. Also, particular kinds of explicitly (self) regulatory instruments such as relatively standard -izing laws, weights and measures, prices, taxes, subsidies, money or budgets take on richer - because more usefully explicitly distinct - meaning than their generally implicit analogues in the single person case.

Summarizing : in what follows it will be seen that single person cases as well as n person cases provide :

i) positive roles for as if purposively induced principles and/ or processes of mathematical/ physical indeterminacy/ incompleteness relative to self among other things including relative indeterminacy/ incomplete -ness/ uncertainty as if purposively induced by an individual or group relative to a relatively abstract self as if thereby to potentiate *more* relative to self/ selves/ another/ others potentially differently located in space-time. *And/or* ;

ii) with contexts of potential principles and processes of as if purposive (self) contradiction as if themselves purposively potentiating/ potentiated via elements of gifts/ thefts/ barters or trades, *both* single person *and* n person cases may provide roles for sequential/ cyclical changes/ exchanges *founded upon* potentials for *exploitations* of principles and/ or processes of contradiction of relatively abstract individual/ collective preference orderings by individuals and/ or groups relative to self/ selves/ another/ others.

The latter points relate directly to central issues and problems in the collective choice literature and will be extended and developed further, again with the aid of Lancaster-like characteristics based individual and collective preference/ indifference/ welfare relations, in Part II.

6.2 Some preliminary analyses and examples

Assume that an individual (Crusoe) has a stock, x_o, of a divisible, non-perishable consumption commodity for which there are no substitutes. He knows that his remaining life span is T periods and that conditions of certainty will prevail throughout the interval from the present (period 1) to period T. His problem is to allocate his stock of this single scarce commodity to his own consumption over this interval.

Following Blackorby and others {2} assume that the individual is able to order all possible potential consumption levels and thereby to determine a strictly quasi-concave and consistent preference ordering of the form:

$$U_t = U_t(x_t,\ U_{t+1}),\quad t = 1,2.,.T\text{-}1,\ U_T = U_T(x_T)$$

where x_t is the planned level of consumption in period t

Now consider a number of apparently equivalent, because apparently alternative, ways of representing and determining this individual's intertemporally optimal consumption plan under these simplified conditions as follows :

1. The optimal plan, if one exists, could be represented by the vector $x^* = \{x_1^*,\ x_2^* \ldots x_T^*\}'$ or, equivalently, as the solution to a choice problem represented as follows:[3]

$$U_1^* = \textit{Maximize}\ U_1(x_1(U_2(x_2,\ U_3(x_3, U\ldots)$$

$$\lambda_{1t} \qquad \text{subject to:} \qquad x_t = x_t^* \qquad (1_t) \quad (I)$$

It might seem that, by associating the indicated Lagrange multipliers λ_{1t} with the conditions (1_t), the following conditions might be generated :

$$\frac{\delta U_1}{\delta x_1} = \lambda_{11},\quad \frac{\delta U_1}{\delta x_t} = \frac{\delta U_1}{\delta U_2}\cdot\frac{\delta U_2}{\delta U_3}\ \frac{\delta U_t}{\delta x_t} = \lambda_{1t} \qquad (1_t)'$$

or, recursively:

$$\frac{\delta U_1}{\delta x_t} / \frac{\delta U_1}{\delta x_{t-1}} = \frac{\lambda_{1t}}{\lambda_{1t-1}}$$

Notice that conditions $(1_t)'$ imply *differentiation* of the measure U_1 which, if considered (as here) in the context of the system (I) - because implying *variations* of the measures x_t -itself implies not just contradictions *of*, but potentials for as if purposive (self) contradictions *via*, elements of conditions (1_t) of that system.

2. The following representation (II) might appear open to interpret -ation as if potentiating an equivalent, yet alternative, representation to (I) by apparently making explicit provision for potential processes of (self) contradiction, among other things via *explicit* potentials for (self) contradiction/ change inherent in the conditions (1t):

$$U_1{}^* = \textit{Maximize } U_1(x_1, U_2(x_2, U_3(x_3 \ldots) - M_t \sum_t (x_t{}^+ + x_t{}^-)$$

subject to:

$$\bar{\lambda}_{1t} \qquad x_t + x_t{}^+ - x_t{}^- = x_t{}^* \qquad (\bar{1}_t) \quad \text{(II)}$$

Again introducing Lagrange multipliers $\bar{\lambda}_{1t}$ as indicated, it might seem that these conditions potentiate relations as if:

$$\frac{\delta U_1}{\delta x_1} = \lambda_{11}, \ \frac{\delta U_1}{\delta x_t} = \frac{\delta U_1}{\delta U_2} \cdot \frac{\delta U_2}{\delta U_3} \ldots \frac{\delta U_t}{\delta x_t} = \bar{\lambda}_{1t} \qquad (\bar{1}_t)'$$

By contrast with (I), in (II) explicit processes of variation of measures x_t and thence of U_t would *not* contradict the specification II, *and yet,* interpreting measures M_t as implicitly of arbitrarily large magnitude, by inspection conditions as if *optimally* $x_t{}^+ = 0$, $x_t{}^- = 0$, $x_t = x_t{}^*$ together constitute an optimal *solution* to (II), as well as an arguably *optimally determined specification* for the system (I).

The optimality of such a specification is arguable in either case since the underlying choice problem might arguably be more appropriately expressed in ways which make the intertemporal consumption resource condition $\Sigma x_t = x_o$ explicit as follows :

$$U_1{}^* = \textit{Maximize } U_1(x_1, U_2(x_2, U_3 (x_3 \ldots)$$

subject to:

$$\varphi_1 \qquad \sum_t x_t = x_o \qquad (1o) \quad \text{(III)}$$

Introducing the Lagrange multiplier φ_1 it might seem that the system (III) implies relations as follows:

$$\frac{\delta U_1}{\delta x_1} = \varphi_1, \ \frac{\delta U_1}{\delta x_t} = \frac{\delta U_1}{\delta U_2} \frac{\delta U_2}{\delta U_3} \ldots \frac{\delta U_t}{\delta x_t} = \varphi_1 \qquad (1_o)'$$

or:

$$\frac{\delta U_1}{\delta x_1} = \frac{\delta U_1}{\delta U_2} = \frac{\delta U_t}{\delta x_t} = \varphi_1$$

According to these conditions x_o would optimally be allocated to periods $t = 1, \ldots T$ such that *at the margin* the individual would currently (i.e. in period 1) secure *indifference* between increments in optimal consumption levels $(x_1{}^*, x_2{}^* \ldots x_T{}^*)$.

Notice that an optimal solution to (III) might in principle be used to generate optimal *specifications*, and thence optimal solutions to problems (I) and (II), or conversely. *But*, by contrast with the system (I), the system (III) in principle allows intertemporally optimally determined variations in the measures x_t and, by contrast with the system (II) – a specification which also allows variations in the measures x_t –the system (III) explicitly incorporates conditions allowing variations to be consistent with the overall resource availability condition $\Sigma x_t = x_o$.

Using rather more stark terminology, the specification (I) apparently *explicitly permits no change* in measures x_t^*, while, by contrast, the specification (II), through the measures x_t^+, x_t^-, apparently *explicitly permits changes* in measures x_t.

Going further, through the conditions $\Sigma x_t = x_o$ the system (III) apparently not only implicitly *permits* changes in measures x_t, but implicitly *requires* that any such changes connote *intertemporally optimal exchanges* at the margin.

Examples include changes such as to *reduce* a measure x_t at the margin as if thereby to *increase* a measure x_{t+1} at the margin and conversely, or, more generally, changes as if purposively to potentiate *less* in one or more periods as if thereby to potentiate *more* in one or more other periods.

Stressing this latter point, whereas in general a reader observing conditions as above as if variously:

$$\frac{\delta U_1}{\delta x_1} = \lambda_{1t}, \frac{\delta U_1}{\delta x_1} = \bar{\lambda}_{1t}, \frac{\delta U_1}{\delta x_1} = \varphi_1$$

might in each case impute interpretations as if $\delta x_t > 0$ and a preference for more at the margin, the conservative conditions $\Sigma x_t = x_o$ of (III) implicitly require that feasible conditions of change $\Delta x_t \neq 0$ *necessarily* connote essentially conservative conditions of exchange of kinds such that, schematically, $\Delta x_t^+ - \Delta x_t^- = 0$, in turn suggesting fundamental signif -icance for as if purposively induced more-for-less processes in relation to elements of (I), (II), (III) and, more simply, optimally intertemporally *exchange* related interpretations for measures x_t^*, x_t of the system (II).

Whereas the system (II) is arguably incomplete insofar as it explicitly omits the overall resource availability conditions $\Sigma x_t = x_o$, the system (III) is arguably incomplete, too, insofar as it apparently explicitly omits analogues of measures x_t^+, x_t^-. With possibilities of change/ exchange in view now consider the following system:

$$U_1^* = \text{Maximize } U_1(x_1, U_2(x_2, U_3(x_3 \ldots\ldots) - M_t \sum_t (x_t^+ + x_t^-)$$

subject to

$$\begin{aligned} &\bar{\bar{\lambda}}_{1t} \qquad x_t + x_t^+ - x_t^- = x_t^* \qquad (1^=_t) \\ &\bar{\varphi}_1 \qquad \sum_t x_t = x_o \qquad (1^-_o) \end{aligned} \qquad \text{(IV)}$$

Associating the indicated Lagrange multipliers with these conditions, apparently they potentiate relations as follows:

$$\cdot \quad \frac{\delta U_1}{\delta x_1} = \bar{\bar{\lambda}}_{11} + \bar{\varphi}_1, \quad \frac{\delta U_1}{\delta x_t} = \frac{\delta U_1}{\delta U_2} \cdot \frac{\delta U_2}{\delta U_3} \cdots \frac{\delta U_t}{\delta x_t} = \bar{\bar{\lambda}}_{1t} + \bar{\varphi}_1 \qquad (1_t)'$$

By inspection (IV) comprehends (II) and (III) as special cases. Apparently, too, relations $(1^=_t)$, (1^-_o) incorporate conditions (1^-_t) of (II) and $(1_o)_t$ of (III) as special cases.

Indeed, considering (IV) with reference to (III), relations $(1^=_t)$in (IV) - and thence measures $\lambda^=_{1t}$ in $(1^=_t)'$ appear *redundant*. Or, considering (IV) with reference (II), relations $(\bar{1}_o)$ in (IV) - and thence measures $\bar{\varphi}_o$ in$(1^=_t)'$ appear *redundant*.

Going further, relations $\Sigma x_t = x_o$ apparently relate explicitly to *overall* resource availabilities and thence, by implication, measures $\bar{\varphi}_o$ to evaluations of potential increases in *overall* availabilities, whereas relations $x_t + x_t^+ - x_t^- = x_t^*$ apparently relate explicitly to resource availabilities x_t and potential changes in resource availabilities x_t^+, x_t^- in *particular periods* t, and thence, by implication, measures $\lambda^=_{1t}$ to evaluators of potential increases/ decreases in resource availabilities in periods t *relative to* the evaluator of potential increases in overall availability $\bar{\varphi}_o$.

Whereas conditions $(1^=_t)$, (1^-_o) suggest potential for intertemporally optimal determinations of changes/ exchanges relative to potential consumption *quantity* measures x_t, x_o, conditions $(1^=_t)'$ suggest potential for *corresponding* intertemporally optimal *determinations of* changes/ exchanges *relative to* potential consumption *price* measures $\lambda^=_{1t}$, $\bar{\varphi}_1$.

These remarks suggest potentials for classes of interpretations according to which this individual might be represented as if potentially *gaining* relative to a system by acting as if purposively to determine intertemporally optimal consumption plans by means of relatively abstract price/ quantity relations, interrelations and processes.

With such potentials in mind now define :

$$\frac{\delta U_s}{\delta U_{s+1}} = \frac{1}{1 + r_{ss+1}}, \quad \frac{\delta U_s}{\delta x_t} = p_{st}$$

where the measure p_{st} is interpreted as a price associated by this individual with the commodity x_t at the margin in period s and r_{ss+1} represents that individual's time preference rate for potential translations between periods s and s+1.

With these definitions conditions $(1^=_t)'$ of (III) yield the conditions:

$$\frac{\delta U_1}{\delta x_t} = \frac{1}{1 + r_{12}} \frac{\delta U_2}{\delta x_t} = p_{1t}$$

and

$$p_{1t} = \frac{1}{1 + r_{12}} p_{2t}$$

The first of these conditions is evidently open to interpretation as if implying that positive time preference rates $r_{ss+1} > 0$ imply optimal intertemporal allocations such that, at the margin:

$$\frac{\delta U_1}{\delta x_t} / \frac{\delta U_2}{\delta x_t} < 1$$

The second goes further and implies that an individual with positive time preference allocating elements of an endowment x_o over time, if looking forward to consumption in a period t, would *optimally choose* essentially *inflationary* pricing rules according to which:[4]

$$p_{1t} < p_{2t} < \ldots\ldots p_{st}$$

Notice two related but more subtle points, both of them stemming from the relatively objective/ non-objective character of the measures $\delta U_s/\delta x_t, p_{st}$. First, if the relatively abstract preference/ indifference measure $U_1(\ )$ is considered as *ordinal* it follows that a condition as if:

$$\frac{\delta U_s}{\delta x_t} = p_{st}$$

is potentially consistent with *arbitrary* (order preserving) transformations θ_s of the preference relation U_s such that:

$$\theta_s U'_s = \text{def } U_s \quad \text{and} \quad \theta_s \frac{\delta U'_s}{\delta x_t} = p_{st}$$

Secondly, *relative* conditions as if :

$$\frac{p_{1t}}{p_{1t+1}} = \frac{\delta U_1}{\delta x_t} / \frac{\delta U_1}{\delta x_{t+1}}$$

appear potentially consistent with *arbitrary* transformations of *prices* such that :

$$\gamma_1 p_{1t} = \text{def } p_{1t} \qquad \text{or} \qquad \frac{p'_{1t}}{p'_{1t+1}} = \frac{\delta U_1}{\delta x_t} / \frac{\delta U_1}{\delta x_{t+1}}$$

These two remarks together suggest explicitly more generally specified optimization systems than those considered thus far. For example an apparently explicitly more generally specified analogue of (II) as follows:

$$U_1^* = \textit{Maximize } \theta_1 U'_1(x_1, \theta_2 U'_2(x_2, \theta_3 U'_3(x_3 \ldots\ldots) - M_t \sum_t (x_t^+ + x_t^-)$$

subject to:

$$\bar{\lambda}_{1t} \qquad x_t + x_t^+ - x_t^- = x_t^* \qquad (\bar{I}_t) \quad (\bar{II})$$

Associating the indicated Lagrange multipliers with the constraints of $(\overline{II})$ yields:

$$\theta_1 \frac{\delta U'_1}{\delta x_1} = \bar{\lambda}_{11}, \quad \theta_1 \frac{\delta U'_1}{\delta x_t} = \frac{\theta_1}{\theta_2} \frac{\delta U'_1}{\delta U'_2} \cdot \frac{\theta_2}{\theta_3} \cdot \frac{\delta U'_2}{\delta U'_3} \ldots \theta_t \frac{\delta U'_t}{\delta x_t} = \bar{\lambda}_{1t}$$

so that

$$\theta_1 \frac{\delta U'_1}{\delta x_t} / \theta_t \frac{\delta U'_1}{\delta x_{t-1}} = \frac{\bar{\lambda}_{1t}}{\bar{\lambda}_{1t-1}}$$

With conditions as if identically

$$\theta_2 \frac{\delta U'_2}{\delta x_t} = \frac{1}{1 + r_{ss+}} \quad \theta_{s+1} \frac{\delta U'_{s+1}}{\delta x_t}$$

and

$$\theta_s \frac{\delta U'_s}{\delta x_t} = \gamma_s p'_{st}$$

such conditions yield analogues of conditions on p.143 as follows:

$$\frac{\delta U'_s}{\delta x_t} / \frac{\delta U'_s}{\delta x_{t+1}} = \frac{p'_{st}}{p'_{st+1}} = \frac{\bar{\lambda}_{st}}{\bar{\lambda}_{s+1t}}$$

$$\theta_s \frac{\delta U'_s}{\delta x_t} / \theta_{s+1} \frac{\delta U'_{s+1}}{\delta x_t} = \frac{1}{1+r_{s.s+1}}$$

- all *relative* conditions and all apparently *invariant* to transformations variously as if $U_t \rightarrow \theta_t U'_t$ and/ or as if $p_{st} \rightarrow \gamma_s p'_{st}$.

As might be anticipated, if such potential transformations are incorporated into analogous extensions and developments of the apparently explicitly more completely specified system (III), the implications are correspondingly more complex. To see this consider the system :

$$U_1^* = \textit{Maximize}\ \theta_1 U'_1(x_1, \theta_2 U'_2(x_2, \theta_3 U'_3(x_3 \ldots .) \quad - M_t \sum_t (x_t^+ + x_t^-)$$

subject to :

$$\bar{\bar{\underline{\lambda}}}_{1t} \qquad x_t + x_t^+ - x_t^- = x_t^* \qquad (\bar{\bar{\underline{1}}}_t)$$

$$\bar{\underline{\varphi}}_1 \qquad \sum_t x_t = x_o \qquad (\bar{\bar{\underline{1}}}_o) \qquad (\bar{\text{I}}\text{V})$$

Associating the indicated Lagrange multipliers with these relations yields conditions as follows:

$$\theta_1 \frac{\delta U'_1}{\delta x_1} = \bar{\bar{\underline{\lambda}}}_{11} + \bar{\underline{\varphi}}_1, \quad \theta_1 \frac{\delta U'_1}{\delta x_t} = \frac{\theta_1}{\theta_2} \frac{\delta U'_1}{\delta U'_2} \frac{\theta_2}{\theta_3} \frac{\delta U'_2}{\delta U'_3} \ldots \theta_t \frac{\delta U'_t}{\delta x_t} = \bar{\bar{\underline{\lambda}}}_{1t} + \bar{\underline{\varphi}}_1$$

With translations/ transformations as if :

$$\frac{\theta_2 \delta U'_s}{\theta_{s+1} \delta U'_{s+1}} = \text{def}\ \frac{1}{1 + r_{ss+1}}$$

and

$$\theta_s \frac{\delta U'_s}{\delta x_t} = \text{def}\ p_{st} = \gamma_s p'_{st}$$

Conditions again emerge similar in structure and interpretations to those considered on pp.143 and 146 as follows:

$$\frac{\delta U'_s}{\delta x_t} \Big/ \frac{\delta U'_s}{\delta x_{t+1}} = \frac{p'_{st}}{p'_{st+1}} = \bar{\bar{\underline{\lambda}}}_{st} + \bar{\underline{\varphi}}_s \Big/ \bar{\bar{\underline{\lambda}}}_{st+1} + \bar{\underline{\varphi}}_s$$

with

$$\theta_s \frac{\delta U'_s}{\delta x_t} = \frac{1}{1 + r_{ss+1}} \theta_{s+1} \frac{\delta U'_{s+1}}{\delta x_t}$$

Via these definitions, potentially related and essentially inflationary choices of price relations according to which :

$$p_{st} = \frac{1}{1 + r_{ss+1}} p_{s+1t}$$

These suggest classes of relations, interpretations and processes according to which φ_s measure system prices and λ_{st} evaluate relative price *changes* (potentially) variously associated with intertemporally distinct quantity *changes* x_t^+, x_t^- themselves marginal to a system endowment x_o, all in a wider context of potentials for intertemporal optimization via (potentially) fundamentally mathematically/ physically (self) contradictory relations between individual and collective elements of the system (IV).

According to that specification, essentially subjective and *personal* measures U_s, $\theta_s U'_s$ potentiate and/or are as if purposively potentiated via *conflicts with* essentially objective system measures x_o, via essentially *relatively* subjective/ objective relations/ interpretations/ processes themselves potentially determining/ determined via measures λ_{st}', θ_s, γ_s and associated classes of potential relations/ interrelations translations/ transformations relative to measures U'_s, x_t, φ_s.

With such contexts, *actions* relative to self may appear as if purposively induced *deviations* from goals relative to a wider system, and conversely. More evocatively, elements of mathematical/ physical actions relative to a system might appear as if *purposively* inducing/ induced via elements of mathematical/ physical uncertainty/ incompleteness/ indeterminacy principles and/ or processes relative to self.

More directly, given interpretations as if optimally :

$$p_{st} = \theta_s \frac{\delta U'_s}{\delta x_t}$$

with

$$p_{st} = \frac{1}{1+r_{ss+1}} \quad p_{s+1t}$$

apparently:

$$p_{s1}x_o = p_{s1}\sum_t x_t = \sum_t p_{s1}x_t = \sum_{t=1}^{T} \prod_{s=0}^{t} \frac{1}{1+r_{ss+1}} \quad p_{st}x_t$$

Now make the latter conditions explicit in a modification of problem (IV) as follows:

$$U_1{}^* = \textit{Maximize}\ \theta_1 U'_1(x_1,\ \theta_2 U'_2(x_2, \theta_3 U'_3(x_3\ldots.) - M_t \sum_t (x_t{}^+ + x_t{}^-)$$

subject to :

$$\rho_1 \qquad \sum_{t=1}^{T} \prod_{s=0}^{t} \frac{1}{1+r_{ss+1}} \quad p_{st}x_t = p_{s1}x_o$$

$$\underline{\overline{\overline{\lambda}}}_{1t} \qquad x_t + x_t{}^+ - x_t{}^+ = x_t{}^* \qquad (V)$$

$$\overline{\overline{\varphi}}_1 \qquad \sum_t x_t = x_o$$

Associating the indicated Langrange multipliers with the constraints of (V) yields the following conditions :

$$\theta_1 \frac{\delta U'_1}{\delta x_1} = \rho_1 p_{11} + \underline{\overline{\overline{\lambda}}}_{11} + \overline{\overline{\varphi}}_1$$

$$\theta_1 \frac{\delta U'_1}{\delta x_t} = \rho_1 \prod_{s=1}^{t} \frac{p_{st}}{1+r_{ss+1}} + \underline{\overline{\overline{\lambda}}}_{1t} + \overline{\overline{\varphi}}_1$$

Recall that definitions as if:

$$\theta_1 \frac{\delta U'_1}{\delta x_t} = p_{1t} = \underline{\overline{\overline{\lambda}}}_{1t} + \overline{\overline{\varphi}}_1$$

were considered in the context of (IV). With such definitions the measures ρ_1, and thence the associated "budget" relations in (V), might appear redundant

More evocatively, if $\theta_1 \delta U_1/\delta x_t$ is considered as a measure of *change* in relatively *abstract* intertemporal preference/ indifference measures relative to self, and $\underline{\lambda}{=}_{1t}$ as a measure of *change* in *revealed* preference/ indifference relative to a wider (sub)system then those conditions suggest more subtle classes of (potentially) mathematically/ physically systematic contradictions/ changes/ exchanges between elements of a relatively abstract self and relatively abstract elements of a wider subsystem as if themselves among other things potentiating/ potentiated via elements of relatively standardized physical, fiscal and/or financial units.

Again notice apparently fundamental and essential roles for relative indeterminacy/ incompleteness/ uncertainty principles according to which, an individual, if defined as if *wholly and only* relative to a relatively *abstract* self (e.g. via elements of a relatively abstract preference/ indifference measure U'_s) apparently *cannot* interact with elements of a wider mathematical/ physical subsystem *because* defined wholly and only relative to self.

Such an individual may act as if purposively to communicate with another/other elements of a wider subsystem *only if*, among other things, thereby acting as if *purposively* to be/ become mathematically/ physically relatively incomplete/ relatively uncertain/ relatively indeterminate and therefore *necessarily* mathematically/ physically (self) contradictory and (self) inconsistent relative to elements of a wholly and only mathematically/ physically abstractly defined self.

Those seeking explicit representations of potential mathematical/ physical self inconsistency or self contradiction will see them in the preemptive goal programming -like structure of elements of the objective and constraints of (V) and, more subtly, in potential interpretations of elements of that subsystem according to which (changes in) relatively *abstract* preference/ indifference measures $\theta_s U'_s$ defined over relatively *abstract* commodities x_t relative to self, might themselves motivate and/ or be as if purposively motivated via (changes in) relatively *non -abstract* consumption commodities x_t.

More technically, a perspective of *duality* principles and processes, especially if taken together with definitions as if contingently:

$$\theta_s \frac{\delta U'_s}{\delta x_t} = \text{def } p'_{st}$$

in the context of conditions as if (as above):

$$\theta_s \frac{\delta U'_s}{\delta x_t} = \rho_s p_{st} + \underline{\bar{\bar{\lambda}}}_{st} + \bar{\bar{\varphi}}_s$$

might suggest consideration of classes of *contingently* applicable processes according to which elements of the system (V) and of the system (VI) which follows may be/ become as if perfectly predictive of - and/or as if perfectly predicted via -each other[5]:

$$\text{Maximize} \quad \sum_t p_{1t} x_t - M_t \sum_t (x_t^+ + x_t^-)$$

subject to:

$$\sum_t p_{1t} x_t \leq p_{10} x_o \qquad \text{(VI)}$$

$$x_t + x_t^+ - x_t^- = x_t^*$$

$$\sum_t x_t = x_o$$

Relations as if *conditionally* $\theta_s U'_s = \Sigma p_{st} x_t$ suggest potential for essentially self contradictory processes according to which an individual might seek to *dominate* abstract preference/indifference relative to a relatively abstract self by means of actions as if themselves potentiated via processes of (self) contradiction relative to a *relatively* abstract system-related "budget" constraint, and conversely.

For example, an individual might act as if to choose a position relatively *interior* to a currently oriented "budget" condition $p_{10} x_o$ in a period as if *purposively* thereby to potentiate a relatively preferred position relatively *exterior* to a relatively future oriented "budget" condition $p_{1t} x_t$ in period t. Elements of sequences of conditions as if potentially *systematically*:

$$\theta_s U_s \neq \sum_t p_{st} x_t$$

might seem potentially *deireable*, among other things *because* open to interpretation as if potentially systematically potentiating/potentiated via elements of sequences of contradictions of elements of relatively abstract preference relations and/ or budget relations relative to self, relative to each other and/ or relative to a wider system.

More narrowly :

i) if the "budget" relation $\Sigma p_{st}x_t \leqq p_{so}x_o$ is treated as if redundant in (VI), then that system alone suggests a (primitively specified) goal programming problem, whereas, if such a budget condition is treated as *not* redundant that same system suggests a correspondingly extended form of such a primitively specified goal programming problem ;

ii) if conditions obtain *as if only* the "budget" constraint is applicable to (VI), i.e. if the "goal" and resource constraint conditions appear redundant, then, to those familiar with standard microeconomic analyses, the consequently reduced system will suggest a standard form of intertemporal choice specification.

Indeed (VI) might not only suggest an explicitly more complete form of intertemporal choice specification than those of standard types, but a specification which implicitly embodies a fundamental critique of such standard approaches through its *explicit* emphasis on potential for *process*(es) of change/ exchange as if themselves potentiating/ potentiated via elements of mathematical/ physical self contradiction in general, and potential principles and processes of mathematical/ physical self contradiction/ change/ exchange as if systematically potentiating/ potentiated via relatively linear/ nonlinear elements of the potentially interrelated systems (V), (VI) in particular.

Here there are potential implications of measures x_t^+, x_t^- *not just* as if potentiating/ potentiated via elements of principles and processes of intertemporally optimizing change/ exchange in general, *but* potential interpretations of those measures as if potentiating/potentiated via essentially goal oriented *regulation* and *control* principles and processes, even for an individual relating only to a relatively abstract self, or to elements of a wider mathematical/ physical subsystem in particular.

Less subtly, by recognizing the (sub)system (VI) as potentially comprehending elements of a relatively primitive goal programming system, the reader might recognize that system as itself suggesting potential for extensions to comprehend apparently more comprehensive production and/ or consumption related specifications.

Particular kinds of "land" and "capital" oriented production processes, as well as particular kinds of characteristics oriented consumption processes are considered in some detail for the single individual case in the following Section and in Section 4 respectively, before turning to consideration of n-individual cases and problems in the next Chapter.

6.3 A single individual economy with production

In the previous Section attention was restricted to a one commodity world with no production (unless inventory holding and disbursement are counted under this head). Concomittantly with the absence of production the only form of capital in the preceding analyses was the initial holding of the commodity in each period. Also labour was omitted from consideration, it being implicitly assumed that the act of consuming was itself a desireable "leisure" activity. The purposes of this Section are twofold. First to extend preceding analyses to comprehend elements of capital, including working capital, and of labour, and, secondly, in doing so, to extend the preemptive goal formulation to include labour and physical capital in particular goal-oriented ways.

These developments will emphasize that in general labour inputs will be essentially heterogeneous in character and, more subtly, that employment activities might contribute variously and positively as well as negatively to preference related characteristics. Also elements of physical capital are necessary inputs to capital formation.

In order to analyse these and related points the formulation of the intertemporal choice problem is extended so that preferences are explicitly defined over leisure as well as consumption related activities and to include two types of capital z_{1t}, z_{2t} as well as an initial endowment.

These two types of physical capital might be thought of as two types of land area, one undeveloped and one developed via conversion to production (e.g. tillage) and the initial endowment x_0 as contingently yielding either elements of input to production or elements of input to consumption.[7]

Consider the following extremal representation:[8]

$$U_1^* = \text{Maximize } \theta_1 U_1(y_1, L_1, \theta_2 U_2(y_2, L_2, \theta_3 U_3(y_3, L_3 \ldots)$$

$$- M_t \sum_t (y_t^+ + y_t^-) - M_t \sum_t (x_t^+ + x_t^-) - M_t \sum_t (z_{1t}^+ + z_{1t}^-)$$

$$- M_t \sum_t (z_{2t}^+ + z_{2t}^-)$$

subject to:

η_{1t}	$L_t + N_t \leq L_{ot}$	(7.1)
$\tilde{\omega}_{1t}$	$\tilde{n}_t y_t \leq L_t$	(7.2)
ω_{1t}	$n_t x_t + n_{1t} z_{1t} + n_{2t} z_{2t} + n_{12t} z_{12} + n_{21t} z_{21t} \leq Nt$	(7 3)
μ_{1t}	$x_t \leq q_1 z_{1t}$	(7.4)
φ_{1t}	$v_t = v_{t-1} + x_t - y_t - a_t x_{t+1}$	(7.5)
ξ_{11t}	$z_{1t} = z_{1t-1} - z_{12t-1} + z_{21t-1}$	(7.6)
ξ_{12t}	$z_{2t} = z_{2t-1} - z_{21t-1} + z_{21t-1}$	(7.7)
$\alpha_{\alpha 1t}$	$y_t + y_t^+ - y_t^- = y_t^*$	(7.8)
α_{1t}	$x_t + x_t^+ - x_t^- = x_t^*$	(7.9)
γ_{11t}	$z_{1t} + z_{1t}^+ - z_{1t}^- = z_{1t}^*$	(7.10)
Υ_{12t}	$z_{2t} + z_{2t}^+ - z_{2t}^- = z_{2t}^*$	(7.11)

All variables non-negative.

Briefly, in (VII) the first condition requires that leisure time and work time not exceed the time available. The second condition relates the act of consuming to leisure time available, and the third acts of production, capacity maintenance and capacity conversion to work time available, where output is constrained by output-specific capacity via condition (7.4), with conditions (7.5) referring to intertemporal product/ endowment availability and (7.6), (7.7) relating to intertemporal availability, via conversion, of elements of production capacity. Finally conditions (7.8) -(7.11) refer to consumption, production and capacity goals for the planning interval.

Now, if an abstractly attainable optimum (y_t^*, L_t^*) exists, and (x_t^*, z_{1t}^*, z_{2t}^*) constitutes a feasible/ efficient means of securing this, then an analyst might recognize (VII) as representing one means whereby such a feasible/ efficient plan might be chosen. If so, the analyst should also recognize in (VII) a central emphasis on potential for (self) contradiction in general and for as if purposive mathematical/ physical contradictions/

changes/ exchanges relative to measures y_t^*, x_t^*, z_{1t}^*, z_{2t}^* via measures (y_t^+, y_t^-), (x_t^+, x_t^-), (z_{1t}^+, z_{1t}^-), (z_{2t}^+, z_{2t}^-), respectively.

The formulation (VII)incorporates both production and consumption variables, with production lags apparently necessitating that output both anticipate and be anticipated via future-oriented final consumption demands, with consequences for pricing and valuation. Such implications will become clearer on examination of conditions potentiated by the Lagrange multipliers associated with the constraints of (VII) as follows:

$$L_t \geqq 0 \qquad \theta_1 \frac{\delta U'_1}{\delta L_t} \geqq \eta_{1t} - \tilde{\omega}_{1t} \qquad (7.12)$$

$$N_t \geqq 0 \qquad 0 \geqq \eta_{1t} - \omega_{1t} \qquad (7.13)$$

$$y_t \geqq 0 \qquad \theta_1 \frac{\delta U'_1}{\delta y_t} \geqq \tilde{n}_{1t}\tilde{\omega}_{1t} + \varphi_{1t} + \alpha_{1t} \qquad (7.14)$$

$$x_t \geqq 0 \qquad n_{1t}\omega_{1t} + \mu_{1t} + a_{t-1}\varphi_{t-1} + \beta_{1t} \geqq \varphi_{1t} \qquad (7.15)$$

$$v_t \geqq 0 \qquad \varphi_{1t} - \varphi_{1t+1} \geqq 0 \qquad (7.16)$$

$$\left(\varphi_{1t} - \frac{\varphi'_{2t+1}}{1+r_{12}} \geqq 0\right) \qquad (7.16)'$$

$$z_{1t} \geqq 0 \qquad \xi_{11t} - \xi_{11t+1} + \mu_{1t}q_1 + n_{1t}\omega_t + \gamma_{11t} \geqq 0 \qquad (7.17)$$

$$z_{2t} \geqq 0 \qquad \xi_{11t} - \xi_{12t+1} + \gamma_{12t} \geqq 0 \qquad (7.18)$$

$$z_{12t} \geqq 0 \qquad \xi_{11t} - \xi_{12t+1} \geqq - n_{12t}\omega_{1t} \qquad (7.19)$$

$$z_{21t} \geqq 0 \qquad \xi_{12t} - \xi_{11t+1} \geqq - n_{21t}\omega_{1t} \qquad (7.20)$$

$$-M_t \leqq \alpha_{1t} \leqq M_t \qquad (7.21)$$

$$-M_t \leqq \beta_{1t} \leqq M_t \qquad (7.22)$$

$$-M_t \leqq \gamma_{11t} \leqq M_t \qquad (7.23)$$

$$-M_t \leqq \gamma_{12t} \leqq M_t \qquad (7.24)$$

$$n_{1t},\ \tilde{\omega}_{1t},\ \omega_{1t},\ \mu_{1t} \geqq 0$$

At an optimum the conditon (7.12) relates the individual's preference for leisure time at the margin to a marginal evaluation of time *per se*, n_{1t}, *less* an evaluation of time appropriated to produced consumption commodities $\tilde{\omega}_{1t}$ at the margin *where*, according to (7.13), at an optimum, the individual will not choose to work (to produce commodities in the current period) unless the evaluation of work time ω_{1t} equates to his more general evaluation n_{1t} of time for that period.

Condition (7.14) relates the individual's preference for chosen consumption(s) of produced commodities to essentially subjective evaluations $\tilde{n}_{1t}\tilde{\omega}_{1t}$ associated with *processes* of consumption and to evaluations φ_{1t} of costs of production (as well as to measures α_{1t} associated with consumption targets)[9] *where*, via conditions (7.15), at an optimum output(s) x_t are not chosen to be positive unless the work (labour) time related cost of production $n_{1t}\omega_{1t}$, the capital rental μ_{1t} potentially associated with production and the variable cost(s) of production $a_{t-1}\varphi_{t-1}$ (as well as costs β_{1t}, if any, implicitly associated with production targets) would be recouped by the production prices φ_t imputed to elements of output.

Conditions (7.16)-(7.20) specify various kinds of optimally determined intertemporal relationships pertaining to potential production prices and/ or capacity rentals, valuations and maintenance costs.

Starting with conditions (7.16), these specify that output *not* be stored (for future production or consumption) if their present price $\varphi 1t$ exceeds the present evaluation of the future price φ_{1t+1}. Conversely, at an optimum output *may* optimally be stored if the present evaluation of the future price φ_{1t+1} equates to the present price φ_{1t}. This relation connotes a rule to the effect that output should optimally not be stored unless anticipated future price φ_{1t+1} is sufficient to recoup present opportunity costs φ_{1t}[10]. The essentially intertemporal nature of such relations may be made clearer by considering conditions as if identically:

$$\frac{\varphi_{2t+1}}{1+r_{12}} = \varphi_{1t+1}$$

so that condition (7.16) then interprets itself as if generating/ generated via the rule ; *do not* retain output for future production or consumption unless the (anticipated) price change will be sufficient to recoup present opportunity costs φ_{1t} plus essentially time related financial costs $r_{12}\varphi_{1t}$.

Under the (reasonable) assumption $r_{12} > 0$, this has essentially *chosen inflationary* implications according to which individuals/ groups would apparently *optimally choose* secularly rising output/ consumption prices – an implication which would apparently be reinforced if non-financial holding/storage expenditure would also be required (see footnote 11).

Turning now to conditions (7.17),(7.18). According to these, capacity of type s (s=1,2) would be retained for (potential) production only if at the margin the present evaluation of its capital value in period (t+1), ξ_{st+1} would be sufficient to recoup its current value ξ_{st} plus accumulated rental and maintenance cost imputations $\mu_s q_s$ and $\eta_{st}\omega_t$ (as well as potentially zero measures γ_{rt} associated with capacity retention targets).

Again the essentially intertemporal nature of such relations can be made clearer if transformations are considered as if identically:

$$\xi_{11t+1} = \frac{\xi_{12t+1}}{1 + r_{12}}$$

With such transformations conditions (7.17), (7.18) extend to include interest related financial costs as well as output related optimal valuations and rentals, in turn suggesting potential for relations to further kinds of financial and accounting relations, interpretations and phenomena.[11]

Finally conditions (7.19), (7.20) relate to another kind of optimal retention condition for capacity of types 1 and 2 according to which capacity of type 1 (respectively type 2) is retained *only as long as* the current evaluation of its alternative usefulness ξ_{12t+1} (respectively ξ_{11t+1}) *less* potential conversion costs does not exceed its current valuation in its current use ξ_{11t+1} (respectively ξ_{12t+1})[12].

The simplified form of the present analysis according to which one type of capacity may be used for production of desired (and potentially) scarce commodities x_t, whereas any remaining units of the other optimally remain unused itself emphasizes that even under an optimally determined intertemporal production, consumption and investment/ capital formation regime particular types of capacity may *optimally* remain unutulized and/ or underutilized for production in any or all periods during which they are available (here capacity of type 2). Whereas, due to potential conversion costs, others may *optimally* be retained even though unutilized or underutilized for some periods (here elements of capacity of type 1) according to rules among other things reflecting conversion costs potentially associated with alternative use(s), as contrasted with maintenance cost for retention, for example, to meet intermittant peak demands for capacity in the current use.[13]

Before closing this Section, I emphasize the central places in it both of a positive role for potentially *chosen* and *essentially inflationary* price increases for produced commodities (here the single scarce produced commodity) and of apparent potentials for *optimal* divergence(s) between evaluations of preferences at the margin for leisure and work (see conditions (7.12), (7.13)), with the difference here stemming essentially from a recognition that consumption as well as production will in general involve *processes* involving commitment of *time* and *so* imputing a spacer variable $\tilde{\omega}_{1t}$ to the relation (7.12).

By placing emphasis on consumption activities as well as production activities the latter remark will recall the main theme of this chapter with its focus on potentially relatively decentralized goal programming-like extensions to Lancaster-like commodities-characteristics analysis - analyses which, even in Lancaster's original work, focused on potential processes of consumption - as will again be apparent in the following Section.

For related reasons, at an intertemporal optimum, in general individual time preference rates for consumption commodities wont equate to individual time preference rates for capital investment or inventory. This point can be made quite neatly by combining elements of developments in Section 2 with elements of (VII)' to obtain:

$$\theta_1 \frac{\delta U'_1}{\delta y_t} = \frac{\theta_1}{\theta_2}\frac{\delta U'_1}{\delta U'_2} \cdot \frac{\theta_2}{\theta_3}\frac{\delta U'_2}{\delta U'_3} \cdots\cdots \frac{\delta U'_t}{\delta y_t}$$

$$\geq \tilde{\eta}_{1t}\tilde{\omega}_{1t} + \varphi_{1t} + \alpha_{1t} \qquad \text{(from (7.14))}$$

Defining:

i) $$\varphi_{1t} = \prod_{s=1}^{t-1} \frac{1}{1 + r_{ss+1}} \quad \varphi'_{tt}$$

ii) $$\frac{\theta_s}{\theta_{s+1}} \quad \frac{\delta U'_s}{\delta U'_{s+1}} = \frac{1}{1 + \rho_{ss+1}}$$

these conditions might be written alternatively as:

$$\prod_{s=1}^{t-1} \frac{1}{1 + \rho_{ss+1}} \quad \frac{\delta U'_t}{\delta y_t} = \tilde{\eta}_{1t}\tilde{\omega}_{1t} + \prod_{s=1}^{t-1} \frac{1}{1 + r_{ss+1}} \quad \varphi'_{tt} + \alpha_{1t}$$

Interpreting ρ_{ss+1} as the individual's time preference rate and r_{ss+1} as a market interest rate, it is immediately evident from these latter relations that there is no logical necessity for the two rates to be equal in *any* period,or for any sequence of periods. That said, notice that the individually related measures $\tilde{n}_{1t}$, ω_{1t}, α_{1t} are such that the individual *may* choose to interact with a wider system in such a way as if to equate such rates relative to self and relative to that wider system.

6.4 Characteristics, prices, "taxes" and "subsidies"

In this Section characteristics are introduced in ways which extend those in which Lancaster uses this term (see {7}, {8}, {9}). Three important classes of distinctions from Lancaster's approach are : *first*, that although the representation of an individual's consumption technology will be linear it will not be assumed that the consumption technology is itself linear.

The argument which suggests this point is closely analogous to that which has just been made with reference to production. That is, a specifically nonlinear formulation of the consumption technology (e.g following Muth {11}) would not here represent a generalization with reference to the representation of the consumption technology, although it may aid the search for it.

Secondly, in the developments which follow, objectivity, in the sense used by Lancaster, will *not* be assumed for the consumption technology. On the contrary, an assumption of *informed subjectivity* will be made, meaning that the analysis will allow for any individual's appreciation of any given situation to differ not only with potential differences of time and place relative to self but, for example, due to colour blindness – itself an embarrassment to Lancaster's "objectivity" assumption - while *also* allowing for an individual to be (potentially) *subjectively* fully informed.

That is to say, differences of subjective appreciation of characteristics will not *necessarily* stem from relative *ignorance* of a relatively abstract "objective" perspectives, but rather from relative differences of, and *fundamentally subjective* perspectives – differences stemming from differences of location of (elements of) individua]s in space-time relative to self/ selves/ another/ others and, more subtly, from differences of potential process of mathematical/ physical action/ reaction/ interaction relative to self/ selves/ another/ others *because* differently located in space-time.

A *third* and crucial kind of distinction between the analysis which follows and Lancaster's pioneering work is that here characteristics-commodities interactions will in principle, extend over *all potential commodities (and all potential characteristics)*, in principle including issues pertaining to free goods and more generally to production and consumption externalities.

These latter remarks suggest connections to analyses pertaining more generally to distributions/ redistributions of *property rights*, which constitute a large part of Chapter 7. More directly they suggest potential classes of interpretations and implications as if themselves potentiating/ potentiated via elements of optimal taxation/ subsidization of commodities *even for the individual case*. A two characteristic, two commodity representation will make this and the preceding points clearer.

Accordingly consider potential choices pertaining to two characteristics $c_1(t)$, $c_2(t)$ and two produced consumption commodities $y_1(t)$, $y_2(t)$ and an individual's optimal production and consumption plan as in (VII) above, but now with the following commodity-characteristic representation of the chosen optimal point :

$$\text{Maximize } U = \theta_1 U_1(c_1(1), c_2(1), \theta_2 U_2(C_1(2), C_2(2, \theta_3 U_3(..\theta_t U_t(c_1(t), c_2(t)...)$$

$$- M\sum_j(y_j^+(t)+y_j^-(t)) - M\sum_j(x_j^+(t)+x_j^-(t)) - M\sum_j(z_j^+(t)+z_j^-t))$$

subject to :

$$\lambda_1(t) \qquad c_1(t) = \bar{\alpha}_{11}(t)y_1(t) + \bar{a}_{21}(t)y_2(t) + \bar{b}_{11}(t)x_1(t) + \bar{b}_{21}(t)x_2(t)$$
$$\bar{d}_{11}(t)z_1(t) + \bar{d}_{21}(t)z_2(t) \qquad (8.1)$$

$$\lambda_2(t) \qquad c_2(t) = \bar{a}_{12}(t)y_1(t) + \bar{a}_{22}(t)y_2(t) + \bar{b}_{12}(t)x_1(t) + \bar{b}_{22}(t)x_2(t)$$
$$\bar{d}_{12}(t)z_1(t) + \bar{d}_{22}(t)z_2(t) \qquad (8.2)$$

$$\omega(t) \qquad \bar{n}_1(t)y_1(t) + \bar{n}_2(t)y_2(t) + n_1(t)x_1(t) + n_2(t)x_2(t) + \bar{\bar{n}}_1(t)z_1(t)$$
$$+ \bar{\bar{n}}_2(t)z_2(t) + n_{12}(t)z_{12}(t) + n_{21}(t)z_{21}(t) \leq L_{ot} \qquad (8.3)$$

$$\mu_1(t) \qquad x_1(t) \leq q_1 z_1(t) \qquad (8.4)$$

$$\mu_2(t) \qquad x_2(t) \leq q_2 z_2(t) \qquad (8.5) \qquad \text{(VIII)}$$

$$\varphi_1(t) \qquad v_1(t) = v_1(t-1)+x_1(t) - y_1(t) - a_{11}(t)x_1(t+1) - a_{12}(t)x_2(t+1) \qquad (8.6)$$

$$\varphi_2(t) \qquad v_2(t) = v_2(t-1)+x_2(t) - y_2(t) - a_{21}(t)x_1(t+1) - a_{22}(t)x_2(t+1) \qquad (8.7)$$

$$\xi_1(t) \qquad z_1(t) = z_1(t-1) - z_{12}(t-1) + z_{21}(t-1) \qquad (8.8)$$

$$\xi_2(t) \qquad z_2(t) = z_2(t-1) - z_{21}(t-1) + z_{12}(t-1) \qquad (8.9)$$

$$\alpha_j(t) \qquad y_j(t)+y_j^+(t) - y_j^-(t) = y_j^*(t) \qquad (8.10)$$

$$\beta_j(t) \qquad x_j(t)+x_j^+(t) - x_j^-(t) = x_j^*(t) \qquad (8.11)$$

$$\gamma_j(t) \qquad z_j(t)+ z_j^+(t) - z_j^-(t) = z_j^*(t) \qquad (8.12)$$

All variables non-negative

This system is open to interpretation as if potentially corresponding to a characteristics-based extension of the system (VII). Expanding on this, conditions (8.4)-(8.12) are isomorphic with conditions (7.4)-(7.11) and, under conditions as if identically $\bar{n}_1(t)y_1(t) + \bar{n}_2(t)y_2(t) = L(t)$, condition (8.3) is open to interpretation as if potentially specializing to an extended form of conditions (7.1), (7.2), (7.3) of the system (VII).

Given such correspondences between elements of (VII) and (VIII) it is instructive to consider conditions under which elements of the objectives of these systems also become as if equivalent to each other. These include conditions :

i) as if identically $c_1(t) = y_1(t)$, $\bar{a}_{11}(t)=1$, $\bar{a}_{21}(t)=0$, $\bar{b}_{11}(t) = 0$, $\bar{b}_{21}(t) = 0$, $\bar{d}_{11}(t)=0$, $\bar{d}_{21}(t)=0$;

ii) as if identically $c_2(t)= L(t)$.

With reference to potential translations/ transformations considered above as if identically $\bar{n}_1(t)y_1(t) + \bar{n}_2(t)y_2(t) = L(t)$, such conditions in turn suggest specializations of (8.2) according to which $\bar{a}_{12}(t) = \bar{n}_1(t)$, $\bar{a}_{22}(t) = \bar{n}_2(t)$, $\bar{b}_{21}(t) = 0$, $\bar{b}_{22}(t) = 0$, $\bar{d}_{21}(t) = 0$, $\bar{d}_{22}(t) = 0$.

Conditions as if identically $\bar{a}_{12}(t) = n_1(t)$, $\bar{a}_{22}(t) = \bar{n}_2(t)$ are open to interpretation as if *requiring*, for equivalence to standard analyses, that measures relative to self be as if *identical* to measures relative to a system. More constructively, such conditions emphasize that in general, in (VIII), measures/observations relative to self will be *different from* measures/observations relative to a system.

Specializations as if identically $\bar{a}_{12}(t) = 0$, $\bar{n}_2(t) = 0$, serve not just to generate correspondences to specializations as if "consumption" y(t) and "leisure" L(t) are mutually exclusive activities, as in conventional analyses, but, in doing so, to emphasize that such specializations impute apparent *timelessness* to consumption activities.

This contradicts everyday experience to the contrary. For this reason alone an individual/ agent/ analyst might reject standard, and in these and other ways essentially simplistic analyses, because anticipating consumption interdependencies and externalities even for the simplest classes of cases.

More constructively, such potential classes of specializations also serve to emphasize ways in which (VIII) generalizes the system (VII) and, more particularly, ways in which the system (VIII) extends and generalizes emphases in (VII) on goal programming-like principles and processes of interaction between elements of individuals and elements of wider systems in ways which incorporate potential for distinctions between relative *subjectivity* of characteristics and commodities relative to self,and relative *objectivity* of characteristics and commodities relative to other elements of a wider system.

Such comparisons emphasize potential for gains or losses by individuals relative to self and/or relative to elements of a wider system as if themselves potentially generating/ generated via difference between measures of commodities and characteristics relative to self and measures of commodities and characteristics relative to another/ other element(s) of a subsystem potentially differently and distinctly located in space-time relative to self.

In (VIII) not just all commodities, but all processes of change in an economy relate via characteristics to the individual and vice versa. That is, in that representation, individual appreciation of any mathematical/ physical subsystem is *not* independent of that individual's (potential) principles and/or processes of *interaction with* that subsystem.

Specifically : in (VIII) characteristics are in principle defined over *all* commodities, including "free" goods,and *all* processes of interaction. More subtly, there is potential for an individual to *learn from* that system, *not just* via the appreciation of characteristics of known commodities and/ or processes of interaction, or via the appreciation through their characteristics of relatively unknown commodities and processes of interaction *but, also*, via the appreciation of relatively *new kinds* of characteristics via the more subtle appreciation of *relatively known* commodities and/or processes, and/or via *new kinds* of appreciation of *relatively unknown* commodities or processes.

Analogous to this, in (VIII) there is potential, too, for an individual to *create* both by generating relatively novel mathematical/ physical manifestations of commodities or characteristics relative to another/ other element(s) of a wider system and, more subtly, by generating relatively novel mathematical/ physical manifestations of relatively new kinds of commodities and characteristics relative to another/ other element(s) of a wider system.

Each of these very general classes of potential mathematical/ physical principles and processes potentiate and/or are as if purposively potentiated via their association with inherently relatively *unknown/ unknowable* and so, at best, relatively mathematically/ physically *incompletely* known/ knowable elements of (VIII).

Indeed, via their association with that system, such potential principles and processes can be seen in a yet more comprehensive context of potentially *optimally determined* principles and processes of relatively *purposive* (self) contradiction/ indeterminacy/ incompleteness/ uncertainty, themselves potentiating and/or potentiated via correspondences to elements of goal programming-like specifications of mathematical/ physical principles, processes and phenomena.

Among other things such specifications imply optimally determining/ determined mathematical/ physical economic *duality* principles, processes and phenomena pertaining to relatively individual/ collective economic action, reaction and interaction- at -a -distance in relative space-time.

With such potentially fundamentally significant roles for elements of duality principles and processes in view, now associate the indicated dual variables with constraints of the system (VIII) and use linear dependence arguments to generate dually related conditions as follows:

$$c_1(t) \qquad \theta_t \frac{\delta U(t)}{\delta c_1(t)} \geqq \lambda_1(t) \qquad (8.13)$$

$$c_2(t) \qquad \theta_t \frac{\delta U(t)}{\delta c_2(t)} \geqq \lambda_2(t) \qquad (8.14)$$

$$y_1(t) \qquad \bar{a}_{11}(t)\lambda_1(t) + \bar{a}_{12}(t)\lambda_2(t) \leqq \bar{n}_1(t)\omega(t) + \varphi_1(t) + \alpha_1(t) \qquad (8.15)$$

$$y_2(t) \qquad \bar{a}_{21}(t)\lambda_1(t) + \bar{a}_{22}(t)\lambda_2 t) \leqq \bar{n}_2(t)\omega(t) + \varphi 2(t) + \alpha_2(t) \qquad (8.16)$$

$$x_1(t) \qquad \varphi_1(t) + \bar{b}_{11}(t)\lambda 1(t) + \bar{b}_{12}(t)\lambda_2(t) \leqq a_1(t)\omega(t) + \mu_1(t)$$
$$+ a_{11}(t)\varphi_+(t-1) + a_{21}(t)\varphi_2(t-1) + \beta_1(t) \qquad (8.17)$$

$$x_2(t) \qquad \varphi_2(t) + \bar{b}_{21}(t)\lambda_1(t) + \bar{b}_{22}(t)\lambda_2(t) \leqq a_2(t)\omega(t) + \mu_2(t)$$
$$+ a_{12}(t)\varphi_2(t-1) + a_{22}(t)\varphi_2(t-1) + \beta 2(t) \qquad (8.18)$$

$$v_1(t) \qquad \varphi_1(t) \geqq \varphi_1(t+1) \qquad (8.19)$$

(VIII)'

$$v_2(t) \qquad \varphi_2 t) \geqq \varphi_2(t+1) \qquad (8.20)$$

$$z_1(t) \qquad \bar{d}_{11}(t)\lambda_1(t) + \bar{d}_{12}(t)\lambda_2(t) \leqq \bar{\bar{n}}_1(t)\omega(t) - \mu_1(t)q_1 + \xi_1(t)$$
$$- \xi_1(t+1) + \gamma_1(t) \qquad (8.21)$$

$$z_2(t) \qquad \bar{\bar{d}}_{21}(t)\lambda_1(t) + \bar{\bar{d}}_{22}(t)\lambda_2(t) \leqq \bar{\bar{n}}_2(t)\omega(t) - \mu_2(t)q_2 + \xi_2(t)$$
$$- \xi_2(t+1) + \gamma_2 t) \qquad (8.22)$$

$$z_{12}(t) \qquad \xi_1(t) + n_{12}(t)\omega(t) \geqq \xi_2(t+1) \qquad (8.23)$$

$$z_{21}(t) \qquad \xi_2(t) + n_{21}(t)\omega(t) \geqq \xi_1(t+1) \qquad (8.24)$$

$$- M \leqq \alpha_j(t) \leqq M \qquad (8.25)$$

$$- M \leqq \beta_j(t) \leqq M \qquad (8.26)$$

$$- M \leqq \gamma_j(t) \leqq M \qquad (8.27)$$

With these conditions the emphasis on potential *process*(es) implicit in the characteristics-like extension (VIII) to the system (VII) becomes starkly apparent. To appreciate this notice the overall similarity of structure between elements of the constraints of (VIII)' and elements of the constraints of (VII)'. In particular compare conditions (8.23)-(8.27) and (8.19)-(8.20) of (VIII)' and (7.19)-(7.23) and (7.16) of (VII)' noting their isomorphism. Then compare conditions (8.21), (8.22) of (VIII)' with (7.17),(7.18) of (VII)',and conditions (8.17), (8.18) with conditions (7.15), noting that in each case in the former constraints, by contrast with the latter, there are apparently explicit correspondences to potentially characteristics *inducing* and/ or characteristics *induced* principles and processes of interaction.

In each case the fact as well as the form of these measures of potential elements of production/ consumption interactions suggests potential processes of production/ consumption interaction *variously* corresponding *not just* to potential production or consumption externalities, but to potentials for optimally determined *interrelations between* elements of production and/ or consumption externalities.

More directly the form of these relations suggests classes of interpretations according to which the measures $\bar{a}_{ij}(t)\lambda_i(t)$, $\bar{b}_{ij}(t)\lambda_i(t)$,

$\bar{a}_{ij}(t)\lambda_i(t)$, as if themselves purposively potentiate and/or are as if themselves purposively potentiated via elements of optimally determined instruments of regulation in general, and elements of optimally determined consumption or investment taxes/subsidies in particular.

I remark here, as I remarked in the Introduction, that even though (VIII) apparently relates to *optimal* intertemporal decisionmaking for a single individual alone in an economy, nevertheless in the dually related system (VIII)' measures emerge which are quite evidently analogous to regulatory taxes and subsidies *as if chosen* by that individual in order to secure intertemporally *preferred* conditions among other things via elements of the "primal" system (VIII).

This emphasizes another point ; in (VIII), (VIII)', not only do interpretations emerge analogous to (optimal regulations of) production and consumption externalities but potentially optimal *interrelations* between elements of (VIII), (VIII)' emerge pertaining to potential *processes* of (re)generation of as if purposively (*dually*) interrelated objectives and *choices* of elements generating production and consumption externalities on the one hand, and production and consumption taxes, subsidies and transfers on the other.

Reinforcing this : by complementary slackness, if $c_i(t) > 0$ at an optimum, then (8.13), (8.14) will hold as equalities. Using such equalities to substitute in (8.15) the following modified condition emerges:

$$y_1(t) \quad \bar{a}_{11}(t)\frac{\delta U_1}{\delta c_1(t)} + \bar{a}_{12}(t)\frac{\delta U_1}{\delta c_2(t)} \geqq n_1(t)\omega(t) + \varphi_1(t) + \alpha_1(t) \qquad (8.15)$$

This condition appears open to an interpretation according to which this individual's *optimal* choice of consumption level $y_1(t)$ of commodity 1 in period t is conditioned by a *tradeoff* at the margin *between*, on the right hand side, opportunity cost related measures of consumption time $\bar{n}_1(t)\omega(t)$ and production resources $\varphi_1(t)$ and, where applicable, an explicitly consumption inducing/reducing regulatory measures $\alpha_1(t)$) *and*, on the left hand side, apparently explicitly preference related measures explicitly preference related measures $\bar{a}_{11}(t)\delta U_1/\delta c_1(t)$, $\bar{a}_{12}(t)\delta U_1/\delta c_2(t)$ of potential contributions at the margin of potentially chosen levels of consumption of commodity 1 in period t.

In this form condition (8.15)'is open to an interpretation according to which an individual will choose to consume commodity 1 in period t, if at all, then up to the point where its return, as measured by contributions to characteristics 1, 2, equates to its potentially regulated opportunity cost at the margin.

Analogous developments would yield an analogous condition (8.16)' via substitutions from (8.13), (8.14) in (8.16) at an optimum.

But conditions (8.13), (8.15) could be used more simply, and more subtly, to obtain :

$$y_1(t) \quad \bar{a}_{11}(t)\frac{\delta U_1}{\delta c_1(t)} \geqq \bar{n}_1(t)\omega(t) + \varphi_1(t)+\alpha_1(t) - \bar{a}_{12}(t)\lambda_2(t) \qquad (8.15)''$$

This relation in turn suggests interpretations according to which a measure $\bar{a}_{12}(t)\lambda_2(t)$ may correspond to an optimally chosen characteristic *inducing* or characteristic *induced* tax/ subsidy. It also suggests potentially related classes of interpretations in relation to potential *processes* according to which for example this individual would optimally *choose* amounts of commodity 1 according to a rule equating its preference -related return at the margin to characteristic 1 to its, opportunity cost based, time and resource cost *net* of *both* a goal related measure $\alpha_0(t)$ *and* a tax/ subsidy measure $\bar{a}_{12}(t)\lambda_2(t)$ implicitly or explicity imputed to potential yield(s) of characteristic 2 at the margin.

Such easily generalizeable and dually interrelated interpretations and results pertaining to elements of the (sub)system (VIII), (VIII)' again suggest potentials in elements of these subsystems to (re)generate classes of essentially *optimally goal oriented* and *optimally regulated,* because essentially characteristic-related processes in relation to intertemporal choice.

The following particular cases will suggest more general ones :

$\frac{\delta U_1}{\delta c_1(t)} > 0$	*or*, more of characteristic 1 is preferred by this individual at the margin.
$\bar{a}_{12}(t)\lambda_2(t) > 0$	*or*, at an optimum with $\bar{a}_{12}(t) > 0$ optimally choose to act as if to subsidize $y_1(t)$.
$\bar{b}_{12}(t)\lambda_2(t) < 0$	*or*, at an optimum with $\bar{a}_{12}(t) > 0$ optimally choose to act as if to tax $x_1(t)$.
$\bar{a}_{12}(t)\lambda_2(t) = 0$	*or*, at an optimum with $\bar{a}_{12}(t) = 0$ optimally choose to act as if to choose neither characteristic 1 taxes nor characteristic 1 related subsidies to $y_1(t)$.

More subtly, interrelations (as in (VIII), (VIII)') between elements of conditions such as (8.13), (8.14) and (8.15)-(8.18) might suggest classes of interpretations according to which commodity related relative taxes and subsidies *potentiate* relatively preferred states relative to an individual via their potentiation of respectively relatively less and relatively more commodities and associated characteristics relative to that individual at the margin.

They may also suggest classes of interpretations according to which characteristic-related preferences may potentiate relatively preferre states relative to a relatively wider system via their potentiation of variously relative taxes or subsidies relative to potentially more and/or relatively novel commodities relative to a wider mathematical/physical system.

More directly, for those familiar with standard microeconomic arguments, a context of particular conditions, such as $\delta U_1/\delta c_1(t) > 0$ which have just been considered, when viewed in conjunction with conditions (8.15)' will directly suggest classes of interpretation according to which measures as if *identically* $\bar{a}_{ij}(t)\lambda_i(t)$, $\bar{a}_{ij}(t)y_i(t)$ ($\bar{b}_{ij}(t)\lambda_i(t)$, $\bar{b}_{ij}(t)y_i(t)$) potentiate and/ or are as if purposively potentiated via relatively positive or negative consumption (respectively consumption related production) *externalities.*

They will also suggest classes of interpretation isomorphic with those considered elsewhere in connection with *public goods*, in turn immediately suggesting potential links to issues pertaining to relative decentralization and regulation, not just as these might relate to a single isolated Crusoe-like individual, but as they might relate to potential n-individual collective choice contexts - in such ways anticipating developments in the next chapter.

6.5 Summary and conclusion

I have looked at individual Crusoe-like economies in ways which emphasize potentially characteristics inducing and/ or characteristics induced processes of interrelation between an individual and elements of a wider mathematical/ physical subsystem.

Arising from these, emphasis has been placed upon as if purposiveIy (self) regulating instruments of optimal intertemporal choice open to interretations isomorphic, even in these single individual cases, with elements of intertemporally optimally determined (first best) transfers, taxes and subsidies.

These have been shown to stem not just from consumption oriented production and consumption activities per se, but from arguably intertemporally optimal processes of interaction with and through elements of wider systems.

In turn such wider systems have been seen to be open to interpretations not just as if potentiating/ potentiated via elements of consumption per se or via consumption/ production externalities or capacity changes per se, but, more actively, as if directly potentiating/ potentiated via elements of processes variously of consumption, production and/ or capital change *each* open to interpretation as if potentiating/ potentiated via particular kinds of interpretation in relation to particular kinds of as if purposively mathematically/ physically decentralized, mathematical/ physically self contradictory and mathematically/ physically indeterminate elements of the dually interrelated goal programming-like (sub)systems (VII),(VII).

Footnotes

1. For an introduction to this type - and to pioneering work in this area see {3}.

2. Notice that the single individual/ n individual distinction is not generally a stark one. In fact the very existence of an individual generally connotes the prior existence of at least one other of that kind and, as the reader may recall, even within the essentially naive context of Defoe's Robinson Crusoe story, one of Crusoe's first actions was to commit time, effort and resources to construct a signal fire in order to increase his potential for contacts with others whom he would recognize as potentially friendly. Indeed Crusoe was surprised by and came to appreciate the company of one whom he at first feared as a potential enemy.

3. From another viewpoint it might seem that this is a statement of a *functional* relationship between U_1* and $x_1*...x_T*$.

4. For developments of this point see also my extensions of work by Swallow {14}, Aarestad {1} and others in Chapter 10.

5. Conditions as if potentially $\theta_1 U_1$ ( ) = $\Sigma p_{1t} x_t$, especially if mediated, as here, via conditions as if contingently $p_{st} = \theta_s \delta u_s / \delta x_t$, may suggest potential relations to integration/ integrability issues.

6. In this respect including not only those such as Samuelson's {13} using conventional calculus, but for example Debreu's well known work {4} using more advanced mathematical methods. For more fundamental critiques see also {12}.

7. Economists familiar with growth models will be familiar with simple (and arguably simplistic) assumptions of this latter kind in analyses omitting/ abstracting from capacity considerations (for an introduction to that literature see Dixit's book {6}).

8. Those familiar with consumption-leisure choice models in the standard microeconomics literature might see (VII) as corresponding to an extension of such models to comprehend not just production of output and of capacity but also explicitly to comprehend potential processes of change/ exchange via the measures y_t+, y_t^-, x_t^+, x_t^-, z_{1t}^+, z_{1t}^-, z_{2t}^+, z_{2t}^- relative to self and/ or relative to a system.

9. Notice that, by contrast with standard microeconomic analyses of consumption-work-leisure choice, the individual's marginal rate of substitution between work time and leisure time will in general not equate to the "real wage rate" ω_{1t}/φ_{1t}. Such a condition would not only require chosen work in positive amounts but would require conditions as if identically $\tilde{\eta}_{1t} = 0$ - the latter conditions apparently contradicting any assumption to the effect that work is one means to a final consumption end.

10. In a more comprehensively specified model the possibility of non-zero requirements for capacity and/ or variable inputs for storage would be incorporated in a suitably respecified extension of (VII) in which, as the analogue of (7.16) would require, that anticipated future price be sufficient to recoup present opportunity costs plus storage costs.

11. See Chapter 9 for related developments, including for example, developments pertaining to optimal depreciation/ amortization and/ or to bonds/ stocks as potential instruments of finance. Notice that such potential extensions, developments and interpretations apparently apply in principle even to a single individual analysis which as is being considered here, even though in practice, except for book keeping purposes, they might seem more appropriate to a multi-individual environment.

12. Again a more general analysis would consideration of potentially multi-period conversion processes as well as potential for conversion to more than one alternative use. On those points see developments in Chapter 8 below as they relate to issues pertaining to *accessibility* in time and space of potentially alternative uses.

13. These remarks do not only suggest potential relations to a well known and long standing peak load pricing literature (see {10}) but potential for quite subtle specializations and modifications and revisions to standard results in that literature according to which peak load priciing rules are understood as only one part of an optimal investment, maintenance and/ or disinvestment programme. For more on this and related poionts see related analyses and developments in Chapter 9.

References

{1} Aarestad, J.,(1990), *Simultaneous Use of Renewable and Non-Renewable Natural Resources*, Resources and Energy 12, pp.253-262.

{2} Blackorby, C., Nissen, D., Primont, D. and Russell, R.R.,(1973), *Consistent Intertemporal Decisionmaking*, Review of Economic Studies 40, pp.239-248.

{3} Charnes, A. and Cooper, W.W.,(1961), *Management Models and Industrial Applications of Linear Programming*, 2 volumes, Wiley, New York.

{4} Debreu, G.,(1951), *Theory of Value: An Axiomatic Analysis of Economic Equilibrium*, Cowles Foundation Monograph 17, Yale University Press.

{5} De v. Graaf, J.,(1957), *Theoretical Welfare Economics*, Cambridge University Press.

{6} Dixit, A.K.,(1976), *The Theory of Equilibrium Growth*, Oxford University Press.

{7} Lancaster, K.,(1975), *Socially Optimal Product Differentiation*, American Economic Review 65, pp.567-585.

{8} Lancaster, K.,(1979), *Variety, Equity and Efficiency*, Basil Blackwell, Oxford.

{9} Lancaster, K.,(1991), *Modern Consumer Theory*, Edward Elgar.

{10}Littlechild, S.C.,(1970), *Marginal Cost Pricing with Joint Costs*, Economic Journal 80, pp.223-235.

{11}Muth, R.F..(1966), *Household Production and Consumer Demand Functions*, Econometrica 34, pp.699-708.

{12}Ryan, M.J.,(1991), *On Impossibility Results and Competitive Systems*, forthcoming.

{13}Samuelson, P.A.,(1947), *Foundations of Economic Analysis*, Harvard University Press, Cambridge, Mass.

{14}Swallow, S.K.,(1990), *Depletion of the Environmental Basis for Renewable and Non-Renewable Resources*, Journal of Environmental Economics and Management 19, pp.281-296.

7 Lancaster-like characteristics and bases for regulation and self regulation in first best economies: N individual cases

7.1 Introduction

The primary purpose of this second part is the same as that of the first : to show how Lancaster's approach to consumer theory can be usefully and powerfully adapted and developed in ways which establish positive roles for regulation, including taxation, subsidies and other forms of government regulation, in determinations of individually and collectively "first best" allocations and (re)distributions of economic products and resources, even in a world of competition.

In the previous Chapter attention was confined to single individual Crusoe economies and to determinations of relatively abstract preference/ indifference relations relative to self as if purposively, via inherently relatively self contradictory interactions with a wider system, to generate potential gain(s) relative to a relatively abstract self differently located in space-time.

With the relaxation of the single individual "Crusoe" assumption, more subtle and complex classes of cases can be considered, including classes of cases according to which two or more individuals may act as if purposively to potentiate *less* relative to self/ selves as if thereby, by variously altruistically or selfishly oriented principles and processes of giving/ taking, bartering or trading, to potentiate relatively *more* to another/ others.[1]

In such more generally specified n person cases not only do relatively standardized physical, fiscal or financial units have more purpose and meaning in general than in the single person case, but clearly, too, particular kinds of *explicitly* (self) *regulatory* instruments, such as relatively standardizing laws, weights and measures, prices, taxes, subsidies, money or budgets, may take on richer - because more usefully explicitly distinct -meaning than their generally implicit analogues in the single person case.

The n person case as well as the single person case provides positive roles for as if purposively induced principles and/ or processes of mathematical/ physical indeterminacy/ incompleteness/ uncertainty relative to self/ selves as well as for sequential/ cyclical changes/ exchanges *founded upon* potentials for *exploitations of* principles and/ or processes of contradiction of relatively abstract individual/ collective preference orderings by individuals and/ or groups relative to self/ selves and/ or another/ others.

These points are developed here with particular reference to taxation and regulation issues of types which have long been seen as presenting intractable problems in the collective choice literature (see particularly Arrow's work and that of others on Impossibility results, {2}, {13} or more narrowly by Lipsey and Lancaster {9} and later authors on Second Best results in particular, and difficulties of specification of Bergson -Samuelson welfare functions more generally {5}).

To establish connections with developments in Part I, and to provide a foundation for later developments in this chapter, Section 2 is given over to a brief review of characteristics-related intertemporal planning and control models which were developed in Part I.

In Section 3 attention turns to relations between these earlier models and n-individual extensions and moves from the earlier focus on *individid -ually* optimizing characteristics-related consumption, production and physical/ financial investment/ divestment rules, to a focus on potentially *collectively -welfare* as well as implicity *macro*-economically optimizing characteristics-related consumption, production and investment/ divestment rules, with associated emphases upon potential classes of interpretations as if themselves potentiating/ potentiated via relatively individually *and/ or* collectively optimizing economic principles and processes.

In Sections 4 and 5 I proceed to a more detailed elucidation and discussion of the potentials immanent in the earlier models for the generation of relative gains or losses to particular individuals, or groups, by means of particular kinds of principles and/ or processes of variously goal oriented price, tax, subsidy or transfer induced giving/ taking, bartering or trading.

More subtly, potentials will be explored for the generation of relative gains or losses to particular kinds of *relatively decentralized* individuals or groups acting as if *purposively* to secure conditions of *contradiction*, incompleteness and indeterminacy relative to relatively abstract preference/ welfare measures relative to self/ selves as if *thereby* to potentiate relatively greater gains/ losses relative to self/ selves and/ or another/ others differently located in space-time.

For those familiar with the standard microeconomics literature it will be of particular interest that a concept of *Reciprocal Revealed Preference* is developed.

This not only gives an empirical role to the *Revealed Preference* idea (originally developed by Samuelson {12}), but does so in ways which do not just emphasize and require relatively abstract *Hicks-like* individual preference/indifference relations, but which also emphasize and operationalize ideas associated with relatively abstract *Bergson-Samuelson* collective preference/indifference welfare analysis.

In Section 5 attention turns to a detailed treatment of particular kinds of relatively decentralized allocation and distribution principles and processes with emphasis upon standard units, budgets, property rights, taxes and transfers in general, and potential by such means for systematically individually and socially beneficial exploitations of relatively individually and collectively applicable mathematical/ physical uncertainty, incompleteness and indeterminacy principles and processes.

7.2 Extremal representations of individually optimal intertemporal choices

In Chapter 6 the following goal programming-like model was developed to represent a Crusoe-like individual's characteristic-related optimal consumption, production and investment/ disinvestment decisions over time :

$$\text{Maximize} \quad U_1 = \Theta_1(c_1(1),\ c_2(1),\ \Theta_2 U_2(c_1(2),\ c_2(2),\ \Theta_3 U_3(.\Theta_t U_t(c_1(t), c_2(t))$$
$$- M \sum_t (y_i^+(t) + y_i^-(t)) - M \sum_t (x_i^+(t) + x_i^-(t))$$
$$- M \sum_t (z_i^+(t) + z_i^-(t))$$

subject to:

$$\lambda_1(t) \quad c_1(t) = \tilde{a}_{11}(t)y_1(t) + \tilde{a}_{21}(t)y_2(t) + \tilde{b}_{11}(t)x_1(t) + \tilde{b}_{21}(t)x_2(t) + \tilde{d}_{11}(t)z_1(t) + \tilde{d}_{21}(t)z_2(t) \quad (1.1)$$

$$\lambda_2(t) \quad c_2(t) = \tilde{a}_{12}(t)y_1(t) + \tilde{a}_{22}(t)y_2(t) + \tilde{b}_{12}(t)x_1(t) + \tilde{b}_{22}(t)x_2(t) + \tilde{d}_{12}(t)z_1(t) + \tilde{d}_{22}(t)z_2(t) \quad (1.2)$$

$$\omega(t) \quad \tilde{n}_1(t)y_1(t) + \tilde{n}_2(t)y_2(t) + n_1(t)x_1(t) + n_2(t)x_2(t) + \tilde{n}_1(t)z_1(t) + \tilde{n}_2(t)z_2(t) + n_{12}(t)z_{12}(t) + n_{21}(t)z_{21}(t) \leq L_{ot} \quad (1.3)$$

$$\mu_1(t) \quad x_1(t) \leq q_1 z_1(t) \quad (1.4)$$

$$\mu_2(t) \quad x_2(t) \leq q_1 z_2(t) \quad (1.5) \qquad \text{(I)}$$

$$\xi_1(t) \quad z_1(t) = z_1(t-1) - z_{12}(t-1) + z_{21}(t-1) \quad (1.6)$$

$$\xi_2(t) \quad z_2(t) = z_2(t-1) - z_{21}(t-1) + z_{12}(t-1) \quad (1.7)$$

$$\varphi_1(t) \quad v_1(t) = v_1(t-1) + x_1(t) - y_1(t) - a_{11}(t)x_1(t+1) - a_{12}(t)x_2(t+1) \quad (1.8)$$

$$\varphi_2(t) \quad v_2(t) = v_2(t-1) + x_2(t) - y_2(t) - a_{21}(t)x_1(t+1) - a_{22}(t)x_2(t+1) \quad (1.9)$$

$$\alpha_j(t) \quad y_i(t) + y_i^+(t) - y_i^-(t) = y_i^*(t) \quad (1.10)$$

$$\beta_j(t) \quad x_i(t) + x_i^+(t) - x_i^-(t) = x_i^*(t) \quad (1.11)$$

$$\gamma_j(t) \quad z_i(t) + z_i^+(t) - z_i^-(t) = z_i^*(t) \quad (1.12)$$

All variables non-negative

Briefly, this specification is consistent with choice by an individual of the intertemporally optimizing consumption, production and investment/ disinvestment plan ($y_i^*(t)$, $x_i^*(t)$, $z_i^*(t)$) as if *via* a relatively abstract intertemporally optimizing preference/ indifference relation U_1 defined over relatively individualized and abstract *characteristics* $c_1(t)$, $c_2(t)$ where, according to conditions (1.1), (1.2), such characteristics may be yielded by commodities, including potentially produced commodities $x_j(t)$ and elements of production capacity $z_j(t)$, as well as apparently more explicitly consumption commodities $y_j(t)$.

Conditions (1.3) relate the times potentially required respectively for consumption, production, capacity maintenance and capacity formation in periods t to time (L_{ot}) potentially available to the Crusoe-like individual in those periods.

The production-related conditions (1.4)-(1.9) are more familiar in form and, respectively, relate potential output(s) to available capacity (conditions (1.4), (1.5)), capacity availability to previous capacity *plus* additions/ conversions *less* relinquishments/ diversions ((1.6), (1.7)), and conditions (1.8), (1.9) relate amounts available for future production or consumption in period t to previous availabilities *plus* production in the current period less final consumption and variable inputs to production in the current period.

Finally, conditions (1.10) - (1.12) relate *realized* plans $y_i(t)$, $x_i(t)$, $z_i(t)$ to *target* plans $y_i^*(t)$, $x_i^*(t)$, $z_i^*(t)$, with $(y_i^+(t), y_i^-(t))$, $(x_i^+(t))$, $(z_i^+(t), z_i^-(t))$ being measures of deviations from these - deviations associated with potentially arbitrarily large penalties M in the objective of the system (I).

It was significant in Part I, and will be more so in subsequent sections of this second Part, that not only do potential production and consumption processes per se have explicit roles to play in the system (I), and the system (I)' below, but potential processes of *change* in production technology and processes of *interraction* between individual production and consumption elements and elements of relatively wider mathematical/ physical (sub)systems have explicit roles to play in the systems (I), (I)'.

Emphasizing these points : systems (I), (I)' make explicit provision for processes of introduction of relatively *new kinds* of production capacity as well as for processes of maintenance or augmentation of existing capacity. They also explicitly recognize explicit *differences* between measurements relative to self/ selves and measurements relative to elements of a wider mathematical/ physical system relatively distant/ distinct from self/ selves.

To see these and related points more sharply associate the indicated dual variables with the constraints of (I) to generate the dually related system (I)' which follows, noticing particularly the "spacer" variables $\alpha_j(t)$, $\beta_j(t)$, $\gamma_j(t)$ in conditions (1.15)- (1.18) and (1.21), (1.22) of (I)'which are open to interpretation as stemming directly from their association with explicitly empirically/ physically measurement- oriented specifications of respectively consumption, production and capacity investment/ disinvestment goals via the conditions (1.10),(1.11),(1.12) of (I):

$$c_1(t)\ \theta_1 \frac{\delta U(1)}{\delta U(2)} \quad \ldots\ \theta_t \frac{\delta U(t)}{\delta c_2(t)} \geqq \lambda_1(t) \qquad (1.13)$$

$$c_2(t)\ \theta_2 \frac{\delta U(1)}{\delta U(2)} \quad \ldots\ \theta_t \frac{\delta U(t)}{\delta c_2(t)} \geqq \lambda_2(t) \qquad (1.14)$$

$$y_1(t)) \qquad \tilde{a}_{11}(t)\lambda_1(t) + \tilde{a}_{12}(t)\lambda_2(t) \leqq \tilde{n}_1(t)\omega(t) + \varphi_1(t) + \alpha_1(t) \qquad (1.15)$$

$$y_2(t) \qquad \tilde{a}_{21}(t)\lambda_1(t) + \tilde{a}_{22}(t)\lambda_2(t) \leqq \tilde{n}_2(t)\omega(t) + \varphi_2(t) + \alpha_2(t) \qquad (1.16)$$

$$x_1(t) \qquad \varphi_1(t) + \tilde{b}_{11}(t)\lambda_1(t) + \tilde{b}_{12}(t)\lambda_2(t) \leqq a_{11}(t)\omega(t) + \mu_1(t) + a_{11}(t)\varphi_1(t-1) + a_{12}(t)_2(t-1) + \beta_1(t) \qquad (1.17)$$

$$x_2(t) \qquad \varphi_2(t) + \tilde{b}_{21}(t)\lambda_1(t) + \tilde{b}_{22}(t)\lambda_2(t) \leqq a_{21}(t)_{\omega}(t) + \mu_2(t) + a_{21}(t)\varphi_1(t-1) + a_{22}(t)\varphi_2(t-1) + \beta_2(t) \qquad (1.18)$$

(I)'

$$v_1(t) \qquad \varphi_1(t) \geqq \varphi_1(t+1) \qquad (1.19)$$

$v_2(t)$ $$\varphi_2(t) \leq \varphi_2(t+1) \tag{1.20}$$

$z_1(t)$ $$\tilde{d}_{11}(t)\lambda_1(t) + \tilde{d}_{12}(t)\lambda_2(t) \leq \tilde{\tilde{n}}_1(t)\omega(t) - \mu_1(t)q_1 + \xi_1(t) - \xi_1(t+1) + \gamma_1(t) \tag{1.21}$$

$z_2(t)$ $$\tilde{d}_{21}(t)\lambda_1(t) + \tilde{d}_{22}(t)\lambda_2(t) \leq \tilde{\tilde{n}}_2(t)\omega(t) - \mu_2(t)q_2 + \xi_2(t) - \xi_2(t-1) + \gamma_2(t) \tag{1.22}$$

$z_{12}(t)$ $$\xi_1(t) + n_{12}(t)\omega_1(t) \geq \xi_2(t+1) \tag{1.23}$$

$z_{21}(t)$ $$\xi_2(t) + n_{21}(t)\omega_2(t) \geq \xi_1\ (t+1) \tag{1.24}$$

$y_i^+(t),\ y_i^-(t)$ $$-M \leq \alpha_i(t) \leq M \tag{1.25}$$

$x_i^+(t),\ x_i^-(t)$ $$-M \leq \beta_i(t) \leq M \tag{1.26}$$

$z_i^+(t),\ z_i^-(t)$ $$-M \leq \gamma_i(t) \leq M \tag{1.27}$$

Conditions (1.13), (1.14) relate characteristics based preferences at the margin relative to self to characteristics-based measures $\lambda_i(t)$ of preferences at the margin generated relative to a system relative to self, with such measures being generated via commodities $y_i(t)$.

According to conditions (1.15), (1.16) consumption commodities $y_i(t)$ are optimally supplied up to the point where (essentially subjective) evaluations of characteristics based gain:

$$\tilde{a}_{i1}(t)\lambda_1(t) + \tilde{a}_{i2}(t)\lambda_2(t)$$

This equates to the system based measure of system resource (opportunity) cost $\varphi_1(t)$ for production of the quantity $y_1(t)$ *plus* a privately measured opportunity cost based evaluation of time associated with consumption of the quantity $y_1(t)$ and the quantity $\alpha_1(t)$ - here open to interpretation as a measure potentially *systematically regulating conformity* between *consumption* related system goals and *consumption* related system achievement.

While production opportunity costs $\varphi_j(t)$ are related to consumption oriented measures via conditions (1.15), (1.16), conditions (1.17) and (1.18) are open to interpretations as if generating optimal decision rules according to which commodities $x_j(t)$ are optimally produced (if at all) up to the point where the potential *returns* $\varphi_j(t)$ from sales to consumers *plus* essentially consumption related externality measures $\tilde{b}_{j1}(t)\lambda_1(t)$ + $\tilde{b}_{j2}(t)\lambda_2(t)$ *equate to* measures of labour input *plus* variable resource input *plus* capacity input *plus* a measure $\beta_j(t)$ open to interpretation as a measure potentially systematically regulating conformity between *production* related system goals and *production* related system achievement.

The form of conditions (1.19), (1.20) emphasizes the intertemporal character of (I). These conditions are open to interpretations as if corresponding to optimal stock-holding conditions according to which produced commodities are held as inputs to future production, or future consumption, as long as discounted future prices are sufficient to compensate for current sales revenue foregone at the margin.

Conditions (1.21), (1.22), (1.23) and (1.24) relate to intertemporally optimal acquisition and retention rules and associated valuation and amortization rules according to which, via (1.21), (1.22), capacity is retained for production *only if*, at the margin, rental/ amortization allowances $\mu_j(t)q_j$ are sufficient to recoup maintenance cost and net capital appreciation/depreciation, *after* allowance for the net effect of essentially consumption related externality measures $\tilde{d}_{j1}(t)\lambda_1(t) + \tilde{d}_{j2}(t)\lambda_2(t)$ and the measures $y_j(t)$ (open to interpretation as potentially systematically regulating conformity between *capacity* related system goals and *capacity* related system achievement).

The form of conditions (1.23) and (1.24) suggests classes of inter -pretation according to which capacity of type 1 (respectively type 2) is *optimally converted* to capacity of type 2 (respectively type 1) *only if* its (discounted) future value equates to its current value *less* potential conversion cost at the margin - and optimally retained in its current use otherwise.

Finally, conditions (1.25), (1.26) and (1.27) respectively relate goal compliance measures $\alpha_i(t)$, $\beta_i(t)$, $\gamma_i(t)$, via system related deviations from goals, $(y^+_i(t), y^-_i(t))$, $(x^+_i(t), x^-_i(t))$, $(z^+_i(t), z^-_i(t))$, to system related measures of compliance/ non-compliance M in the objective function of (I).

This in turn suggests not just potential classes of interpretations in relation to relatively *preemptive* natural or manmade *laws*, but, via the emphasis on potential relativity of compliance, on relative *enforceability* of laws, e.g. by means of various kinds of potential penalty or inducement, including taxes and subsidies.

Such classes of interpretations do not just suggest potential classes of potentially optimal *consistency/ conformity* and/ or potential classes of potentially optimal *inconsistency/ nonconformity* between relatively abstractly decentralized elements of these (sub)systems and *other* relatively decentralized elements of these (sub)systems, but between relatively abstractly decentralized elements of these (sub)systems and *themselves*.

They do this in a variety of ways which, since associated with the single individual specification (I), (I)', imply potential *optimality* of relative tax/subsidy inducing principles and processes *even for the single individual case*, according to rules *as if* : i) *themselves potentiating/ potentiated via* conditions as if among other things *purposively* generating/ generated via elements of relatively *purposive* (self) indeterminacy/ (self) incompleteness/ (self) uncertainty principles and processes *and* as if ; ii) both through their algebraic structures, and through their potential for goal programming-like principles and processes of solution, *themselves suggesting/suggested via* potential classes of extensions to comprehend classes of n-individual examples. Such n-individual extensions and examples are the subject of Section 3.

8.3 Extremal representations of intertemporal choices : extensions to extensions to n-individual cases

Consider first the following extensions to the goal programming-like extremal representation (I) (p.167):

$$\text{Maximize } W = \sum_i \theta_{i1}U_{i1}(c_{i1}(1), c_{i2}(1), \theta_{i2}U_{i2}(c_{i1}(2), c_{i2}(2), \theta_{i3}(c_{i1}(3) \ldots \ldots \theta_{it}U_{it}(c_{i1}(t), c_{i2}(t))$$

$$+ M\sum_j(y^+_j(t)+y^-_j(t)) - M\sum_j(x^+_j(t)+x^-_j(t)) - M\sum_j(z^+_j(t)+z^-_j(t))$$

subject to:

$$\lambda_{i1}(t) \qquad c_{i1}(t) = \tilde{a}_{i11}(t)y_{i1}(t) + \tilde{a}_{i21}(t)y_{i2}(t) + \tilde{b}_{i11}(t)x_1(t) + \tilde{b}_{i21}(t)x_2(t) + \tilde{d}_{i11}(t)z_1(t) + \tilde{d}_{i21}(t)z_2(t) \qquad (2.1)$$

$\lambda_{i2}(t) \qquad c_{i2}(t) = \tilde{a}_{i12}(t)y_{i1}(t) + \tilde{a}_{i22}(t)y_{i2}(t) + \tilde{b}_{i12}(t)x_1(t)$
$+ \tilde{b}_{i22}(t)x_2(t) + \tilde{d}_{i12}(t)z_1(t) + \tilde{d}_{i22}(t)z_2(t) \qquad (2.2)$

$\omega_i(t) \qquad \tilde{n}_{i1}(t)y_{i1}(t) + \tilde{n}_{12}(t)y_{i2}(t) + E_i(t) \leq L_{io}(t) \qquad (2.3a)$

$\omega(t) \qquad n_1(t)x_1(t) + n_2(t)x_2(t) + \tilde{n}_1(t)z_1(t) + \tilde{n}_2(t)z_2(t)$
$+ n_{12}(t)z_{12}(t) + n_{21}(t)z_{21}(t) \leq \sum_i E_{it} \qquad (2.3b)$

$\psi_j(t) \qquad \sum_i y_{ij}(t) = y_j(t) \qquad (2.4)$

$\mu_1(t) \qquad x_1(t) \leq q_1 z_1(t) \qquad (2.5)$

(II)

$\mu_2(t) \qquad x_2(t) \leq q_2 z_2(t) \qquad (2.6)$

$\xi_1(t) \qquad z_1(t) = z_1(t-1) - z_{12}(t-1) + z_{21}(t-1) \qquad (2.7)$

$\xi_2(t) \qquad z_2(t) = z_2(t-1) - z_{21}(t-1) + z_{12}(t-1) \qquad (2.8)$

$\varphi_1(t) \qquad v_1(t) = v_1(t-1) + x_1(t) - y_1(t) - a_{11}(t)x_1(t+1)$
$- a_{12}(t)x_2(t+1) \qquad (2.9)$

$\varphi_2(t) \qquad v_2(t) = v_2(t-1) + x_2(t) - y_2(t) - a_{21}(t)x_1(t+1)$
$- a_{22}(t)x_2(t+1) \qquad (2.10)$

$\alpha_j(t) \qquad y_j(t) + y^+_j(t) - y^-_j(t) = y^*_j(t) \qquad (2.11)$

$\beta_j(t) \qquad x_j(t) + x^+_j(t) - x^-_j(t) = x^*_j(t) \qquad (2.12)$

$\gamma_j(t) \qquad z_j(t) + z^+_j(t) - z^-_j(t) = z^*_j(t) \qquad (2.13)$

All variables non-negative

By analogy with (I) this system (II) is open to interpretation as if giving an extremal representation to intertemporally optimal consumption, production and investment/ disinvestment choices $y_j^*(t)$, $x_j^*(t)$, $z_j^*(t)$ but now for a *group* of individuals i = 1, 2...n.

With this context the most obvious interpretation of the measure W is that of a *Welfare Functional* as if composed from a weighted sum $\Sigma\theta_{i1}U_{i1}(\;)$ of individual preference/ indifference measures $U_i(\;)$.

Notice that according to this specification each individual's pref -erence/ indifference measure $\theta_{i1}(\;)$ is defined *solely and only* with reference to that individual's *own* measurements on characteristics.

In that sense each individual's preference/ indifference relation is clearly relatively *abstract* and, *because* in that sense relatively abstract, in that sense, too, *necessarily unknown/ unknowable i.e.*necessarily only *relatively* knowable relative to another/ others differently located in space-time.

Reinforcing this crucially important point, not only does the specification (II) imply that each individual's preference/ indifference relations are defined uniquely with reference to measures on own characteristics relative to self, but the conditions (2.1), (2.2) imply that if individuals choose to measure relative to a wider system, then such measurements are necessarily relatively subjective.

By contrast with Lancaster's original work on characteristics analyses, therefore, *subjectivity* of measurement is central and crucial here. Among other things potentials for differences of measurement between individuals and each other and/or between individuals and their relatively abstract selves can *themselves* provide sufficient motivations for potentially mutually beneficial changes/ exchanges.

Potential for gains to individuals as if fundamentally stemming from their potentially different perceptions of "the same" reality, e.g. the same commodity, suggests potentially fundamental significance for as if purposive individual and/or collective *exploitations* of fundamental and pandemically applicable mathematical/ physical relative indeterminacy, relative incompleteness and relative uncertainty principles and processes as if purposively thereby to secure elements of individual and/or collective mathematical/ physical gain(s).

Pursuing conditions (2.1), (2.2) of the system (II) from another perspective, analogy with conditions (1.1), (1.2) of the system (I) suggests classes of interpretation according to which each individual i, potentially measures characteristics *not just* via *own* consumption commodities $y_{ij}(t)$ but via *overall levels* of production commodities $x_j(t)$, and of available production capacities $z_j(t)$.

While the incidence of the magnitudes $y_{ij}(t)$ in conditions (2.1), (2.2) suggest potentiations of privately appreciated characteristics relative to self, among other things potentially derived from relatively individually and privately obtained consumption commodities relative to a system, the incidence of the magnitudes $x_j(t)$ and $z_j(t)$ in those conditions will also suggest potentiations of privately appreciated characteristics relative to self, among other things derived from relatively collectively and publicly obtained produced commodities and elements of production capacity relative to a wider (sub)system.

In such ways the form of (2.1), (2.2) suggests classes of inter-pretation in relation to production and consumption *externalities*. It also suggests further classes of extensions according to which some or all individuals' measurements on characteristics depend on others' consumption levels as well as their own and/ or *not just* on overall *levels* of prod-uction or of production capacity but on individual *commitments* $E_j(t)$ of labour inputs, on particular individuals' particular *claims* $x_{ij}(t)$ (with $\Sigma x_{ij}(t) = x_j(t)$) to elements of produced output and/ or particular *claims* $z_{ij}(t)$ (with $\Sigma z_{ij}(t) = z_j(t)$) to elements of production capacity.

Extensions of these kinds suggest potential classes of interpretation in relation to potentially yet more comprehensive classes of consumption externality and/or issues pertaining to distributions/ redistributions of property rights.

With a wider context of collective social choice, they suggest potential classes of extension in relation to relatively more/less *just/ unjust* patterns of individual as well as collective production and consumption opportunities and/or relatively more/less *just/unjust* patterns of individual as well as collective (re)distribution of relatively individual and/or collective property rights, including as particular cases potential for the generation, analysis and critical comparison of different kinds of relatively regulated/ unregulated, centralized/ decentralized market oriented changes/ exchanges.

I will develop these and other kinds of possibilities in more detail in Section 5. Until then, in the interests of clarity, attention will be confined to the relatively simpler relative aggregation/ disaggregation, individual/ collective choice issues, processes and phenomena potentially generating/ generated via elements of the system (II).

Even this relatively simple specification can focus attention *both* :

on the relative *inevitability* of relative individual/ collective mathematical/ physical economic uncertainty/ incompleteness/ indeterminacy principles, processes and phenomena *and*, more subtly ; on the relative *desireability* of relatively individual/ collective mathematical/ physical economic uncertainty/ incompleteness/ indeterminacy principles, processes and phenomena.

Exploring these latter observations notice : *first* that if the relation:

$$W = \sum_{i} \theta_{i_1} U_{i_1}(\ \ )$$

in the system (II) is interpreted as if corresponding to a mathem-atical/ physical economic Welfare Functional composed from a weighted sum of individual preference/ indifference measures $U_{i1}(\ \ )$, then it can be stated with certainty that *none* of those individuals i can completely specify W *either* relative to another/ others *or* relative to elements of a wider mathematical/ physical (sub)system *because* each may (only) certainly, completely specify his/ her/ its individual/ collective preference/ indifference measure $U_{i1}(\ \ )$ relative to self.

Second, it apparently follows directly from an interpretation of $W = \Sigma\theta_{i_1}U_{i_1}(\ \ )$ as a welfare functional that, given *any* collection of initial states, say $U_{i_1}{}^{*}(\ \ )$, *no* individual may change *or* be changed relative to that state - which is as if fixed and certain wholly and only relative to his/ her own preference/ indifference, *unless* acting as if purposively to be/ become relatively *less* certain/ *less* completely determinate wholly and only relative to a particular time and state dependent *definition of* self.

In such contexts, therefore, elements of relatively decentralized individual/ collective actions, reactions and/ or interactions *necessarily* connote *as if purposive* operations of relative mathematical/ physical uncertainty/ incompleteness/ indeterminacy principles and processes.

One important class of examples: individuals acting as if *ultimately* to generate more/less preferred states relative to self/ selves via the generation of *currently* less/more preferred states relative to self/ selves apparently must *necessarily* act as if *choosing* to generate relatively *less* determinate, *less* complete, *less* certain time-states relative to self/ selves.

In a mathematical/ physical economic environment the wording of this statement suggests kinds of individual and/or collective circumstances for which such kinds of as if individually and collectively relative uncertainty, incompleteness and indeterminacy may not just be individually and collectively *inevitable*, but individually and collectively *desireable*. For example, in such contexts as well as others, apparently individuals may choose to act as if by means of gifts, barters or trades *certainly* to potentiate less relative to self/ selves as if thereby *certainly* to potentiate offers of otherwise relatively unknown (in some situations otherwise unknowable) opportunities relative to another/ others differently / distantly located in space-time relative to self/ selves.

In more detail, apparently individuals may choose to act as if *purposively to dominate* relatively decentralized elements of a relatively abstract preference/ indifference/welfare measure $W = \Sigma\theta_{i_1}U_{i_1}(\ \ )$ relative to self/ selves and, in doing so, to generate conditions of relative uncertainty/ incompleteness/ indeterminacy relative to self/ selves as if thereby *not just to potentiate but to exploit* otherwise relatively *unknown* (or unknowable) opportunities for relative gain/loss (e.g. of commodities, rights, information) relative to self/ selves and/ or another/ others differently located in space-time relative to self/ selves.

To generate relations which will pave the way for further, more detailed and technical preference and welfare related developments of these and other kinds, and, more generally, because individually and collectively optimal decision rules which are generated are of considerable interest in their own right, now associate the indicated dual variables with the constraints of (II) to generate the system of relations (II)' as follows:

$c_{i_1}(t)$ $$\frac{\theta_{i_1}}{\theta_{i_2}} \frac{\delta U_{i_1}}{\delta U_{i_2}} \cdots \theta_{it} \frac{\delta U_{it}}{\delta c_{i_1}(t)} \geqq \lambda_{i_1}(t) \tag{2.14}$$

$c_{i_2}(t)$ $$\frac{\theta_{i_1}}{\theta_{i_2}} \frac{\delta U_{i_1}}{\delta U_{i_2}} \cdots \theta_{it} \frac{\delta U_{it}}{\delta c_{i_2}(t)} \geqq \lambda_{i_2}(t) \tag{2.15}$$

$y_{i_1}(t)$ $$\tilde{a}_{i_{11}}(t)\lambda_{i_1}(t) + \tilde{a}_{i_{12}}(t)\lambda_{i_2}(t) \leqq \tilde{n}_{i_1}(t)\omega_i(t) + \psi_2(t) \tag{2.16}$$

$y_{i_2}(t)$ $$\tilde{a}_{i_{21}}(t)\lambda_{i_1}(t) + \tilde{a}_{i_{22}}(t)\lambda_{i_2}(t) \leqq \tilde{a}_{i_2}(t)\omega_i(t) + \psi_2(t) \tag{2.17}$$

$y_j(t)$ $$\psi_j(t) \geqq \varphi_j(t) + \alpha_j(t) \tag{2.18}$$

$E_i(t)$ $$\omega_i(t) \leqq \omega(t) \tag{2 19}$$

$x_1(t)$ $$\varphi_1(t) + \sum_i \tilde{b}_{i_{11}}(t)\lambda_{i_1}(t) + \sum_i \tilde{b}_{i_{12}}(t)\lambda_{i_2}(t) \leqq a_1(t)\omega(t) + \mu_1(t) + a_{11}(t)\varphi_1(t-1) + a_{21}(t)\varphi_2(t-1) + \beta_1(t) \tag{2.20}$$

$x_2(t)$ $$\varphi_2(t) + \sum_i \tilde{b}_{i_{21}}(t)\lambda_{i_1}(t) + \sum_i \tilde{b}_{i_{22}}(t)\lambda_{i_2}(t) \leqq a_2(t)\omega(t) + \mu_1(t) + a_{12}(t)\varphi_1(t-1) + a_{22}(t)\varphi_2(t-1) + \beta_2(t) \tag{2.21}$$

$v_1(t)$ $$\varphi_1(t) \leqq \varphi_1(t+1) \tag{2.22}$$

$v_2(t)$ $$\varphi_2(t) \leqq \varphi_2(t+1) \tag{2.23}$$

(II)'

$z_1(t)$ $$\sum_i \tilde{d}_{i_{11}}(t)\lambda_{i_1}(t) + \sum_i \tilde{d}_{i_{12}}(t)\lambda_{i_2}(\tilde{t}) \leqq \tilde{n}_1(t)\omega(t) - \mu_1(t)q_1 + \xi_1(t) - \xi_1(t+1) + \gamma_1(t) \tag{2.24}$$

$z_2(t)$ $$\sum_i \tilde{d}_{i_{21}}(t)\lambda_{i_1}(t) + \sum_i \tilde{d}_{i_{22}}(t)\lambda_{i_2}(t) \leqq \tilde{\tilde{n}}_2(t)\omega(t) - \mu_2(t)q_2 + \xi_2(t) - \xi_2(t+1) + \gamma_2(t) \tag{2.25}$$

$y^+_j(t)$, $y^-_j(t)$ $$-M \leqq \alpha_j(t) \leqq M \tag{2.26}$$

$x^+_j(t)$, $x^-_j(t)$ $$-M \leqq \beta_j(t) \leqq M \tag{2.27}$$

$z^+_j(t)$, $z^-_j(t)$ $$-M \leqq \gamma_j(t) \leqq M \tag{2.28}$$

By comparing (II)' with (I)' on the reader can verify that all of the differences between these systems occur in constraints (2.14) - (2.21) and (2.24), (2.25) (respectively (1.13) - (1.18) and (1.21), (1.22)).

These differences reflect the introduction of distinct n-person consumption plans (via conditions (2.1), (2.2) of (II)) and explicitly distinct individual time allocations for consumption, work and leisure and individual times made available for work respectively via the conditions (2.3a), (2.3b) of (II), as opposed to the single, elided condition (2.3) of (I) which represented the single Crusoe-like individual case.

With these observations in mind now concentrate on the implications and interpretations of the particular differences in conditions (2.14) - (2.21) and (2.24), (2.25).

Taking these in turn : *first*, at an optimum the conditions (2.14), (2.15) imply that an individual i would choose to consume levels of characteristic $c_{i_1}(t)$, $c_{i_2}(t)$ relative to a wider system, if at all, then up to the point where the measure of return $\lambda_{ij}(t)$ relative to the system equates to a preference related, and essentially subjective, measure of opportunities foregone relative to a relatively abstract self.

Next, according to the relations (2.16), (2.17), any individual i would optimally choose to consume levels $y_{ij}(t)$ of commodities j, if at all, then up to the point where the (subjective) characteristics-related returns to that consumption were sufficient to compensate for the personally time related and system consumption related opportunity costs, $\tilde{n}_{ij}(t)$, $\omega_i(t)$ and $\psi_j(t)$ respectively, at the margin, where, according to conditions (2.18), these latter magnitudes are optimally sufficient to recoup a measure $\varphi_j(t)$ of system resource cost potentially imputed to consumption *plus* a target compliance related measure $\alpha_j(t)$ associated with an overall availability target for consumption commodities of type j in period t.

(Notice here that conditions (2.16), (2.17) optimally elide with (2.18) to give conditions isomorphic with (1.15), (1.16) of (I)' for the single individual case. More technically if overall (target) consumption levels are optimally positive then, by conditions (2.4) of (II), target consumption levels are necessarily positive for at least one individual, and conversely).

Conditions (2.19) have straightforward interpretations as earned income conditions according to which : i) *no* individual would choose to work *unless*, at the margin, the system-related income for doing so, $\omega_i(t)$, was sufficient to compensate that individual for his/her non consumption and/or leisure alternatives to work at that rate at that margin, *and* according to which ; ii) with the wider context provided by conditions (2.19), a system marginal wage rate is open to interpretation as if optimally determined via an essentially competitive labour market structure, with the lowest rate necessary (and sufficient) to induce productive contributions of labour time by that optimally determined marginal collection of workers.

I stress here that uniformity of individual wage rates constitutes only one particular class of *special cases* stemming essentially from an assumption implicit in the *specification* of the systems (II), (II)' that individuals and/ or groups act as if individually and collectively *indifferent to* the specification of any targets either for overall labour time supplied, or for distributions of labour times between workers.

Underlining this crucially significant point, if, for example, the system (II) were extended so that total quantities of labour time and/ or individuals' own or other individual's quantities of labour times were represented/ recognized as potentially directly yielding particular kinds of consumption related characteristics, then that modified system would generate a modified system of dual relations in which wages would in general be/ become optimally differentiated between workers.

The optimal wage rate determining criterion would in general then be/ become optimally different from that associating the optimal wage with the lowest consumption/ leisure time related opportunity cost for the worker marginal to the (endogenously) optimal act of workers choosing to work.

These remarks suggest further classes of extensions and developments in relation to (II) - for example to comprehend considerations pertaining to overtime to unemployment benfits and to subsistence income.

They also further encourage the reader to understand the fundamental nature of the goal programming specifications (I)', (II) through the suggestion implicit in them of potentially *dually related* goal programming-like extensions not just *of* elements of these systems, but potentially attainable *via* elements of these systems.

Turning now to the output related conditions (2.20), (2.21): In a manner analogous to the consumption related conditions (2.16), (2.17), these relations apparently have quite straightforward interpretations according to which : output of type j is optimally produced in period t, if at all, then up to the point where its marginal cost $\varphi_j(t)$ is equal to the *sum* of labour input cost $a_j(t)\omega(t)$, capacity cost $\mu_j(t)$, costs of variable inputs to production $a_{1j}(t)\varphi_1(t-1) + a_{2j}(t)\varphi_2(t-1)$ and a goal compliance inducing measure $\beta_j(t)$ *less* the sum of individual-related measures $\tilde{b}_{ij_1}(t)\lambda_{i_1}(t) + \tilde{b}_{ij_2}(t)\lambda_{i_2}(t)$.

It is these measures which are of particular interest here. In the context of (II)', their structure suggests interpretations according to which these latter totals may correspond to *variously* individually *inducing* and/ or individually *induced* production related net taxes or net subsidies, depending on whether the individually related measures $\tilde{b}_{ij_1}(t)$, $\tilde{b}_{ij_2}(t)$ are negative or positive.

Since they are of central significance it is worth analyzing their wider implications in more detail. First, in the relations (2.16), (2.17), the measures $\tilde{b}_{ij_1}(t)\lambda_{i_1}(t)$, $\tilde{b}_{ij_2}(t)\lambda_{i_1}(t)$ together constitute a sum of essentially individually and essentially subjectively related measures. Stressing the essential subjectivity of these measures, not only does their *incidence* depend on the individually related indices i, but their *magnitude* depends on the essential subjectivity of the related measures $\tilde{b}_{ij_1}(t)$, $\tilde{b}_{ij_2}(t)$.

That is, contrary to Lancaster's objectivity assumption, not only will the *incidence* of these measures be expected to differ between individuals but so will their *magnitudes*. Different individuals may expect (and be expected) not just to appreciate different *magnitudes* of particular charact -eristics in particular objects but different *kinds* of characteristics in particular objects.

Even if,coincidentally, conditions indeed obtained as if identically $\tilde{b}_{ij_1}(t) = \tilde{b}_{j_1}(t)$, $\tilde{b}_{ij_2}(t) = \tilde{b}_{j_2}(t)$ according to which perceptions of particular objects' characteristics *were as if* invariant across individuals, these conditions would become equivalent to the following:

$$\varphi_j(t) + \sum_i b_{j_1}(t)\lambda_{i_1}(t) + \sum_i b_{j_2}(t)\lambda_{i_2}(t) \leq a_j(t)\omega(t) + \mu_j(t)$$
$$+ a_{1j}(t)\varphi_1(t-1) + a_2(t)\varphi_2(t-1) + \beta_j(t)$$

In these conditions measures analogous to relatively individually/ collectively determined taxes and subsidies remain essentially *individually* and *subjectively* determined. This is due to the essentially individually and subjectively relativistic nature of the measures $\lambda_{i_1}(t)$, $\lambda_{i_2}(t)$, quantities essentially individually and subjectively related to marginal preference/ indifference relations via conditions (2.16), (2.17).

The *form* of conditions (2.16), (2.17), which extend conditions (1.15), (1.16) of (I) from the single individual case to the n-individual case, itself suggests *optimality of essentially collectively deterministic processes* of decisionmaking as preconditions if individually optimal production decisions are to be attained.

Before proceeding to investigate this point further I briefly consider the conditions (2.24) and (2.25), which are also open to interpretation as if implying optimality for ultimately *essentially collective* means of determining *individual* investment/ disinvestment decisions, and, conversely, for ultimately *essentially individual* means of determining *collective* investment/ disinvestment decisions.

In each of these classes of cases the very form of the constraints, through the measures $\tilde{b}_{ij_1}(t)$, $\tilde{b}_{ij_2}(t)$ and $\tilde{d}_{ij_1}(t)$, $\tilde{d}_{ij_2}(t)$ in (2.16), (2.17) and (2.24), (2.25), does not just suggest potential *processes* of relatively individually/ collectively ultimately characteristic-oriented consumption, production, investment or disinvestment decisions, but *processes* of relatively individual/ collective decisionmaking giving central roles to taxes and subsidies as if among other things potentiating/ potentiated via essentially *First Best* (because essentially optimally chosen) conditions of individually/collectively mathematical/physical optimality.

The nature of such potential processes is easily indicated if the reader recalls that, via conditions (2.14), (2.15), according to which:

$$\frac{\theta_{i1}}{\theta_{i2}} \frac{\delta U_{i1}}{\delta U_{i2}} \ldots \theta_{it} \frac{\delta U_{it}}{\delta c_{i_1}(t)} \geqq \lambda_{i_1}(t),$$

$$\frac{\theta_{i1}}{\theta_{i2}} \frac{\delta U_{i1}}{\delta U_{i2}} \ldots \theta_{it} \frac{\delta U_{it}}{\delta c_{i_2}(t)} \geqq \lambda_{i_2}(t)$$

an individual would *optimally* choose to experience characteristics relative to a wider system rather than experiencing them relative to a relatively abstract self, if at all, then (only) to the point where marginal returns to realized characteristics $\lambda_{i_1}(t)$, $\lambda_{i_2}(t)$ were sufficient to compensate for the essentially subjectively evaluated marginal opportunity costs of realizing them :

$$\theta_{it} \frac{\delta U_{it}}{\delta c_{i1}(t)}, \theta_{i1} \frac{\delta U_{it}}{\delta c_{i1}(t)}$$

In particular, if at an optimum $c^*_{i_1}(t) > 0$, then, via conditions (2.14) at an optimum relative to that individual i, conditions obtain as if:

$$\frac{\theta_{i_1}}{\theta_{i_2}} \frac{\delta U_{i_1}}{\delta U_{i_2}} \ldots \theta_{it} \frac{\delta U_{it}}{\delta U_{i_1}(t)} = \lambda_{i_1}(t) \qquad (2.29)$$

Or, using conditions as if identically:

$$\frac{\theta_{is}}{\theta_{is+1}} \quad \frac{\delta U_{is}}{\delta U_{is+1}} = \frac{1}{1+r_{is.s+1}}$$

conditions arguably obtain as if identically, relative to that individual:[2]

$$\prod_{s=1}^{t-1} \frac{1}{1+r_{is.s+1}} \theta_{it} \frac{\delta U_{it}}{\delta c_{i1}(t)} = \lambda_{i_1}(t) \qquad (2.30)$$

And, via conditions (2.16), (2.17), (2.20), (2.21), (2.22), (2.23) at an optimum relative to the wider (sub)system conditions obtain as if:

i) for *consumption* commodities $y_{ij}(t)$:

$$\tilde{a}_{ij_1}(t) \prod_{s=1}^{t-1} \frac{1}{1+r_{is.s+1}} \theta_{it} \frac{\delta U_{it}}{\delta c_{i_1}(t)} \leqq \tilde{n}_{ij}(t)\omega_i(t)$$

$$+ \psi_j(t) - \tilde{a}_{ij_2}(t)\lambda_{i_2}(t) \qquad (2.31)$$

with equality if *realized* $y^{**}_{ij}(t) > 0$

ii) for *production* commodities $x_j(t)$:

$$\varphi_j(t) + \tilde{b}_{ij_1}(t) \prod_{s=1}^{t-1} \frac{1}{1+r_{is.s+1}} \theta_{it} \frac{\delta U_i}{\delta c_{i_1}(t)} \leq a_j(t)\omega(t)$$

$$+ \mu_j(t) + a_{1j}(t)\varphi_1(t-1) + a_{ij(t)}\varphi_2(t-1) + \beta_j(t) \qquad (2.32)$$

$$- \sum_{r\neq 1} \tilde{b}_{rj_1}(t)\lambda_{r_1}(t) - \sum_r \tilde{b}_{rj_2}(t)\lambda_{r_2}(t)$$

with equality if *realized* $x^{**}{}_j(t) > 0$

iii) for elements of *production capacity* $z_j(t)$:

$$\tilde{d}_{ij_1}(t) \prod_{s=1}^{t-1} \frac{1}{1+r_{is.s+1}} \theta_{it} \frac{\delta U_{it}}{\delta c_{i_1}(t)} \geq \tilde{\tilde{n}}_j(t)\omega(t)$$

$$- \mu_j(t)q_j + \xi_j(t) - \xi_j(t+1) + \lambda_j(t) - \sum_{r\neq i} d_{rj_1}(t)\lambda_{r_1}(t) \qquad (2.33)$$

$$- \sum_r d_{j_2}(t)\lambda_{r_2}(t)$$

with equality if *realized* $z_j^{**}(t) > 0$

Conversely, an individual with preference/ indifference relations $\theta_{it}U_{it}(\quad)$ as in (II) would apparently act as if freely to consent to *realized choices* of consumption commodities $y_{ij}^{**}(t)$, produced commodities $x_j^{**}(t)$ and production capacities $z_j^{**}(t)$ relative to a wider system as if *thereby* to potentiate *optimally*, and essentially relatively *subjectively*, determined quantities $c_{ij_1}(t)$, $c_{ij_2}(t)$ of characteristics 1, 2 relative to their relatively abstract selves.

The form of these various relations itself suggests classes of processes of relative self contradiction/ change/ exchange according to which individuals may act consciously and optimally to choose non-zero levels of consumption commodities, produced commodities and production capacity.

(Incidentally individuals may act as if to choose zero values relative to a wider system, in which case some, or all, of the measures $\tilde{a}_{ijr}(t)$, $\tilde{b}_{ijr}(t)$, $\tilde{d}_{ijr}(t)$ would be/ become as if zero).

If non zero levels were optimally chosen, then, according to the above relations, they would be so up to the point where relatively tax/ subsidy adjusted measures of opportunity cost(s) relative to the system equate to essentially subjectively determined and characteristics related measures of opportunity cost(s) relative to a relatively abstract self.

Interpreting measures $\lambda_{i_1}(t)$, $\lambda_{i_2}(t)$ as elements of potential relatively individual "tax-prices", conditions (2.16), (2.17) potentially correlate relatively *higher* tax prices relative to a system with relative *preference* by individuals to participate in (potentially essentially collective) decisionmaking relative to that system over participation in (essentially isolated/ individual) decisionmaking relative to a relatively abstract self.

In this sense individuals apparently arguably *prefer higher* system taxes-prices relative to a relatively abstract self/ selves - a result which might initially appear paradoxical because, relative to any particular individual/ group, apparently essentially and fundamentally self- contradictory.

The wider and essentially relative individual/ collective context provided by elements of the related systems (II), (II)' reinforces this by suggesting individual and collective *purpose* for apparently universally applicable mathematical/ physical principles and processes which not only potentially *generate*, but which potentially systematically/ algorithmically *exploit* conditions of individual self contradiction and paradox.

Illustrating this : Still with interpretations of measures $\lambda_{i_1}(t)$, $\lambda_{i_2}(t)$ in relation to elements of tax-prices, the relations just considered are open to interpretations according to individuals may act as if to *choose* relatively *higher* taxes-prices relative to self/ selves as if thereby to offer potentially *preferred* consumption, production, investment/ disinvestment opportunities *via* relatively *lower* taxes-prices relative to self/ selves/ another/ others (potentially) differently located in space-time.

That is : apparently in the related systems (II), (II)' a relatively *higher* tax-price relative to self may act as if purposively to potentiate - and by that means as if potentially perfectly to *predict* - a relatively *lower* tax-price relative to another/ others, while *also* predicting relatively *higher* price(s) (e.g. $\xi_j(t)$, $\varphi_j(t)$) relative to a wider system (and conversely).

These remarks again emphasize potentially fundamental individual and collective *desireability* for particular kinds of apparently paradoxical (e.g. consciously inflationary) principles and/or processes of (self) *contradiction* implicit in elements of (II), (II)'.

According to conditions (2.16), (2.17) individuals *choosing* to measure characteristics relative to the wider system (as opposed to choosing to measure them, if at all, exclusively relative to a relatively abstract self) would implicitly choose according to output and capacity conditions (2.20), (2.21) and (2.24), (2.25) as if, respectively:

$$\sum_i \tilde{b}_{ij_1}(t)\lambda_{i_1}(t) + \sum_i \tilde{b}_{ij_2}(t)\lambda_{i2}(t) \leq a_j(t)\omega(t) + \mu_j(t) + a_{1j}(t)\varphi_1(t-1) + a_{2j}(t)\varphi_2(t-1) + \beta_j(t) - \varphi_j(t)$$

and

$$\sum_i \tilde{d}_{ij_1}(t)\lambda_{i_1}(t) + \sum_i \tilde{d}_{ij_2}(t)\lambda_{i_2}(t) \leq \tilde{\tilde{n}}_j(t)\omega(t) - \mu_j(t) + \xi_j(t) - \xi_j(t+1) + \gamma_j(t)$$

The weights $\tilde{b}_{ij_1}(t)$, $\tilde{b}_{ij_2}(t)$, $\tilde{d}_{ij_1}(t)$, $\tilde{d}_{ij_2}(t)$ do not just differ between individuals i. Even for the same individual weights relative to "the same" characteristic may systematically differ depending on the nature of potentially associated consumption, production or capacity retention/ investment/ disinvestment processes. In that sense far from being consistent with Lancaster's original objectivity assumption such weights become subjective a fortiori.

These weights can be variously positive, negative or zero, with such conditions associated respectively with preference for *more*, preference for *less* and *indifference* toward the contributions (if any) of respectively production and investment/ disinvestment generating activities to individuals' appreciation of their particular characteristics at the margin.

These remarks will suggest classes of interpretation in relation to individual/ collective taxes/ subsidies in general - and interpretations as if potentially yielding tax/ subsidy-free "competitive" cases only as particularly naive (and therefore ultimately essentially uninteresting) special cases. They will also suggest classes of potential interpretations as if themselves potentially *empirically* generating/ generated via a potentially rich and varied plethora of alternative processes.

These include essentially *altruistically* motivated cases and as if *entrepreneurially* motivated production/ investment/ disinvestment processes according to which :

i) *positive* measures of these kinds constitute measures of willingness to pay for *more* output/ capacity, without recompense beyond directly wage/ capacity related income and ;

ii) *negative* measures of this kind constitute willingness to generate more output/ capacity only if compensated *beyond* direct wage/ capacity income for any particular individual or group.[3]

More generally such cases include examples according to which for any two complementary subsets m, $\bar{m}$ of individuals i conditions obtain as if:

$$\sum_{i\in m} \tilde{b}_{ij_1}(t)\prod \frac{1}{1+r_{is.s+1}}\,\theta_{it}\,\frac{\delta U_{it}}{\delta c_{i_1}(t)} + \sum_{i\in m} b_{ij_2}(t)\prod \frac{1}{1+r_{is.s+1}}\,\theta_{it}\,\frac{\delta U_{it}}{\delta c_{i_2}(t)}$$

$$\leq a_j(t)\omega(t) + \mu_j(t) + a_{1j}(t)\varphi_1(t-1) + a_{2j}(t)\varphi_2(t-1) + \beta_j(t) - \varphi_j(t)$$

$$- \sum_{i\in m} \tilde{b}_{ij_1}(t)\lambda_{i_1}(t) - \sum_{i\in m} \tilde{b}_{ij_2}(t)\lambda_{i_2}(t)$$

And :

$$\sum_{i\in m} \tilde{d}_{ij_2(t)}\prod \frac{1}{1+r_{is.s+1}}\,\theta_{it}\,\frac{\delta U_{it}}{\delta c_{i_1}(t)} + \sum_{i\in m} \tilde{d}_{ij_2(t)}\prod \frac{1}{1+r_{is.s+1}}\,\theta_{it}\,\frac{\delta U_{it}}{\delta c_{i_2(t)}}$$

$$\leq \tilde{\tilde{n}}_j(t)\omega(t) - \mu_j(t)q_j + \xi_j(t) - \xi_j(t+1) + \gamma_j(t)$$

$$- \sum_{i\in m} \tilde{d}_{ij_1}(t)\lambda_i(t) - \sum_{i\in m} \tilde{d}_{ij_2}(t)\lambda_{i_2}(t)$$

If these relations hold with strict equality they are consistent with actively *preferred* (potentially variously individually/ collectively taxed/ subsidized) choices of strictly positive amounts $x_j(t)$, $z_j(t)$ for individuals $i\in m$ - and conditions of as if *indifference* to such (processes) of production for individual $i\in m$.

In such a situation the above relations would potentially "add up" in ways consistent with individually/ collectively optimally determined - and potentially *optimally* taxed or subsidized - accounting and financial relations.

Whereas, conditions according to which these relations hold with strict inequality appear *variously* consistent *first* with outputs $x_j(t)$ and capacities $z_j(t)$ as if optimally zero and, *second*, and more interestingly, with actively *preferred* (and potentially variously individually/ collectively taxed/ subsidized) choices of *relatively* greater/ positive or relatively less/ negative amounts $x_j(t)$, $z_j(t)$, thus potentially inducing/ induced via the *evolution of* potentially strictly preferred conditions $x_j(t)$, $z_j(t)$ relative to individuals $i\in\bar{m}$ by individuals $i\in m$, or conversely.

Together these classes of interpretations suggest many different kinds of principles and processes, including essentially self contradictory principles and processes of self dominance/ change/ exchange according to which individual(s) $i\in m$ may act as if *purposively* to dominate preferences and/ or imputations of rights/ commodities/ characteristics relative to self/ selves as if *thereby* to potentiate *more*, e.g. knowledge, rights, commodities, characteristics, relative to self/ selves/ another/ others differently/ distantly located in space-time.

Such principles and processes are open to interpretations as if themselves potentiating/ potentiated via goal programming-like extensions and interpretations in relation to elements of (II), (II)'. I explore aspects of these points in more detail in the following Section.[4]

7.4 Self contradiction, self dominance, change and exchange

I have already noted that in (II) the relation $W = \Sigma\theta_{i_1}U_{i_1}(\ )$ might take on the interpretation of an as if optimally determining and/or optimally determined Welfare Functional. More particularly this relation is open to interpretation as if an explicitly Bergson- Samuelson- like welfare functional (see {12}, {5} and {10}) being potentially consistent with both of the necessary properties, namely *positive weights* ($\theta_{i_1} > 0$ all i) for individual preference relations and a *Pareto property* according to which, if any individual i were made better off according to his/ her own relatively abstract preference relation $U_{i_1}(\ )$, then society would be/become better off according to the socially related welfare measure W since, for example:

if $$W = \sum_i \theta_{i_1} U_{i_1}(\ )$$

then $$dW = \sum_i \theta_{i_1} \frac{\delta U_{i_1}}{\delta c_{i_1}} dc_{i_1}$$

and, if $\theta_{i_1} > 0$ all i, *then* dW > 0 for cases where:

$$dc_{i_1} > 0,\ \frac{\delta U_{i_1}}{\delta c_{i_1}}(\ ) > 0,\ \frac{\delta U_{r_1}}{\delta c_{i_1}}(\ ) > 0 \quad r \neq i$$

Notice here :

i) That, according to such characteristics-related measures W( ), $U_{i_1}(\ )$, apparently a state potentially constitutes a *social improvement* if potentially yielding, or yielded via, essentially characteristics-related improvements *to any, or to all* individuals i.

ii) That potentially Bergson-Samuelson-like welfare interpretations do indeed constitute only one class of special cases in relation to the measures W. Others include examples for which, implicitly or explicitly, conditions obtain as if $\theta_{it} = 0$, $\theta_{it} < 0$, some or all i, thereby comprehending the as yet relatively *unknown* preferences of as yet relatively *unknown* individuals.

Lest the reader become beguiled by the apparent precision either of analysis or of interpretations apparently thus potentially attainable via elements of the relation $W = \Sigma\theta_{i_1}U_{i_1}(\ )$, I again stress that, although this relation constitutes the objective of an essentially collectively specified (and welfare maximizing) specification (II), according to that same specification *no* individual i may *discover* the relation W by completely discovering all individuals' preference/ indifference relations $U_{r_1}(\ )$ and weighting them with measures θ_{r_1} *since* in that system *each* individual i is essentially relatively *abstractly* defined with reference to his/her own relatively *different* and *subjective* measurements on characteristics relative to self and/or another/ other elements of a wider mathematical/ physical system.

Very simply, this specification recognizes that *your* measurement of a characteristic or a commodity relative to *me* is *necessarily different* from *my* measurement of a characteristic or of a commodity relative to me.

In the system (II), *realizations* of magnitudes of mathematical/ physical quantities (of whatever kind) relative to self/ another/ others *are not independent* of *processes of measurement* relative to self/ selves/ another/ others. If $c^*_{ij}(t)$. $y^*_{ij}(t)$ $x^*_{ij}(t)$, $z^*_{ij}(t)$ represent a particular state of elements of subsystems of the system (II) relative to self/ selves, then no such element can measure itself/ be measured *differently* relative to self/ another/ others *except* by being/ becoming *changed* relative to self/ another/ others.

If a representation of a contingently intertemporally optimal plan $y^*_{ij}(t)$, $x^*_{ij}(t)$, $z^*_{ij}(t)$ is seen as corresponding to elements of an overtly *cardinal* specification (II) then, according to that same specification, individuals i *either* already constituting elements of that subsystem (via conditions as if $\theta_{i_1} > 0$, $U_{i_1}(\ ) > 0$), *or* as if individuals/ analysts/ agents as yet only potentially construed via elements of that system (via conditions as if $\theta_{i_1}>0$, $U_{i_1}(\ )>0$), may act as if to *specify* potential principles or processes according to which relatively individually/ collectively *ordinally* preferred/ less preferred welfare gains/ losses, including among others classes of gain(s)/loss(es) in the Pareto sense, via elements of principles and/ or processes of (self) contradiction/ change/ exchange as if themselves purposively potentiating/ potentiated via particular elements of that system.

One sweepingly applicable class of such principles and/ or processes are those open to interpretation as if purposively *altruistically* induced according to which *any* individual (be he/she/they expert or lay) operating either within a subsystem, or relative to it, may act as if potentially to choose *less* (e.g. rights, desireable commodities or desireable character -istics) for self/ selves as if thereby purposively to potentiate *more* (e.g. rights, desireable commodities or desireable characteristics) for another/ others relatively differently and distantly located in space-time relative to self/ selves.

It is illuminating to consider particular classes of examples of behaviours potentiating/ potentiated via elements of (II) in more detail as one way of bringing out more fundamental principles from which they are composed as follows:

First notice a fundamentally applicable principle of mathematical/ physical self contradiction. According to behaviours of the kind just described any individual, whether expert or lay, analyst or executive agent, if relatively abstractly endowed with a particular amount of (potential knowledge of) a particular right, desireable commodity or desireable characteristic relative to self, *must* act as if purposively to have relatively *less* of that relatively abstract endowment relative to self if to act as if purposively to potentiate relatively *more* of (potential knowledge of) that particular right, desireable commodity, desireable characteristic relative to another/ other/ others relatively differently and distantly located in relative space-time.

A fortiori any individual relatively abstractly preferring relatively *more* endowments of rights, commodities, characteristics relative to a relatively abstract self, yet nevertheless acting as if purposively to potentiate relatively *less* endowments of rights, commodities, characteristics relative to a relatively abstract self/ selves as if purposively thereby to potentiate relatively *more* endowments of rights, commodities, characteristics relative to another/others, *must* act as if, in general to *dominate* and, in particular, to *contradict* relatively abstract preference relations relative to a relatively abstract self as if in order thereby to potentiate gains relative to another/ others.

Secondly notice a related principle of as if purposive relative mathematical/ physical (self) indeterminancy/ incompleteness/ uncertainty according to which an individual acting as if certainly/ completely/ deterministically initially endowed with a particular quantity of relatively abstract rights, commodities, characteristics, acts as if *purposively* to potentiate relatively *less* of these relatively abstract rights, commodities, characteristics relative to a relatively abstract self, i.e. acts as if to potentiate a relatively *less* determinate/ complete/ certain state relative to his/her relatively abstract initial endowment of rights, commodities, characteristics as if purposively *thereby* to potentiate relatively *more* of those rights, commodities, characteristics via a relatively more complete/ certain/ determinate amount of such rights, commodities, characteristics relative to another/ others.

Here there are not just relative mathematical/ physical uncertainty/ incompleteness/ indeterminancy principles per se, but principles according to which individuals and groups may act as if purposively to potentiate *gains* relative to relatively abstract self/ selves via elements of processes as if *explicitly designed to exploit* relative mathematical/ physical indeterminacy/ incompleteness/ uncertainty principles and processes relative to self/ selves/ another/ others.

Even altruistically motivated principles and processes of the kinds just considered do *not inevitably* connote *welfare* gains since individual subjective preferences vary and (knowledge of) what is relatively *more* preferred relative to one may be/become (knowledge of) what is relatively *less* preferred relative to another/ others.

Even in essentially altruistic environments, individuals or groups of altruistic donors may act as if potentially to offer relatively *less* preferred states of information, rights, commodities, characteristics relative to relatively abstract self/ selves (as if thereby to potentiate (offers of) *potentially* more preferred states of information, rights, commodities, characteristics relative to another/ others).

Nevertheless there are classes of essentially altruistically motivated cases for which both donor(s) and recipient(s) would gain.

Generally, if realized outcomes with respect to information, rights, commodities and/ or characteristics were indeed preferred by both donor(s) and recipient(s) then, *because* both would gain in their own estimation, and according to their own relatively abstract preference measures, *any* measure of welfare positively weighting (all) individuals relatively abstract preference measures would *necessarily* increase.

More particular examples include the following : if a freely made offer were freely *accepted*, then apparently the donor, *because* having freely revealed a preference to give, could be argued to have *gained* according to his/ her characteristics-related preferences *and* as having gained information about another's/ others' (revealed) preferences, even though having mathematically/ physically *lost* information, rights, commodities, characteristics relative to self *because of* such another's/ others' actions as if to accept (knowledge of) rights, commodities and/ or characteristics.

More subtly ; if a freely made offer of (knowledge of) rights, commodities and/or characteristics were freely *refused* then the potential donor might be argued potentially *also* to gain because, *via that refusal*, and *relative to the unaccepted offer*, now potentially generating *more* knowledge, rights, commodities and/or characteristics relative to a relatively abstract self than would have been attainable had that offer been accepted, *as well as*, via that refusal by another/ others, gaining knowledge of another/ others relatively abstract knowledge, rights, commodities and/or characteristics related preference/ indifference measures.

In summary these remarks suggest classes of interpretations with reference to offers of *gifts* of commodities to another/ others according to which an individual/ group may act as if to potentiate *less* rights, commodities, characteristics relative to self/selves as if thereby perfectly predictively to potentiate (offers of) relatively *more* rights, commodities, characteristics relative to another/ others *all* in such a way that if such gifts were *freely accepted* both would gain according to their individually characteristics related preference/ indifference measures. And, if such potential gifts were *freely refused* arguably each would nevertheless potentiate gains according to their own and according to another/ others characteristics related preference/ indifference measures.

In turn these essentially individually gift-related interpretations suggest further and more complex kinds of behaviours, including the following:

A. Reciprocated (Offers of) Gifts/ Sequences of (Offers of) Gifts - behaviours according to which individuals/ groups (re)act as if freely to potentiate *less* rights, commodities, characteristics relative to self/ selves as if thereby to potentiate (offers of) *more* rights, commodities, characteristics relative to another/ others differently located in space-time, who, *in turn*, act as if freely to potentiate *less* rights, commodities, characteristics relative to self/ selves as if thereby to potentiate (offers of) *more* rights, commodities, characteristics relative to another/ others differently located in space-time... .

Such terminologies and potential reciprocations in turn suggest interpretations with reference to:

B. (Offers of) Barter/ Sequences of (Offers of) Barters - behaviours according to which individuals/ groups (re)act as if freely to potentiate *less* rights, commodities, characteristics relative to self/ selves as if thereby to potentiate (offers of) *more* rights, commodities, characteristics relative to another/ others, (those offers being) *conditional upon* particular kinds of conditional, and essentially commodity related, (re)actions by that other/ those others to potentiate *less* rights, commodities, characteristics relative to self/selves as if thereby to potentiate conditional and essentially commodity related (offers of) *more* rights, commodities, characteristics relative to another, others ... .

Again such terminologies, together with potential reciprocations of these latter kinds, suggest further classes of interpretations with reference to:

C. (Offers of) Trade(s)/ Sequences of (Offers of) Trade(s) - behaviours according to which individuals/ groups (re)act as if freely to potentiate *less* rights, commodities, characteristics relative to self/selves as if thereby to potentiate (offers of) *more* rights, commodities, characteristics relative to another/ others, these offers being *conditional upon* particular kinds of conditionally - and essentially both commodity and currency related - (re)actions by that other/ those others to potentiate *less* rights, commodities, characteristics relative to self/ selves as if thereby to potentiate essentially both currency and commodity related (offers of) *more* rights, commodities, characteristics relative to another/others ... .

The latter cases suggest central and fundamentally positive roles for currency, taxes, subsidies as well as for standard units, including not only standard monetary, fiscal and financial units per se, but potential principles and processes as if themselves potentiating/ potentiated via principles and processes of (self) contradiction relative to relatively individually/ collectively standardized mathematical/ physical units, principles and processes more generally.[5]

These types of potentially interactive behaviours will also prompt various kinds of technical questions, including questions pertaining to relative *starting/ stopping* of (sequences of) processes pertaining to offers to give/take, barter or trade, and associated questions pertaining to *magnitudes* of individual/ collective gain(s)/ loss(es) relative to self/ selves/ another/ others and relative to a wider mathematical/physical (sub) system - questions which I have explored elsewhere in considerable depth and detail with particular emphasis upon potentially positive roles:

i)For (Potentially) *Reciprocal Revealed Preference Principles* and processes of contradiction change/ exchange relative to self/ selves/ another/ others and/ or relative to elements of a wider mathematical/ physical system;[6]

ii)For relatively standardized physical/ fiscal/ financial units in general, and for elements of essentially integer and self axiomatizing currency units in particular[7], as well as ;

iii)For potentially as if purposively *cyclically* (self) contradictory individual/ collective decision principles, processes and phenomena.[8]

Here it is sufficient to recognize that, if one individual/ group may predictably *gain* according to their *own* preferences via another's/ others' *chosen* loss according to *their own* preferences, and conversely, then apparently *all* such groups may potentially act as if (unanimously) to potentiate gains to all - incidentally including gains *of* as well as gains *via* knowledge of the feasibility of otherwise relatively unknowable/ unattainable *socially* preferable states- *whoever* initiates a sequence of change/ exchanges.

Apparently via an exchange or sequence of exchanges, *all* groups of individuals may gain with reference to preferences as well as to commodities *if* those relatively more well endowed (the relatively *larger*) potentiate gain(s) to the relatively less well endowed (the relatively *smaller*) and, in turn, if accepted, the relatively *smaller* potentiate gain(s) relative to the relatively *larger* ... .

If such a sequence were freely continued apparently individual *and* mutual gain(s) could and would become *arbitrarily large* (unbounded) - i.e. with such a context potential for (relative) *unboundedness* of solutions to (II), (II)' may be/ become collectively *desireable*.

Any individual or group freely choosing to *stop* such a sequence of gifts/ barters/ trades would apparently stop otherwise potentially *still more preferred* outcomes for the stopping individual/ group relative to the wider system in such a way as *both* to secure a relatively abstract and implicitly relatively preferred state for that stopping individual/ group relative to self/ selves *and* to potentiate relatively yet more preferred outcomes for the other individual(s)/ group(s) thereby stopped, *because* enabling them to retain/ consume relatively desireable commodities otherwise offered as gifts/ as inducements to (further) barter/ trade.

Such potential sequences emphasise individual/ collective mathematical/ physical *relativity* in general and *relativity of futurity* in particular according to which *what is/ was* (e.g. a gift, barter good, trade good or currency unit) relative to one individual/ group is as if perfectly predictive of and/ or potentially as if perfectly predicted via *what will be/ become* relative to another/ others, and conversely.[9]

They also emphasize potentially associated and central roles for relative mathematical/ physical *indeterminacy*, *incompleteness*, *and/ or uncertainty* principles relative to self/ another/ others according to which individuals may act as if *purposively* to potentiate *less* certain, *less* complete, *less* determinate elements of endowments relative to self/ selves as if thereby *more* certainly, *more* completely, *more* determinately to potentiate them relative to self/ selves/ another/ others relatively differently/ distantly located in space-time.

Of course processes of giving/ taking, bartering/ trading, are not necessarily essentially constructive in the sense of essentially mutually advantageous: they may be individually and so, ultimately, collectively *destructive*.

Principles and processes according to which individuals *lose* relative to self/ selves as if thereby to potentiate relatively *larger losses* relative to another/ others will suggest a large class of possible examples.

More technically, narrowly "competitive" principles and processes according to which individuals/ groups potentially *lose* relative to self/selves as if to potentiate *gains* via *price* and *income determined* trade(s) relative to another/ others are open to interpretations as consistent with such examples of potentials for individual/ mutual/ collective *annihilation*. (Such processes are consistent inter alia with loss(es) *by* - and ultimately loss *of* relatively *smaller* as if to potentiate gain(s) relative to relatively *larger*).

Finally the systematic and essentially *algorithmic* nature of the potential principles and processes of (self) contradiction/ change/ exchange which have just been considered themselves suggest - and have themselves been suggested via - particular kinds of essentially systematic and algorithmic interpretations as if potentiating/ potentiated via elements of relatively *dually interrelated* linear/ nonlinear, integer/ noninteger (self) contradictions/ changes/ exchanges corresponding to (changes in) elements of the goal programming - like systems (II), (II)'.

The potential in these systems for the generation of such very generally applicable and dually interrelated mathematical/ physical principles, processes and phenomena will become more evident with the extensions of these systems in the following Section.

7.5 Further analyses and developments of relatively decentralized individual and collective decision processes

In Section 3 I remarked that the system (II) might be extended to comprehend explicit classes of interpretations relating to individuals' property rights. With such possibilities in mind now consider the following extensions of that so that not only are *rights* to potential outputs of consumption commodities $y_j(t)$ explicitly allocated to individuals via conditions $\Sigma y_{ij}(t) = y_j(t)$ as in (II) but *rights* to (potentially) produced outputs $x_j(t)$ and rights to (potential) production capacities $z_j(t)$ are also explicitly allocated to individuals via the analogous conditions $\Sigma x_{ij}(t) = x_j(t)$, $\Sigma z_{ij}(t) = z_j(t)$ in the extended system (III) which follows:

$$\begin{aligned} \textit{Maximize } W = \sum_i &\theta_{i_1}U_{i_1}(c_{i_1}(1), c_{i_2}(1), \theta_{i_2}U_{i_2}(c_{i_1}(2), c_{i_2}(2), \\ &\theta_{i_3}U_{i_3}(c_{i_1}(3), c_{i_2}(3) \ldots \theta_{it}U_{it}(c_{i_1}(t), c_{i_2}(t) \ldots) \\ - M \sum_j(y_j^+(t) + y_j^-(t)) &- M \sum_j(x_j^+(t) + x_j^-(t)) - M \sum_j((z_j^+(t) + z_j^-(t)) \end{aligned}$$

subject to:

$$\begin{aligned} \lambda_{i_1}(t) \qquad c_{i_1}(t) = \; &\tilde{a}_{i_{11}}(t)y_{i_1}(t) + \tilde{a}_{i_{21}}(t)y_{i_2}(\tilde{t}) + \tilde{a}_{i_{11}}(t)y_1(t) \\ &+ \tilde{\tilde{a}}_{i_{21}}(t)y_2(t) + \tilde{\tilde{b}}_{i_{11}}(t)x_{i_1}(t) + \tilde{\tilde{b}}_{i_{21}}(t)x_{i_2}(t) \\ &+ \tilde{b}_{i_{11}}(t)x_1(t) + \tilde{b}_{i_{21}}(t)x_2(t) + \tilde{\tilde{d}}_{i_{11}}(t)z_{i_1}(t) \\ &+ \tilde{\tilde{d}}_{i_{21}}(t)z_{i_2}(t) + \tilde{d}_{i_{11}}(t)z_1(t) + \tilde{d}_{i_{21}}(t)z_2(t) \end{aligned} \qquad (3.1)$$

$$
\begin{aligned}
&\lambda_{i2}(t) \qquad c_{i2}(t) = \tilde{\tilde{a}}_{i12}(t)y_{i1}(t) + \tilde{a}_{i22}(t)y_{i2}(t) + \tilde{a}_{i12}(t)y_1(t) \\
&\qquad + \tilde{\tilde{a}}_{i22}(t)y_2(t) + \tilde{\tilde{b}}_{i12}(t)x_{i1}(t) + \tilde{\tilde{b}}_{i22}(t)x_{i2}(t) \\
&\qquad + \tilde{b}_{i12}(t)x_1(t) + \tilde{b}_{i22}(t)x_2(t) + \tilde{\tilde{d}}_{i12}(t)z_{i1}(t) \qquad (3.2)\\
&\qquad + \tilde{\tilde{d}}_{i22}(t)z_{i2}(t) + \tilde{d}_{i12}(t)z_1(t) + \tilde{d}_{i22}(t)z_2(t)
\end{aligned}
$$

$$\omega_i(t) \qquad \tilde{n}_{i1}(t)y_{i1}(t) + \tilde{n}_{i2}(t)y_{i2}(t) + E_i(t) \leq L_{io}(t) \qquad (3.3a)$$

$$
\begin{aligned}
&\omega(t) \qquad n_1(t)x_1(t) + n_2(t)x_2(t) + \tilde{\tilde{n}}_1(t)z_1(t) + \tilde{\tilde{n}}_2(t)z_2(t) \\
&\qquad + n_{12}(t)z_{12}(t) + n_{21}(t)z_{21}(t) \leq \sum_i E_i(t) \qquad (3\ 3b)
\end{aligned}
$$

$$\psi_j(t) \qquad \sum_i y_{ij}(t) = y_j(t) \qquad (3.4a)$$

$$\tilde{\psi}_j(t) \qquad \sum_i x_{ij}(t) = x_j(t) \qquad (3.4b) \qquad . \ (III)$$

$$\tilde{\tilde{\psi}}_j(t) \qquad \sum_i z_{ij}(t) = z_j(t) \qquad (3.4c)$$

$$\mu_1(t) \qquad x_1(t) \leq q_1 z_1(t) \qquad (3.5)$$

$$\mu_2(t) \qquad x_2(t) \leq q_2 z_2(t) \qquad (3.6)$$

$$\xi_1(t) \qquad z_1(t) = z_1(t-1) - z_{12}(t-1) + z_{21}(t-1) \qquad (3.7)$$

$$\xi_2(t) \qquad z_2(t) = z_2(t-1) - z_{21}(t-1) + z_{12}(t-1) \qquad (3.8)$$

$$
\begin{aligned}
&\varphi_1(t) \qquad v_1(t) = v_1(t-1) + x_1(t) - y_1(t) - a_{11}(t)x_1(t+1) \\
&\qquad - a_{12}(t)x_2(t+1) \qquad (3.9)
\end{aligned}
$$

$$
\begin{aligned}
&\varphi_2(t) \qquad v_2(t) = v_2(t-1) + x_2(t) - y_2(t) - a_{12}(t)x_1(t+1) \\
&\qquad - a_{22}(t)x_2(t+1) \qquad (3.10)
\end{aligned}
$$

$$\alpha_j(t) \qquad y_j(t) + y_j^+(t) - y_j^-(t) = y^*_j(t) \qquad (3.11)$$

$$\beta_j(t) \qquad x_j(t) + x_j^+(t) - x_j^-(t) = x^*_j(t) \qquad (3.12)$$

$$\gamma_j(t) \qquad z_j(t) + z_j^+(t) - z_j^-(t) = z^*_j(t) \qquad (3.13)$$

Notice that, if the measure W interprets itself/ is interpreted as (potentially) corresponding to a welfare functional then, apparently, according to this specification, *welfare* would theoretically increase *directly*, other things being equal:

a) with numbers of individuals i.

b) with increases in numbers and/or in quantities of relatively desireable characteristics $c_{is}(t)$ relative to particular individuals i.

In fact, of course, elements, usually of *both* (and *always* of at least one) of these various kinds of theoretical possibilities are empirically *always* attainable by members of societies. Existing individuals might empirically as well as theoretically choose, respectively:

a) to act as if purposively to *have* less relative to self/selves as if thereby purposively to potentiate further numbers of individuals relative to a wider system and, perhaps more easily;

b) to act as if purposively, at least immediately, to *know* less characteristics as if (only) relative to their own relatively abstract self/selves as if thereby potentially to convey more characteristics relative to another/others ... .

And, if, in the specification (III), the measure W interprets itself/ is interpreted as potentially corresponding to a welfare functional then, apparently, via the measures $c_{is}(t)$, *welfare* would theoretically increase *indirectly*, other things equal:

c) with increases in endowments of individual rights $x_{ij}(t)$ to potentially produced commodities $x_j(t)$;

d) with endowments of individual rights $z_{ij}(t)$ to potentially produced production capacities $z_j(t)$;

e) with endowments of individual rights $y_{ij}(t)$ to potentially attainable consumption levels $y_j(t)$.

Again in fact elements of these various kinds of increases are *always* potentially empirically attainable. Individuals initially endowed with rights variously to potentially produced commodities $x_{ij}(t)$, to potential production capacity $z_{ij}(t)$ and/or to potential consumption levels $y_{ij}(t)$ may act as if purposively to potentiate *more* relative to another/ others - by acting as if purposively to potentiate relatively *less* rights, commod -ities *and/or* characteristics as if exclusively relative to relatively abstract self/ selves.

Also, with interpretations as before, according to the specification (III), in general elements of measures $c_{i_1}(t)$, $c_{i_2}(t)$, and thence elements of measures $U_i(\ )$ and W will variously *directly and indirectly* increase, ceteris paribus :

f) with increases in *aggregated* output(s) $x_j(t)$;

g) with increases in *aggregated* consumption(s) $y_j(t)$;

h) with increases in *aggregated* capacity (capacities) $z_j(t)$.

Apparently here individuals and/ or groups may potentiate gains not just by potentiating personal gains exclusive to self/ selves but by potentiating aggregate gains relative to a wider mathematical/ physical (sub)system.

(In turn suggesting developments according to which individuals might be recognized and represented as potentially gaining *or* losing via others' gains or losses).

More subtly, if the various measures $x_j(t)$, $x_{ij}(t)$, $z_j(t)$, $z_{ij}(t)$ interpret themselves/ are interpreted as essentially current or future *income* related and the measures $y_j(t)$, $y_{ij}(t)$ as essentially current or future *expenditure* related measures, then the measure W is open to interpretation as if potentially increasing *both* with increases in (rights to) income *and* with increases in (rights to) expenditure.

With a *macroeconomic* context these remarks would suggest a focus on the former measures $x_j(t)$, $z_j(t)$, $y_j(t)$ in relation to relatively aggregated income-expenditure analyses. With a *microeconomic* context these remarks would suggest a contrasting focus on the latter measures $x_{ij}(t)$, $z_{ij}(t)$, $y_{ij}(t)$ in relation to relatively disaggregated and decentralized income - expenditure analyses.

More interestingly, because theoretically and empirically more naturally, these remarks taken together emphasize scope here for more generally and more fundamentally applicable micro - macroeconomic analyses, in turn focussing attention on potentially interrelated principles and processes according to which relatively *decentralized* individuals and groups may act as if purposively to potentiate gains (or losses) relative to relatively larger and/or relatively *centralized* agencies, individuals or groups - and *vice versa*, thereby among other things returning attention to (elaborations of) classes of potential processes of relatively individual/ collective, giving/ taking, bartering/ trading such as those considered in the preceding Section.

Formally these remarks suggest searches :

i) for *more precise representations* of particular kinds of relatively (de)centralized mathematical/ physical economic decision processes as if generating/generated via particular kinds of refinements of the system (III) and/or ;

ii) for individually and collectively optimal mathematical/physical economic decision rules as if potentially generating/generated via relations dual to the system (III).

In the former category of potentially more precisely (de)centralizable structures, optimal solutions to (III) appear consistent with appending further goals analogous to conditions (3.11), (3.12), (3.13) to that system as follows:

$a_{ij}(t) \qquad y_{ij}(t) + y^+_{ij}(t) - y^-_{ij}(t) = y_{ij}^*(t) \qquad (3.11a)$

$\beta_{ij}(t) \qquad x_{ij}(t) + x^+_{ij}(t) - x^-_{ij}(t) = x_{ij}^*(t) \qquad (3.12a)$

$\gamma_{ij}(t) \qquad \tilde{z}_{ij}(t) + z^+_{ij}(t) - z^-_{ij}(t) = \tilde{z}_{ij}^*(t) \qquad (3.13a)$

To obtain results in the latter category now associate the indicated dual variables with conditions (3.1)...(3.13) on p. and conditions (3.11a) ..(3.13a) here and linear dependence arguments can be used to generate relations analogous to those of (II)' on p.175.

In fact such relations will be *identical* to those of (II)' *except* those pertaining to measures $y_{ij}(t)$, $x_{ij}(t)$, $z_{ij}(t)$, $x_j(t)$, $z_j(t)$ generated by the modifications to (II) : i) via the extension of (2.1), (2.2) to give

(3.1), (3.2) in (III) and ; ii) via the extension of (analogues of) conditions (2.4) via (3.4a), (3.4b), (3.4c) and ; iii) via (3.11a), (3.12a), (3.13a) to include explicitly individually related consumption, production and investment goals.

With these points in mind only relations dual to (III) distinct from those dual to (II) are considered explicitly as follows:

$$y_{i_1}(t) \qquad \tilde{a}_{i_{11}}(t)\lambda_{i_1}(t) + \tilde{a}_{i_{12}}(t)\lambda_{i_2}(t) \leq \tilde{n}_{i_1}(t)\omega_i(t) + \psi_1(t) + \alpha_{i_1}(t) \qquad (2.16)'$$

$$y_{i_2}(t) \qquad \tilde{a}_{i_{21}}(t)\lambda_{i_1}(t) + \tilde{a}_{i_{22}}(t)\lambda_{i_2}(t) \leq \tilde{n}_{i_2}(t)\omega_i(t) + \psi_2(t) + \alpha_{i_2}(t) \qquad (2.17)'$$

$$x_{i_1}(t) \qquad - \tilde{\tilde{b}}_{i_{11}}(t)\lambda_{i_1}(t) - \tilde{\tilde{b}}_{i_{12}}(t)\lambda_{i_2}(t) + \tilde{\psi}_1(t) + \beta_{i_1}(t) \geq 0$$

$$x_{i_2}(t) \qquad - \tilde{\tilde{b}}_{i_{21}}(t)\lambda_{i_1}(t) - \tilde{\tilde{b}}_{i_{22}}(t)\lambda_{i_2}(t) + \tilde{\psi}_2(t) + \beta_{i_2}(t) \geq 0$$

$$\tilde{z}_{i_1}(t) \qquad - d_{i_{11}}(t)\lambda_{i1}(t) - \tilde{d}_{i_{12}}(t)\lambda_{i_2}(t) + \tilde{\tilde{\psi}}_1(t) + \gamma_{i_1}(t) \geq 0$$

$$\tilde{z}_{i_2}(t) \qquad - d_{i_{12}}(t)\lambda_{i_1}(t) - \tilde{d}_{i_{22}}(t\lambda_{i_2}(t) + \tilde{\tilde{\psi}}_2(t) + \gamma_{i_2}(t) \geq 0$$

$$y_j(t) \qquad \psi_j(t) \geq \varphi_j(t) + \alpha_j(t) \qquad (2.18)$$

$$x_j(t) \qquad \varphi_j + \sum_i \tilde{b}_{ij_1}(t)\lambda_{i_1}(t) + \sum_i \tilde{b}_{ij_2}(t)\lambda_{i_2}(t) \leq a_j(t)\omega(t) + a_{ij}(t)\varphi_1(t-1) + a_{2j}(t)\varphi_2(t-1) + \psi_j(t) + \beta_j(t) \qquad (2.20)',(2.21)'$$

$$z_j(t) \qquad \sum_i d_{ij_1}(t)\lambda_{i_1}(t) + \sum_i d_{ij_2}(t)\lambda_{i_2}(t) \leq \tilde{n}_1(t)\omega(t) - \mu_j(t)q_j + \xi_j(t) - \xi_j(t+1) + \tilde{\psi}_j(t) + \gamma_j(t) \qquad (2.24)',(2.25)'$$

$$y^+_{ij}(t),\ y^-_{ij}(t) \qquad - M \leq \alpha_{ij}(t) \leq M$$

$$x^+_{ij}(t),\ x^-_{ij}(t) \qquad - M \leq \beta_{ij}(t) \leq M$$

$$z^+_{ij}(t),\ z^-_{ij}(t) \qquad - M \leq \gamma_{ij}(t) \leq M$$

By comparing the corresponding relations in (II)' p.174 the reader can see how these relations extend and modify those earlier results by requiring that, in general, intertemporally optimal *individual* decisions, as well as intertemporally optimal *collective* decisions, will *optimally* comprehend *both* individually *and* collectively (self) regulatory instruments analogous to individually and collectively *optimally chosen* levels of operation for laws, taxes, subsidies or transfers.

In these ways these results again emphasise underlying themes of this paper while further extending its range of application. For example under (weak) conditions as if an individual i optimally chooses $c_{ir}{}^*(t) > 0$ then, by complementary slackness from (2.14), (2.15), p.174 :

$$\frac{\theta_{i1}}{\theta_{i2}} \quad \frac{\delta U_{i1}}{\delta U_{i2}} \cdots \quad \theta_{it} \frac{\delta U_{it}}{\delta c_{ir}(t)} = \lambda_{ir}(t)$$

Because this implies $y_{ij}(t) > 0$ for some j, again by complementary slackness, at an optimum,from (2.16)',(2.17)' p.189, *for some* j :

$$\tilde{a}_{ij_1}\lambda_{i_1}(t) \quad + \quad \tilde{a}_{ij_2}(t)\lambda_{i_2}(t) \quad = \quad \tilde{n}_{ij}(t)\omega_i(t) + \psi_j(t) + \alpha_{ij}(t)$$

These conditions together imply conditions as if *op*timally :

$$\sum_r \tilde{a}_{ijr}(t) \frac{\theta_{i1}}{\theta_{i2}} \; \frac{\delta U_{i1}}{\delta U_{i2}} \cdots \theta_{it} \frac{\delta U_{it}}{\delta c_{ir}(t)} = \tilde{n}_{ij}(t)\omega_j(t) + \alpha_{ij}(t)$$

according to which an individual would optimally choose quantities $y_{ij}(t)$, if at all, then only up to the point where their marginal characteristics -related returns equalled a *marginal supply cost* made up of an opportunity cost based evaluation consumption time, factor requirements to produce $y_{ij}(t)$ and an individual goal compliance measure aij(t).

Since $y_{ij}(t)$ for some i implies $y_j(t) > 0$, then, at an optimum, by complementary slackness from condition (2.18), p. :

$$\varphi_j(t) \quad = \quad \psi_j(t) \quad + \quad \alpha_j(t)$$

or, considering the last two relations together, at an optimum conditions obtain as if :

$$\sum_r \tilde{a}_{ijr}(t) \frac{\theta_{i1}}{\theta_{i2}} \quad \frac{\delta U_{i1}}{\delta U_{i2}} \quad \cdots \theta_{it} \frac{\delta Uit}{\delta c_{ir}(t)} \quad - \quad \tilde{n}_{ij}(t)\omega_i(t)$$

$$= \quad \varphi_j(t) \quad - \quad \alpha_j(t) \quad + \alpha_{ij}(t)$$

That is, at an optimum, *subjective* evaluations of characteristics-related returns net of consumption time relative to a wider system are related to a relatively *objective* system related measure of opportunity cost $\varphi_j(t)$ *less* a relatively collective measure of goal compliance $\alpha_j(t)$ *net* of a relatively individual measure of goal compliance $\alpha_{ij}(t)$.

(While here *preemptive* weights have been associated with potential deviations from individual or collective goals, these relations again suggest potentially *non-preemptive* individual and/or collective inter -pretations in relation to regulatory laws, taxes and subsidies, a point which is developed further below).

Stressing the potentially comprehensive nature of the specification (III) from a different perspective specialist economic theorists might notice more narrowly academic points : that that specification in principle comprehends as particular classes of special cases :

i) "no trade" cases according to which individuals meet their own demands (only) from their own endowments ;

ii) gifts or thefts according to which individuals may act as if purposively to generate *less* relative to self (respectively another/ others) as if thereby to generate *more* relative to another/ others (respectively self), as well as ;

iii) classes of cases potentially open to interpretations in relation to principles and processes of "barter" or (monetized) "trade".

More subtly notice potential for principles and processes of as if *purposive* contradiction relative to relatively abstract preference/ indifference relations relative (only) to self/ selves as if thereby to act as if *purposively thereby* to potentiate relatively more/less relative to another/ others according to principles and processes open to interpretation among other things as if *purposively* potentiating/ potentiated via elements of (potentially reciprocated) revealed preference behaviours.

Observe here that although elements of the specification (III), are open to interpretation as if themselves potentiating/ potentiated via elements of mathematical/physical externalities, the apparent incompleteness even of *that* specification appears to suggest still more subtle forms of externality inducing or externality induced specifications according to which individuals' measures on characteristics relative to a system are contingent *not just* on *own* consumptions $y_{ij}(t)$ and *own* rights (if any) to output(s) $x_{ij}(t)$ and elements of capacity $z_{ij}(t)$, *but also* upon those of others. This suggests modifications of relations in (III) so that, for example, (3.1) would extend to:

$$\begin{aligned} c_{i_1}(t) = & \sum_r \sum_j \tilde{a}_{irj_1}(t) y_{rj}(t) + \sum_j \tilde{\tilde{a}}_{ij_1}(t) y_j(t) \\ & \sum_r \sum_j \tilde{b}_{irj_1}(t) x_{rj}(t) + \sum_j \tilde{\tilde{b}}_{ij_1}(t) x_j(t) \qquad (3.1)' \\ & \sum_r \sum_j \tilde{d}_{irj_1}(t) z_{rj}(t) + \sum_j \tilde{\tilde{d}}_{ij_1}(t) z_j(t) \end{aligned}$$

with evident implications for suitably modified (and relatively yet more complex) dual relations.

More technically (III) again has an essentially goal programming-like structure, with consequences inherent in the implicitly individually and/ or collectively regulatory interpretations of elements of the dually related system (III)', and conversely.

Indeed the specifications of these systems themselves do not just suggest goal programme -like structures and implications, but correspond to a particular class of examples of apparently universally applicable Heisenberg-like mathematical/physical relative (in)determinacy principles, processes and phenomena according to which elements of such mathematical/ physical economic subsystems are *necessarily* potentially *mathematically/ physically/ economically changed* relative to self and/or another and relative to elements of a wider system, among other things *because* potentially measured differently relative to self and/or another and relative to elements of a wider system.

This suggests relations to more fundamental mathematical and physical issues which I will not pursue further here except to note potentially very positive implications of potentially universally applicable relative indeterminacy/ incompleteness/ uncertainty principles and processes both for relatively individualistic and for relatively collective economies.

Briefly, in very generally applicable classes of cases such principles can, for example, potentiate processes according to which relatively (de)-centralized individuals/ groups may act as if purposively to know/ have *less* knowledge, rights, commodities, characteristics relative to their relatively abstract self/ selves as if thereby purposefully to potentiate *more* knowledge, rights, commodities and/or characteristics relative to another/ others relatively abstract to self/ selves *via* elements of a wider mathematical/ physical (sub)system.

If, as has already been noted, an individual analyst/ agent recognizes the mathematical/ physical *necessity* of relative *incompleteness* of mathematical/ physical knowledge/ measurement relative to self and relative to elements of a wider (sub)system, then roles immediately emerge for relatively individually and/ or collectively standardizing measures, modes of behaviour and language, and for standard units pertaining to elements of particular relatively (de)centralized scientific or economic mathematical/ physical experiments or experiences in particular.

Here mathematical (micro)economists and others will recall the central theme of this chapter and look to elements of (III), when modified by (3.1)', as if potentiating/ potentiated via elements of relatively decentralized principles and processes relating to relatively abstract individual preference/indifference relations relative to that system as follows:

$$
\begin{aligned}
\text{Maximize}\quad & \theta_{i_1}U_{i_1}(c_{i_1}(1),\ c_{i_2}(1),\ \theta_{i_2}U_{i_2}(\ \ldots\ \theta_{it}U_{it}(c_{i1}(t),\ c_{i2}(t)) \\
& + \sum_j[\psi_j(t) - \sum_{s\neq i}\tilde{a}_{sijf}(t)\lambda_{sf}(t)]y_{ij}(t) \\
& - \sum_j[\tilde{\psi}_j(t) + \sum_{s\neq i}\tilde{\tilde{b}}_{sijf}(t)\lambda_{sf}(t)]x_{ij}(t) \\
& - \sum_j[\tilde{\tilde{\psi}}_j(t) + \sum_{s\neq i}\tilde{\tilde{d}}_{sijf}(t)\lambda_{sf}(t)]z_{ij}(t) \\
& + \sum_j[\varphi_j(t) + \alpha_j(t) - \psi_j(t) - \sum_{s\neq i}\tilde{\tilde{a}}_{sjf}(t)\lambda_{sf}(t)]y_j(t) \\
& + \sum_j[-\varphi_j(t) + \beta_j(t) + \tilde{\psi}_j(t) + n_j(t)\omega(t) + \mu_j(t) \\
& + \sum_{k=1,2} a_{jk(t)}\varphi_{r2}(t\ 1) - \sum_{s\neq i}\tilde{b}\ _{sjf}(t)\lambda_{sf}(t)]x_j(t) \\
& + \sum_j[\xi_j(t) - \xi_j(t+1) + \tilde{\tilde{\psi}}_j(t) + \gamma_j(t) + n_j(t)\omega(t) - \mu_j(t)q_j \\
& - \tilde{d}_{sjf}(t)\lambda_{sf}(t)]z_j(t) \quad - \omega(t)E_i(t) \\
& - M\sum_j(y_{ij}^{+}(t) + y_{ij}^{-}(t)) - M\sum_j(x_{ij}^{+}(t) + x_{ij}^{-}\ (t)) \qquad (IV)_i \\
& - M\sum_j(z_{ij}^{+}(t) + z_{ij}^{-}\ (t))
\end{aligned}
$$

subject to:

$$\lambda_{if}(t) \qquad c_{if}(t) = \sum_{r,j}\tilde{a}_{irjf}(t)y_{rj}(t) + \sum_j\tilde{\tilde{a}}_{ijf}(t)y_j(t)$$

$$+ \sum_{r,j}\tilde{\tilde{b}}_{irjf}(t)x_{rj}(t) + \sum_j\tilde{b}_{ijf}(t)x_j(t)$$

$$+ \sum_{r\ j}\tilde{\tilde{d}}_{irjf}(t)z_{rj}(t) + \sum_j\tilde{d}_{ijf}(t)z_j(t) \qquad (4.1)$$

$$\omega_i(t) \qquad n_{i_1}(t)y_{i_1}(t) + n_{i_2}(t)y_{i_2}(t) + E_i(t) \leq L_{io}(t) \qquad (4.2)$$

$$\alpha_{ij}(t) \qquad y_{ij}(t) + y_{ij}^{+}(t) - y_{ij}^{-}\ (t) = y_{ij}*(t) \qquad (4.3)$$

$$\beta_{ij}(t) \qquad x_{ij}(t) + x_{ij}^{+}(t) - x_{ij}^{-}(t) = x_{ij*}(t) \qquad (4.4)$$

$$\gamma_{ij}(t) \qquad z_{ij}(t) + z_{ij}^{+}(t) - z_{ij}^{-}(t) = z_{ij}*(t) \qquad (4.5)$$

All variables non-negative

Associating the indicated dual variables with the constraints of the systems (IV)i yields dual relations as follows:

$c_{if}(t)$ $$\frac{\theta_{i1}}{\theta_{i2}}\ \frac{\delta U_{i1}}{\delta U_{i2}}\ \ldots\ \theta_{it}\frac{\delta U_{it}}{\delta c_{if}(t)} \geq \lambda_{if}(t) \qquad (4.6)$$

$y_{if}(t)$ $$\sum_j \tilde{a}_{ijf}(t)\lambda_{if}(t) \geq \psi_j(t) - \sum_{s\neq i} \tilde{a}_{sijf}(t)\lambda_{sf}(t) + \alpha_{ij}(t) \qquad (4.7)$$

$E_i(t)$ $$\omega_i(t) \geq \omega(t) \qquad (4.8)$$

$x_{ij}(t)$ $$\sum_j \tilde{\tilde{b}}_{iijf}(t)\lambda_{if}(t) \geq \tilde{\psi}_j(t) - \sum_{f,s\neq i} \tilde{\tilde{b}}_{sijf}(t)\lambda_{sf}(\ ) + \beta_{ij}(t) \qquad (4.9)$$

$z_{ij}(t)$ $$\sum_f \tilde{\tilde{d}}_{iijf}(t)\lambda_{if}(t) \geq -\tilde{\tilde{\psi}}_j(t) - \sum_{f,s\neq i} \tilde{\tilde{d}}_{sijf}(t)\lambda\ (t) + \gamma_{ij}(t) \qquad (4.10)$$

$y_j(t)$ $$\sum_f \tilde{\tilde{a}}_{ijf}(t)\lambda_{if}(t) \geq -\varphi_j(t) - \psi_j(t) - \sum_{f,s\neq i} a_{sjf}(t)\lambda_{sf}(t) + \alpha_j(t) \qquad (4.11)$$

$x_j(t)$ $$\sum_f \tilde{b}_{ijf}(t)\lambda_{if}(t) \geq -\varphi_j(t) + n_j(t)\omega(t) + \mu_j(t)$$

$$+ \sum_{k=1,2} a_{jk}\varphi_k(t\ 1) - \sum_{f,s\neq i} \tilde{b}_{sjf}(t)\lambda_{sf}(t) + \beta_j(t) \qquad (4.12)$$

$z_j(t)$ $$\sum_f \tilde{d}_{ijft}\lambda_{if}(t) \geq \xi_j(t) - \xi(t+1) + \tilde{\tilde{n}}_j(t)\omega(t) + \mu_j(t)q_j$$

$$- \sum_{f,s\neq i} \tilde{d}_{sjf}(t)\lambda_{sf}(t) + \gamma_j(t) \qquad (4.13)$$

$y_{ij}^+(t),\ y_{ij}^-(t)$ $$-M \leq \alpha_{ij}(t) \leq M \qquad (4.14)$$

$x_{ij}^+(t), x_{ij}^-(t)$ $$-M \leq \beta_{ij}(t) \leq M \qquad (4.15)$$

$z_{ij}^+(t), z_{ij}^-(t)$ $$-M \leq \gamma_{ij}(t) \leq M \qquad (4\ 16)$$

Elements of these relations suggest further kinds of analysis and interpretations. In particular : in conjunction with conditions (4.2) of the relatively centralized/ collective primal problem (IVi), conditions (4.8) apparently correspond to elements of a work - leisure decision according to which an individual i will decide to work at a wage rate $\omega(t)$, if at all, then only up to the point where that system rate equates to his (subjectively evaluated) personal opportunity rate $\omega_i(t)$.

Or, in the absence of individually related consumption and (potential) production externalities apparently :

i) conditions (4.7) would correspond to conditions according to which an individual i would consume quantities $y_{ij}(t)$ of commodity j, if at all, then up to the point where (subjectively evaluated and characteristics related) opportunity costs relative to relatively abstract self equate to price relative to the system plus an essentially process related self-system compliance measure $\alpha_{ij}(t)$. And ;

ii) conditions (4.9), (4.10) would correspond to conditions according to which an individual i would retain quantities $x_{ij}(t)$, $z_{ij}(t)$ of produced commodities and production capacity of types j, if at all, then up to the point where (subjectively evaluated and characteristic related) opportunity costs relative to relatively abstract self equate to price relative to the system, again, respectively plus essentially process related self-system compliance measures $\beta_{ij}(t)$, $\gamma_{ij}(t)$.

In the absence of individually related potential consumption or production property rights/ externalities *and* under conditions as if aggregate goal compliance measures $\alpha_j(t)$, $\beta_j(t)$, $\gamma_j(t)$ equate to zero, the various conditions (4.11), (4.12), (4.13) would take on forms familiar to economists according to which, from (4.11), relative to the system, consumption commodity *supply price* $\varphi_j(t)$ equated to consumption commodity *demand price* $\psi_j(t)$, where, from (4.12), consumption commodity supply price optimally equates to intermediate input, labour and capacity costs of production at the margin. In turn, the rental costs of production capacity $\mu_j(t)$ would optimally amortize that capacity according to conditions (4.13) by optimally equating earned rentals $\mu_j(t)q_j$ to change in capacity value plus maintenance cost ... .

In each of these cases the relevant relations thus take on forms which will be familiar, for their respective markets, to those familiar with standard economic theories of *variously* individual,or corporate, or financial, decisionmaking in ways here clearly interrelating with each other through a wider (sub)system -ways which, even in the absence of measures of individually related production and consumption externalities, will suggest potential classes of interpretations in relation to relatively (dis)aggregated macro-micro economic income- expenditure systems and budget relations.

As richer examples the reader may notice *returns* via measures $\lambda_{if}(t)$ relative to relatively abstract self on the left hand sides of conditions (4.7) and (4.9) - (4.13), versus measures of *opportunity cost* relative to a wider mathematical/ physical (sub) system relative to self on the right hand sides of those conditions.

In the absence of individually related consumption and production externality and goal compliance measures, these relations could apparently be as if chosen as *optimally* consistent with equations between relatively decentralized expenses and returns for each particular individual's choises of each commodity - and thence for each individual's budget related income-expenditure choices over all commodities.

But in more generally applicable - and more empirically plausible - classes of cases for which production and consumption externalities were *not* absent, these relations (4.7) and (4.9)-(4.13) would in general be optimally chosen as *inconsistent with* essentially anonymous equations between *prices* uniform for all units demanded of each particular commodity demanded and *opportunity costs* uniform for all units supplied. *And* a fortiori, in general optimally chosen as *inconsistent with* as if optimally essentially anonymously individually related *and/ or* as if bargaining process free, fully decentralized, balanced income-expenditure budget specifications.

Especially with a macro-micro economic context the latter remarks will suggest classes of interpretations in relation to individually and collectively goal-oriented income and expenditure taxes and subsidies and, more generally, in relation to *deficit budgeting* per se and to principles and processes of individual and collective gain or loss themselves potentially generating/ generated via relatively individually or collectively *purposively* relatively *unbalanced* budgeting opportunities inherent in the interrelated systems (III) and (IV).

These possibilities emphasize a more fundamental point, namely that the focus here is not just upon the presence or otherwise of individually or collectively system related measures, but ; i) upon ways in which such measures may be seen as essentially deriving from goal programming representations of extended Lancaster-like goods-characteristics analyses and ; ii) upon ways related to individual and/ or collective *processes* of interaction via elements of relatively (de)centralized (sub)systems.

From these points of view the relations dual to (IV_i) which have just been considered can take on much richer and, I believe, theoretically and empirically more interesting interpretations. Not only do those relations incorporate essentially process-related and relatively (de)centralized goal compliance measures ($\alpha_{ij}(t)$, $\alpha_j(t)$)), ($\beta_{ij}(t)$, $\beta_j(t)$)), ($\alpha_{ij}(t)$, $\alpha_j(t)$), they also incorporate potentials for much more subtle kinds of principles and processes of (self) contradiction between elements of relatively abstract self and elements of wider (sub)systems.

Illustrating this ; consider a class of special (and highly restrictive) cases which will be familiar to mathematical economists and in which, *by assumption*, for a given individual i there is a 1 : 1 correspondence between characteristics and commodities. In that case the objective and the constraints of the relatively decentralized system $(IV)_i$ specialize to:[10]

$$\text{Maximize} \quad \theta_{i_1}U_{i_1}(c_{i_1}(1),\ c_{i_1}(2),\ \theta_{i2}U_{i_2}(\ \dots\ \theta_{it}U_{it}(c_{i_1}(t),\ c_{i_2}(t))$$

$$+ \sum_j \psi_j(t)y_{ij}(t) - \sum_j \tilde{\psi}_j(t)x_{ij}(t) - \sum_j \tilde{\psi}_{ij}(t)z_{ij}(t) - \omega(t)E_i(t)$$

$$+ \sum_j [\psi_j(t) + \alpha_j(t) - \psi_j(t)]y_j(t)$$

$$+ \sum_j [-\varphi_j(t) + \beta_j(t) - \tilde{\psi}_j(t) + n_j(t)\omega(t) + \mu_j(t)$$

$$+ \sum_{k=1,2} a_{jk}(t)\varphi_k(t-1)]x_j(t)$$

$$+ \sum_j [\xi_j(t) - \xi_j(t+1) + \tilde{\tilde{\psi}}_j(t) + \gamma_j(t) + \tilde{\tilde{n}}_j(t)\omega(t)]z_j(t)$$

$$- M \sum_j [y_{ij}^+(t) + y_{ij}^-(t)] - M \sum_j [x_{ij}^+(t) + x_{ij}^-(t)]$$

$$- M \sum_j [z_{ij}^+(t) + z_{ij}^-(t)]$$

subject to:

$$c_{if}(t) = y_{ij}(t) \qquad f = j$$

$$\tilde{n}_{i1}(t)y_{i1}(t) + \tilde{n}_{i2}(t)y_{i2}(t) + E_i(t) \leqq L_{io}(t)$$

$$y_{ij}(t) + y_{ij}^+(t) - y_{ij}^-(t) = y_{ij}^*(t)$$

$$x_{ij}(t) + x_{ij}^+(t) - x_{ij}^-(t) = x_{ij}^*(t)$$

$$z_{ij}(t) + z_{ij}^+(t) - z_{ij}^-(t) = z_{ij}^*(t)$$

All variables non-negative

In more detail, the first of these constraints is open to interpretation as if potentiating 1:1 correspondences between relatively *abstract* measures $c_{if}(t)$ relative to self and relatively *non-abstract* measures $y_{ij}(t)$ on commodities relative to a wider subsystem.

The second production and leisure *time* related constraint remains as in the more general system $(IV)_i$ and the third conditions again relate to measures $y_{ij}(t)$, but in doing so now contrast strongly with the first by explicitly relating to *processes* of measurement of commodities relative to a system according to goal programming-like principles and processes of mathematical/ physical (self) contradiction as if potentially *inevitably* changing/ changed by individuals' measurements relative to relatively abstract self.

Such conditions recall developments pertaining to more fundamentally applicable mathematical/ physical (self) (in)determinacy/ (in)completeness/ (un)certainty principles and processes such as have been considered in some detail in Section 4 as well as in Chapters 1 and 4.

Those developments among other things include relations to - and new kinds of motivations for -generally applicable Heisenberg-like relative mathematical/ physical (un)certainty principles pertaining to potential (self) contradictions between states of elements of (sub)systems and measurements on elements of (sub)systems.

They also include, in apparently more narrowly applicable mathematical/ physical economic contexts, relations to potential principles and processes of individually and/or collectively oriented, and essentially self contradictory, Reciprocal Revealed Preference, according to which relatively larger/ smaller groups/ individuals may (re)act as if purposively to choose less (more) relative to relatively abstract self/ selves as if thereby - e.g. via elements of tax reliefs, gifts, barters, trades - to potentiate relatively more (less) relative to another/ others differently/ distantly located in space-time relative to self/ selves. (On such points again see developments in Chapters 1, 2 and 4, as well as in Section 4 above).

In a context of relatively (de)centralized microeconomic interpret -ations the apparently *chosen* fixity of the measures $x_{ij}(t)$, $z_{ij}(t)$ in the preceding system might appear consistent with conditions according to which *property rights* $x_{ij}^*(t)$, $z_{ij}^*(t)$, $L_{io}(t)$ are exogenously determined as fixed and inviolable -assumptions which, in conjunction with apparently given input and output prices would suggest interpretations of the remainder of the objective function in relation to elements of an indiv -idually oriented budget constraint.

Indeed mathematical economists seeking to relate developments here to standard microeconomic representations and analyses of individual constrained choice problems, will notice emphases here on explicit representations of potential *process* whereby budgets and/ or rights may be fixed, or changed, as well as *processes* whereby consumption or leisure choices may be fixed or changed, with implicitly associated *opportunities* for individual and/ or collective gains/ losses to potentials for exploitations of associated relative indeterminacy, incompleteness and uncertainty principles.

Such emphases contrast starkly with the explicit *absence* of measures potentially associated with the relatively individually oriented processes of changes as well as the insistence on conditions of certainty, or certainty equivalence, and complete information characteristic of standard economic representations and analyses. (The developments in Chapter 4 have focused directly on these points).

While these preceding developments stress conditions of mathematical/ physical change in general -and conditions of giving, taking, bartering or trading in particular- the inevitability of the applicability of mathematical/ physical indeterminacy, incompleteness and uncertainty principles here *also* suggests new and positive kinds of roles for standard units, and for standardized principles and processes of measurement relative to relatively standardized units, (including standardized units of language).

Especially in such essentially socioeconomic contexts, apparently individuals may be seen as potentially individually and/or collectively gaining through gifts, thefts, barters or trades relative to elements of wider mathematical/ physical subsystems *because* measures relative to self/ selves *inevitably* differ even from relatively standardized measures relative to another/ others and relative to elements of a wider mathematical/ physical economic system.

More formally the primal specifications (I) - (IV) are all consistent with essentially *predictive* processes according to which actions as if *purposively* to *generate* (self)*contradictions*/ changes/ exchanges relative to elements of those problems may systematically potentiate, or be as if purposively potentiated via, systematically related changes in correspondingly dual relations, and vice versa.

For example, via dually related elements of these systems, changes in demand for a commodity j by an individual i are open to interpretation as if not only potentially systematically induced or promoted by dually related changes in prices for commodity j, but, more subtly, potentiated or promoted by changes in supplies of such a commodity *variously* : i) directly or indirectly via supplies of factors of production by another/ others differently located in space-time *and/or* ; ii) directly or indirectly via supplies of elements of taxes or subsidies related to individual i's potential purchase of commodity j by another/others relatively differently located in space-time ... .

7.6 Conclusion

The structure (IV)i just considered clearly illustrates central messages of this Chapter - and of this book. These are : firstly that regulatory and self regulatory structures may be seen as stemming fundamentally and directly from relatively decentralizeable goal programming extensions of Lancaster-like principles and processes of interaction between individuals,their relatively abstract selves, and elements of wider mathematical/ physical subsystems. Second ; such principles and processes of measurement relative to self/ another/ others and/ or relative to elements of wider mathematical/ physical subsystems *necessarily* connote applications of fundamental mathematical/ physical relative indeterminacy/ incompleteness/ uncertainty principles and processes.

It has been shown how such principles, if appropriately recognized and exploited, may potentiate opportunities for individual or collective mathematical/ physical gains - including gains of knowledge and information in general - and opportunities for individually and collectively socioeconomic gains, including gains of socioeconomic knowledge and information in particular.

With such contexts it will be clear that the systems (IV)i are not the only possible ways of attaining relatively decentralized structures from suitably modified forms of the system (III). As the reader can easily verify, one could straightforwardly decentralize relative to that wider system to yield specifications relative to particular enterprises, or to particular time periods, and in those ways directly relate developments here to Chapter 9 and Chapter 10.

Conversely, the system (III) might be seen as corresponding to a particular region and thereby as directly suggesting developments to comprehend more generally applicable interregional analyses such as are considered in Chapter 8.

From the perspective of the next and subsequent chapters the present

Chapter can be seen as providing individually and collectively more fundamental socioeconomic motivations for the objectives of those systems as potentially fundamentally deriving from relatively abstract Lancaster-like characteristic - commodity formulations which can motivate individual and collective principles and processes of regulation and self regulation via relatively (de)centralized goal programming and duality principles, processes and phenomena.

Footnotes

1. I remarked on page 162 and emphasize here that a single individual/n individual distinction is not generally a stark one. In fact the very existence of an individual generally connotes the prior existence of at least one other of that kind. And, as the reader may recall, even within the essentially naive context of Defoe's Robinson Crusoe story, one of Crusoe's first actions was to commit time, effort and resources to construct a signal fire in order to increase his potential for contacts with others whom he would recognize as potentially friendly. As you may also recall, Robinson Crusoe was in fact surprised by - and came to appreciate the company of - one whom he at first feared as a potential enemy.

2. Notice that measures $r_{is\ s+1}$ here correspond to individual *time preference rates* which, if positive, are open to interpretation as implying essentially *chosen* inflationary pricing policies. For more on this point see Part I.

3. Microeconomic analysts will immediately recognize that such an approach can for example be understood as potentially explicitly including "entrepreneurial" "normal profit" imputations in this way - thus providing, perhaps for the first time, an unexceptionally rigorous foundation for that essentially risk and managerially related concept.

4. I have pursued other aspects of these topics elsewhere (and in Chapter 3) including arguably more comprehensively and fundamentally established mathematical/ physical relative uncertainty, incompleteness and indeterminancy principles and processes and including, also, relations to various kinds of *game-like* principles and processes. Among the latter are principles and processes as if potentiating/ potentiated via *coalitional* behaviours as if purposively to *dominate* imputations relative to self/ selves as if thereby to potentiate gain relative to another/ others and, incidentally, as if purposively relative emptiness of *core*(s) relative to self/ selves.

5. For more on these and related points pertaining to relative desireability as well as to relative inevitability of mathematical/ physical uncertainty/ incompleteness/ indeterminancy principles again see developments in Chapter 4.

6. In turn these extensions and developments among other things extend Samuelson's (essentially empirically based) Revealed Preference idea in ways potentially essentially coherent with *and yet* essentially contradictory to essentially Hicksian abstract and ordinal preference/ indifference ideas, as well as to essentially collective Bergson-Samuelson Welfare ideas.

7. For more on this see developments in Section 3 of Chapter 2.

8. By contrast with acyclicity, intransitivity and other (self) consistency preconditions for individual/ collective preference/ indifference/ welfare relations and processes typically imposed in the collective choice literature in general, and for Arrow's Impossibility results in particular (on thesse points see Chapter 2 Section 1 and Chapter 3).

9. For development of this particular point as well as its more generally relativistic connotations see Chapter 4.

10. Notice here that while for simplicity in the preceding analyses each commodity has been assumed to yield amounts of at most two characteristics for each individual i such an assumption is emphatically not essential to those analyses and results. These extend straightforwardly to subjectively varying numbers as well as appreciations of characteristics, as the reader can easily verify.

References

{1} Aarestad,J., (1990),*Simultaneous Use of Renewable and Non-Renewable Natural Resources*, Resources and Energy 12, pp.253-262.

{2} Arrow,K.J., (1951), *Social Choice and Individual Values*, Cowles Foundation Monograph No 12, Yale University Press.

{3} Charnes,A. and W.W. Cooper, (1961), *Management Models and Industrial Applications of Linear Programming*, 2 volumes, Wiley, New York.

{4} Charnes,A., R.W. Clower and K.O. Kortanek, (1967), *Effective Control Through Coherent Decentralization with Preemptive Goals* Econometrica 35.

{5} de V. Graaff, J., (1957), *Theoretical Welfare Economics*, Cambridge University Press.

{6} Lancaster, K., (1966), *A New Approach to Consumer Theory*, Journal of Political Economy, 84, pp.132-157.

{7} Lancaster, K., (1975), *Socially Optimal Product Differentiation*, American Economic Review, 65, pp.567-585.

{8} Lancaster, K., (1979), *Variety, Equity and Efficiency*, Basil Blackwell, Oxford.

{9} Lipsey R.G.and K. Lancaster, (1956), *The General Theory of The Second Best*, Review of Economic Studies, 24, pp.11-32.

{10}Quirk J.and R.Saposnik, (1968), *Introduction to General Equilibrium Theory and Welfare Economics*, McGraw-Hill, New York.

{11}Ryan M.J., (1978), *Qualitative Interpretations of Urban Phenomena*, Journal of Regional Science, pp.383-394.

{12}Samuelson P.A., (1947), *Foundations of Economic Analysis*, Harvard University Press, Cambridge.

{13}Sen A.K., (1970), *Collective Choice and Social Welfare*, Holden Day, San Francisco.

{14}Swallow S.K., (1990), *Depletion of the Environmental Basis for Renewable and Non-Renewable Resources*, Journal of Environmental Economics and Management, 19, pp.281-296.

8 A goal programming approach to land use economics, planning and regulation

8.1 General introduction

The topic of land use planning and regulation is of considerable current interest. National, state and local legislation is being introduced to regulate the conflicting demands of industrial output with residential and recreational developments and those of environmental protection and conservation.

Insofar as land uses constitute production capacities, and production capacity constrains the output of commodities for further production and for consumption, the regulation of land use constrains the path and configuration of the development of an economy. The instruments of land use regulation may be property taxes or subsidies, discriminatory taxes or subsidies for the augmentation of specified types of production capacity or discriminatory zoning ordinances.

These types of regulation, however, form only part of an overall development plan, for a society typically has a multiplicity of goals relating, for example, to the level of employment, to the distribution of income and wealth, to the rate of depletion of nonrenewable resources, as well as to the rate of formation and the character of production capacity. Examples of such goals and the instruments directed toward their attainment are target rates of employment and payroll taxes and welfare payments, viable incomes to farmers and subsidies to agricultural commodities, and upper limits on waste discharges with penalties for discharges in excess of these targets.

Ultimately the purpose of production is consumption and the prices of consumption commodities may be regulated by means of sales taxes and subsidies as a matter of social policy. The demand for consumption commodities is, however, a function of income and wealth (and its distribution). These, in turn, are derived from the levels and distributions of current and future production, taxation, subsidies, and prices.

A land use plan may thus only be appraised as part of an overall development plan for an economy. The interrelationship of goals, plans and control is set out by Collomb ({17} Ch. 1). He quotes Steiner {61} as follows ;

> . . . the definition of control is usually given as the process of making sure that performance takes place in conformance with plans

and goes on to note that :

> . . . it would be foolish to prepare plans independently of the means and ways used to implement them, and the distinction between what is planning and what is control can be difficult to make in practice.

Chenery {15}, p.131 states that "A planning model specifies the relationship between the goals of the society and the instruments that the government (has available to achieve them." In practice a number of government and statutory authorities have planning and regulatory functions. Their jurisdictions may overlap (e.g. river authorities may span several states) and their goals conflict (e.g. national goals of expanding oil refining capacity and regional goals of refinery-free coastlines).

In order to represent these variations a multi-region model is required which embodies a multi-level regulatory structure. Here the term multi-level connotes only levels of government, for a single model is developed. Kornai {31} defines multi-level planning as follows :

> Multi-level planning is operating in all cases when there are top level (economy wide) middle level (branch or regional) and perhaps lower level models within one country, for the same period and an organized information flow exists between them.

Here a unified model is developed by means of which land use plans and regulatory policies may be evaluated. The model is neutral with respect to the process of planning except insofar as a multi-level political or regulatory structure is modelled.

Since land use planning involves the regulation of the location and character of production capacity, a multi-region model is required, with the magnitudes, types and locations of production capacities being endogenously determined, in order that they may be susceptible to regulation and that mutatis mutandis rates of compensation for loss or curtailment of property rights may be determined.[1] A multi-period model is thus required with horizon conditions such that investment, disinvestment and maintenance as well as consuznption decisions are made in the light of their futurity.

The following paragraphs give an overview of the genesis and structure of the goal programming model which is developed for the evaluation of land use plans and regulatory policies and of the interpretations which may be elicited from the associated dual program. The connections between this model and related work are outlines following the overview.

In the following chapters a normative multi-period multi-region goal programming model for regional land use planning and economic development is developed extensively. This model generalizes the results of previous linear programming approaches by simultaneously taking explicit account of the magnitude, timing, location, and the processes of formation of capital, the social goals, the regulatory structure, and the configurations of production, pricing, and consumption of a closed economy consisting of geologically distinct regions over a predetermined planning interval.

The functional of the model, which differs from those of previous formulations, is the maximization of the discounted added value imputed to consumption over the planning interval. Added value is defined as the quantity of commodities consumed, evaluated at prescribed market prices, less the value of renewable resources foregone by the future, due to current consumption and capital formation ; the value of leisure foregone by labor in employment ; and the social regret associated with deviations from social goals.

These goals may be set directly by regulatory authorities such as national, state, and local legislative bodies, but also by statutory authorities such as, for example, the Environmental Protection Agency. (These authorities may have overlapping jurisdictions and conflicting goals).

By associating piecewise linear regret functions with deviations above and below social goal levels, which may relate to levels of employment, consumption, production, production capacity, increments of production capacity, and the horizon land use configuration, interpretations which correspond to instruments of regulation are obtained. These include payroll taxes, welfare payments, investment grants, fines for excessive waste discharges, property taxes, sales taxes and subsidies, etc. The nature and magnitude of the instruments which apply are determined endogenously for each commodity, region and time period.

The full implications of the fact that the area of each region is fixed in a multi-region model appear to have been unexplored before. The fact that these areas are given necessarily requires that the augmentation of any type of production capacity connotes the reduction of at least one other type of capacity. That is, capital formation or land use change, *in their essence*, involve replacement or conversion processes, with the character of the process being specific to the conversion, or conversions, which together constitute the increment of capacity.

By considering the totality of possible land uses and of feasible land use conversions, and maintaining the requirement that new capacity may only be obtained at the expense of existing capacity, the optimal sequence of land uses is endogenously determined for each site in each region over the planning interval. These sequences of conversions or processes of capital formation, are determined with full regard for the geology of the site, for the current and future spatial configuration of markets for all commodities, for all forms of production capacity, (where both these markets may be regulated), in each region and time period.

From the dual program mutatis mutandis evaluations for each form of production capacity are obtained for the first time. These valuations reflect both the current and future markets for the product of each form of production capacity, and for the capacity itself. The latter markets arise from the introduction of the possibility of converting production capacity from one process to another. The costs of augmenting production capacity and the, time taken are specific to the conversions undertaken. These, together with the value of the capacity, both prior to and following conversion, are *all* determined endogenously.

It is shown that from the identification of production capacity with land use, only by a semantic contrivance may value be imputed to "land," per se for the value of any site is given by the value of the production capacity with which it is associated. (The fact that the area of each region is given is reflected in the fact that increments of capacity require conversions of existing capacity and this, in turn, is reflected in its value.)

The value of an increment of capacity is shown to be made up of two components -the terminal value of the existing capacity and the conversion cost. These terminal values are defined at the point of purchse of capacity for conversion to another process, and hence the appropriate marginal rate of compensation for foregoing continuous production to the owners of that capacity is determined.

By generalizing Littlechild's results {37} to the case where the interval of production is determined endogenously, it is shown that the cost of capacity is recouped exactly from the sale of commodities during the interval of production and its terminal value for each type of capacity. As a corollary of this result the interval of production must be sufficiently long for the capital and maintenance costs associated with each increment of capacity to be recouped from the sale of production.

A perfect capital market is assumed in which funds may be borrowed and lent at an interest rate p in each period. Since the value of capacity and the financial requirements for its finance are both determined endogenously, a bond market is motivated wherein capacity is financed by means of bonds carrying interest of ρ%. The magnitude and timing and location of capital flows may then be determined.

From this approach well-known macroeconomic relationships are also recouped from the dual pair of programs at the optimum, including the equality between consumption and investment and income and transfer payments.

Among further significant results arising from the dynamic model are representations for a variety of urban phenomena and the generation of a generalized optimal replacement policy for physically depreciating assets.

I now turn to the connections between the specifications and inter -pretations of this model and those of related work. Stevens {42} develops a single period interregional linear programming model for a closed economy in which the quantities of labor, fuel and mineral re- sources and of production capacity are assumed to be fixed exogenously for each region. A single linear production process is associated with each commodity, including extraction processes for raw materials. Here the technology, or technologies, used for the production of each commodity is determined endogenously for each region and time period, and joint production, which Stevens excludes, is admissible.

The process of capital formation which is excluded from Stevens' model is given a central place in the multi-period models for open economies developed by Eckaus and Parikh {20} and Goreaux, Manne et, al.{22}.[2] In these models a fixed coefficient process is assumed for augmenting each form of production capacity. Fixed lags are assumed for the introduction of these increments and horizon posture conditions for production capacity are modeled as constraints. The only capacity conversion processes which are considered are those relating to the conversion of older production capacity to new capacity of the same type. It is implicitly assumed that capacity once purchased is retained indefinitely, with allowance being made for phsycial depreciation over time. Values are obtained from the associated dual programs which are imputed by the current and future market for the product for each form of capacity alone.

In the model which is developed here the augmentation of production capacity necessarily requires the reduction of at least one other type of capacity. All feasible conversions are incorporated and the optimal sequence of conversions with the inputs specific to them is determined for each site in each region over the planning interval. The time taken for each conversion is determined endogenously, reflecting the fact that the time required depends upon the conversion (e.g. shops to apartments versus parkland to apartments). By introducing conversion processes, values are obtained for all types of capacity, which reflect current and future market considerations both for their products and for the production capacity. Both of these markets may be regulated. Horizon posture goals are specified for production capacity in each region, with weights reflecting social regret being associated with deviations above or below these goal levels in the functional. Hence the interval during which each form of capacity is available for production in each region is determined endogenously.

In the Stevens, Eckaus and Parikh, and Goreux and Manne models, minimal levels are prescribed for the supply of each consumption commodity in each region. In the model developed here, goal levels for the supply of consumption commodities are prescribed, with allowance for shortfalls and excesses from these goals with associated penalties in the functional.

Since the models of Goreaux and Manne and Eckaus and Parikh are aggregative, they do not consider constraints imposed by fuel and mineral resource availabilities. In Stevens' model these are expressed simply as upper bounds on the quantity extracted. In the model developed here, the nonrenewable character of these resources and the consequent loss to the future due to current depletion is modelled by piecewise linear supply functions from the future (beyond the planning horizon) to the planning interval. The area beneath these supply functions is taken to be the appropriate measure of value foregone in the future due to depletion during the planning interval and is entered with a negative sign in the functional.

The model of Goreux, Manne et. al. includes constraints on labor force availability, as does that of Stevens. In the model developed here employment goals are considered with penalties representing social regret being associated with deviations from these and other regulatory goals in the functional.

The functional of each of the three linear programming models, those of Eckaus and Parik, Goreux, Manne et, al., and Stevens, is the maximization of the value of commodities consumed in the economy during the planning interval, where these are evaluated at predetermined prices. In the former two models the path of development is conditioned by preemptive goals or constraints relating to rates of growth of consumption and to horizon posture for production capacity. In the model developed here there and other goals are incorporated in the functional, thus opening the way for tradeoffs between them and the simultaneous determination of a structure of market prices and regulatory instruments. These together provide the means of implementation and regulation of the development plan and the associated land use plan for the economy over the planning interval.

The following work was inspired in large part by the multi-level goal programming models developed for manpower planning by Charnes, Cooper, Niehaus et.al.{10} as part of the research program of the U.S. Department of the Navy. Their multi-level models incorporate input-output analysis in order to determine manpower requirements and utilize Markov processes to model manpower transitions (e.g. geographical movements, skill changes). The objective of these models is the minimization of a weighted sum of deviations from output and manpower goals.

It was apparent that social policies with respect to employment, production and environmental protection might properly be approached by means of a goal programming model. Only after prices for consumption commodities and costs for labor do the weights associated with deviations from social goals take on the interpretations, at the optimum, of the instruments of regulation.

The work of Charnes and Collomb {7} on goal interval programming is drawn upon to allow increasing social regret to be associated with increasing deviations from social goals. Their results also enable indifference regions to be introduced in the neighborhood of goals and bounds to be placed on deviations from goals. By associating potential penalties of non-Archimedean order with deviations beyond specified levels, legal prohibitions (for example, exclusionary zoning ordinances) may be modified.

Littlechild's results {36}, {37} on marginal cost pricing valuation and amortization are obtained in a generalized form. Production capacity supplies its output jointly to temporally separated markets. He assumed that the marginal variable costs of production are known and that increments of capacity may be purchased at known marginal cost in each period up to a horizon period and that the terminal value of the capacity at the horizon is known. Assuming given demand functions for each period, he shows that under a marginal cost pricing regime, prices are set such that capacity costs (including maintenance costs) are exactly recouped from the sale of production and the terminal value of the capacity. He further shows that the capacity cost component of the price (or the rental for capacity) determines an optimal amortization policy for the capacity. Implicit in Littlechild's analysis is the assumption that capacity once purchased is retained (with allowances for physical depreciation) up to the horizon.

The directions of generalizations which I have made follow from the treatment of capital formation as involving conversion processes. From this it follows that the interval of production is determined endogenously for each form of capacity as axe the initial costs, the variable production costs and the terminal values for each type of capacity. Thus values for all forms of production capacity are defined with respect both to the current and future markets for their products and for the capacity itself.

By a direct extension of Littlechild's results, it is shown that the amortization policy must then be such as to recoup net capacity costs from the sale of production over the endogenously determined production interval. As a corollary, it follows that the interval of production must be sufficiently long for capacity costs to be recouped.

The locations of employment and of housing are determined simultan -eously in the multi-period model developed below. This simultaneous determination may be contrasted with the simulation approach of the urban residential model developed by the National Bureau of Economic Research, as reported by Kendrick {29}.

In this latter model employment locations and levels are determined exogenously in each planning period, and the number of movers is then calculated. These movers are then allocated to housing, which is made up of vacancies created by movement, vacancies held over from the previous period and new housing. This allocation is modelled by a linear program of distribution type whose functional is the minimization of housing and transportation costs and whose constraints are given by the number of workers working in each zone requiring housing of each type and the quantity of housing of each type available in each zone.

> Shadow prices on dwelling units by type and location are used to determine which units it is profitable to repair or let decay and what new units will be constructed or transformed from existing units. {29}

The important point here is that marginal opportunity costs or rentals of housing in one period are being used to determine housing stock for the subseauent period. There is, however, no theoretically sound basis for this procedure, since rentals measure current opportunity costs alone.

There is, in general, no direct relationship between rental levels in one period and those in the next. Rentals measure the *change* in value of capacity, rather than the value itself. By considering employment, demand, housing and transportation in a single model, we determine the changing spatial configuration of housing with full regard for the system costs and benefits of such transformations in a theoretically rigorous manner.

The model is developed extensively in the following chapter in order that attention may be focused sequentially on particular aspects or its development with their associated interpretations.

In Chapter 8.2 a goal programming model is motivated and formulated in which goals are set for employment and consumption and from which all investment, disinvestment and maintenance requirements are excluded in order to establish the relationships between goals and regulatory instruments. In this instance the regulatory instruments are payroll taxes and welfare payments and sales taxes and subsidies, respectively. In the part of that chapter the model is extended to a goal interval formulation in which increasing social regret may be associated with increasing deviations above and below social goals. By means of this extension indifference regions may also be introduced in the neighborhood of goals and bounds paced on deviations from them.

In Chapter 8.3 attention is focused upon the processes of land use conversion, or capital formation. The totality of land uses including housing and transportation are considered, as well as all feasible land use conversions together with the associated requirements for maintenance and conversion. The feasibility of conversion is determined by the times required for the stages of conversion to be completed, and then nature is conditioned upon the nature of the conversion and related to the geology of the region. The timing and configuration of the conversions undertaken is determined by the configuration of current and future markets for commodities and those for production capacity.

In Chapter 8.4 the following interpretations are recouped from the dual relationships of the program which is developed in Chapter 8.3. Firstly, it is shown that under a marginal cost pricing regime, capital costs are exactly recouped either from the sale of products or from the technical value over the interval of production for each production process in each region. Secondly, mutatis mutandis valuations are obtained for types of production capacity in each region and time period. Thirdly, a new motivation for peak load pricing is set forth wheree in capacity is retained although underutilized in order to meet future demand only in cases where this is the most efficient means of supplying that demand. Fourthly, the spatial relationship of property values is outlined. Finally, the identification of production capacity with land use and the consequent identity of "land" values with the value of production capacity is used to motivate qualitative explanations of urban phenomena.

In Chapter 8.5 the emphasis is turned from the concentration on issues of valuation and compensation of Chapter 8.4 to the development of an institutional and regulatory structure for the economy. In the earlier part of the chapter a future market for nonrenewables resources, a bond market for finance of production capacity and a corporate structure are motivated. The magnitude and timing of capital flows to and from production capacity are analyzed. The macroeconomic relationship of equality between consump -tion and investment and income and transfer payments is recouped from the equality of the functionals of the dual pair of programs at the optimum. This result then introduces the topic of macroeconomic regulation.

In the latter part of Chapter 8.5 regulatory goals are introduced for production capacity, output and new capacity. These goals may be set by regulatory authorities at one or more levels of the economy. These authorities may be federal, state or local governments or statutory bodies and may have overlapping jurisdictions and their goals may conflict. It is shown that, at the optimum, the social regrets associated with deviations from these goals take on the interpretations of the relevant instruments of regulation.

In Chapters 8.2 through 8.5, for purposes of clarity of presentation and interpretation, it is assumed that at most one technology is available for the production of each commodity (excluding increments of production capacity) in each region, that the productivity and maintenance requirements of production capacity are independent of its age, that joint production is confined to transportation capacity and that there are no inventories in economy or lags in production processes.

In Chapter 8.6 it is shown that all of these assumptions may be related straightforwardly and that the interpretations of the preceding chapter are thereby generalized. These modifications complete the development of the multi-period multi-region goal programming model.

8.2 Goals, taxes and subsisidies

8.2.1 *Introduction*

This chapter may be regarded as preliminary to the developments of the following one. Investment, disinvestment and maintenance are excluded here in order that attention may be focused on the interrelationship of goals, prices, taxes and subsidies. A single period goal programming model for regional planning is motivated and developed which extends the results which have been obtained by means of linear programming approaches by explicitly recognizing the target (or goal) nature of the stipulations associated with such formulations while at the same time retaining the pricing structure characteristic of them.

These results are achieved by associating penalties representing social regret in the functional with deviations within specified ranges from prescribed goal levels for the production of commodities for consumption, for the levels of employment of labor and for the depletion of fuel and mineral resources.

It is shown that these penalties may be interpreted at the optimum as sales taxes or subsidies for consumption commodities if the deviation lies above or below the goal level respectively.

For employment the penalties represent at the optimum marginal welfare payments or payroll taxes if labor in underemployed or overemployed respectively. In the case of fuel and mineral resources the increasing penalties reflect the increasing marginal costs or marginal opportunity costs associated with increasing depletion of resources.

In the latter part of the chapter a goal interval formulation of the problem is developed. This formulation enables indifference regions to be introduced in the neighborhood of the goals and piecewise linear regret functions to be associated with increasing deviations above or below the goal levels.

The content of this chapter does not exhaust the possibilities of the goal programming approach for the modeling of the regulation of an economy by means of taxes and subsidies to conform to an overall plan related to social goals. Further classes of regulation and associated interpretations are introduced in Chapter 5 where also the possibility of conflicting goals for authorities having overlapping jurisdictions is introduced.

8.2.2 *Linear programming approaches to regional planning*

Kendrick {30} provides a survey of mathematical models for regional planning including a discussion of alternative spproaches for single period linear programming formulations. Further examples of single period linear programming models drawn from a large literature may be found in public -ations on applications of activity analysis {32}, {39},[3] and of Lefeber {35}, Stevens {42} and Takayama and Judge {43}.

In order to provide the basis and motivation for the goal programming approach of the following section, rather than survey extensively the variations among the aforementioned models with respect to the inclusiveness of the economy considered, the functional adopted and the constraints incorporated, we next present, for simplicity, a model which incorporates the central features of all of the linear programming approaches to the single period planning problem with respect to consumption, pricing and resource constraints.

Consider the program[4]

$$\text{Minimize} \sum_i \sum_k c_i^k x_i^k + \sum_i \sum_{\substack{k,\ell \\ \ell \neq k}} c_i^{k\ell} x_i^{k\ell}$$

$$\varphi_i^k \geq 0 \quad \text{s.t.} \quad x_i^k + \sum_{\substack{\ell \\ \ell \neq k}} x_i^{\ell k} \geq \sum_{\substack{\ell \\ \ell \neq k}} x_i^{k\ell} + \sum_j a_{ji}^k x_j^k + d_i^k \qquad \text{all } i$$

$$\lambda_i^k \geq 0 \qquad x_i^k \leq R_i^k \qquad i \epsilon I_3^k$$

$$\theta_i^k \geq 0 \qquad x_i^k \leq E_i^k \qquad i \epsilon I_2$$

$$x_i^k, x_i^{k\ell} \geq 0$$

The variables and parameters of the program have the following interpretations:

x_i^k is the output of commodity i in region k during the period where i = 1,2...n k = 1,2..K

$x_i^{k\ell}$ is the quantity of commodity i shipped from region k to region ℓ ($\ell \neq k$) during the period.

c_i^k is the marginal production cost or rental for capacity of type i in region k.

$c_i^{k\ell}$ is the marginal transportation cost for shipments of commodity i from region k to region ℓ ($\ell \neq k$). This cost is assumed to include both the costs of variable inputs to transportation and transportation capacity costs.

a_{ij}^k is the quantity of commodity j required per unit output of commodity i in region k. It is assumed that there is at most one process or technology for the production of each commodity in each region.

d_i^k is the exogenously prescribed minimal level of supply of commodity i in region k for final consumption. This quantity may be zero in cases where the commodity in question is used purely as an input to production -- an intermediate commodity. Let the set of consumption commodities be I_1.

R_i^k. is the quantity of a fuel or mineral resource of type i in region k available as input to production after allowance for capacity conversion, maintainance and transportation requirements $I_3{}^k$ is the set of fuel and mineral resources in region k.

Following Stevens {42} an extraction process is associated with the extraction of each fuel and mineral resource.

E_i^k is the quantity of labor type $i \epsilon I_2$ resident in region k, available for employment in production after allowance for capacity conversion maintenance and transportation requirements I_2 is the set of labor types. Also, since there is no production process for labor

$$c_i^k = a_{ij}^k = 0 \qquad i \epsilon I_2$$

The functional of the program may be interpreted at the optimum (if a feasible solution is attainable[5]) as the minimization of the costs of production and transportation of produced commodities for the economy. The marginal costs of production and transportation are determined exogenously and are assumed to reflect an optimal adjustment of production capacity utilization. It is also assumed that all commodities may be produced during the period .

Associating the indicated dual variables with the constraints of the primal problem the dual program is:

$$\text{Maximize} \sum_k \left(\sum_{i \epsilon I_1} \varphi_i^k d_i^k - \sum_{i \epsilon I_2} \theta_i^k E_i^k - \sum_{i \epsilon I_3} \lambda_i^k R_i^k \right)$$

$$x_i^k \geq 0 \qquad \text{s.t.} \qquad \varphi_i^k - \Sigma a_{ij}^k \varphi_j^k \leq c_i^k \qquad i \notin I_3^k \qquad (2.2.1)$$

$$x_i^k \geq 0 \qquad \varphi_i^k - \Sigma a_{ij}^k \varphi_j^k - \lambda_i^k \leq c_i^k \qquad i \epsilon I_3^k \qquad (2.2.2)$$

$$x_i^{\ell k} \geq 0 \qquad \varphi_i^k - \varphi_i^\ell \leq c_i^{\ell k} \qquad i \epsilon I_1 \qquad (2.2.3)$$

$$x_i^k \geq 0 \qquad \varphi_i^k - \theta_i^k \leq 0 \qquad i \epsilon I_2 \qquad (2.2.4)$$

$$\varphi_i^k, \quad \theta_i^k, \quad \lambda_i^k \geq 0.$$

The quantities $\varphi_i{}^k$, $\theta_i{}^k$, $\lambda_i{}^k$ are interpreted at the optimum as the marginal costs or prices of the commodities, labor types, or fuel or minerals resources with which they are associated respectively. We interpret the functional at the optimum as the optimal value added by production in the economy during the period.

Now interpret the constraints at the optimum as

$$x_i^k > 0 \quad i \epsilon I_3^k, \quad I_2 \Rightarrow$$

$$\varphi_i^k = c_i^k + \Sigma_j a_i^k \varphi_j^k \qquad (2.2.1)$$

That is the marginal cost of commodity i in region k is equal to the marginal production cost plus the marginal capacity cost or rental $c_i{}^k$.

For extraction processes ($i \epsilon I_3{}^k$) the marginal cost or price of the fuel or mineral resource $\lambda_i{}^k$ must be added as an input cost. Thus :

$x_i^k > 0, \quad i \in I_3^k \quad \Rightarrow$

$$\varphi_i^k = c_i^k + \Sigma a_{ij}^k \varphi_j^k + \lambda_i^k \qquad (2.2.2)$$

The transportation constraints apply to all commodities excluding resources "in the ground." (Extracted resources are however transpor -table.) The transportation constraints may then be interpreted at the optimum as follows:

$x_i^{\ell k} > 0, \; i \in I_1 \quad \Rightarrow$

$$\varphi_i^k = \varphi_i^\ell + c_i^{\ell k} \qquad (2.2.3)$$

That is, if shipments of commodity i are made between regions ℓ and k the price of the commodity in the two regions differs by the shipping cost.

For labor $x_i^k > 0, \quad i \in I_2 \quad \Rightarrow$

$$\varphi_i^k = \theta_i^k \qquad (2.2.4)$$

That is, the marginal cost of labor type i in region k is equal to the wage rate $\theta_i{}^k$. Notice that labor may be "shipped" from region to region with, in this case, the marginal transportation cost $c_i{}^{\ell k}$ being equal to the commuting cost. (2.2.3), (2.2.4). Restrictions on labor movements imposed by commuting times may be incorporated by restricting the set of regions accessible from and to each region for each type of labor. This would involve modifying the constraints for labor to, for employment:

$$x_i^k + \sum_\ell x_i^{\ell k} \geqq \sum_j a_{ji}^k x_j^k \qquad i \in I_2$$

and for the labor force availability

$$x_i^k + \sum_\ell x_i^{k\ell} \leqq E_i^k$$

and restricting the set of regions ℓ accessible from region k. The dual variables and relationships remain unchanged in this more restricted case, which may lead more easily to more isolated labor markets than a formulation based on costs alone.[6]

The stipulations of the primal program have the force of preemptive goals with respect to output, resource utilization, and maximal rates of employment, for a solution is required which lies on the boundary of the constraint set which they prescribe. Such a solution may not be attainable however as long as the minimal consumption constraints and the resource and labor availability constraints are opposed, for the prescribed resource limitations may preclude the attainment of the prescribed minimal levels of output $d_i{}^k$ of commodities for consumption.

If, on the other hand a feasible, (and thence an optimal), solution is attainable, shadow prices of zero are apt to be imputed to labor and resources.[7] Such shadow prices clearly run counter to observation, for "labor" typically receives income even if only in the form of welfare payments in cases of unemployment or underemployment, and resources not consumed in the current period, if they are of interest for planning purposes, derive value from their availability for the future. A goal programming model is developed in the following section which incorporates these possibilities while at the same time guaranteeing a feasible solution.

8.2.3 *A single period goal programming model*[8]

In this section a model is developed in which the quantities d_i^k, E_i^k and R_i^k are taken to be goal levels for consumption, employment and resource utilization respectively with allowance being made for cases where the optimal configuration of production, resource utilization and employment does not meet these goal levels by the introduction of variables for the deviations in the constraints and the association of penalties with these deviations in the functional. Transportation is made endogenous to the model[9] and the requirements for the maintenance and conversion of production capacity including transportation capacity are assumed to be determined exogenously. This consumption implies that the availabilities of capacity of resources, and of labor for production, are given by the total availabilities net of the exogenously determined requirements for maintenance and conversion.

The constraints of the problem are as follows:

Let d_i^k be the prescribed goal level for the output of consumption commodities i in region k and let I_1 be the set of consumption commodities. Then if y_i^{k+} represents the deviation below the goal level and y_i^{k-} the deviation above the goal level and y_i^k the actual quantity produced for consumption

$$y_i^k + y_i^{k+} - y_i^{k-} = d_i^k \qquad i \epsilon I_1 \qquad (2.3.1)$$

Let E_i^k be the target rate of employment in production (as opposed to employment in the maintenance or conversion of production capacity) of labor of type i in region k where I_2 is the set of labor types. Then, if x_i^k is the actual employment, x_i^{k+} is underemployment and x_i^{k-} is employment in excess of the goal level E_i^k for labor type i in region k:

$$x_i^k + x_i^{k+} - x_i^{k-} = E_i^k \qquad i \epsilon I_2 \qquad (2.3.2)$$

The quantity x_i^{k-} may be bounded above by the total labor force availability in region k (after allowance for overtime, maximal participation, etc.). Further consideration is given to such bounds at a later stage in the development.

Let R_{i1}^k $(i \epsilon I_3^k)$ represent the target rate of utilization of resource i for production in region k during the period where I_3^k is the set of fuel and mineral resources in the region. Let R_i^k be the actual quantity of resources available for production in region k. If x_i^k is the quantity of resources i $(i \epsilon I_3^k)$ extracted during the period and w_{i1}^k represents the utilization of resource i in excess of the target rate R_{i1}^k then

$$\begin{aligned} & x_i^k - w_i^k \leq 0 \\ & w_i^{k-} - w_{il}^k \leq R_{il}^k \qquad (2.3.3) \\ & w_{il}^{k-} \leq R_i^k - R_{il}^k \end{aligned}$$

It is assumed that a single direct route is prescribed for shipments of each commodity between each distinct pair of regions. As in the previous model all commodities with the exceptions of resources "in the ground" and production capacity are assumed to be transportable. Let the route for the shipment of commodity i from region k to region ℓ consist of the set of links $I_i^{k\ell}$.

Production capacity is assumed fixed exogenously in each region at a level D_i^k for each commodity produced in the region so :

$$x_i^k \leq D_i^k \qquad (2.3.4)$$

Let I_4^k be the set of transportation links in region k and D_{jk} be the capacity on link $j_k \epsilon I_4^k$. 10 If $e_{ijk}^{\ell m}$ is the quantity of production capacity required (after allowance for peak load effects, if appropriate) on link j_k per unit shipment of commodtyi over the route ℓm:

$$\sum_{\substack{i\ell m\\ \ell \neq m}} e_{ij_k}^{\ell m} x_i^{\ell m} \leq D_{j_k} \qquad j_k \epsilon I_i^{\ell m} \qquad (2.3.5)$$

The supply and demand relationship is modified to include the requirements for variable transportation inputs or:

$$x_i^k + \sum_\ell x_i^{\ell k} \geq \sum_j a_{ji}^k x_j^k + \sum_j a_{ji}^{\ell m} x_j^{\ell m} + \sum x_i^{k\ell} + y_i^k \qquad k \epsilon I_j^{\ell m} \qquad (2.3.6)$$

where a_{ji}^k is the quantity of commodity i required as input per unit output of commodity j in region k and $a_{ji}^{\ell m}$ is the quantity of commodity i required per unit of commodity j shipped to, from or through region k on the route ℓm. The quantity y_i^k is zero if i is not a consumption commodity.

Let c_i^k be a prescribed wage rate for labor of class i in region k $(i \epsilon I_2)$ and p_i^k a prescribed price for consumption commodity i $(i \epsilon I_1)$ in region k.

Penalties c_i^{k+}, c_i^{k-} are associated with deviations below or above the goal levels in the functional and represent the marginal social regret imputed to such deviations. With these penalties the functional of the primal program may be interpreted at the optimum as the maximization of the added-value to inputs to production. The overall program is

$$\text{Maximize} \ \sum_k \Big(\sum_{i \epsilon I_1} (p_i^k y_i^k - c_i^{k+} y_i^{k-} - c_i^{k-} y_i^{k-})$$

$$- \sum_{i \epsilon I_2} (c_i^k x_i^k + c_i^{k+} x_i^{k+} + c_i^{k-} x_i^{k-})$$

$$- \sum_{i \epsilon I_3} (c_i^{k-} w_i^{k-} + c_{i_1}^{k-} w_{i_1}^{k-}) \Big)$$

subject to:

$$\pi_i \qquad y_i^k + y_i^{k+} - y_i^{k-} = d_i^k \qquad i \epsilon I_1 \qquad (2.3.1)$$

$$\varphi_i \geq 0 \qquad y_i^k + \sum_j a_{ji}^k x_j^k + \sum_{\substack{j\\ k \epsilon I_i^{\ell m}}} a_{ji}^{\ell m} x_j^{\ell m} + \sum_\ell x_i^{k\ell} \leq x_i^k + \sum_\ell x_i^{\ell k} \qquad (2.3.6)$$

$$\mu_i \geq 0 \qquad x_i^k \leq D_i^k \qquad i \epsilon I_1^k \qquad (2.3.4)$$

$$\mu_{ik} \geq 0 \qquad \sum_{i_k \epsilon I_i^{\ell m}} e_{ji_k}^{\ell m} x_j^{\ell m} \leq Di_k \qquad i_k \epsilon I_4^k \qquad (2.3.5)$$

θ_i^k $\quad x_i^k + x_i^{k+} - x_i^{k-} = E_i^k \quad i \epsilon I_2 \quad (2.3.2)$

$\lambda_i \geqq 0 \quad x_i^k - w_i^{k-} \leqq 0$

$\lambda i \geqq 0 \quad w_i^{k-} - w_{i_1}^{k-} \leqq R_{i_1}^k \quad i \epsilon I_3^k \quad (2.3.3)$

$\lambda_{i_2}^k \geqq 0 \quad w_{i_1}^k - \leqq R_i^k - R_{i_1}^k = R_{i_2}^k$

All variables non-negative

This program always has a feasible solution (e.g. $x_i{}^k = y_i{}^k = x_i{}^{k\ell} = 0$ all i, k, ℓ, $x_i{}^{k+} = E_i{}^k$, $y_i{}^{k+} = d_i{}^k$). Its value is bounded above by the capacity constraints as well as the resource constraints.

Associating the indicated dual variables with the constraints of the primal problem the associated dual program is

$$\text{Minimize} \quad \sum_k \Big[\sum_{i \epsilon I_1^k} \mu_i^k D_i^k + \sum_{i \epsilon I_4^k} \mu_{i_k} D_{i_k} + \sum_{i \epsilon I_3^k} (\lambda_{i_1}^k R_{i_1}^k$$

$$+ \lambda_{i_2}^k R_{i_2}^k) + \sum_{i \epsilon I_2} \theta_i^k E_i^k + \sum_{i \epsilon I_1} \pi_i^k d_i^k \Big]$$

subject to :

consumption

$y_i^k \geqq 0 \quad \varphi_i^k + \pi_i^k \geqq p_i^k \quad (2.3.7)$

$i \epsilon I_1$

$y_i^{k+}, y_i^{k-} \geqq 0 \quad -c_i^{k+} \leqq \pi_i{}^k \leqq c_i^{k-} \quad (2.3.8)$

production

$-\varphi_i^k + \Sigma a_{ij}^k \varphi_j^k + \mu_i^k \geqq 0 \quad (2.3.9)$

$x_i^k \geqq 0 \quad i \epsilon I_1^k$

$-\varphi_i^k + \sum_j a_{ij}^k \varphi_j{}^k + \mu_i^k + \lambda_i^k \geqq 0 \quad (2.3.10)$

$i \epsilon I_3^k$

resources

$w_i^k \geqq 0 \quad -\lambda_i^k + \lambda_{i_1}^k \geqq -c_i^{k-} \quad (2.3.11)$

$i \epsilon I_3^k$

$w_{i_1} \geqq 0 \quad -\lambda_{i_1}^k + \lambda_{i_2}^k \geqq -c_{i_1}^{k-} \quad (2.3.11a)$

transportation

$x_i^{\ell m} \geqq 0 \quad -\varphi_i^m + \varphi_i^\ell + \sum_{i \epsilon I_i^{\ell m}} a_{ij}^{\ell m} \varphi_j^k + \Sigma \mu_{jk} a_{ij_k}^{\ell m} \geqq 0 \quad (2.3.12)$

labor

$$x_i^k \geqq 0 \qquad -\varphi_i^k + \theta_i^k \geqq -c_i^k \qquad (2.3.13)$$

$$x_i^{k+}, x_i^{k-} \geqq 0> \qquad -c_i^{k+} \leqq \theta_i^k \leqq c_i^{k-}. \qquad (2.3.14)$$

The dual functional may be interpreted at the optimum as the minimization of the opportunity costs associated with production, where these relate to production capacity costs incurred during the period, the cost of the resources used, and the social costs associated with deviations (if any) from the target levels for comsumption and employment.

At the optimum the relationships of tho dual program have the following interpretations :

$$y_i^k \geqq 0 \Rightarrow$$

$$\varphi_i^k + \pi_i^k = p_i^k \qquad i \epsilon I_1 \qquad (2.3.7)$$

From (2.3.7) for consumption commodities the price equals the marginal production cost plus the value imputed to the goal for each commodity $i \epsilon l_1$ where

$$- c_i^{k+} \leqq \pi_i^k \leqq c_i^{k-} \qquad (2.3.8)$$

If $y_i^{k+} > 0$

$$\pi_i^k = c_i^{k+} \quad \Rightarrow p_i^k + c_i^{k+} = \varphi_i^k$$

If $y_i^{k-} > 0$

$$\pi_i^k = c_i^{k-} \quad \Rightarrow p_i^k = \varphi_i^k + c_i^{k-}$$

If $y_i^{k+} = y_i^{k^-} = 0$

$$-c_i^{k+} < \pi_i^k < c_i^k$$

This latter case is considered after the introduction of goal intervals below.

Thus if consumption falls short of the goal, ($y_i^{k+} > 0$) the commodity is sold below cost and, if it exceeds the goal, ($y_i^{k-} > 0$) it is sold above cost.

Now $y_i^k > 0$, φ_i^k, $p_i^k \geqq 0 \Rightarrow$

$$+c_i^{k-} \leqq p_i^k$$

$$+c_i^{k+} \leqq \varphi_i^k$$

That is, if the commodity is consumed in region k at the optimum and consumption exceeds the target the quantity $c_i^{k-} \leqq p_i^k$ has the inter -pretation of a sales tax and similarly if consumption falls short of the target a unit subsidy $c_i^{k+} \leqq \varphi_i^k$ is applied toward the cost of the commodity.

$$x_i^k > 0, \quad i \epsilon I_1^k \quad =>$$

$$\varphi_i^k = \sum_j a_{ij}^k \varphi_j^k + \mu_i^k . \qquad (2.3.9)$$

From (2.3.9) for production processes excluding extraction processes the marginal cost of each commodity in each region is given by the marginal variable cost of production plus the marginal capacity cost μ_i. The marginal capacity cost is zero if the production capacity is not fully utilized during the period for $x_i{}^k < D_i{}^k \Rightarrow \mu_i{}^k = 0$ by complementary slackness.

A distinction should be made between the marginal opportunity cost or rental μi^k of production capacity for the period under consideration and its actual value. The former quantity is the appropriate marginal rental for the capacity and is quite distinct from its value. This distinction and the relationship of the rental to the value of production capacity is made sharply in Chapter 8.4.

For extraction processes the marginal cost or value of the extracted commodity includes the marginal cost of purchasing the unprocessed commodity or

$$x_i^k > 0, \quad i \epsilon I_3^k \quad =>$$

$$\varphi_i^k = \sum_j a_{ij}^k \varphi_j^k + \mu_i^k + \lambda_i^k \qquad (2.3.10)$$

A price schedule for each resource wherein the marginal opportunity cost or price increase with increasing withdrawals is determined according to the following system

$$x_i^k > 0,\ i \epsilon I_3^k \quad => \quad w_i^{k-} > 0 \quad => \quad \lambda_i^k = c_i^{k-} + \lambda_{i_1}^k \qquad (2.3.11)$$

$$x_i^k < R_{i_1}^k \quad => \quad w_{i_1}^{k-} = 0 \quad => \quad \lambda_{i_1}^k = 0$$

$$R_{i_2}^k \geqq x_i^k > R_{i_1}^k \quad => \quad w_{i_1}^{k-} > 0 \quad => \quad \lambda_{i_1}^k = c_{i_1}^{k-} + \lambda_{i_2}^k \qquad (2.3.11a)$$

or

$$\lambda_i^k = c_i^{k-} + c_{i_1}^{k-} + \lambda_{i_2}^k$$

and

$$w_i^{k-} < R_{i_2}^k \quad => \quad \lambda_{i_2}^k = 0.$$

The rising price of the resource with quantity utilized reflects the trade-off between current and future usage of the resource or the future opportunities foregone due to current depletion.

$$x_i^{\ell m} > 0 \quad =>$$

$$\varphi_i^m - \varphi_i^\ell = \sum_{k \epsilon I_1^{\ell m}} a_{ij}^{\ell m} \varphi_j^k + \sum_{j_k \epsilon I_i^{\ell m}} e_{ij_k}^{\ell m} \mu_{j_k} \qquad (2.3.12)$$

That is if commodity i is shipped from region ℓ to region m the difference in marginal cost or price prevailing in the two regions is equal the the sum of the variable and capacity costs incurred in transportation. As for all types of capacity the capacity requirements may be adjusted for peak loads if appropriate.

Labor may, in general, be imported to, or exported from each region - such labor movements correspond to commuting trips, so that the marginal cost of labor differs between connected labor markets by the commuting cost. Labor costs are however also related to the wage rates c_i^k ($i \epsilon I_2$) by the quantities θ_i^k where

$x_i^k > 0 \quad =>$

$$- \varphi_i^k + \theta_i^k = - c_i^k \qquad (2.3.13)$$

$$- c_i^{k+} \leq \theta_i^k \leq c_i^{k-} \qquad (2.3.14)$$

$$x_i^{k+} > 0 \quad => \quad \theta_i^k = - c_i^{k+} \quad => \quad \varphi_i^k = c_i^k - c_i^{k+}$$

If $x_i^{k+} > 0$, labor is underemployed and the quantity c_i^{k+} may be interpreted as an unemployment benefit or a welfare payment to underemployed labor of type i resident in region k while employed labor resident in region k receives income both from the employer and from the subsidizing agency. The payment of the subsidy c_i^{k+} may be effected either through the employer or directly to the employee corresponding to a payroll subsidy and a negative income tax respectively). In the absence of transactions costs these two alternatives are equivalent.[11]

$$\text{If} \quad x_i^{k-} > 0, \quad \theta_i^k = c_i^{k-} \quad => \varphi_i^k = c_i^k + c_i^{k-} \qquad (2.3.13)$$

In this case labor in excess of the target quantity for region k is employed and the quantities c_i^{k-} designate appropriate marginal payroll tax rates. Such taxes may reflect for example the "cost push" inflationary effect of high wages.

8.2.4 *Goal intervals*

In the goal program developed above the penalties which are associated with deviations above or below the consumption or employment goals are independent of the magnitudes of the deviations. Penalties which increase with the magnitude of the deviation may be introduced by the introduction of piecewise linear regret functions drawn from the work of Charnes and Collomb {7} and Collomb {17} on goal interval programming.

In this case if the additional constraints

$$y_i^{k+} - y_{ir}^{k+} \leq D_{ir}^{k+} \qquad r=0,1\ldots h_i^{k+}$$

$$i \epsilon I_1 \qquad (2.4.1)$$

$$y_i^{k-} - y_{ir}^{k-} \leq D_{ir}^{k-}, \qquad r=0,\ldots h_i^{k-}$$

$$x_i^{k+} - x_{ir}^{k+} \leq D_{ir}^{k+} \qquad r=0,\ldots h_i^{k+}$$

$$i \epsilon I_2 \qquad (2.4.2)$$

$$x_i^{k-} - x_{ir}^{k-} \leq D_{ir}^{k-} \qquad r=0,\ldots h_i^{k-}$$

are introduced and penalties are associated with the quantities x_{ir}^{k+}, x_{ir}^{k-}, y_{ir}^{k+}, y_{ir}^{k-} in the functional, the overall program becomes:

$$\text{Maximize} \sum_k (\sum_{I_1} (p_i^k y_i^k - c_{ir}^{k+} y_{ir}^{k+} - c_{ir}^{k-} y_{ir}^{k-})$$

$$- \sum_{I_2} (c_i^k x_i^k + c_{ir}^{k+} x_{ir}^{k+} + c_{ir}^{k-} x_{ir}^{k-})$$

$$- \sum_{I_3} {}_k (c_i^k w_i^k - c_{i_1}^k w_{i_1}^k))$$

consumption

π_i^k $\quad y_i^k + y_i^{k+} - y_i^{k-} = d_i^k. \quad i \epsilon I_1$

$x_{ir}^{k+} \geq 0$ $\quad y_i^{k+} - y_{ir}^{k+} \leq D_{ir}^{k+}$ (2.4.1)

$\pi_{ir}^{k-} \geq 0$ $\quad y_i^{k-} - y_{ir}^{k-} \leq D_{ir}^{k-}$

demand-supply

$\varphi_i^k \geq 0$ $\quad y_i^k + \sum_j a_{ji}^k x_j^k + \sum_{\substack{j \\ k \epsilon I_j}} {}_{\ell m} a_{ji}^{\ell m} x_j^{\ell m} + \sum_\ell x_i^{k\ell} \leq x_i^k + \sum_\ell x_i^{\ell k}$

production capacity

$\mu_i \geq 0$ $\quad x_i \leq D_i^k$

$\mu_{i_k} \geq 0$ $\quad \sum_{i_k \epsilon I_j} {}_{\ell m} e_{ji_k}^{\ell m} x_j^{\ell m} \leq D_{i_k}$

employment

θ_i^k $\quad x_i^k + x_i^{k+} - x_i^{k-} = E_i^k. \quad i \epsilon I_2$

$\theta_{ir}^{k+} \geq 0$ $\quad x_i^{k+} - x_{ir}^{k+} \leq D_{ir}^{k+}$

$\theta_{ir}^{k-+} \geq 0$ $\quad x_i^{k-} - x_{ir}^{k-} \leq D_{ir}^{k-}$ (2.4.2)

resources

$\lambda_i^k \geq 0$ $\quad x_i^k - w_i^k \leq 0$

$\lambda_{i_1}^k \geq 0$ $\quad w_i^k - w_{i_1}^k \leq R_{i_1}$

$\lambda_{i_2}^k \geq 0$ $\quad w_{i_1}^k \leq R_{i_2}^k$

All variables are non-negative and, by assumption $D_{io}{}^{k+} = D_{io}{}^{k-} = 0$, all $i \epsilon I_1$, I_2.

Associating the indicated dual variables with the constraints of the primal problem, by inspection, all of the dual relationships remain the same as in the previous program except those with which the variables y_i^{k+}, y_i^{k-}, $i \epsilon I_1$, and x_i^{k+}, x_i^{k-} ,$i \epsilon I_2$ are associated. The modified dual relationships are as follows for consumption commodities:

$$y_i^{k+} \geqq 0 \qquad \pi_i^k + \sum_{r=0}^{h_i^{k+}} \pi_{ir}^{k+} \geqq 0 \qquad (2.4.3)$$

$$y_i^{k-} \geqq 0 \qquad -\pi_i^k + \sum_{r=0}^{h_i^{k-}} \pi_{ir}^{k-} \geqq 0$$

$$y_{ir}^{k+} \geqq 0 \qquad -\pi_{ir}^{k+} \geqq -c_{ir}^{k+}$$

$$y_{ir}^{k-} \geqq 0 \qquad -\pi_{ir}^{k-} \geqq -c_{ir}^{k-}$$

Hence

$$-\sum_{r=0}^{h_i^{k+}} \pi_{ir}^{k+} \leqq \pi_i^k \leqq \sum_{r=0}^{h_i^{k-}} \pi_{ir}^{k-}$$

$$\text{Now } y_i^{k+} > 0 \quad \Rightarrow y_{io}^{k+} > 0 \quad \Rightarrow \pi_{ir}^{k+} = c_{io}^{k+}$$

$$y_i^{+} > D_{i_1}^{k+} \quad \Rightarrow y_{i_1}^{k+} > 0 \quad \Rightarrow \pi_{i_1}^{k+} = c_{i_1}^{k+}$$

$$\text{and} \quad D_{ir-1}^{k+} < y_i^{k+} < D_{ir}^{k+} \quad \Rightarrow y_{is}^{k+} > 0 \qquad s=0,\ 1 \ldots (r-1)$$

$$\Rightarrow \pi_{is}^{k+} = c_{is}^{k+} \qquad s=0,\ 1 \ldots .(r-1)$$

$$\text{or} \qquad \pi_i^k = -\sum_{s=0}^{r-1} c_{is}^{k+}$$

That is, the subsidy associated with the deviation below the goal level increases as the deviation increases. By a similar argument an increasing tax is applied as the deviation above the goal level increases.

For employment of type $i \epsilon I_2$ similar relationships and interpretations obtain at the optimum.The following relationships imply that subsidies snd taxes to labor increase as "under" and "over" employment increase respectively.

$$x_i^{k+} \geqq 0 \qquad \theta_i^k + \sum_{r=0}^{h_i^{k+}} \theta_{ir}^{k+} \geqq 0$$

$$x_i^{k-} \geqq 0 \qquad -\theta_i^k + \sum_{r=0}^{{}^k h_i} \theta_{ir}^{k-} \geqq 0$$

$$x_{ir}^{k+} \geqq 0 \qquad -\theta_{ir}^{k+} \geqq -c_{ir}^{k+}$$

Hence $$-\sum_{r=0}^{h_i^{k+}} \theta_{ir}^{k+} \leq \theta_i^k \leq \sum_{r=0}^{h_i^{k-}} \theta_{ir}^{k-}$$

8.2.5 *Indifference regions and bounds on deviations*

Following Charnes and Collomb {7} and Collomb {17}, the introduction of goal intervals opens the way for the incorporation of indifference regions with respect to price in the neighborhood of the goals. If $y_i^{k+} < D_{i_1}{}^{k+}, y_i^{k-} < D_{i_1}{}^{k-}$:

$$-c_i^{k+} < \pi_i^k < c_i^{k-} \qquad i \epsilon I_1$$

If $c_{io}^{k+} = c_{io}^{k-} = 0$, then in the range $d_i^k + y_{io}^{k-}$, $d_i^k - y_{io}^{k+}$, the price for the consumption commodity i in region k is p_i^k. The introduction of such indifference regions ensures that if the consumption goals are met exactly ($y_i k+ = y_i^{k-} = 0$) the price of the commodity i in region k is p_i^k. By a similar argument if employment exactly equals the target rate in region k for labor type $i \epsilon I_2$, the wage rate in region k is c_i^k, if an indifference region is introduced in the neighborhood of the employment goals for each type of labor $i \epsilon I_2$.

Bounds on deviations may either be introduced explicitly as above or by the association of increments of regret of non-Archimedean order with deviations beyond the acceptable range in the functional.

In the following chapter the goal programming model is extended to include investment and disinvestment in production capacity in a multiperiod formulation.

8.3 A multi-period goal programming model for regional land use planning

8.3.1 *Introduction*

The principal focus of this chapter is on the determination of the optimal magnitude, timing and location of investment in production capacity be means of a multi-period goal programming model. This model may be regarded as a generalization of the model developed in the previous chapter.

A closed economy consisting of k = 1,2,...,R regions is considered over a planning interval $t_o < t < t_H$ where t_o is the initial planning period and period (t_H+1) is the planning horizon.A production process is associated with each commodity produced in each region. Commodities here include production capacity at various stages of construction, fuel and mineral resources, labor, and goods produced both as inputs to production processe[6] and for consumption. As in the previous chapter, labor availabilities are determined exogenously, and an extraction process is associated with each fuel and mineral resource in each region. Processes, or technologies, represent the means whereby commodities, with the exceptions of labor and fuel and mineral resources, are produced.

In this and the following chapter it is assumed that there exists at most one production process whereby each commodity may be produced in each region. The modifications required to extend the model to include multiple production processes are introduced in Chapter 8.6. Each process (or technology) is assumed to require a linear combination of a designated set of commodities as inputs for each unit of output.

Production capacity is identified with land use for each process, region, and time period by defining the capacity for each process as the bound on output set by the area devoted to it in each region and planning period multiplied by the productivity per unit area for the process. The existence of production capacity does not imply then that it is fully utilized in each period, or any period.

Changes in production capacity constitute the outputs of sequences of conversion processes which are contingent on the nature, location, and timing of the conversions. These processes, together with production processes constitute the totality of alternative land uses.

Investments and disinvestments in production capacity are represented by the inputs to conversion processes, which have the distinction from production processes that output equals capacity for each conversion process undertaken.

Maintenance expenditures specific to the capacity type and its location are associated with each production (as distinct from conversion) process in each region and time period. These expenditures are assumed to be sufficient to ensure that the productivity of the production capacity is independent of its age.

Goals for the output of consumption commodities and employment, and resource constraints similar to those developed in the previous chapter are incorporated in the model, and supply-demand relationships are developed which include the additional requirements for the conversion and maintenance of production capacity. The central additions to the model of the previous chapter are the equations relating to capacity conversions over time and the initial and prescribed horizon conditions for the land use or production capacity configuration.

The dual of the goal program developed in the earlier part of this chapter provides the basis for a number of interpretations which are developed partially at the end of this chapter and extensively in the following two chapters where further topics including the regulation of the output of wastes and zoning are introduced.

8.3.2 *Regions*

The geology of each region $k = 1,2,\ldots,K$ is assumed to be uniform. That is, it is assumed that the strata underlying each point of the surface of each region are at the same depths and have the same structure. (This, of course, may be taken as an "average" stratigraphy for the region). Given this assumption, the foundation requirements for any class of structure,or more generally, the preparation required for any land use or conversion of land use is known. Thus, given any pair of alternative land uses any possible sequence of conversion processes required may be defined both with respect to geological and with respect to technical and economic considerations. The level of disaggregation assumed for theoretical purposes is thus large if the geology is sufficiently hetorogeneous, and suitable aggregations may be required empirically.[12] Given the assumption of a uniform third dimension in each region a two-dimensional analysis of production and land use conversion may be undertaken.

8.3.3 *Production and conversion processes*

Let $I_0^k(t)$ be the set of alternative land uses in region k and period t. This set includes proccesses for the production, import, and export of commodities. Changes in production capacity (or land use conversions) themselves constitute the output of production processes wherein the output is the transformed or converted production capacity. For the purposes of analysis, however, a distinction is made between production processes and conversion processes where $I_1^k(t)$ is the set of alternative production processes and $I_2^k(t)$ is the set of alternative conversion processes in region k and period t and $I_1^k(t) \cup I_2^k(t) = I_0^k(t)$. That is the totality of alternative production and conversion processes in region k and period t constitutes the set of alternative land uses in region k and period t.

Production processes Let $x_i^k(t) \geq 0$, $i \epsilon I^k(t)$ be the marketable[13] output of production process i in region k and period t and $z_i^k(t)$ be the surface area devoted to process i in region k during period t. Let q_i^k be the production capacity per unit area for process i in region k, then if output of commodity i is not to exceed capacity,

$$x_i^k(t) \leq q_i^k z_i^k k(t) \qquad i \epsilon I_1^k(t) \qquad (3.3.1)$$

The quantity q_i^k is by assumption independent of time, it being assumed that all time, it being assumed that maintenance inputs (to be introduced below) are sufficient in each period to ensure that the productivity of production capacity is independent of its age.

It is further assumed that a single process, or technology, is associated with each commodity which may be produced in each region and time period. The particular process associated with the production of a commodity will, however, in general vary regionally due to geological considerations, and market considerations both for the commodity itself and for the production capacity be means of whlch it is produced. Not every commodity may be produced in every region, for regional endowments of fuel and mineral resources will generally vary, thus restricting the possible locations for extraction processes, and industrial location may be regulated due to environmental considerations.

Extensions to include physical depreciation and the endogenous determination of production technologies are made in Chapter 8.6. Multi-level environmental regulation is introduc~d in Chapter 8.5.

Conversion processes In general the conversion of productlon capacity from one process to another may require more than one planning period for its completion with the minimal time interval required varying with the nature of the oonversion and the actual time interval taken depending upon the alternative uses open to the site both currently and in the future. That is, there may be a number of stages in a conversion sequence corresponding, for example, to the removal of an existing structure, holding the site in a "cleared" state, excavating for foundations for a new structure and constructing it. Each of these stages corresponds to a process either of conversion or of production. In this case the "marketable" output of the production capacity ("Ucleared land") may be zero. As an alternative to being left "cleared" the site may be used for car parking, although it it were macadamed additional conversion processes would be required both for installing and removing the macadam. The actual sequence of land uses at each site depend upon an optimal adjustment to the market conditions prevailing during the planning interval. The nature of this dependence is the subject of the following chapter.

Rather than pursue a discussion of alternative sequences of land uses the following approach is taken.

The production process β in period (t+l) is defined to be *accessible* from the production process α during period t if the conversion from process β to process α may be completed during period t. It is assumed that if the conversion is undertaken the time required for the conversion process $\alpha\beta$ is exactly one period, and thus that for conversion processes output equals capacity in all cases.

Let the set of processes accessible from process α at the beginning of period t be ${}_{\alpha}I^k(t)$ and the set of processes to which the process α is accessible during period t be $I_{\alpha}{}^k(t)$.

It is assumed that accessibility follows a logical sequence insofar as, for example, the excavations for a new structure must follow the removal of an existing one (if any) and precede the installation of new foundations and the completion of the structure.[14] As noted above, restrictions may be placed on accessibility by means of legal prohibitions (zoning) of designated subsets of conversions. Such restrictions are introduced in a more general framework in Chapter 8.5. By its definition accessibility is related empirically to the length of the time assumed for each planning interval.

Let $z_{\alpha\beta}^k(t)$ be the area of region k converted from process α to process β ($\alpha,\beta \epsilon I_2^k(t)$) during period t. Then the total area in land use i in region k and period t is given by the quantity $z_i^k(t-1)$ carried over from period (t-1), plus the capacity converted to process i during period (t-1) the capacity removed from production for conversion during period (t).Hence :

$$z_i^k(t) = z_i^k(t-1) + \sum_{i\epsilon_\beta I^k(t-1)} z_{\beta i}(t-1) - \sum_{\alpha\,\epsilon I_i^k(t)} z_{i\alpha}^k(t) \qquad (3.3.2)$$

Multiplying through (3.3.2) by q_i^k the relationship becomes

$$q_i^k z_i^k(t) = q_i^k \, [z_i^k(t-1) + \sum_{i\epsilon_\beta I^k(t-1)} z_{\beta i}^k(t-1) - \sum_{\alpha\epsilon I_i^k(t)} z_{i\alpha}^k(t)] \qquad (3.3.3)$$

Equation (3.3.3) gives a relationship for production capacity changes for process i in region k over time. Clearly, relationships (3.3.2) and (3.3.3) are linearly dependent and thus either the capacity change or the land use conversion relationships are redundant for purposes of computation and interpretation. Anticipating the interpretation of the dual program the value of each site in a region is given by the value of the production capacity associated with it in each planning period, either for purposes of contlnued production through maintenance, or for conversion.

Initial conditions and "Land" constraints. At the beginning of the initial planning period t_0 the land use configuration is known.[15] Hence

$$z_i^k(t_o) + \sum_{\alpha\epsilon_i I^k(t)} z_{i\alpha}^k(t_0) = z_i^{**k}(t_0-1) + \sum_{i\epsilon_\beta I^i(to-1)} z_{\beta i}^{k**}(t_0-1) \qquad (3.3.4)$$

$$= \text{constant} = z_i^{k*}(t_0-1) \qquad (3.3.5)$$

Also

$$\sum_{i\epsilon I^k} z_i^{k*}(t_0-1) = L^k \qquad (3.3.6)$$

where L^k is the surface area of region k. Then

$$\sum_{i\epsilon I^k(t)} z_i^k(t_0) + \sum_{i\epsilon I^k(t)} \sum_{\alpha\epsilon I_i^k(t)} z_{i\alpha}^k(t_0) = L^k \qquad (3.3.7)$$

and by induction

$$\sum_{i\epsilon I^k(t)} z_i^k(t) + \sum_{i\epsilon I^k(t)} \sum_{\alpha\epsilon I^k(t)} z_{i\alpha}^k(t) = L^k \qquad (3.3.8)$$

$$(t_0+1) \leq t \leq t_H$$

The relationships (3.3.8) may be interpreted as overall "land" constraints for each region and time period and are seen to be redundant as linear combinations of land use conversion constraints. Hence it might be anticipated that the value of "land" in a region may be obtained only as the value of the capacity associated with the marginal land use in each region and time period.

Horizon posture constraints for production capacity. A target capacity $z_i{}^{k*}(t_H+1)$ is assumed to be prescribed for each production process at the end of period t_H in order that production be maintained beyond the horizon either by maintenance or conversion of the production capacity at the horizon. The production capacity available for each process $i \epsilon I^k(t_H+1)$ at the horizon is given by [16] :

$$z_i^k(t_H) + \sum_{iA\alpha} z_{\alpha i}(t_H) \qquad (3.3.9)$$

Then

$$- z_i^k(t_H) - \sum_{iA\alpha} z_{\alpha i}^k(t_H) + z_i^{k-}(t_H+1) - z_i{}^{k+}(t_H+1) = - z_i{}^{k*}(t_H+1) \qquad (3.3.10)$$

where $z_i{}^{k-}(t_H+1)$, $z_i{}^{k+}(t_H+1)$ are respectively the deviations above and below the horizon capacity goals. Alternative horizon conditions may be :

$$-z_i^k(t_H) - \sum_{iA\alpha} z_{\alpha i}^k(t_H) = z_i^{k-}(t_H+1) \qquad (3.3.11)$$

or more complex conditions relating to capacity requirements for groups of regions may be introduced, corresponding for example to national and regional as well as local postures and policies.

8.3.4 *Resource, labor, production and market relationships*

As in the preview chapter an extraction process is associated with each fuel and mineral resource in each region. Assuming that the rate of formation of new deposits is so small in comparison to the planning interval as to be negligible, the total withdrawals of these commodities during the planning interval may not exceed their initial endowments or:

$$\sum_{i=t_o}^{t+i} x_i^k(t) \leq R_i^k(t_o-1) \qquad i \epsilon I_3^k \qquad (3.4.1)$$

where $I_3{}^k$ is the set of fuel and mineral resources in region k, and $R_i{}^k(t_o-1)$is the initial endowment of resource i in region k.

Relationships (3.4.1) do not generally prescribe the relevant bounds for planning and pricing purposes, for resources will generally be demanded of each type beyond the horizon. In order to reflect the future requirements a price or time-preference schedule may be defined for the depletion of each resourcesby the relationships:

$$\sum_{t=t_o}^{t+1} x_i^k(t) - w_i^k(t_H+1) \leq 0 \qquad (3.4.2)$$

$$w_i^k(t_H+1) - w_i^k(t_H+1) \leq R_i^k(t_H+1)$$

$$w_{i_1}^k(t_H+1) \leq R_i^k(t_H+1) - R_i^k(t_H-1) = R_{i_2}^k(t_{H+1})$$

where an increasing penalty is associated with increasing depletion of each fuel or mineral resource in the functional, with the number of price increments being given by the number of intervals considered. The horizon price increments are given by quantities $c_i{}^k(t_H{}^+1)$ associated with the quantities $w_i{}^k(t_H{}^+1)$, $w_{i_1}{}^k(t_H{}^+1)$ in the functional.

In order to enable the resource to be exhausted at, or prior to, the horizon a potential final increment of magnitude ε where ε is arbitrarily small, but finite, may be assumed with an associated non-Archimedean penalty in the functional. That is, exhaustion is modelled by potential supply at arbitrarily high marginal cost.

Water differs from the fuel and mineral resources introduced in the previous paragraphs insofar as the quantity of water available as inputs to production varies in each planning period due to the spatial interrelations between rainfall, runoff, and return flows in each period.

Heaney {24} develops a long-range river basin planning model in which relationships between precipitation, runoff, extraction, storage, and return flows for a river system are extensively developed, in order to appraise water pricing and river basin development policies.[17] Here a much simplified water supply model is embedded within the overall model.

It is assumed that the run-off in region k and period t is $H_o^k(t)$ and the quantity of water extracted from the aquifer in region k during period t is $x_o^k(t)$, and consequently, under the assumption of the present model that no inventories are maintained,[18] the following relationships apply ln each region and time period:

$$x_o^k(t) \leqq H_o^k(t) \tag{3.4.3}$$

Water may be transported between regions by means of streams, rivers, and pipelines, with the former being a local transportation link and the latter being arterial link under the dichotomy which is made between local and arterial transportation capacity below. For completeness a sink would be required for each river system where the quantity of water reaching the sink would be, for example.[19]

$$\sum_{k \epsilon S_r} H_o^k(t) - \sum_{k \epsilon S_r} x_o^k(t) \tag{3.4.4}$$

where S_r is the set of links serving the sink r (constituting the river system). These latter constraints are omitted below. Return flows to aquifers may augment the runoff with these flows being either treated or untreated, and thus their magnitudes are determined by the level or output of waste treatment processes.

Return flows to river systems and storage are derived from treated or untreated waste water and thus constitute additions to the water supply. Treated water is the output of waste water treatment processes whose inputs consist of waste water, treatment capacity and variable inputs including labor. The determination of the optimal capacity, design and finance of waste water treatment facilities is the subject of Lynn's dissertation {38} in which a multi-period model is developed for the design and staged growth of treatment facilities.

Deininger {19} develops a model for the optimal location and capacity of treatment plants in which wastes may either be treated prior to discharge or discharged into rivers for treatment downstream. Constraints imposed by the treatment capacity at each location and by regulatory authorities for water quality for each reach of the river are included in Deininger's model.[20]

Here a single waste water treatment process is assumed for the water requirements of each process in each region, and the contribution made by the output of the treatment processes to the water supply in a region is modelled by the negativity of the sign of the quantity a_{io}^k where a_{io}^k is the quantity of water required per unit of treated water in region k, i.e., $a_{io}^k = -1$.Multiple treatment processes may be incorporated by means of modifications to the overall model to include multiple technologies (these are made in Chapter 8.6). The output or capacity of water treatment plants may be regulated and controlled on environmental grounds. These possibilities are introduced in Chapter 8.5.

Labor. Let I_2 be the set of labor types and $E_i(t)$ be the target employment rate for labor of class i in period t. Then if $x_i^k(t)$ is the quantity of labor of class i resident in region k in period t and $x_i^{k+}(t)$, $x_i^{k-}(t)$ measure respectively global underemployment and overemployment of labor of class i in period t

$$\sum_k x_i^k(t) + x_i^{k+}(t) - x_i^{k-}(t) = E_i(t) \qquad i \epsilon I_2 \qquad (3.4.5)$$

Here local labor availability $x_i^k(t)$is assumed to be constrained by the condition, introduced below, that sufficient housing be available locally. The global constraint (3.4.5) may be contrasted with the local constraint on labor availabllity developed in the previous chapter. In practice both types of constraints may apply. This possibility is examined in Chapter 8.5.The deviations $x_i^{k+}(t)$, $x_i^{k-}(t)$ may be divided into intervals and bounded by means of additional goal interval constraints and associated penalties, as shown in the latter part of the previous chapter. Here,in order only to reduce complexity, a single interval is assumed, and it is also assumed that upper bounds (given for example by the maximum possible labor force participation for each type of labor) are not violated at the optimum.

The quantities $E_i(t)$ may be linked temporally by demographic considerations relating to birth rates, retirement ages, and educational and training policies. Linkages of this kind are incorporated by means of Markov transition matrices in a series of multi-period goal programming models for manpower planning developed by Charnes, Cooper, Niehaus and others {10} and in the constraints of a model for social development (Charnes, Kirby, and Walters {13}). In the manpower models these transition matrices include transitions over space as well as transitions over time.

The interpretations of overemployment and underemployment associated with the quantities $x_i^{k+}(t)$,$x_i^{k-}(t)$ are defined with respect to the goal level and may reflect the impact of cost push inflation and the loss of desired production possibilities, respectively.

Housing. Let I_3 be the possible set of housing types and α_{ij}^k be the quantity of housing of type j required by labor of type i resident in region k. Then :

$$\sum_{i \epsilon I_2} \alpha_{ij}^k x_i^k(t) \leq x_j^k(t) \qquad i \epsilon I_3 \qquad (3.4.6)$$

Transportation. It is assumed that all commodities, with the exception of production capacity, (either in production or under construction), and fuel and mineral resources,[21] may be transported within each region or between regions. In order to transport these commodities both transportation capacity and variable transportation inputs are required. Transportation capacity may take the form of roads, railways pipelines, power lines, etc., as well as capacity at transshipment points, e.g., ports and marshalling yards. Variable transportation inputs include the vehicles appropriate to the form of transportation capacity (if any) and their associated maintenance requirements and fuel and labor.A distinction is made between local and arterial transportation capacity and inputs.

Changes in local transportation capacity are compounded with the inputs to land-use conversions and variable inputs to local transportation specific to each production process with the inputs of the process. Local transportation capacity includes, for example, access roads, feeder lines for water and waste water, and local power and telephone connections. It will be seen that the association of local transportation capacity directly with land use conversions implies that capital costs associated with local transportation are imputed to local land uses.In the case of access roads, the purpose of the road implies that local land users are the beneficiaries of the roads, either directly or by services provided to them. In the case of utility connections the users of the capacity are the owners of the property served.

The character of existing local road and utility connections has a bearing on conversion processes for each accessible use of a site in a region.For example, existing access roads and utility connections may be utilized when houses are converted to apartments.

It is assumed that there is a prescribed direct arterial route whereby each transportable commodity may be shipped between each distinct pair of regions. These routes may incorporate links utilizing different trans -portation modes, e.g. road-rail-road, and sufficient capacity must be availsble on each link and also at transhipment points to accommodate the scheduled shipment quantities after allowance, where appropriate, for peak loads, and differences in vehicles used for shipment.[22] The prescription of direct routes does not preclude the indirect shipment of commodities via one or more intervening regions, if this should be less costly.

Extensions may be made to include alternative direct routes between regions but are omitted here due to the notational complexity introduced thereby. Such extensions would be required in order to accommodate modal split possibilities for direct shipments.

It is assumed that the endogenous expansion of capacity precludes the occurrence of congestion on arterial transportation links, and that they are constructed for specified design flows or speeds.

Let the direct route for shipment of commodity i from region k to region ℓ consist of the set of links $I_i^{k\ell}$ and the quantity shipped be $x_i^{k\ell}(t)$ in period t.

Let the set of arterial links in region k be I_4^k. Then if $q_{i_k} z_{i_k}(t) \geq 0$ is the capacity on link i_k in period t the relationship between transport capacity on link i_k and the flow over link i_k in period t is given by

$$\sum_j \sum_{i_k \epsilon I_i^{\ell m}} e_{ji}^{\ell m} x_j^{\ell m}(t) \leq q_{i_k} z_{i_k}(t) \qquad (3.4.7)$$

where $e_{ji}^{\ell m}$ is the quantity of capacity required on link i_k per unit shipment of commodity i over the route $I_i^{\ell m}$ given that $i_k \epsilon I_j^{\ell m}$. The quantity $e_{jik}^{\ell m}$ may be adjusted for peak loads where appropriate.

Thus link i_k supplies capacity jointly to the set of shipments $x_j^{\ell m}(t)$ for which $i_k \epsilon I^{\ell m}$. In order to maintain a general form for production capacity constraints and the demand and supply constraints the quantity x_{ik} is introduced where :

$$x_{i_k} \leq q_{i_k} z_{i_k} \qquad (3\ 4\ 8)$$

and

$$\sum_i \sum_{\ell m} e_{ji_k}^{\ell} x_j^{\ell m}(t) \leq x_{i_k} \qquad (3.4.9)$$

It will be assumed that a linear combination of variable inputs specific to the commodity shipped and the link over which it is shipped is required for each interregional unit shipment of a comnodity. A more detailed analysis would include the scheduling of the movements of vehicles and their crews over the transportation network. Such analyses are undertaken by Charnes, et.al.{14}.

Turning now to consumption commodities, let the quantity of commodity i consumed in region k and period t be $yi^k(t)$ and let consumption goals $di^k(t)$ be prescribed for each region k = 1, 2,...,K and planning period $t_o \leq t \leq tH$. Then equations (3.4.1) express the relationship between the quantity of commodity i consumed in each region and time period and the goal levels where $y_i^{k+}(t)$ and $y_i^{k-}(t)$ are respectively the shortfall from the goal and the amount consumed in excess of it.

$$y_i^k(t) + y_i^{k+}(t) - y_i^{k-}(t) = d_i^k(t) \qquad i \epsilon I_1 \qquad (3.4.10)$$

Housing has the distinction of being an immobile consumption commodity. Thus for housing :

$$y_i^k(t) \leq q_i^k z_i^k(t) \qquad i \epsilon I_3 \qquad (3.4.11)$$

As in the case of transportation capacity, to preserve the general form of the capacity and supply and demand constraints the quantities $x_i^k(t)$, $i \epsilon I_3$ are introduced as follows:

$$y_i^k(t) \leq x_i^k(t) \leq q_i^k z_i^k(t) \qquad i \epsilon I_3 \qquad (3.4.12)$$

In each region and time period commodities are required as inputs to production processes, including construction, maintenance, and transportation requirements, as well as those for consumption.

Following the assumption that input requirements are linear functions of the output quantities for each of these processes the overall demand $D_i^k(t)$ in region k for commodity i in period t is given by:

$$D_i^k(t) = y_i^k(t) + \sum_j a_{ji}^k x_j(t) + \sum_j b_{ji}^k i z_i^k k(t) + \sum_{\alpha,\beta} b_{\alpha\beta i}^k z_{\alpha\beta}^k(t)$$

$$+ \sum_i \sum_{k \epsilon R^{\ell m}} a_{ji}^{\ell m} x_j^{\ell m}(t) + \sum_\ell x_i^{k\ell}(t) \qquad (3.4.13)$$

In order, the terms of equation (3.4.13) are the demands for consumption, for production, for maintenance, for conversion, for variable transportation inputs, and for export. Thus

a_{ji}^k is the quantity of commodity i required per unit output of commodity ; in region k (for $j \epsilon I_2$, the set of labor types these are zero).

b_{ij}^k is the quantity of commodity i required for the maintenance of capacity of type j in region k (where capacity is given by the area devoted to the production process in the region or $b_{ij}^k = \bar{b}_{ij}^k q_i^k$).

$b_{\alpha\beta i}^k$ is the quantity of commodity i required per unit area converted from production process a to process β in region k, where the process α is accessible to β in the period.

$a_{ji}^{\ell m}$ is the aggregate quantity of commodity i required for shipment of commodity j through, from, or to region k in period

This demand is to be supplied either from production in region k or from imports or :

$$D_i^k(t) = y_i^k(t) + \sum_j a_{ji}^k x_j^k + \sum_j b_{ji}^k z_i^k(t) + \sum_{\alpha,\beta} b_{(\alpha\beta)i}^k z_{\alpha\beta i}^k(t)$$

$$+ \sum_{j,\ell} a_{ji}^{\ell} x_j^{\ell m}(t) + \sum_{\ell} x_i^{k\ell}(t) \leq x_i^k(t) + \sum_{\ell} x_i^{\ell k}(t) \qquad (3.4.14)$$

8.3.5 *The functional*

A perfect capital market in which funds may be freely borrowed or lent at an interest rate ρ in each planning period is assumed to exist. Target prices $p_i{}^k(t)$ $(i \epsilon I_1)$ are assumed to be prescribed for each consumption commodity, region, and time period, as well as a target wage rate $c_i(t)$ $(i \epsilon I_2)$ for each class of labor and time period .

\` Weights are associated with deviations from goals relating to consumption, employment and horizon capacity, as well increments in the use of fuel and mineral resources. These weights reflect the marginal social regret associated with deviations from social goals in the range to whlch the deviations are confined.

The functional of the program may be interpreted at the optimum as the discounted sum of the added value in the economy during the planning interval after allowance for transfer payments.[23]

8.3.6 *The overall program*

Maximize $$\sum_{k,t} \frac{1}{(1+p)^t} \Big(\sum_{i \epsilon I_1} p_i^k(t) y_i^k(t) - c_i^{k+}(t) y_i^{k+}(t) - c_i^{k-}(t) y_i^{k-}(t)$$

consumption

$$- \sum_{i \epsilon I_2} [c_i k(t) x_i k(t) + c_i +(t) x_i +(t) + c_i -(t) x_i -(t)]$$

employment

$$- \frac{1}{(1+p)^{t_H+1}} \sum_k \sum_{i \epsilon I_3} (c_{i1}^k(t_H+1) w_i^k(t_H+1) + c_{i2}^k(t_H+1) w_{i2}^k(t_H+1))$$

resources

$$+ \sum_{i \epsilon I_3} {}_k[\, c_i^{k+}(t_H+1) z_i^{k+}(t_H+1) + c_i^{k-}(t_H+1) z_i^{k-}(t_H+1) \,)\Big)$$

horizon conditions

subject to:

consumption

$$\frac{\pi_i^k(t)}{(1+p)^t} \qquad y_i^k(t) + y_i^{k+}(t) - y_i^{k-}(t) = d_i^k(t) \quad i \epsilon I_1 \qquad (3.4.10)$$

demand-supply

$$\frac{\varphi_i^k(t)}{(1+p)^t} \geq 0 \qquad y_i^k(t) + \sum_j a_{ji}^k i x^k(t) + \sum_j b_{ji}^k z_j^k(t)$$

$$+ \sum_{\alpha} b_{(\alpha\beta)}^k z_{\alpha\beta}^k(t) + \sum_{k \epsilon I_i^{\ell m}} a_{ji}^{\ell m} x_j^{\ell m}(t) \qquad (3.4.14)$$

$$+ \sum_{\ell} x_i^{k\ell}(t) \leq x_i^k(t) + \sum_{\ell} x_i^{\ell k}(t)$$

employment

$$\frac{\theta_i(t)}{(1+p)^t} \qquad \sum_k x_i^k(t) + x_i^{k+}(t) - x_i^{k-}(t) = E_i^k(t) \qquad i \epsilon I_2 \qquad (3.4.5)$$

labor-housing

$$\frac{\delta_j(t)}{(1+p)^t} \geqq 0 \qquad \sum a_{ij}^k x_i^k(t) \leq x_j^k(t) \qquad j \epsilon I_3 \qquad (3.4.6)$$

capacity conversion

$$\frac{\xi_i^k(t)}{(1+p)^t} \qquad z_i^k(t) = z_i^k(t-1) + \sum_{iA\alpha} z_{\alpha i}^k(t-1) - \sum_{\beta Ai} z_{i\beta}^k(t)$$

$$(3.3.8)$$

$$(t_o+1) \leq t \leq t_H$$

production capacity

$$\frac{\mu_i^k(t)}{(1+p)^t} \qquad x_i^k(t) \leq q_i^k z_i^k(t) \qquad i \epsilon I_1^k(t) \qquad (3.3.1)$$

transportation capacity

$$\frac{\mu_i^k(t)}{(1+p)^t} \qquad \sum_j \sum_{ik \epsilon I_i^\ell m} e_{ji}^{\ell m} x_k^{\ell m}(t) \leq q_i z_i \left(\frac{t}{k}\right) \qquad (3.4.7)$$

initial conditions

$$\frac{\xi_i^k(t_o)}{(1+\rho)^t} \qquad z_i^k(t_o) + \sum_\beta z_{i\beta}^k(t_o) = z_i^{k*} (t_o-1) \qquad t=to \qquad (3.3.5)$$

horizon conditions

$$\frac{\xi_i^i(t_H+1)}{(1+p)^t} \qquad z_i^k(t_H) - \sum_{\alpha Ai} z_{\alpha i}^k(t_H+1) + z_i^{k-}(t_H+1) \qquad t=t_{H+1}$$

$$(3.3.10)$$

$$- z_i^{k+}(t_H+1) = - z_i^{k*}(t_H+1)$$

water supply[24]

$$\frac{\lambda_o^k(t)}{(1+p)^t} \qquad x_o^k(t) \leq H_o^k(t) \qquad (3.4.3)$$

fuel and mineral resources

$$\frac{\lambda_i^k(t_H+1)}{(1+\rho)^{t_H+1}} \qquad \sum_{t=t_o}^{t_H} x_i^k(t) - w_i^k(t_H+1) \leq 0$$

$$\frac{\lambda_{i1}(t_H+1)}{(1+\rho)^{t_H+1}} \qquad w_i^k(t_H+1) - w_{i_1}^k(t_H+1) \leq R_{i_1}^k(t_H+1) \qquad i \epsilon I_3^k \qquad (3.4.2)$$

$$\frac{\lambda_{i2}(t_H+1)}{(1+\rho)^{t_H+1}} \qquad w_{i_1}^k(t_H+1) - w_{i_2}^k(t_H+1) \leq R_{i_2}^k(t_H+1)$$

All variables non-negative

The primal program always has a feasible and hence an optimal solution by arguments similar to those of Chapter 8.2. Briefly, feasibility may be attained by setting all output and consumption equal to zero. The program is bounded above by the overall capacity constraints.

8.3.7 *The dual program*

Associating the indicated dual variables with the constraints of the primal problem the dual program is:

$$\text{Minimize} \quad \sum_k \sum_i \left(\frac{\xi_i^k(t_0)\, z_i^k(t_0-1)}{(1+\rho)^{t_0}} - \frac{\xi_i^k(t_H+1) z_i^k(t_H+1)}{(1+\rho)^{t_H+1}} \right.$$

production capacity

$$+ \sum_{t=t_0}^{t_H^1} \sum_{i\epsilon I_1 I_2} \frac{1}{(1+p)^t} [\pi_i^k(t) d_i^k(t) + \theta_i(t) E_i(t)]$$

goal evaluations

$$+ \sum_{t=t_0}^{t_H^1} \sum_k \frac{1}{(1+p)^t} \lambda_o^k(t) H_o^k(t)$$

water

$$+ \frac{1}{(1+\rho)^{t_H+1}} \sum_k \sum_{i\epsilon I_3^k} (\lambda_{i_1}^k(t_H+1)\, R_{i_1}^k(t_H+1) + \lambda_{i_2}^k(t_H+1))$$

resources

subject to:

consumption

$$y_i^k(t) \geq 0 \qquad \pi_i^k(t) + \varphi_i^k(t) \geq p_i^k(t) \qquad (3.7.1)$$

$$y_i^{k-}(t), y_i^{k+}(t) \geq 0 \qquad -c_i^{k+}(t) \leq \pi_i(t) \leq c_i^{k-}(t) \qquad (3.7.2)$$

housing

$$x_j^k(t) \geq 0 \qquad -\varphi_i^k(t) - \delta_i^k(t) + \mu_i^k(t) \geq 0 \qquad i\epsilon I_3 \qquad (3.7.3)$$

labor

$$x_i^k(t) \geq 0 \qquad -\varphi_i^k(t) + .\sum_{j\epsilon I_3} \alpha_{ij}^k \delta_j(t) + \theta_i(t) \geq c_i(t) \quad i\epsilon I_2 \qquad (3.7.4)$$

$$x_i^+(t),\ x_i^-(t) \geq 0 \qquad -c_i^{k+}(t) \leq \theta_i(t) \leq c_i^{k-}(t) \qquad i\epsilon I_2 \qquad (3\ 7\ 5)$$

transportation

$$x_i^{\ell k}(t) \leq 0 \qquad -\varphi_i^k(t) + \varphi_i^\ell(t) + \sum_{m\epsilon I_i^{\ell k}} a_{ij}^{\ell k} \varphi_j^m \qquad (3.7.6)$$

$$+ \sum_{j_m \epsilon I_i^{\ell k}} e_{ij}^{\ell k} \mu_{j_m}(t) \geq 0$$

production (excluding housing, extraction, and conversion processes)

$$x_i^k(t) \geq 0 \qquad - \varphi_i^k(t) + \sum_j a_{ij}^k \varphi_j^k(t) + \mu_i^k(t) \geq 0 \tag{3.7.7}$$

extraction processes

$$x_i^k(t) \geq 0 \qquad - \varphi_i^k(t) + \sum_j a_{ij}^k \varphi_j^k(t) + \mu_i^k(t) + \frac{\lambda_i(t_H+1)}{(1+\rho)^{t_H+1-to}} \geq 0 \tag{3.7.8}$$

water

$$-\varphi_o^k(t) + \sum_j a_{oj}^k \varphi j(t) + \mu_o^k(t) + \lambda_o{}^k(t) \geq 0 \tag{3.7.9}$$

resource prices

$$w_i^k(t) \geq 0 \qquad -\lambda_i^k(t_H+1) + \lambda_{i_1}^k(t_H+1) \geq -c_{i_1}^k(t_H+1) \tag{3.7.10}$$

$$w_{i_1}^k(t) \geq 0 \qquad \lambda_{i_1}^k(t_H+1) + \lambda_{i_2}^k(t_H+1) \geq -c_{i_2}^k(t_H+1) \tag{3.7.11}$$

capacity

$$z_i^k(t) \geq 0 \qquad -q_i^k \mu_i^k k(t) + \xi_i^k(t) - \frac{\xi_i(\overset{k}{t}+1)}{(1+p)} + \sum_j b_i^k \varphi_j^k(t) \geq 0 \tag{3.7.12}$$

horizon period

$$z_i^{k+}(t_H+1),\ z_i^{k-}(t_H+1) \geq 0$$

$$-c_i^{k-}(t_H+1) \leq \xi_i^k(t_H+1) \leq c_i^{k+}(t_H+1) \tag{3.7.13}$$

capacity conversion

$$z_{\alpha,\beta}^k(t) \geq 0 \qquad -\xi_\beta^k(t+1)/(1+\rho) + \xi_\alpha^k(t) + \sum_j b_{\alpha\beta j}^k\ \varphi_j^k(t) \geq 0 \tag{3.7.14}$$

The constraints of the dual problem may be interpreted at the optimum as follows:

Consumption commodities. The relationship between prices and marginal costs for consumption commodities is as in the previous chapter.

$$y_i^k(t) > 0 \Rightarrow \qquad \varphi_i^k(t) + \pi_i^k(t) = p_i^k(t) \qquad I \epsilon I_1 \tag{3.7.1}$$

where

$$-c_i^{k+}(t) \leq \pi_i^k(t) \leq c_i^{k-}(t) \tag{3.7.2}$$

The quantity $\pi_i{}^k(t)$ may be interpreted as a sales tax when $y_i{}^{k-}(t) > 0$ ($\Rightarrow \pi_i{}^{k-}(t) = c_i{}^{k-}(t)$), and as a subsidy when $y_i{}^{k+}(t) > 0$ ($\Rightarrow \pi_i{}^k(t) = -c_i{}^{k+}(t)$). Further intervals may be introduced and the solution perturbed to ensure that when $y_i{}^{k+}(t) = y_i{}^{k-}(t) = 0$, $\pi_i k(t) = 0$, by the arguments of the latter part of the previous chapter.

Housing. Housing is a consumption commodity, so that the above relationships and interpretations for consumption commodities apply but also :

$$x_i^k(t) > 0 \quad \Rightarrow \quad \varphi_i^k(t) + \delta_i^k(t) = \mu_i^k(t) \qquad i \epsilon I_3 \qquad (3.7.3)$$

That is, the marginal rental $\mu_i{}^k(t)$ of housing of type i in region k is equal to the marginal rental of the house itself plus the location premium $\delta_i{}^k(t)$. The quantity $\delta_i{}^k(t)$ is associated with the constraint relating labor to housing and is zero if the supply of housing is sufficient to house all locally resident employees. In case $\delta_i{}^k(t) > 0$ then the housing of type i houses only employees and the quantity $\delta_i{}^k(t)$ either be collected from all tenants or allocated among tenants on the basis made possible by the relationship (3.4.6):

$$\delta_i^k(t) > 0 \quad \Rightarrow \quad \sum_{j \epsilon I_2} \alpha_{ji}^k x_j^k(t) \delta_i^k(t) = x_i^k(t) \delta_i^k(t) \qquad i \epsilon I_3 \qquad (3.4.6)$$

That is, a tenant of class j pays a rent premium of $\alpha_{ji}{}^k \delta_i{}^k(t)$ for housing of type i. Each alternative,I believe, has a real world correspond

Labor $x_i(t) > 0$, $i \epsilon I_2 \Rightarrow$

$$\varphi_i^k(t) = \sum_j \alpha_{ij}^k \delta_j^k(t) + \theta_i(t) + c_i(t) \qquad (3.7.4)$$

where

$$-c_i^{k+}(t) \leqq \theta_i(t) \leqq c_i^{k-}(t) \qquad (3.7.5)$$

That is the marginal cost of labor of type $i \epsilon I_2$ to an employer is given by the guaranteed economy wide wage $c_i(t)$ plus or minus the payroll subsidy or tax $\theta_i(t)$ plus the marginal location premium which the marginal locally resident employee must pay for accommodation. Recall that labor is assumed to be mobile subject to the condition that sufficient housing is available and that the commuting distance for labor may be restricted by the time which is required. The difference in marginal cost of labor between two markets connected by commuting is thus equal to the marginal commuting cost, as is shown below by relating (3.7.6) which apply to all transportable commodities including labor.

Transportation $x_i k\ell\ (t) > 0 \Rightarrow$

$$\varphi_i^\ell(t\ ) = \varphi_i^k(t\ ) + \sum_j a_{ij}\varphi_j(t) + \sum_{j_k \epsilon I_i^{k\ell}} e_{ij_k}^{k\ell} \mu_{j_k}(t) \qquad (3.7.6)$$

Hence if commodity i is shipped from region k to region ℓ in period t the marginal cost in region ℓ exceeds that in region k by the sum of the variable and capacity costs required for the shipment.

Production (excluding extraction and conversion processes) $x_i{}^k(t) > 0 \Rightarrow$

$$\varphi_i^k(t) = \sum_j a_{ij}^k \varphi(t) + \mu_i^k(t) \qquad (3.7.7)$$

That is, the marginal cost of commodity i produced in region k in period t is given by the marginal cost of the variable inputs plus the marginal production capacity cost.

Extraction processes. $x_i^k(t) > 0 \Rightarrow$

$$\varphi_i^k(t) = \sum_j a_{ij}^k \varphi_i^k(t) + \mu_i^k(t) + \frac{\lambda_i^k(t_H+1)}{(1+\rho)^{t_H+1-t}} \qquad (3.7.8)$$

For extraction processes the marginal cost of the resource is added to the marginal costs of variable inputs and production capacity to determine the marginal cost of the extracted commodity. Let

$$\frac{\lambda_i^k(t_H+1)}{(1+\rho)^{t_H+1-t}} = \lambda_i^{1k}(t)$$

Then

$$\lambda_i^{1k}(t+1) = (1+\rho)\lambda_i^{1k}(t)$$

That is, the marginal cost of fuel and mineral resources in the ground ($i \epsilon I_3^k$) increases in each period at the rate ρ (if they are not exhausted prior to the horizon)-an inherent inflationary effect. The developments of Chapter 8.5 will show that this result holds whether or not the rate of extraction is regulated. This phenomenon been unnoticed has a straight -forward explanation, namely that at the margin a resource owner may either hold resources in the ground or sell them for extraction currently or in the future and invest the proceeds of the sale.

Resource prices. For fuel and mineral resources the price or marginal opportunity cost prevailing at the horizon is given by $\lambda_i^k(t_H+1)$ where

$$0 < \sum_{t=t_o}^{t+1} x_i^k(t) \leq R_i^k(t_H+1) \Rightarrow \qquad (3.7.10)$$

$$\lambda_i^k(t_H+1) = c_i^k(t_H+1)$$

$$R_{i_1}^k(t_H+1) < \sum_{t=t_o}^{t+1} x_i^k(t) \leq R_{i_1}^k(t_H+1) \Rightarrow \qquad (3.7.11)$$

$$\lambda_i^k(t_H+1) = c_j^k(t_H+1) + \lambda_{i1}^k(t_H+1) + c_{i_1}^k(t_H+1)$$

Hence the horizon price or marginal opportunity cost of each resource increases as the quantity used increases. Since the current marginal cost of resources $i \epsilon I_3^k$ is related to the horizon marginal cost by relations (3.7.8) increasing utilization over the planning interval is associated with increasing marginal costs of resources in each period during the interval.

Water resources. In the case of water resources, since it is here assumed that water may not be stored from period to period, the marginal cost or price of water is given by the relationship (3.7.9). The interpretation for

$x_o^k(t) > 0 \Rightarrow$

$$-\varphi_o^k(t) + \sum_j a_{oj}^k \varphi_j^k(t) + \mu_o^k(t) + \lambda_o^k(t) = 0 \qquad (3.7.9)$$

this relationship is the same as those for fuel and mineral resources except that in the case of water, additional supplies are made available in each planning period and consequently the supply price for water is determined de novo in each scheduling period. (Inventories and storage are considered in Chapter 8.6.)

Production capacity. $z_i{}^k(t) > 0$ =>

$$q_i^k \mu_i^k(t) = \xi_i^k(t) - \frac{\xi_i^k(t+1}{(1+p)} + \sum_j b_{ij}^k \varphi_j^k(t) \qquad (3.7.12)$$

This relationship may be interpreted at the optimum as follows. The marginal income to production capacity of type i in region k in period t is equal to the change in the discounted marginal value of the capacity during the period plus the marginal maintenance cost incurred during period t. This and the following relationship will be shown to yield a number of further interpretations in the following two chapters.

Capacity conversion. $z_{\alpha\beta}{}^k(t) > {}^0$, $\beta A \alpha$ =>

$$\xi_\alpha^k(t) + \sum_j b_{\alpha\beta j}^k \varphi_j^k(t) = \frac{\xi_\beta^k(t+1)}{1+p} \qquad (3.7.14)$$

That is, the marginal value of capacity of type β in period t in region k must equal the marginal value of capacity of type α in period t and region k plus the conversion cost if capacity of type α is to be converted to type B during period t.

Horizon posture constraints. $z_i{}^{k+}(t_H+1) > 0$ =>

$$\xi_i^k(t_H+1) = c_i^{k+}(t_H+1) \qquad (3.7.13)$$

That is the marginal value of capacity of type i at the horizon (the beginning of period (tH+1) is positive if less capacity of type i is made available for production or conversion than is required and, correspondingly if ;

$$z_i^{k-}(t_H+1) > 0 \Rightarrow \xi_i^k(t_H+1) = -c_i^{k-}(t_H+1) \qquad (3.7.13)$$

the marginal value of capacity of type i at the horizon is negative. For completeness, if :

$$z_i^{k+}(t_H+1) = z_i^{k-}(t_H+1) = 0$$

then
$$-c_i^{k-}(t_H+1) < \xi_i^k(t_H+1) < c_i^{k+}(t_H+1)$$

It has been assumed throughout this chapter that the specification of the program is such that an optimal solution is obtained. In particular, it is assumed that the price and tax structure is such that the links of the arterial transportation system are of uniform dimension over their length and that they are connected in the optimal program. Given the assumption of regret functions and goals this assumption is not a strong one theoretically, but the case of unconnected arterial transport systems in particular is liable to prove a source of considerable difficulty in suboptimal empirical applications. This difficulty arises due to the fact that the land uses adjacent to a transportation link for the purpose of expansion of that link are related to its magnitude.

The dual functional may be interpreted at the optimum as the discounted net cost of production (change in the value of production capacity) plus the net social costs associated with deviations, if any, from the social goals. A more extensive interpretation of the functionals of the primal and dual programs is given in Chapter 8.5 where it is shown that at the optimum their equality may be interpreted as requiring that the present value of consumption plus that of investment equals the income to capacity, to labor, and to resource owners plus net transfer payments.

8.4 Capital costs and valuation

8.4.1 *Introduction*

The goal program developed in the previous chapter determines the optimal sequence of land users for each site in each region k = 1, 2...K over the planning interval $t_o < t < t_H$. Due to the identification of production capacity with land use the optimal sequence of land uses determines the optimal sequence of capacities for production processes for each site over the interval. Thus any site supplies production capacity, either through maintenance or conversion, jointly to a sequence of production processes over time. Further, the production capacity at any site is not required to be fully utilized in any region or time period.

In an important work, Littlechild {36}, {37} considers questions of pricing, valuation, and amortization when production capacity is supplied jointly to varying outputs over time for a single production process.[25] He shows that under a marginal cost pricing policy, capacity costs are exactly recouped from revenues or terminal values over the interval of produccion, where the marginal variable costs of production and the marginal costs of increments of capacity are assumed to be known for each scheduling period. In Littlechild's model {37} as in that of Goreaux and Manne {22} capacity once purchased is retained and allowance is made for physical depreciation over time.

In the model developed in chapter 8.4 both the marginal variable costs of production and the marginal capacity costs are determined endogenously and reflect the full opportunity set for each process, region and time period. Thus marginal opportunity costs or values for capacity may be determined which are contingent not only on the current and future demands for their products but in general on those for all products since the current and future production opportunities for the site are embodied in the model by means of the site conversion relationships and thus the future markets of the commodities associated with these alternative site uses determine, in part, the value of the current production capacity. The interrelatlonship of site uses is determined by relationships (3.7.14) which state that a site is retainod for a productlon process only as long as the marginal value of the production process exceeds its value in any other process plus the conversion cost.

In this chapter Littlechild's results are generalized since production costs and capacity values are determined endogenously. It is shown that using relationships (3.7.14), (3.7.I2), marginal capacity costs are recouped exactly for each production process over the interval of production in each region either from revenues or from the terminal value of the production capacity, at the time of its conversion to a subsequent production process. The following section is devoted to a further analysis of the relationships (3.7.12). It is shown that these relationships may be interpreted as bidding relations based on the land use conversion costs and the marginal value of a site for production or the opportunity costs associated with the removal of production capacity.

It has been emphasized at a number of points in the development of the multi-period model that production capacity need not be fully utilized for the production of marketable commodities in every, or any, planning period. While in this case the marginal income to, or marginal rental of, production capacity is zero the marginal value of the capacity may be positive or negative with the current maintenance or conversion costs being financed by means of the change in value during each period during each excess capacity is available. This case is examined more closely and an application is made to peak load pricing.

Following an analysis of the spatial relationship between the marginal values of production capacity for each process based on relations (3.7.6) the interpretation of the values of production capacity as the values of land uses is employed to define values for land in each region and time period. These specializations provide explanations for a variety of urban phenomena including the development of outlying suburbs and low rental uses of high valued sites.

8.4.2. *Capital costs, pricing and amortization*

In this section the relationships (3.7.14) are shown to yield the result, that the discounted capital costs of capacity[26] are exactly recouped from the capitalized revenues dervied from the sale of any marketed products plus the terminal value of the capacity for each process in each region over the interval of production on that capacity.Capital costs here include the initial acquisition co~t of the site, plus the conversion cost, (if any), plus the maintenance costs incurred during the interval of production.

In order to keep notational complexity to a minimum a specific example is considered without loss of generality.

Let the interval of production be $t_1 < t < t_2$ for process 4 in region k. Let an increment of capacity be converted from process 6 to process 4 during the period (t_1-1) and retained in production through period t_2. At the end of period t_2 let it be wholly or partially purchased for conversion to process 8.

From (3.7.14) at the optimum :

$$z^k_{64}(t_1-1) > 0 \quad \Rightarrow$$

$$\frac{\xi^k_4(t_1)}{1+\rho} = \xi^k_6(t_1-1) + \sum_j b^k_{64j}\varphi(t_1-1) \qquad (4.2.1)$$

And at the end of period t_2 :

$$z^k_{48}(t_2+1) > 0 \quad \Rightarrow$$

$$\xi_4(t_2+1) = \frac{\xi_8(t_2+2)}{(1+\rho)} + \sum_j b^k_{48}\varphi_j(t_2+1) \qquad (4.2.2)$$

From relations (3.7.12) :

$$z^k_i(t) > 0, \quad t_1 < t < t_2 \quad \Rightarrow$$

$$q^k_4\mu^k_4(t) = \xi^k_4(t) - \frac{1}{(1+\rho)}\xi^k_4(t+1) + \sum_j b^k_{4j}\varphi^k_j(t) \qquad (4.2.3)$$

Introducing discount factors and summing over the interval $t_1 < t < t_2$ (the period of production)

$$\sum_{t=t_1}^{t_2} \frac{q^k_4\mu^k_4(t)}{(1+\rho)^t} = \frac{\xi^k_4(t_+)}{(1+\rho)^t} - \frac{\xi^k_4(t_2+1)}{(1+\rho)^{t_2+1}} + \sum_{t=t_1}^{t_2} b^k_{4j}\varphi^k_j(t) \qquad (4.2.4)$$

The left hand side of equation (4.2.4) is the capitalized sum of the capacity cost components of the price over the interval or the capitalized income to capacity during production. (Recall that if $x_i^k(t) < q_i^k z_i^k(t)$, $\mu_i^k(t) = 0$. This is the case of underutilized capacity and is discussed further below.)

The term $\xi_4^k(t)/(1+\rho)^{t_1}$ is the discounted marginal cost of a unit of capacity in period t_1 and consists (from (4.2.1)) of the discounted marginal costs incurred in compensating the owners of capacity of type 6 for foregoing production in the region plus the discounted marginal cost converting the production capacity.

In a similar way the quantity $\xi_4^k(t_2+1)/(1+\rho)^{t_2+1}$ is the discounted marginal terminal value of production capacity in region k at the end of period t_2 for increments purchased for conversion to process 8 during period (t_2+1), and is equal to the marginal value of capacity of type 8 in period (t_2+2) discounted to period t_2 plus the conversion costs.

The final term on the right hand side of equation (4.2.4) is the discounted sum of the marginal maintenance costs incurred by a unit of production capacity of type 4 in region k during the interval of production.

Thus equation (4.2.4) may be interpreted to state that net marginal capacity costs are recouped exactly from revenues over the period of production.

A corollary of this result is that the production period must be sufficiently long for each process and region for capital costs to be recovered from revenues and the tenminal value of production capacity. The length of the interval is dependent, in part, on the cost of converting capacity to the current use and subsequently reconverting it to the succeeding use during the period following the final period of production as well as market considerations and maintenance costs. If the definition of the terminal value of capacity is broadened to include the value of capacity retained for production of the same commodity in the succeeding period as well as the, case where it is purchased for conversion, the general result holds.

The quantity $\mu_i^k(t)q_i^k$ is at the same time the marginal income to capacity retained in production during period t and the change in its value after allowance for maintenance costs during period t and thus may be interpreted as the optimal allowance for amortization of outstanding debt during period t. [27]

8.4.3 *The value of production capacity*

As noted in the previous section, the current marginal opportunity cost, or value, of production capacity for each process, region and time period is determined in part by the market relationships (3.7.12) for its product. These relationships involve both the current and future state of the market for the product of each production process in each region and time period, for in each time period relations (3.7.12) involve both the current marginal value of the production capacity and its marginal value in the succeeding period.

The value of production capacity is also related spatially for connected markets for commodity by the combination of relations (3.7.12) with (3.7.7), (3.7.8) and (3.7.9). This section is, however, devoted primarily to a deeper analysis of the capacity conversion, or production capacity market relationshlps (3.7.14).

Through relations (3.7.14) the marginal value of production capacity for each process in each region and planning period is related to the values of all accessible processes during each planning period or

$$\frac{\xi_{\beta}^{k}(t)}{(1+\rho)} \leq \xi_{\alpha}^{k}(t-1) + \sum_{\beta A\alpha} b_{\alpha\beta j}^{k}\varphi_{j}^{k}(t-1) \qquad (4.3.1)$$

These relations may be rearranged to give

$$\frac{\xi\beta_2^k\ (t+1)}{(1+\rho)} - \sum_j b_{\alpha\beta j}^k \varphi_j^k(t) \leq \xi_\alpha^k(t) \leq (1+\rho)[\xi_\beta^k(t-1) + \sum_j b_{\beta_1\alpha j}^k \varphi_j^k(t-1)] \quad (\beta_2 A\alpha,\ \alpha A\beta_1) \tag{4.3.2}$$

Now the system (4.3.2) may be interpreted at the optimum as follows. The marginal opportunity cost or value of capacity of type α in region k and period t lies between the highest value of the capacity in that location in any alternative process to which it is accessible by means of conversion, and the lowest cost of compensating the owners of capacity accessible to the process α for the loss of their production facilities and converting them to process i during period (t+1).

Alternatively the system (4.3.2) may be interpreted as a set of bidding relations for sites in each region and time period with a site being sold to or maintained by the highest bidder for the existing production capacity in each period. The size of a bid is constrained both by the magnitude of the conversion costs involved (if any) and the freedom with which competitors (the owners of other sites in the region) may offer equivalent alternative sites to the bidders by conversion of the site during the preceding period.

At the point of conversion of production capacity from one process α to another process β in region k and period t the quantity $\xi_\alpha{}^k(t)$ may be interpreted as the terminal value of the production capacity α or the appropriate marginal rate of compensation to the owners of the production capacity for loss of their property rights where these are defined with respect to the specific process or land use.[28] Since the marginal purchase cost of production capacity for conversion includes expenditures both for compensation and for conversion, the purchase cost is only indirectly related to the construction or conversion expenditure.

There is no requirement that all production capacity be converted simultaneously or that all additional capacity be converted from the same preceding use. From the equality prevailing in (4.3.1), for all conversions the total marginal cost or value is the same in each period, for each increment of capacity for a process regardless of the preceding use.It is only in this highly restricted sense, however, that capacity conversion costs are independent of the previous use of a site in a region.

Since the quantities $\xi_i{}^k(t)$ are associated with equalities in the primal problem, they are unrestricted in sign, and thus the marginal value of capacity may be negative at the optimum. This case may arise where the minimal marginal cost of purchasing and converting the production facilities exceeds their value in the converted process in the region and abandonment of the production facilities during the revelant planning period is precluded by legislation. In these cases the owners of the production facilities must either maintain them at a current loss[29] or bear part, or all, of the costs of conversions. Such cases arise in practice, for example, when mine shafts are required to be filled or land reclaimed following coal or mineral extraction.

8.4.4 *Underutilized capacity and peak load pricing*

If capacity for a production process i is not fully utilized in a planning period t ($x_i{}^k(t) < q_i{}^k z_i{}^k(t)$), the marginal income to capacity from sales of the comoodity is zero during that period. From (3.7.12)

$z_i^k(t) > 0 \quad \Rightarrow$

$$q_i^k \mu_i^k(t) = \xi_i^k(t) - \frac{\xi_i^k(t+1)}{(1+\rho)} + \sum_j b_{ij}^k \varphi_j^k(t) \qquad (4.4.1)$$

$x_i^k(t) < q_i^k z_i^k(t) \quad \Rightarrow \quad \mu_i^k(t) = 0$. Thus :

$$\xi_i^k(t) = \frac{\xi_i^k(t+1)}{(1+\rho)} - \sum_j b_{ij}^k \varphi_j^k(t) \qquad (4.4.2)$$

Hence the appreciation in the marginal value of capacity of type i in region k during period t must be sufficient to meet the cost of the capital plus interest required to finance the capacity during period t, or rearranging (4.4.2) the relationship (4.4.3) obtains at the optimum

$$(1+\rho)[\xi_i^k(t) + \sum_j b_{ij}^k \varphi_j^k(t)] = \xi_i^k(t+1) \qquad (4.4.3)$$

Another way to view these relationships is to consider that the owners of production capacity are distinct in each planning period and that capacity is purchased from the lowest cost source, be it by importing, creating additional capacity or by maintaining excess capacity during one or more periods to meet the current demand, with full regard for time lags and costs associated with the augmentation of capacity and the transportation costs associated with imports.

The case of peak load pricing[30] is one wherein capacity is under -utilized for one or more periods and then fully utilized. In this case customers are not charged for capacity costs during "off peak" periods ($x_i^k(t) < q_i^k z_i^k(t) \Rightarrow \mu_i^k(t) = 0$), while capacity costs are charged in peak periods ($x_i^k(t) = q_i^k z_i^k(t) \Rightarrow \mu_i^k(t) > 0$). Off peak capacity costs are zero due to the increase in value imputed to the capacity arising from future demand both for the output of the capacity and the capacity itself. (This latter demand arises from a different process). That is, the lowest cost method of meeting peak loads is, in this case, by purchasing and maintaining assets during off peak periods to meet the peak loads.Since the value of production capacity is contingent upon all alternative present and future demands for the site as well as those for its product during the interval of production and the spatial configuration of these markets, the current value of production capacity will, in general, vary in each planning period, and hence between peak periods, even if the quantity of the commodity supplied is the same in each peak period.

In a linear programming formulation of a pricing policy developed by Turvey {44}, Littlechild showed that in the case of equal demands peak load prices would be degenerate.[31] This result followed from the a priori assumption by Turvey that additional capacity may be purchased at a known marginal cost in the initial period, and that it is retained throughout a predetermined interval thereafter without regard for purchase and sales opportunities for the capacity itself, during the interim.

In the model developed here, since capacity values in general vary for each type of capacity during each planning period the change in value will also vary, and hence the capacity cost component of price will generally vary between peak periods.

Since demand may be supplied either locally or by means of imports, there is no requirement that all production capacity for a particular commodity be fully used simultaneously. That is, the analysis applies to local as well as to system peak loads.

8.4.5 *Transportation, trade and property values*

From relation (3.7.6) at the optimum

$x_i^{\ell k}(t) > 0 \Rightarrow$

$$\varphi_i^k(t) = \varphi_i^\ell(t\ ) + \sum_j a_{ij}^{\ell k} \varphi_j^\ell(t) + \sum_{j_m} e_{ij_m}^{\ell k} \mu_{j_m}\ (t) \qquad (4.5.1)$$

Where $\varphi_i^k(t)$, $\varphi_j^\ell(t)$ are respectively the marginal costs or supply prices for commodity i in region k and in period t and their difference is equal to the sum of the marginal costs of transportation services and tran~portation capacity incurred in shipping the marginal unit of production from region ℓ to region k. These transportation costs include those of transhipment where required and their components are subject to the same analysis and interpretations as costs for other commodities. In particular, transportation capacity costs are imputed to users in such a way that net capital costs of capacity are recouped exactly over the interval during which each link in the route is utilized.

Since links in arterial routes must logically be connected throughout their extent and transitions in land use are endogenously determined as capacity is increased or decreased on each link over time, the location of subsets of sequences of land uses in each region are necessarily. determined; these must lie along the arterial route for which they provide capacity or from which they derive capacity over the planning interval. The nature of the difficulty which this introduces if a suboptimal approach is employed was discussed at the end of the preceding chapter

Since $\varphi_j^\ell(t)$, $\mu_{jm}(t) > 0$, all j, ℓ, m, transportation costs are non-negative, thus two-way trade between distinct regions is precluded.More generally, no trade pattern may be such that shipments may be made by an indirect route from a region to itself. For example,there can be no relations of the form

$$A \rightarrow B \rightarrow C \rightarrow D \rightarrow A$$

Where $\rightarrow$ denotes "exports to" and the letters represent regions. If all regions in which a commodity is utilized are connected by trade[32], their prices are related by relations (3.7.6) so that the difference in prices in any two of them may be represented by a difference in transportation cost. In principle the region in which the lowest supply price for a commodity prevails may be determined and the supply prices in all other markets related to this "base" price.

Consider two regions k, ℓ in which commodity i is produced in period t. From relations (3.7.7), (3.7.8), (3.7.9)

$$x_i^k(t) > 0 \Rightarrow \qquad \varphi_i^k(t) = \sum_j a_{ij}^k \varphi_j^k(t) + \mu_i^k(t) + \lambda_i^k(t)$$

$$x_i^\ell(t) > 0 \Rightarrow \qquad \varphi_i^\ell(t) = \sum_j a_{ij}^\ell \varphi_j^\ell(t) + \mu_i^\ell(t) + \lambda_i^\ell(t) \qquad (4.5.2)$$

where the last terms, $\lambda_i^k(t)$, $\lambda i^\ell(t)$ arise only if commodity i is an extracted material and an extractive process is under consideration.

By the assumption of connectedness of markets above, from (3.7.6):

$$\varphi_i^k(t) = \varphi_i^\ell(t) + \text{"}c_i^{k\ell}(t)\text{"} \qquad (4.5.3)$$

where "$c_i^{k\ell}(t)$"is unrestricted in sign and represents the difference in transportation costs with respect to the base price above.

Substituting from (4.5.2) and (4.5.3) it is seen that the difference in transportation costs associated with the two regions is equal to the sum of the differences between the costs of variable inputs, of raw materials and of capacity prevailing in period t.

Thus the relative income to capacity in a region is determined by the transportation costs associated with alternative sources of supply, by the variation in the production costs due to production processes which differ due both to their location and their duration, and to differing costs of resources (for extractive industries). Since production capacity costs are recouped exactly for each process, no profit or rent arises due to the "advantageous" location of production facilities. Such a rent must be distinguished from the rental of production capacity per se. This point is taken up in the next section.

8.4.6 *Values for "land" and urban issues*

If production and construction processes are considered as land uses and the marginal values of production capacity as "land" values, then it is clear that there are as many "land" values in a region in general as there are land uses, and that "land" is a highly heterogeneous commodity. Further, there are in general, as many values for the rental of capacity ($q_i^k \mu_i^k(t)$) as there are land uses and these rentals only have indirect relationships to "land" values ($\xi_i^k(t)$).

The relationships in question are (3.7.12) and are clearly dynamic in character, for current "land" values and rentals there reflect future production opportunities either through the maintenance or conversion of production capacity as well as market opportunities. Maintenance and conversion expenditures are thus essential to the analysis of current "land" rentals and uses.

It was shown in the previous chapter that the "land" constraints (3.3.8) could be constructed as aggregations of the land use constraints in each period. Herbert and Stevens {26}, in a linear programming formulation for the distribution of residential activity in an urban area, include such constraints but exclude the production capacity constraints for housing and hence obtaining apparent "land" rents, independent of the housing type for each region. The "land" constraints of their problem are of the form (using the notation above)

$$\sum_i \frac{x_i^k}{q_i^k} \leq L^k \qquad (4.6.1)$$

These constraints may be derived from the elision of the production capacity constraints (3.3.1) and the "land" constraints (3.3.8) :

$$x_i^k(t) \leq q_i^k z_i^k(t) \qquad (4.6.2)$$

$$\Rightarrow \quad \frac{x_i^k(t)}{q_i^k} \leq z_i^k(t) \qquad (4.6.3)$$

and from (3.3.9) :

$$\sum_i z_i^k(t) + \sum_{aAi} z_{i\alpha}^k(t) = L^k \qquad (4.6.4)$$

$$\Rightarrow \quad \sum_i \frac{x_i^k(t)}{q_i^k} \leq L^k \qquad (4.6.1)$$

Such "land" constraints are thus illusory and arise from an incomplete specification of the problem. Alonso considered the subject of location and land rent extensively in {1}. Space limitations preclude an extensive comparison between the analysis here and his work, but some salient points of difference are made in the following paragraphs,

Alonso considers a single period and initially assumes a featureless homogeneous plain rather than the heterogeneous initial configuration of land uses in geologically distinct regions assumed above. Land is treated as a homogeneous commodity with the size of the site per unit of output acting as a surrogate for variations in technology or production capacity, rather than congidering the varying conversion and maintenance costs associated with specific land uses.

It has been shown that the inclusion of maintenance and conversion costs together with future production opportunities and the initial land use configurations leads to a *value* for each type of capacity in each region in each period which is quite distinct from its *rental* in that period, and further, that the inclusion of conversion costs leads to distinct values and rentals for each type of capacity (or land use or "land") in each region and time period .

In Alonso's analysis site values and site rentals are confused, since site conversion costs are omitted. He maintains that a site is used by the bidder willing to pay the highest *rental* in each period, whereas in the anal~sis of section (8.4.3) it was shown that bidding relationships apply for the ownership of sites and that bids are based on the *value* of the site, in each period and that a site goes to the highest bidder for the ownership of the site in each period.

Rentals are given by the *change in value* of a site in each period both due to maintenance requirements and the current and future market opportunities open to it, as was shown in section (8.4.2). Thus the magnitudes of rentals have no necessary correlation with the magnitudes of values. High rentals do not imply high values, and conversely. Rather, high rentals imply high *changes* in value and conversely low rental[9] imply low *changes* in value.

This observation forms the basis for an explanation quite distinct from Alonso's for the appearance of low rental housing in downtown areas. Alonso explains this phenonmenon on the basis of a difference between the density, (or type), of housing in downtown and suburban areas and notes that although the rental per unit may be lower downtown than in outlying areas, the rental per unit area may be higher.

A complementary explanation is that the change in value of certain downtown housing is lower per unit area than that in suburban areas due to the future demand for sites downtown for incoming for expanding processes (e.g.office blocks). Indeed, if excess housing is available currently, the optimal rental is zero.

Since conversion costs are determined in part by the geology of each region, insofar as this affects drainage and foundation requirements, and conversion oosts must be recouped from rentals or the terminal value of production capacity, the geology of a region affects rentals and values of production capacity, in general, for all processes located in the region.

This dependence of values and rentals on geology may be thought of as a dependence on the " fertility" of each region as well as its location in time and space for each production process. Thus quoting Marshall, "The industrial demand for land is in all respects parallel to the agricultural"[33] {40}. Alonso {1} maintains that this parallel does not extend to fertility.

A multi-period model taking into account future as well as current demands for production capacity (or sites) will generally yield a heterogeneous optimal land use configuration for each region and time period, since not all capacity is necessarily converted simultaneously. This heterogenaeity arises from purely economic considerations rather than environmental ones.

That is "mixed" neighborhoods in terms of a variety of housing types and commercial and industrial processes may arise through the optimization. Thus some classes of adjacency of land uses or "neighborhood" characteristics, may be seen to be consequences of an optimal distribution of economic activity rather than preconditions for it.[34]

A goal programming model based upon a vector of site attributes for differing classes of uses is developed by Courtney, Klastorin and Ruefli {18} with preference tradeoffs being given through weights attached to deviations from the goal levels.

Apart from differences in site preferences,[35] the development of outlying suburbs for urban areas may be explained through the fact that conversion costs must be recouped over the interval of production, either from rentals, or from the terminal value of the production capacity, for each land use and region, and that this requirement implies as a corollary that the length of the production interval must be sufficient for those costs to be recovered.

The current configuration of land uses is dependent on the changing configuration of land uses in the future in each region and time period and, in particular, sites between the core and an outlying suburb of a city may be held during an interval for future development of industrial, commercial and other types of residential processes.

So the current configuration of economic activity in an "urban" area is contingent upon the character and rate of change of the production capacity of which it is comprised. Here urban is placed in inverted commas for, by the argument of the previous paragraph, it is quite possible that agricultural processes may be efficiently located between the core and outlying suburbs of a city for an interim period.

Since the surface area of any region is fixed, the growth of one type of production capacity is necessarily associated with the decline of at least one other (the type, or types, of capacity which are converted) and thus the terms "growth" and "decline" for production capacity must, in order to be operational, be defined with respect to a subset of processes. With this caveat the arguments developed in this chapter tend to support the hypothesis that the spatial configuration of urban areas with respect to issues of density and congestion is related more to their expected rate of change (relative growth or decline) than to current "size," as measured by population or level of economic activity.

8.5 Institutions and multi-level regulation

8.5.1 *Introduction*

In the first part of this chapter markets for fuel and mineral resources and for the finance of production capacity are introduced by further analysis and interpretation of the dual relationships of the multi-period goal programming model.

In the latter part the planning and regulation aspects of the model are reviewed by means of macroeconomic interpretations which may be elicited from the multi-period goal programming model and its dual at the optimum. The model is then extended to comprehend further classes of regulation by regulatory authorities at various levels of government having conflicting goals and overlapping jurisdictions.

8.5.2 *Asset valuation, income, and wealth*

The quantity $\xi_i^k(t)$ represents simultaneously the marginal cost or value of a unit of capacity of type i in region k and the current value of a claim to future income either from the future sale of production or from the sale of the production capacity.

The quantity $\lambda_i^k(t)$ represents simultaneously the current marginal opportunity cost or value of a unit of fuel or mineral of type i in region k and period t "in the ground," and the current marginal income to owners of the fuel or mineral resource from its extraction

The distribution of the ownership of resources and of production capacity determines the associated distribution of wealth in the economy. This distribution has not been considered explicitly in the development of the goal programming model. Resources and production capacity may, however, be owned by individuals either directly through corporations, or by government agencies. Both income and wealth may be subject to taxation and redistribution by government agencies. A model in which the distribution of income is codetermined with the quantities of production and consumption commodities under an associated pricing structure is the subject of a recent paper by Charnes and Cooper {9}.

For completeness, income is also imputed to labor, either employed or unemployed, by means of wages $c^k t$),and where appropriate, by welfare payments, and to the owners of water rights in each region and planning period.

8.5.3 *The finance of production capacity*

Consider a unit of production capacity in region k purchased at the beginning of period (t_{1-1}) for conversion from process a to process i during period t_{1-1}), retained in production during the interval $t_1 \leq t < t_2$, and sold for conversion to process β at the end of period t_2. (This is the example considered in section (8.3.2)). It is kassumed that process i is accessible to process α during period (t_1-1) and that process β is accessible to process i during period (t_2+1).

Now $z^k_{\alpha i}(t_1-1) > 0 \Rightarrow$

$$\xi^k_\alpha(t_{1-1}) + \sum_{iJA\alpha} b^k_{\alpha i,j}\varphi^k_j(t_{1-1}) = \frac{\xi^k_i(t_1)}{(1+p)} \qquad (5.3.1)$$

The quantity $\xi_i^k(t_1)/(1+p)$ may be interpreted as the value of a one period bond in period (t_{1-1}) secured against the marginal value of production capacity type i in region k in period t_1. This bond may then be used to finance the marginal purchase cost of a unit of production capacity of type α at the beginning of period (t_{1-1}) and its conversion to process i during period (t_{1-1}).

In the interval $t_1 \leq t \leq t_2$, by assumption, $z_i^k(t) > 0$ so that :

$$\frac{\xi^k_i(t+1)}{(1+\rho)} + q^k_i\mu^k_i(t) = \xi^k_i(t) + \sum_j b^k_{ij}\varphi^k_j(t) \qquad (5.3.2)$$

This relationship may be interpreted as giving the relationship between the sources and uses of capital for a marginal unit of production capacity of type i in region k in the interval $t_1 < t < t_2$. The right-hand side of the equation gives the value of a unit of capacity at the beginning of period t and the maintenance costs incurred during period t. These are then financed in each period either by current income ($q_i^k\mu_i^k(t) > 0$) or by one period bonds of face value $\xi_i^k(t+1)/(1+p)$ for redemption at the end of the period.

At the end of the production interval, by assumption, capacity of type i is purchased for conversion to type β during period (t_{1+1}). For a unit so converted[36] the sale price at the beginning of period (t+1)is $\xi_i^k(t+1)$ and this quantity is sufficient to redeem the outstanding debt on the capacity thus removed from production. (Not all capacity of a certain age and type is necessarily converted simultaeneously).

The analysis of this section serves to motivate the assumption of a capital market functioning through the purchase and sale of one period bonds. Evidently bonds of longer maturity may be constructed by aggregation of the one period capital flows. This point will become clearer following the developments of the next section where a diferent approach is taken to the analysis of the capital requirements of production processes.

8.5.4 *Capital flows: an accounting approach*

An alternative approach to the analysis of the finance of production capacity and of the conversion of production capacity may be derived by multiplying the relationships of the previous section throughout by the quantity $(1+\rho)$

At the end of period (t_1-1) and the beginning of the first period of production, period t_1, the following relationship holds:

$$(1+\rho)\ \sum_j b^k_{\alpha i j}\varphi^k_j(t_1-1) + \rho\xi^k_\alpha(t_1-1) \quad = \quad [\xi^k_i(t) \ - \xi^k_i(t_1-1)]$$

That is, the change in the marginal value of the capacity converted from process α to process i during period (t_1-1) must be equal to the accumulated marginal conversion costs plus the cost of servicing the debt incurred in purchasing a marginal unit of capacity of type α at the beginning of period (t_1-1).[37] Hence the incremental quantity of capital to be raised at the end of period (t_1-1) is $[\xi_i{}^k(t_1) - \xi_i{}^k(t_1-1)]$.

During the interval $t_1 < t < t_2$, $z_i{}^k(t) > 0 \Rightarrow$

$$(1+\rho)q^k_i\mu^k_i(t) + [\xi^k_i(t+1) - \xi^k_i(t)] = \rho\xi^k_i(t) \ + c^k_i(t)(1+\rho).$$

Thus in each period $t_1 < t < t_1$ for marginal units of production capacity, the accumulated income from production plus the net capital raised to finance production equals the interest on outstanding debt plus the accumulated maintenance cost.

The quantity $[\xi_i{}^k(t+1) - \xi_i{}^k(t)]$ may be positive, negative, or zero corresponding to cases in which additional capital is raised, aggregate debt is reduced and the level of debt remains unchanged.

At the end of period t_1 the quantity $\xi_i{}^k(t_{2+1})$ is either paid or encumbered to be paid with interest by the purchaser of the capacity of type i for conversion to process β.

Corporations. Corporations may control one or more types of production capacity in one or more regions in each time period. From the asumptions of the linearity of production processes and the consequent omission of considerations of economies or diseconomies of scale for their operations the aggregate net capital requirements for corporations may be determined in each period by the aggregation of the marginal capital requirements weighted by the magnitude of the types of capacity controlled tn each period.

Multi-level jurisdictions, conflicting goals and regulation .Planning and regulatory functions have been implicit throughout the developments of this chapter through the assumption of goals for the economy under consideration and the determination of taxes and subsidies. The likelihood that social goals may conflict provided the initial motivation for the development of the goal programming approach in Chapter 8.2. Employment, consumption and resource utilization goals have been considered throughout the development of the single and multi-period goal programming models. As a means of reviewing the multi-period goal programming model from the aspect of regulation further macroeconomic interpretations are elicited from it in the following section.

In reality a closed economy generally includes within it organizations and statutory authorities at various levels of government as well as corporations, financial institutions and individuals. These authorities may correspond to national, state, and local governments but also include statutory authorities with jurisdiction over spocific sectors of the economy (e.g.river and port authorities). Each of these bodies has powers of regulation within its jurisdiction and its own set of goals and rogulatory instruments for its jurisdiction. Unless a social structure is assumed wherein all decisions are made prescriptively there is no reason to suppose that the goals of those bodies will be consonant with each other.

For example, a nation may set goals for additional oil refinery capacity for imported oil while states seek to maintain refinery-free coastlines.

In the concluding sections of this chapter the multi-period goal program is modified to include these additional types of regulation within a multi-level structure of regulatory authorities. These extensions relate to the regulation of the production of commodities, the location of production facilities, and the level of investment activity.

8.5.6 *Macroeconomic regulation*

By the following argument it follows that at the optimum, the macroeconomic relationship that consumption plus investment equals income plus taxes holds for the economy. At the optimum the equality of the primal and dual functionals of the multi-period goal programming model yields the following relationship:

$$\sum_k [\sum_{t_0}^{t_H} (\sum_i \frac{p_i^k(t) y_i^k(t)}{(1+\rho)^t}) \quad + \quad (\sum_i \frac{\xi_i^k(t_H)}{(1+\rho)^{t_H}} z_i^{k*}(t_H+1) - \sum_i \frac{\xi_i^k(t_0)}{(1+\rho)^{t_0}} z_i^{k*}(t_0-1)$$

consumption

$$-\sum_i \frac{1}{(1+\rho)^{t_H+1}} (c_i^{k+}(t_H+1) z_i^{k+}(t_H+1) - c_i^{k-}(t_H+1) z_i^{k-}(t_H+1))]$$

net investment

$$= \sum_k (\sum_{t=t}^{t_H} \frac{1}{(1+\rho)^t} [\sum_i c_i(t) x_i(t) + \lambda_o^k(t) H_o^k(t)]$$

wages income to water

$$+ \sum_{t=t_0}^{t_H} \frac{1}{(1+\rho)^t} (\sum_i \pi_i^k(t) y_i^k(t) + \sum_i \theta_i(t) x_i(t))$$

transfer payments

$$+ \sum_i \frac{1}{(1+\rho)^t} [\lambda_i^k(t_H+1) R_{i_1}^k(t_H+1) + \lambda_{i_2}^k(t_H+1) w_{i_2}^k(t_H+1)]$$

$$+ \sum_i \frac{1}{(1+\rho)^{t_H+1}} [c_i^{k+}(t_H+1) w_i^k(t_H+1) + c_{i_1}^{k-}(t_H+1) w_{i_1}^k(t_H+1] \qquad (5.6.0)$$

income to resources

Where, at the optimum, the transfer payments to labor and consumption are derived as follows

To prove :

$$\theta_i(t)E_i(t) + c_i^{+}(t)x_i^{+}(t) + c_i^{-}(t)x_i^{-}(t) = \theta_i(t)x_i(t) \quad (5.6.1)$$

Since

$$E_i(t) = x_i(t) + x_i^{+}(t) - x_i^{-}(t) \quad (3.4.5)$$

Then, substituting for $E_i(t)$ from (3.4.5) in (5.6.1):

$$\theta_i(t)\,[x_i(t) + x_i^{+}(t) - x_i^{-}(t)] + c_i^{+}(t)x_i^{+}(t)$$
$$+ c_i^{-}(t)x_i^{-}(t) \quad = \quad \theta_i(t)x_i(t) + \theta_i(t)x_i^{+}(t)$$
$$- \theta_i(t)x_i^{-}(t) + c_i^{+}(t)x_i^{+}(t) - c_i^{-}(t)x_i^{-}(t)$$

At the optimum

$$\theta_i(t) + ci^{+}(t)x_i^{+}(t) = (\theta_i(t) - c_i^{-}(t)x_i^{-}(t) = 0$$

Since $x_i^{+}(t) > 0 \Rightarrow \quad \theta_i(t) = -c_i^{+}(t)$

and $\quad x_i^{-}(t) > 0 \Rightarrow \quad \theta_i(t) = c_i^{-}(t)$ Q.E.D.

Similarly,

$$\pi_i^k(t)d_i^k(t) + c_i^{k+}(t)y_i^{k+}(t) + c_i^{k-}(t)y_i^{k-}(t)$$
$$= \pi_i^k(t)y_i^k(t) \quad (5.6.2)$$

By an inductive proof given in the Appendix it is shown that at the optimum :

$$\sum_i [\sum_k \frac{\xi_i^k(t_H+1)}{(1+\rho}{}^{t_H+1} \quad (z_i^{k*}(t_H+1) - c_i^k(t_H+1)z_i^{k+}(t_H+1)$$
$$-c_i^{k-}(t_H+1)z_i^{k-}(t_H+1)\;) - \frac{\xi_i^k(t_o)}{(1+\rho)^{t_o}} \quad z_i^k(t_o-1)]$$

$$= \sum_{t=t_o}^{t_H} \sum_k \frac{1}{(1+\rho)^t} [\sum_{i,j} b_{ij}^k\varphi_j^k(t)z_i^k(t)$$
$$+ \sum_{\beta j_{Ai}} b_{i\beta j}^k\varphi_j^{k}k(t)z_{i\beta}^k(t) - \sum_i q_i^k\mu_i^k(t)z_i^k(t)] \quad (5.6.3)$$

Now the right hand side of this expression may be interpreted as the discounted sum of the investment in production capacity during the planning interval either in the form of maintenance expenditures or of expendltures on conversion, less the discounted income from the sale of production during the interval $t_o \leq t \leq t_H$

Substituting from (5.6.3) for the "net investment" terms in (5.6.0) the desired relationship is at hand, for then the discounted value of commodities consumed plus the discounted value of investment in capacity over the interval $t_o \leq t \leq t_H$ is equal to the income to production plus wages, income to resource owners, and transfer payments or, more briefly, consumption plus investment equals income plus net taxes. Recall that income from resources or from production capacities may itself be taxable so that the total tax revenue is given by the transfer payments plus any income taxes. The relationship may be expressed as where C is

$$"C + I = Y + T" \qquad (5.6.4)$$

consumption, I is investment, Y is income, and T is taxes. It may be verified by setting $t_H = t_0$ that this relationship holds in each period. The assumption of a perfect capital market implies that, at the optimum, savings are equal to investments in production capacity in each period at the interest rate ρ.[38]

This may be seen more clearly from the developments of the earlier part of this chapter. There it was shown that each type of production capacity may be conceptualized as being financed by means of one-period bonds in each planning period, with the purchase price of the bonds being equal to the capital requirements of the capacity for the period.

It may be verified that the designated wage rates $c_i(t)$ and the increments $c_i^+(t)$, $c_i^-(t)$, associated with underemployment and over employment, respectively, constitute a piecewise linear labor supply function for labor of type i; for increasing real wage rates are associated with increasing employment for each class of labor.

The derivation of the foregoing macroeconomic relationships serves to emphasize the instruments of macroeconomic regulation. Consumption is regulated by means of taxes and subsidies to consumption commodities.[39] Employment levels are regulated by means of payroll taxes and welfare policies, and investment levels may be regulated by means of the interest rate (here assumed to be constant).

Tax rates on wealth or on income from investments and the distribution of the ownership of resources and production capacity are not explicitly considered in the model. Thus it may not be used in its present form for the appraisal of budgetary policies or, in cases where subsets of regions are considered, for trade policies. Budgetary onsiderations are given a central place in a multi-level multi-period goal programming model developed by Charnes, Colantoni, Cooper and Kortanek {6}.

8.5.7 *Multi-level regulation of output*

Although the following analysis may be applied in principle to the output of any production process for purposes of illustration a waste treatment process is considered.

It has been assumed that a single waste treatment process is associated with each type of waste discharge in each region. By regulating the output of waste treatment processes the outputs of wastes may then be regulated and consequently the levels of activity of waste producing processes.

Let the output of a waste treatment process iin region k and period t be $x_i^k(t)$. Then local regulatory constraints for the output of wastes of type i in region k in period t may be incorporated in the overall model of Chapter 8.3 by the following relationships :

$$\frac{\pi_i^{k-}(t)}{(1+\rho)^t}\, x_i^k(t) + x_i^{k+}(t) - x_i^{k-}(t) = G_i^k(t) \qquad (5.7.1)$$

The quantities $c_i^{k+}(t)$, $c_i^{k-}(t)$[40] are associated with the quantities $x_i^{k+}(t)$, $x_i^{k-}(t)$, in the functional. It may be anticipated from the developments of Chapter 8.2 that these quantities will have interpretations at the optimum of local subsidies and taxes on the output of the waste treatment process depending on the level of the output.

Regional waste treatment output or waste production, may be regulated for a subset of regions S by regulatory constraints of the form :

$$\frac{\bar{\pi}_i^S(t)}{(1+\rho)^t} \sum_{k\epsilon S} x_i^k(t) + x_i^{S+}(t) - x_i^{S-}(t) = G_i^S(t) \qquad (5.7.2)$$

The quantities $c_i^{-S+}(t)$, $c_i^{-S-}(t)$ are associated with the quantities $x_i^{S+}(t)$, $x_i^{S-}(t)$ in the functional. All of the other constraints developed in Chapter 8.3 remain the same, and thus the only dual relationship which is modified is (3.7.7)[41]. On associating the dual variables $\pi_i^{-k}(t)$, $\pi_i^S(t)$ with relations (5.7.1), (5.7.2), respectively:

$x_i^k(t) > 0$ at the optimum =>

$$\varphi_i^k(t) = \sum_j a_{ij}^k \varphi_j^k(t) + \mu_i^k(t) + \bar{\pi}_i^k(t) + \bar{\pi}_i^S(t) \qquad (5.7.3)$$

Also,

$$-\bar{c}_i^{k+}(t) \leq \bar{\pi}_i^k(t) \leq \bar{c}_i^{k-}(t) \qquad (5.7.4)$$

$$-\bar{c}_i^{S+}(t) \leq \bar{\pi}_i^S(t) \leq \bar{c}_i^{S-}(t) \qquad (5.7.5)$$

Now if $x_i^{k+}(t) > 0$, $\quad \bar{\pi}_i^k(t) = -\bar{c}_i^{k+}(t)$

$x_i^{k-}(t) > 0$, $\quad \bar{\pi}_i^k(t) = \bar{c}_i^{k-}(t)$

The quantities $c_i^{-k+}(t)$, $c_i^{-k-}(t)$ then have the interpretations of local taxes and subsidies. Regional taxes or subsidies may also apply at the optimum. If[42]

$x_i^{S+}(t) > 0$, $\quad \bar{\pi}_i^S(t) = -\bar{c}_i^{S+}(t)$

$x_i^{S-}(t) > 0$, $\quad \bar{\pi}_i^S(t) = \bar{c}_i^{S-}(t)$

Thus a combination of a local tax and a regional subsidy may be applied to waste output of the waste treatment process at the optimum. Alternatively a local subsidy and a regional tax may apply. In each of these cases the local and regional policies are opposed. If $G_i^S(t)$, $G_i^k(t) = 0$, then all output is liable to taxation.

The prohibition of waste outputs of the type treated by means of process i in region k either by local or regional legislation may be modelled as follows. In this case $G_i^k(t)$ or $G_i^S(t)$ is equal to zero and the weight $c_i^{-k-}(t)$ or $c_i^{-S-}(t)$ is of non-Archimedean order. The dual relationship associated with the variable $x_i^k(t)$ is:

$$\varphi_i^k(t) \leq [\sum_j a_{ij}^k \varphi_j^k(t) + \mu_i^k(t) + \bar{\pi}_i^k(t) + \bar{\pi}_i^S(t)] \qquad (3.7.7)$$

If $x_i^{k-}(t) > 0$, $\bar{\pi}_i^k(t)$ is of non-Archimedean order and consequently $x_i^{k-}(t) = 0$ at the optimum if the local regulatory prohibition is feasible. Similarly, if a regional prohibition applies $x_i^{k-}(t) = 0$ if the regional regulatory policy is feasible at the optimum.

The preceding analysis has been much simplified by the assumption that a single waste treatment process is available in each region for each type of waste output. In reality, there will generally be a choice of alternative technologies with the optimal technology both for the treatment process and for the waste -producing processes being determined in part by the regulatory policy.

A more comprehensive model would include cases where desirable waste discharge levels could be related to, for example, the flows in reaches of river systems. In practice, environmental standards for effluent discharges for water borne effluent are expressed in terms of maximal permissable concentrations of effluent per unit of flow of water. Some of these considerations are incorporated in the work of Deininger {19} and non-linear problems in the abatement of stream pollution are considered by Charnes and Gemmell {11}.

It was noted at the beginning of this section that multi-level regulatory constraintg may be applied in principle to the output of any production process (includlng extraction processes). The degree of mobility and the level of employment of labor may also be affected by local, regional, and national payroll tax and welfare policies. The introduction of regulatory constraints for this case closely parallels the development for production processes except that in place of inputs to production, wage rates and housing premiums (if any) are incorporated. Thus the real wage rate $\varphi_i{}^k(t)$ for labor of type i in region k in period t is related to the money wage rate $c_i(t)$ and local and regional taxes or subsidies $\bar{\pi}_i{}^k(t)$, $\bar{\pi}_i{}^s(t)$ by relations of the form:

$$\varphi_i^k(t) = \sum_j \alpha_{ij}^k \delta_j^k(t) + c_i(t) + \bar{\pi}_i^k(t) + \bar{\pi}_i^s(t)$$

8.5.8 *Multi-level regulation of the location of production capacity*

In the preceding section regulatory constraints were introduced for the outputs of production processes. An alternative or complementary way of regulating output is to regulate the magnitude and location of production capacity, to conform to social goals and policies. These goals and policies may reflect environmental considerations as well as national and regional development objectives.

The development of this section closely parallels the developments of the preceding one. Consider a process i in region k for which capacity is subject to regulation both locally and nationally where the nation consists of the set of regions S. Then the regulatory constraints are

$$\frac{\nu_i^k(t)}{(1+\rho)^t} \qquad z_i^k(t) + z_i^{k+}(t) - z_i^{k-}(t) = z_i^{k*}(t) \qquad (5.8.1)$$

$$\frac{\nu_i^s(t)}{(1+\rho)^t} \qquad \sum_{k\epsilon S} z_i^k(t) + z_i^{s+}(t) - z_i^{s-}(t) = z_i^{s*}(t) \qquad (5.8.2)$$

Associating the indicated dual variables with these constraints and unit social regret terms $c_i{}^{k+}(t)$, $c_i{}^{k-}(t)$, $c_i{}^{s+}(t)$,$c\ {}_i{}^{s-}(t)$ with the deviations in the functional, these constraints together with the constraints developed in Chapter 8.8.3 yield the following moaified dual relationships associated with the variable $z_i{}^k(t)$.

$$q_i^k \mu_i^k(t) \leq \xi_i^k(t) - \frac{\xi_i^k(t+1)}{(1+\rho)} + \sum_j b_{ij}^k \varphi_j^k(t) + v_i^k(t) + \nu_i^s(t) \qquad (5.8.3)$$

where

$$-c_i^{k+}(t) \leq v_i^k(t) \leq c_i^{k-}(t) \qquad (5.8.4)$$

$$-c_i^{s+}(t) \leq v_i^s(t) \leq c_i^{s-}(t) \qquad (5.8.5)$$

By arguments similar to those of the previous section the quantity $v_i{}^k(t)$ may be interpreted as a tax or subsidy at the optimum. If $z_i{}^k(t) > 0$ and $z_i{}^{s-}(t) > 0$ or $z_i{}^{s+}(t) > 0$ a regional tax or subsidy applies.

If, for example, $c_i{}^{k-}(t)$ is of non-Archimedean order, then at the optimum capacity of type i will be excluded from region k in period t if an Archimedean price structure is attainable. This case corresponds to a local exclusion of capacity of type i or a zoning ordinance. Local subsidies may be applied to favor particular specified types of capacity in specified regions. Examples of such favorable treatment are those of local authorities where office and administrative buildings are exempted from local property taxation. In cases where local taxes are applied these correspond to property taxes. National taxes and subsldies may reflect discriminatory development policies for specific industries or types of housing. For example :

If $z_i{}^k(t) > 0$ at the optimum :

$$q_i^k \mu_i^k(t) = \xi_i^k(t) - \frac{\xi_i^k(t+1)}{(1+\rho)} + \sum_j b_{ij}^k \varphi_j^k(t) + \nu_i^k(t) + \nu_i^s(t) \qquad (5.8.6)$$

The analyses of the earlier parts of this chapter and the precealng chapter with reference to rental values, capital requirements, etc., are thus only slightly moaified. All the arguments there may be applied without change if the relevant taxes and subsidies are considered to be part of a generalized "maintenance" cost in those arguments

8.5.9 *Multi-level taxes and subsidies to new production capacity*

In tbe previous section the manner in which the magnitude and location of production capacity may be regulated by means selective property taxes and subsidies or by zoning ordinances was outlined. In this section incentives and disincentives for specified land use are considered. These evidently correspond to incentives and disincentives to the augmentation of specified types of production capacity.

These incentives ana disincentives may be modelled by means of the following local and regional constraints :

$$\frac{\psi_i^k(t)}{(1+\rho)^t} \qquad \sum_{iA\alpha} z_{\alpha i}^k(t) + \Delta z_i^{k+}(t) - \Delta z_i^{k-}(t) = \Delta z_i^{k*}(t) \qquad (5.9.1)$$

$$\frac{\psi_i^s(t)}{(1+\rho)^t} \qquad \sum_{iA\alpha} \sum_{k\epsilon s} z_{\alpha i}^s(t) + \Delta z_i^{s+}(t) - \Delta z_i^{s-}(t) = \Delta z_i^{s*}(t) \qquad (5.9.2)$$

Introducing the indicated dual variables the capacity conversion relationships associated with the variables $z_{\alpha i}{}^k(t) \geq 0$ become:

$$\xi_\alpha^k(t) + \sum_j b_{\alpha ij}^k \varphi_j^k(t) + \psi_i^k(t) + \psi_i^s(t) \geq \frac{\xi_i^k(t+1)}{(1+\rho)} \qquad (5.9.3)$$

$$-c_{i_1}^{k+}(t) \leq \psi_i^k(t) \leq c_{i_1}^{k-}(t) \qquad (5.9.4)$$

$$-c_{i_1}^{s+}(t) \leq \psi_i^s(t) \leq c_{i_1}^{s-}(t) \qquad (5.9.5)$$

The quantities $c_{i_1}{}^{k+}(t)$, $c_{i_1}{}^{k-}(t)$, $c_{i_1}{}^{s+}(t)$, $c_{i_1}{}^{s-}(t)$ are associated wlth the deviations $\Delta z_i{}^{k+}(t)$, $\Delta z_i{}^{k-}(t)$ and $\Delta z_i{}^{s+}(t)$, $\Delta z_i{}^{s-}(t)$ in the functional.

If $\psi_i{}^k(t) + \psi_i{}^s(t) > 0$ at the optimum conversions from process ${}_iI^k(t)$ to process i are promoted. These two cases correspond to the case where a net tax is imposed on new capacity of type i and that in which new capacity of type i in region k is subsidized. It should be noted that $\xi_i{}^k(t+1)$ is the marginal value for all capacity of type i in region k in period (t+1) and thus the investment taxes and subsidies although only applied to increments of capacity affect the value and capital requirements for the enterprise as a whole.

8.6 Extensions and generalizations

8.6.1 *Introduction*

The multi-period goal programming model which was developed in Chapter 8.3 and the extensions and interpretations of Chapters 8.4 and 8.5 all incorporate simplifying assumptions concerning the processes by which commoaities are proauced. Apart from the overriding assumption of linearity for production processes, the following assumptions have been made. Firstly, that at most one process is available for the production of each commodity (apart from production capacity) in each region. Secondly, that the productivity of production capacity is independent of its age. Thirdly, it has been assumed that, with the exception of transportation capacity, a single production process is associated with each type of production capacity. Fourthly, it has been assumed that commodities may be produced within a single planning period and that there are no inventories in the economy.

In this chapter modifications and extensions of the goal program which relax these assumptions are outlined. In each case only the constraints of the goal program which are extensively modified are introduced explicitly, and eacb case is considered independently. In every case analyses and interpretations which parallel those of Chapters 8.3, 8.4, and 8.5 may be derived.

8.6.2 *Multiple production technologies*

It has been assumed throughout the preceding analysis that at most one technology is available for the production or extraction of a commodity in each region and time period. This assumption precludes the endogenous determination of the most efficient technology or combination of technologie for the production of each commodity where an efficient combination of technologies reflects economic and, through regulatory constraints, environmental factors. These possibilities may be incorporated by means of the following developments.

Consider a commodity i and a set of processes (or technologies) S^k whereby commodity i may be produced in region k. Let $x_{i_s}{}^k(t)$ be the output commodity i on production capacity of type i_s in period t where $s \epsilon S^k$. Then if the total output of commodity i in region k and period is $x_i{}^k(t)$

$$\frac{\eta_i^k(t)}{(1+\rho)^t} \qquad x_i^k(t) = \sum_{s \epsilon S^k} x_{i_s}^k(t) \qquad (6.2.1)$$

Let the production capacity of type i_s in region k and period t be $q_i{}^k z_i{}^k(t)$. Then

$$\frac{\mu_{i_s}^k(t)}{(1+\rho)^t} \geq 0 \qquad x_{i_s}^k(t) \leq q_{i_s}^k z_{i_s}^k(t) \qquad (6.2.2)$$

$$\frac{\xi_i^k(t)}{(1+\rho)^t} \qquad z_{i_s}^k(t) = z_{i_s}^k(t-1) + \sum_{i_sA\ \alpha} z_{\alpha i_s}^k(t-1) - \sum_{\beta Ai} z_i^k \beta(\underset{s}{t}) \qquad (6.2.3)$$

The set of processes accessible to process i_s by means of conversion includes, in general, other processes within the set S^k, either directly (if the conversion takes one period), or indirectly, through a sequence of conversion processes. Using relations (6.2.1), (6,2.2), (6 2.3) in place of relations (3.3.1), (3.3.8), and associating the indicated dual variables with the former constraints, the dual relationships become:

$z_{i_s}^k(t) \geq 0 \quad =>$

$$q_{i_s}^k \mu_{i_s}^k(t) \leq \xi_{i_s}^k(t) - \frac{1}{(1+\rho)} \xi_{i_s}^k(t+1) + \sum_j b_{i_s j}^k \varphi_j^k(t) \qquad (6.2.4)$$

If $z_i{}^k(t) > 0$ at the optimum of the modified multi-period goal program then

$z_{i_s}^k(t) > 0 \quad =>$

$$q_{i_s}^k \mu_i^k(t) = \xi_{i_s}^k(t) - \frac{1}{(1+\rho)} \xi_{i_s}^k(t+1) + \sum_j b_{i_s j}^k \varphi_j^k(t) \qquad (6.2.5)$$

Also

$x_{i_s}^k(t) \geq 0 \quad => \quad \mu_i^k(t) \leq \eta_i^k(t) \qquad$ all $s \epsilon S^k$

At the optimum

$$x_{i_s}^k(t) > 0 \quad => \quad \mu_{i(t)}^k = \eta_i^k(t) \qquad (6.2.6)$$

That is, the marginal income to capacity $\eta_i{}^k(t)$ from production of commodity i in region k and period t is the same regardless of the type of capacity on which it is produced. Recall that the current marginal value of capacity is determined in part by the character and cost of the resources requires for its future conversion to other production processes. Since different current production processes may be converted to different processes in the future an optimal *mix* of technologies for the production of commodity i is determined in each region and time period, since the future conversion costs for each type of capacity will in general vary. The capacity conversion relations are

$$z_{i_s\beta}^k(t) \geq 0 \quad => \quad \xi_{i_s}^k(t) + \sum_{\beta A i_s} b_{i_s \beta j}^k \varphi_j^k(t) \geq \frac{\xi_\beta^k(t+1)}{(1+\rho)} \qquad (6.2.7)$$

From equations (6.2.5) it may be seen that each technology in tbe set S^k is associated in general with a different combination of variable inputs, including labor and capital, per unit of output

$$\mu_i^k(t) = \frac{1}{q_{i_s}^k} \left[\xi_{i_s}^k(t) - \frac{1}{(1+\rho)} \xi_{i_s}^k(t+1) + \Sigma b_{i_s j}\varphi_j^k(t)\right] \qquad (6.2.8)$$

For technoiogy seS^k the financial requirements per unit of production are :

$$\frac{1}{q_{i_s}^k} \quad \frac{\xi_{i_s}^k(t+1)}{(1+\rho)}$$

units of capital and specified quantities of a designated subset of commodities specific to the capacity type, where the quantity of commodity j required per unit of production of commodity i in region k is $a_{i\ j}{}^k$. The quantity of capital which is expended per unit of production is $\mu_i{}^k(t)$ and this quantity is imputed to the price of commodity i in period t and region k. These latter observations establish a link with the production function of neoclassical economics.[43]

8.6.3 *Physical depreciation*

In the preceding analysis it has been assumed that maintenance expenditures were sufficient to ensure that the productivity of production capacity ($q_i{}^k$) is independent of the age, or ages, of the capacity with which it has been associated.

In this section the output capacity and the land-use conversion constraints of the multi-period model of Chapter 8.8.3 are modified to reflect the physical depreciation of production capacity over time.

A single type of production capacity, i, is considered over the interval $t_o \leqq t \leqq t_H$. Here it is assumed that $t_o = 1$ and that at the beginning of period t_o the oldest capacity of type in in region k is of age $r_i{}^k$. Alternatively, an approximation may be assumed whereby all capacity of type i in region k of age $r_i{}^k$ or greater at the beginning of period to has the same productivity, maintenance requirements, and requires the same inputs for all subsequent conversions.

Let the quantity of capacity of type α and age r, converted to process i ($iA\alpha$) during period (t-1) be $z_{\alpha i}{}^k(t-1,r)$ then :

$$\frac{\xi_{i_o}^k(t)}{(1+\rho)^t} \qquad z_i(t,o) = \sum_{i_o A\alpha} \sum_{r=o}^{r_i^k+t} z_{\alpha i_o}(t-1,r) - \sum_{\beta A i_o} z_{i_o \beta}(t,o)) \qquad (6.3.1)$$

where $z_i{}^k(t,0)$ is the quantity of new capacity of type i in region k available for production during period t. The right-hand side of constraint (6.3.1) is the capacity converted to process i during period (t-1) less the capacity converted immediately to further processes $\beta\epsilon_i I^k(t)$. The immediate conversion of oapacity corresponds, for example, to the case of continuous construction where construction takes place in stages.

Capacity of type i and age $r_i{}^k+t \geqq r \geqq 1$ in region k and period t is either maintained or converted or :

$$\frac{\xi_{i_r}^k(t)}{(1+\rho)^t} \qquad z_i^k(t,r) = z_i^k(t-1,r-1) \quad -_{\beta A i}\sum_r z_{i_r\beta}^k(t,r) \qquad (6.3.2)$$

If $q_i{}^k$ is the productivity of production capacity of type i and age r in region k, the relationship between the total oukput of commodity i in region k ana period t and the total capacity is :

$$\frac{\mu_i^k(t)}{(1+\rho)^t} \geq 0 \qquad x_i^k(t) \leq \sum_{r=o}^{t+r_i^k} q_{i_r}^k z_i^k(t,r) \tag{6.3.3}$$

Associating the indicated dual variables with constraints (6.3.1), (6.3.2), (6.3.3) and using these constraints in place of constraints (3.3.1), (3.3.8) of the multi-period goal programming model, the dual constraints associated with the variables $z_i{}^k(t,r)$, $z_{\alpha i}(t,r)$ are:[44]

$$z_i^k(t,r) \geq 0$$

$$q_{i_r}^k \mu_i^k(t) \leq \xi_{i_r}^k(t) - \frac{\xi_{i_{r+1}}^k(t+1)}{(1+\rho)} + \sum_j b_{i_r}^k \varphi_j^k(t) \tag{6.3.4}$$

$$z_{\alpha i}^k(t,r) \geq 0, \quad i_o A \alpha$$

$$\xi_{\alpha_r}^k(t) + \sum_j b_{\alpha i_o j}^k \varphi_j^k(t) \leq \frac{\xi_{i_o}^k(t+1)}{(1+\rho)} \tag{6.3.5}$$

These relationships are of the same form as (3.7.12), (3.7.14) and have the same interpretations. In general, new capacity of type i_o in region k is accessible either directly or through a sequence of land use conversions from capacity of type i_r. Assuming, for simplicity, that the conversion $z_i{}^k{}_i(t,r) > 0$ may take place during perioa t then:

$$\xi_{i_r}^k(t) + \sum_j b_{i_r i_o j}^k \varphi_j^k(t) = \frac{\xi_{i_o}^k(t+1)}{(1+\rho)} \tag{6.3.6}$$

That is, equipment of type i and age r is replaced by new equipment of type i during period t, at the margin. Recall that this replacement takes place with full regard for the opportunities of continuing production on the old equipment of type i and of replacing it by any type of equipment which is accessible to process i_r during period t. Thus the actual replacement is determined as part of an overall (generalized) optimal replacement policy.[45]

8.6.4 *Joint production*

With the exception of transportation capacity,it has been assumed that each type of production capacity is used for the production of a single commodity in each period. Joint production arises where the same type of production capacity may be used for the production of more than one commodity in each period where commodities are distinguished by the process of their production rather than the character of their use. Joint production may be moaelled in two equivalent ways.

First, let production capacity of type N^k be supplied jointly to the set of processes N^k in region k.

Constraints (3.3) are then replaced by:

$$\sum_{i \epsilon N^k} \frac{x_i^k(t)}{q_i^k} \leq z_{N^k}^k(t) \tag{6.4.1}$$

Associating the dual variables $\mu^k{}_{Nk}(t)/(1+\rho)t$ with these constraints the dual constraints of the modified multi-period goal program become at the optimum:

$$\varphi_i^k(t) = \sum_j a_{ij}^k \varphi_j^k(t) + \frac{\mu^k{}_{Nk}(t)}{q_i^k} \qquad (6.4.2)$$

and for $z_{Nk}^k(t) > 0$

$$\mu_{Nk}^k(t) = \xi_{Nk}^k(t) - \frac{\xi_{Nk}^k(t+1)}{(1+\rho)} + \sum_j b_{Nk}^k \varphi_j^k(t) \qquad (6.4.3)$$

These relationships bear a close general resemblance to relationships (3.7.7)[46], (3.7.12) of the dual of the multi-period goal program. This similarity may be made exact by the following substitutions.

Let $\quad \mu_{Nk}^k(t) = q_i^k \mu_i^k(t) \qquad (6.4.4)$

$$\xi_i^k(t) = \xi_{Nk}^k(t) \qquad (6.4.5)$$

$$b_{Nkj}^k = b_{ij}^k \qquad t_o \leq t \leq t_N \qquad i \epsilon N^k \qquad (6.4.6)$$

Then, substituting in (6.4.2), (6.4.3) :

$$\varphi_i^k(t) = \sum_j a_{ij}^k \varphi_j^k(t) + \mu_i^k(t) \qquad (6.4.7)$$

and

$$q_i^k \mu_i^k(t) = \xi_i^k(t) - \frac{\xi_i^k(t+1)}{(1+\rho)} + \sum_j b_{ij}^k \varphi_j^k(t) \qquad (6.4.8)$$

The preceding developments and substitutions suggest an alternative way in which cases of joint production may be modelled.

Consider output-capacity relations of the same form as in the program of Chapter 8.3 (3.3.1) and the augmented land use conversion constraints (6.4.10) :

$$\frac{\mu_i^k(t)}{(1+\rho)^t} \qquad x_i^k(t) \leq q_i^k z_i^k(t) \qquad (6.4.9)$$

$$\frac{\xi_i^k(t)}{(1+\rho)} \qquad z_i^k(t) = z_i^k(t-1) + \sum_{iA\alpha} z_{\alpha i}^k(t-1) + \sum_{s\epsilon N^k} z_{si}^k(t) - \sum_{\beta Ai}^k z_{i\beta}(t) \qquad (6.4.10)$$

The nature of the augmentation of the land use conversion constraints (6.4.10) is to make processes within the set immediately accessible to each other. It is assumed(as logically it must be since they are timeless) that conversions within the set N^k are costless. At the optimum: $z_i{}^k(t) > 0 \Rightarrow$

$$q_i^k \mu_i^k(t) = \xi_i^k(t) - \frac{\xi_i^k(t+1)}{(1+\rho)} + \sum_j b_{ij}^k \varphi_j^k(t)$$

and $z_{ij}^k(t) > 0 \Rightarrow$

$$\xi_j^k(t) = \xi_i^k(t) \qquad\qquad i,j \in N^k$$

Cases of joint production arise, for example, when agricultural land uses are considered, for certain classes of crops may be raisea on the same type of agricultural land. (Each type of agricultural land constitutes a different type of production capacity). Types of agricultural land here differ at least with respect to their geology. Further and more exemplary variations with respect to the type of land for agriculture are, at the macro level, the distinction between irrigated and non-irrigated land and, at the micro level, the varying requirements for preliminary preparation with fertilizers. The dependence of the current value of production capacity on the future sequence of land use conversions may be seen in the case of agricultural production processes in the economies which are associated with crop rotations, or specific land use conversion sequences.[47]

8.6.5 *Inventories and production lags*

It has been assumed that commodities may be both produced and consumed during each planning period of the planning interval considered in the multi-period planning model of Chapter 8.8.3. It has also been assumed that no inventories are maintained in the economy. In this section the modifications required in order that these features may be incorporated in the multi-period goal programming model are outlined.

It is assumed for simplicity of presentation that all produced commodities (with the exceptions of transportation and production capacity) may be stored from one period to the next within the planning interval. In reality some commodities may be stored whereas perishable commodities and personal services may not.

Consider a commodity i.Let $v_i^k(t)$ be the quantity of commodity in inventory during period t in region k. Let $v_i^{k+}(t)$, $v_i^{k-}(t)$ be respectively the quantity of commodity i added to inventory and withdrawn from inventory in region k during period t. Then the inventory levels $v_i^k(t)$ are related over the interval $t_0 \leq t \leq t_H$ by the system.

$$\frac{\tau_i(t)}{(1+\rho)^t} \qquad v_i^k(t) = v_i^k(t-1) + v_i^{k+}(t) - v_i^{k-}(t) \tag{6.5.1}$$

Let the quantity of inventory capacity for commodity i in region k and period t be $q_i^k z_i^k(t)$, then

$$\frac{\mu_{i_1}^k}{(1+\rho)^t} \geq 0 \qquad v_i^k(t) \leq q_{i_1}^k z_{i_1}^k \tag{6.5.2}$$

Inventory may be used to augment the supply of commodity i in region k during period t. Also, evidently,inventory provides an alternative use for oommodity i to uses for further production, consumption, transportation, or maintenance. Resources are required both for the augmentation and depletion of inventory, in general. All of these factors are evidenced by modifications, of the relationships between the source of supply and the uses of commodity i in region k and period t. This relationship must be further modified if allowance is made for production processes to take more than one planning period for their completion. In the latter case, of production lags, current demands for inputs are related to the future level of outputs. Only one period lags need be considered for, given the linear relationship between the inputs to, and outputs from, production processes, any production process may be divided into a sequence of connected one-period stages.

If for simplicity it is assumed that all production processes take at least one period for their completion then tbe overall supply-demand constraints (3.4.14) of Chapter 8.3 must be modified to :

$$\frac{\varphi_i^k(t)}{(1+\rho)^t} \qquad y_i^k(t) + v_i^{k+}(t) + \sum_j a_{ji}^k x_j^k(t+1) + \sum_j b_{ji}^k z_j^k(t)$$

$$+ \Sigma b_{\alpha,\beta,i}^k z_{\alpha\beta}^k(t) + \sum_j a_{ji}^{\ell m} x_j^{\ell m}(t) + \sum_\ell x_i^{k\ell}(t)$$

$$+ \sum_j f_{ji}^{k+} v_i^{k+}(t) + \sum_j f_{ji}^{k-} v_i^{k-}(t) \qquad (6.5.3)$$

$$\leq x_i^k(t) + \sum_\ell x_i^{\ell k}(t) + v_i^{k-}(t)$$

Associating the indicated dual variables with constraints (6.5.1), (6.5.2), (6.5.3) the dual constraints associated with the variables $x_i{}^k(t)$ are modified to:

$x_i^k(t) > 0 \quad =$

$$\varphi_i^k(t) \leq (1+\rho) \sum_j a_{ij}^k \varphi_j^k(t) + \mu_i^k(t) \qquad (6.5.4)$$

That is, the marginal cost of production is related to the marginal costs of inputs at the beginning of the production period plus the marginal capacity costs, with equality in the case where $x_i{}^k(t)>0$ at the optimum.

The relationships for inventories are given by the dual constraints associated with the variables $v_i{}^k(t), v_i{}^{k+}(t), v_i{}^{k-}(t)$, at the optimum

$v_i^k(t) > 0 \quad =>$

$$0 = \tau_i^k(t) - \frac{\tau_i^k(t+1)}{(1+p)} + \mu_i^k(t) \qquad (6.5.5)$$

$v_i^{k+}(t) > 0 \quad =>$

$$\tau_i^k(t) = \varphi_i^k(t) + \sum_j f_{ij}^{k+} \varphi_j^k(t) \qquad (6.5.6)$$

$v_i^{k-}(t) > 0 \quad =>$

$$\tau_i^k(t) = \varphi_i^k(t) - \sum_j f_{ij}^{k-} \varphi_j^k(t) \qquad (6.5.7)$$

Here $\mu_{i_1}{}^k(t)$ may be interpreted as the marginal rental cost of inventory capacity, and $\tau_i{}^k(t)$ as the marginal value of inventoried quantities of commodity i in region k and period t.

In order to illustrate the relationship between inventory and market values more clearly, assume that a unit of commodity i is placed in inventory in region k in period t and removed in period (t+1). Then, substituting from (6.5.6), (6.5.7), into (6.5.5) :

$$0 = \varphi_i^k(t) + \sum_j f_{ij}^{k+}\varphi_j^k(t) - \frac{1}{(1+\rho)}\left[\varphi_i^k(t+1) - \sum_j f_{ij}^{k-}\varphi_j^k(t+1)\right] + \mu_{i_1}^k(t) \tag{6.5.8}$$

Rearranging (6.5.8)

$$\frac{\varphi_i^k(t+1)}{(1+\rho)} = \varphi_i^k(t) + \sum_j f_{ij}^{k+}\varphi_j^k(t) + \frac{1}{(1+p)}\sum_j f_{ij}^{k-}\varphi_j^k(t+1) + \mu_{i_1}^k(t) \tag{6.5.9}$$

The relationships and interpretations for the rentals and values of inventory capacity are the same as those for other forms of production capacity, for, at the optimum:

$z_i^k(t) > 0 \quad \Rightarrow$

$$q_i^k\, \mu_i^k\,(t) \;=\; \xi_{i_1}^k(t) - \frac{\xi_{i_1}^k(t+1)}{(1+p)} + \sum_j b_{ij}^k\varphi_j^k(t)$$

The introduction of production lags and inventory positions carries with it a requirement to specify initial conditions and horizon posture levels for inventories. At the beginning of tbe initial planning period inventory on hand and for all projected productions is known for all processes during the first planning interval. Horizon levels for inventory may be specified either directly or indirectly by means of horizon posture constraints for each type of inventory.

The analysis of this section is applicable to a wide class of inventories, including warehousing, storage of liquids and gases in tanks, in-pipe storage for pipelines, and in-process inventories for production processes.

8.8.7 Conclusion

In the preceding chapters a unified multi-period multi-region goal programming model has been developed extensively whereby a land use plan is determined within an overall development plan for a closed economy. By incorporating goals relating to levels of production, consumption, employment and capacity, it has been shown that the magnitude character and incidence of regulatory instruments may be determined simultaneously with the configuration of resource depletion, production, consumption, investment, and employment.

The model provides the means of evaluating, *mutatis mutandis*, the effects of regulatory policies on the distribution of production, income and wealth throughout the economy. The fact that capital formation, (or land use change), involves conversion or replacement processes has been shown to determine values for each type of production capacity which are contingent both on the current and future market for its product, or products, and on those for the capacity itself. In particular, terminal values at the point of conversion of capacity are determined. These values are of central interest to land use planners for they are the appropriate values for oompensation for loss or curtailment of property rights.

The model which has been developed in the preceding chapters is deterministic. It is anticipated that further insights and interpretations will be immediately attainable by extensions of the model to a state preference formulation {2}, {36}. In reality, questions of compensation often involve stochastic considerations. In particular, they arise when the loss of the use of property has been anticipated at best in distribution by its owner, or owners, and they have sustained a loss. Conversely, there is pressure to tax the gains or purchasers of property whose value increases due, for example, to rezoning.

By modelling a finite number of future states of the economy with associated goals, prices and regulatory policies, and associating a discrete probability with each state, it is anticipated that insights into tbese issues may be obtained. The initial (or current) configuration of land uses and ownership is the same for all forthcoming states and an expected value for each site would be determined. Given that a specified state is then forthcoming, the difference between the actual and the expected values would then determine the gains and losses to the owners of the capacity and thus the appropriate rate of taxation or oompensation for them. (These may be subsumed in an insurance scheme.)

It has been shown that the value of production capacity is related directly to the path of the development of each site in each region over the planning interval. Consequently, the regulation of the location of production capacity affects the path of development of the economy as a whole. It remains for empirical studies to determine the sensitivity of the path of development to the various instruments of regulation.

In conclusion the model which has been developed is normative. Ancilliary researh is required to model the processes of decision making of federal, state and local governments as well as statutory authorities, for these are the processes whereby goal levels and regulatory policies are established.

Appendix

The purpose of this appendix is to prove the following relationship:

$$\sum_{t=k_o}^{t_H} \sum_{i,k} \Big[\frac{\xi_i^k(t_0) z_i^{k*}(t_0-1)}{(1+\rho)^{t_0}} - \frac{\xi_i^k(t_H+1) z_i^{k*}(t_H+1)}{(1+\rho)^{t_H+1}}$$

$$+ \frac{\xi_i^k(t_H+1)}{(1+\rho)^{t_H+1}} \left(z_i^{k-}(t+1) + z_i^{k+}(t_H+1)\right)\Big]$$

$$= \sum_{t=t_0}^{t_H} \sum_k \frac{1}{(1+\rho)^t} \Big(\sum_i \big[\mu_i^k(t) q_i^k z_i^k(t)$$

$$- \sum_j b_{ij}^k \varphi_j^k(t) z_i^k(t)\Big) - \sum_{\beta j_{A\alpha}} b_{i\beta j}^k \varphi_j^k(t) z_{i\beta}^k(t)\big] \qquad \text{(A)}$$

The initial land use conditions are for each process $i \epsilon I_0{}^k(t_0)$ and region k = 1,2,..,,K.

$$z_i^k(to) + \Sigma z_{i\beta}^k(t_0) = z_i^{k*}(t_0-1) \qquad (3.3.5)$$

If $z_i^k(t_0) > 0$

$$\mu_i^k(t_0)q_i^k = \xi_i^k(t_0) - \frac{\xi_i^k(t_0+1)}{(1+\rho)} + \sum_j b_{ij}^k \varphi_j^k(t_0) \qquad (3.7.12)$$

From (3.7.12) :

$$\xi_i^k(t_0)z_i^k(t_0) = \mu_i^k(t_0)q_i^k z_i^k(t_0) + \frac{\xi_i^k(t_0+1)}{(1+\rho)} z_i^k(t_0)$$

$$- \sum_j b_{ij}^k \varphi_j^k(t_0)z_i^k(t_0) \qquad (1)$$

And from (3.3.5)

$$\xi_i^k(t_0)z_i^k(t_0) = \xi_i^k(t_0)z_i^{k*}(t_0-1) - \sum_{\beta Ai} \xi_i^k(t_0)z_{i\beta}^k(t_0) \qquad (2)$$

Substituting (1) in (2) and rearranging

$$\xi_i^k(t_0)z_i^{k*}(t_0-1) = \mu_i^k(t_0)q_i^k z_i^k(t_0)$$

$$+ \frac{\xi_i^k(t_0+1)z_i^k(t_0)}{(1+\rho)} - \sum_j b_{ij}^k \varphi_j^k(t_0)z_i^k(t_0) \qquad (3)$$

$$+ \sum_{\beta Ai} \xi_i^k(t_0)z_{i\beta}^k(t_0)$$

But $z_{i\beta}^k(t_0) > 0 \Rightarrow$

$$\xi_i^k(t_0) + \sum_j b_{i\beta,j}^k \varphi_j^k(t_0) = \frac{\xi_\beta^k(t_0+1)}{(1+\rho)} \qquad (3.7.14)$$

So

$$\sum_{\beta Ai} \xi_i^k(t_0)z_{i\beta}^k(t_0) = \sum_{\beta Ai} \frac{\xi_\beta^k(t_0+1)}{(1+\rho)} z_{i\beta}^k(t_o) \qquad (4)$$

$$- \sum_{\beta Ai} \sum_j b_{i\beta,j}^k \varphi_j^k(t_0)z_{i\beta}^k(t_o)$$

Substituting (4) into (3):

$$\sum_i \xi_i^k(t_0)z_i^k(t_0-1) = \sum_i \mu_i^k(to)q_i^k z_i^k(t_0)$$

$$- \sum_j b_{ij}^k \varphi_j^k(t_0)z_i^k(t_0) - \sum_{\beta Ai} \sum b_{i\beta j}^k \varphi_j^k(t_0)z_{i\beta}(t_0) \qquad (5)$$

$$\sum_i \frac{\xi_i^k(t_0+1)}{(1+\rho)} z_i^k(t_0) + \sum_{\beta Ai} \frac{\xi_\beta^k(t_0+1)}{(1+\rho)} z_{i\beta}^k(t_0)$$

From (3.3.2)

$$z_i^k t_0+1) = z_i^k(t_0) + \sum_{iA\alpha} z_{\alpha i}^k(t_0-1) - \sum_{\beta Ai} z_{i\beta}^k(t_0+1) \quad (6)$$

Thus

$$\sum_i \frac{\xi_i^k(t_0+1)}{(1+\rho)} z_i^k(t_0) \quad + \sum_{\beta Ai} \frac{\xi_\beta^k(t_0+1)}{(1+\rho)} \quad z_{i\beta}^k(t_0)$$

$$= \sum_i \frac{\xi_i^k(t_0+1)}{(1+\rho)} [z_i^k(t_0+1) \quad + \sum_{\beta Ai} z_{i\beta}^k(t_0+1)] \qquad (7)$$

By definition of the horizon condition (3.3.10)

$$z_i^k(t_H+1) + \sum_{\beta Ai} z_{i\beta}^k(t_H +1) = z_i^{k*}(t_H +1) - z_i^{k+}(t_H +1)$$

$$-z_i^{k-}(t_H+1) \qquad (8)$$

Hence, by induction, the relationship (A) is proved. That relationship, may be interpreted as requiring that the (discounted) change in value of production capacity is equal to the income from production less the investment in production capacity over the planning interval $t_0 \leq t \leq t_H$. At the optimum :

$$z_i^{k-}(t_H+1) > 0 \Rightarrow$$

$$\frac{\xi_i^k(t_H +1)}{(1+\rho)^{t_H+1}} = \frac{c_i^{k-}(t_H+1)}{(1+\rho)^{t_H+1}} \qquad (9)$$

$$z_i^{k+}(t_H+1) > 0 \Rightarrow$$

$$\frac{\xi_i^k(t_H+1)}{(1+\rho)^{t_H+1}} = \frac{c_i^{k+}(t_H+1)}{(1+\rho)^{t_H+1}} \qquad (10)$$

So

$$\sum_{t=t_0}^{t_H} \sum_{i,k} \left(\frac{\xi_i^k(t_0) z_i^{k*}(t_0-1)}{(1+\rho)^{t_0}} - \frac{\xi_i^k(t_H+1) z_i^{k*}(t_H+1)}{(1+\rho)^{t_H+1}}\right.$$

$$\left. + \frac{\xi_i^k(t_H+1)}{(1+\rho)^{t_H+1}} \quad (z_i^{k-}(t_H+1) + z_i^{k+}(t_H+1)\right)$$

$$= \sum_{t=t_0}^{t_H} \sum_{i,k} \frac{1}{(1+\rho)^t} [\mu_i^k(t) q_i^k z_i^k(t)$$

$$- \sum_j b_{ij}^k \varphi_j^k(t) z_i^k(t) - \sum_{\beta j A\alpha} b_{i\beta j}^k \varphi_j^k(t) z_{i\beta}^k(t)] \qquad (A)$$

Q.E.D.

Footnotes

1. Land use planning is discussed extensively from the legal point of view in the collection of papers edited by Haar {23}.

2. The model which is discussed here is DINAMICO.

3. See also Charnes and Cooper {8} where Koopmans' results {33} are obtained by a linear programming approach.

4. A program similar to this is discussed in a survey by Kendrik {30}. No dual programs, however, are presented.

5. Feasibility is discussed further below.

6. These observations are novel in this context but will not be pursued further here.

7. Recall that at most one production process for each commodity has been assumed so that no substitution may take place.

8. Charnes and Cooper {8}. For an extensive review of goal programming see Lane {34}.

9. See Stevens {42} for a model in which variable transportation requirements are determined endogenously.

10. Strictly these capacities are set after allowance for investment and maintenance requirements have been met.

11. Transactions costs may be incorporated by suitable modifications of the supply-demand relationships.

12. One type of aggregation, that of a "Land Capability Unit" is being developed by the Bureau of Economic Geology at the University of Texas. It is anticipated that these units will provide a basis for environmental legislation in Texas. (See Brown et. al. {4} and Charnes et.al. {12}.)

13. Note that $x^{k}{}_{i}(t)$ may be zero. The distinction between marketable and nonmarketable production is dropped henceforward, it being assumed that all production referred to is marketable.

14. Land use conversion is not restricted to removal and reconstruction. Structures may be modified or forests converted to croplands.

15. Values of variables which are known a priori are designated throughout by the superscripts **or*.

16. aAi is equivalent to $i \epsilon_{\alpha} I^{k}(t_{H})$ or "i accessible to α".

17. Heaney's model and those of Lynn {38} and Deininger {19} introduced below are variations and specializations of the original (unpublished) 1958 models of Charnes, Logan and Pipes. The use of ground water as a source of supply is considered by Buras {5}.

18. Inventories are introduced in Chapter 6.

19. The correct relationships in each case would require an extensive development of the water distribution system. For such development see Heaney {24}.

20. Allowance is made in the model for the natural self-purification of rivers. See also Charnes and Gemmell {11}.

21. Recall that an extraction process is associated with each fuel and mineral resource. The extracted commodity is transportable.

22. If peak loads factors are specified exogenously the system peak must be known a priori. Alternatively, if sufficient large number of scheduling intervals are considered the peak period may be determined endogenously.

23. In this model deviations for employment and consumption, commodities are restricted only by the magnitude of the goal below and by the overall production capacity above. Goal intervals and bounds may be introduced in the manner introduced in the latter part of the previous chapter.

24. The overall "sink" conditions (3.4.4) have been omitted for all river systems.

25. Strictly he considers a single product, or in cases of joint production, a designated set of products, allowing for the product(s) to be produced by means of more than one technology. At this stage in this analysis a single technology is associated with each product.

26. Here and henceforth the arguments are given for the marginal capacity costs per unit area, rather than per unit output. In order to convert to costs per unit of output, the capacity relationships of this and the following chapters must be divided throughout by q_i, the output per unit area.

27. See Littlechild {37}, Baumol {3}.

28. Koopmans {33} defines "the use of land of various grades, including land giving access to mineral resources" as commodities. Coase {16} states that "(A factor of production) is usually thought of as aphysical entity which a businessman acquires and uses (an acre of land, a ton of fertilizer), instead of as a right to perform certain (physical) actions".

29. There is no *overall* loss, for the analysis of the previous section holds regardless of the sign of the quantities $\xi_i{}^k(t)$.

30. See Littlechild {37}, Turvey {44}.

31. For this reason Littlechild developed a covex programming model with the maximization of consumers' plus producers' surplus as the objective {37}.

32. With the exception of housing which is an immobile consumption commodity in this model (and the only one).

33. Agricultural land uses are discussed further when joint production is introduced in Chapter 6.

34. Recall that the spatial relationship of markets based on transportation considerations is endogenously determined.

35. In the model developed here, these are incorporated for housing in the goals and the weights associated with deviations in the relevant region.

36. Recall that not all capacity is necessarily converted simultaneously.

37. It may be assumed that maintenance costs are paid one period in arrears.

38. A varying interperiod interest rate may be readily incorporated in the model by specifying that the rate prevailing in period t is p_t.

39. It is assumed that the target quantities and the tax and subsidy schedules reflect demand considerations.

40. Strictly $c_i^{k+}(t)/(1+p)^t$, $c_i^{k-}(t)/(1+p)^t$. Discount factors are omitted through the end of this chapter.

41. If an extraction process is regulated (3.7.8) or (3.7.9) is modified in an analogous manner.

42. If $x_i^{S+}(t) = 0$ then $\pi_i^{-S}(t) = 0$. An indifference region may be assumed in the immediate neighorhood of the optimum.(See section 8.2.5).

43. See e.g. Henderson and Quant {25}. Notice that $1/\ {}^kq_{is}$ units of "land" or surface area are required per unit of commodity i produced on capacity s in region k.

44. Horizon values for all types and ages of production capacity are assumed to be given either directly or by means of horizon posture constraints.

45. See Jorgensen, McCall, Radner {28}, Chapter 1 for a discussion of deterministic replacement policies.

46. In the case of extraction processes, marginal resource costs are added to the righ-hand side of (6.4.2) and relationships analogous to (3.7.8), (3.7.9) are obtained.

47. An early discussion of the factors bearing on the choice of an optional crop plan using a linear model is that of Hildreth and Reiter {27}.

References

{1} Alonso, W.,(1964), *Location and Land Use*. Cambridge, Mass., Harvard University Press.

{2} Arrow, K.J.,(1964), "Optimal Capital Policy: The Cost of Capital and Myopic Decision Rules," *Annals of the Institute of Statistical Mathematics*, Vol. 16, Nos. 1-2, Tokyo.

{3} Baumol, W.J.,(1971), "Optimal Depreciation Policy: Pricing the Products of Durable Assets," *Bell Journal of Economics and Manaqement Science*, Vol. 2, No. 2.

{4} Brown, L.F., Fisher, W.L., Erxleben, A.W. and McGowen, B.H.,(1971), *Resource Capability Units* Geological Circular 71-1, Bureau of Economic Geology, University of Texas, Austin.

{5} Buras, N., (1963), "Conjunctive Operation of Dams and Aquifers," *Journal of the Hydraulics Division, Proceedings of the American Society of Civil Engineers*, November.

{6} Charnes, A., Colantoni, C.,Cooper, W.W., Kortanek,K.O.,(1973), "Revenue Sharing, Regionalized Economic Activity and Social Goals," *Manaqement Science*, Vol. 19, No. 10, June.

{7} Charnes, A. and Collomb, B.P.,(1972), "Optimal Economic Stabilization Policy: Linear Goal Interval Programming Models," *Socio-Economic Planning*, Vol. 6.

{8} Charnes, A. and Cooper, W.W.,(1961), *Management Models and Industrial Applications of Linear Programming*. Vols.I and II, New York, Wiley.

{9} Charnes, A. and Cooper W.W.,(1974), *An Extremal Principle for Accounting Balance of a Resource Value Transfer Economy: Existence, Uniqueness, and Computation*. Research Report 165, Center for Cybernetic Studies, University of Texas, Austin, January.

{10}Charnes, A., Cooper, W.W., Niehaus, R.,(1972), *Studies in Manpower*. Planning Office of Civilian Manpower Management, Department of the Navy, Washington, D.C.

{11}Charnes, A. and Gemmell, R.E.,(1964), *A Method of Solution of Some Non-Linear Problems in the Abatement of Stream Pollution*. Systems Researcb Memorandum No. 103, Northwestern University, May.

{12}Charnes, A., Haynes, K., Hazelton, J., Ryan, M.J.,(1973), "Texas Coastal Zone Management Project, *Proceedings NATO Conference on Mathematical Analysis of Decision Problems in Ecology*, Istanbul, July.

{13}Charnes, A., Kirby, M.J.L., Walters, A.S.,(1970), "Horizon Models for Social Development," *Management Science*, Vol. 17, No. 4, December.

{14}Charnes, A. and Miller, M.H.,(1956), "A Model for Optimal Programming of Railway Freight Train Movements," *Management Science*, Vol. 3, No. 1, October.

{15}Chenery, H.B., "Notes on the Use of Models in Development Planning," in {21}.

{16}Coase, R., (1960), "The Problem of Social Cost," *Journal of Law and Economics*, Vol. 3, October.

{17}Collomb, B.P., (1971), *Goal Interval Approaches to Intertemporal Analysis and Decentralization in Management*. Unpublished Ph.D.dissertation, University of Texas, Austin.

{18}Courtney, B.P., Klastorin T.D., Ruefli, T.W., (1972), "A Goal Programming Approach to Urban-Suburban Location Preferences," *Management Science*, Vol. 18, No. 6, February.

{19}Deininger, R.A., (1965), *Water Ouality Management: The Planninq of Economically Optimal Pollution Control Systems*. Unpublished Ph.D. dissertation, Northwestern University.

{20}Eckaus, R.S. and Parikh, K.S., (1968), *Planninq for Growth*. Cambridge, Mass.

{21}Faber, M. and Seers, D., (1972), *The Crisis ln Planning*, Vol. I. Edinburgh, Sussex University Press.

{22}Goreux, L,M., Manne A.S. [Eds].,(1973), *Multi-Level Planning Case Studies in Mexico*. Amsterdam, North Holland.

{23}Haar, C.M. [Ed]., (1964), *Law and Land*. Cambridge, Mass, Harvard University Press.

{24}Heaney, J.P., (1968), *Mathematical Proqramming Models for Long Range River Basin Planning with Emphasis on the Colorado River Basin*. Unpublished Ph.D. dissertation, Northwestern University.

{25}Henderson, J.M. and Quandt, R.E., (1958), *Microeconomic Theory*. New York, McGraw-Hill.

{26}Herbert, J.D. and Stevens, B.H., (1960), "A Model for the Distribution of Residential Activit in Urban Areas," *Journal of Regional Science*, Vol. 2, No. 2.

{27}Hildreth, C. and Reiter, S."On the Choice of a Crop Rotation Plan," in {32}.

{28}Jorgensen, D.W., McCall, J.J.and Radner R., (1967), *Optimal Replacement Policy*. Amsterdam, North Holland.

{29}Kendrick, D.A., (1972), "Numerical Models for Urban Planning," *Swedish Journal of Economics*, Vol.74, 1972.

{30}Kendrick, D.A.,(1971), "Mathematical Models for Regional Planning," *Regional and Urban Economics*, Vol. 1, No. 3, 1971.

{31}Kornai, J. "Thoughts on Multi-Level Planning Systems," in {22}.

{32}Koopmans, T.C., (1951), *Activity Analysis of Production and Allocation*, Wiley, 1951.

{33}Koopmans, T.C. "Analysis of Production as an Efficient Combination of Activities," in {32}.

{34}Lane, M.N., (1970), *Goal Programming and Satisficing Models in Economic Analysis*. Unpublished Ph.D. dissertation, University of Texas, Austin, 1970

{35}Lefeber, L. *Allocation in Space*. Amsterdam, North Holland

{36}Littlechild, S.C., (1969), *On Some Applications of Linear Programming in Economics*. Unpublished Ph.D.dissertation, University of Texas, Austin.

{37}Littlechild, S.C., (1970), "Marginal Cost Pricing with Joint Costs," *Economic Journal*, Vol. 80, No. 318, June.

{38}Lynn, W.R., (1963), *Process Design and Financial Planning of Sewage Treatment Works*. Unpublished Ph.D. dissertation, Northwestern University.

{39}Malinvaud, E and Bacharach, M.O.L. [Eds], (1967), *Activity Analysis in the Theory of Growth and Plaaning*. New York, St. Martins Press.

{40}Marshall, A., (1916), *Principles of Economics*. 7th edition, London, Macmillan.

{41}Steiner, H., (1969), *Top Management Planning*. New York, Macmillan.

{42}Stevens, B.H., (1968), "An Interregional Linear Programming Model," *Journal of Regional Science*, Vol. 1.

{43}Takayama, T. and Judge, G.G., (1971), *Spatial ana Temporal Price and Allocation Models*. Amsterdam, North Holland.

{44}Turvey, R., (1969), "Marginal Cost." *Economic Journal*, Vol.17, No. 314, June.

9 Limited liability and corporate control under uncertainty

9.1 Introduction

In a recently published paper Innes focused on incentive effects of limited liability conditions for an enterprise operating under conditions of uncertainty. In his model he assumed given technology and given and continuous and twice differentiable production relations, thus effectively ignoring any kind of discreteness necessarily involved in processes of capacity change, and a fortiori in switching ex post between forthcoming sequences of states of the world. Indeed Innes himself suggested that "the most provocative of the limitations (of his analysis lay) in the entrepreneurial choice of an investment level and an investment policy assumed to be fixed and known by all agents" (Innes (6) p.62).

From one perspective what follows here can be seen as providing straightforward ways of addressing issues pertaining to planning and control under conditions of uncertainty and limited or unlimited liability without the necessity of such restrictive assumptions in the specification of the models used.

More positively, by using the linear/ goal programming specification which is introduced in the following Section, it will be seen that not only can such discreteness issues be directly addressed in the primal problem in essentially new and enlightening ways, but, through the duality properties of that specification, access is gained to investigations of wider issues and potential processes of accounting, finance and control, including those pertaining to limited or unlimited liability and corporate merger, takeover and diversification decisions which are the subject of Sections 3 to 6.

9.2 Extremal representations of optimal production plans

Assume that an intertemporally optimal production and investment/ divestment plan $x^*_{\ell rt}$, $z^*_{\ell srt}$ exists for an enterprise potentially producing a single type of output in amounts x_{rt} over a sequence of forthcoming time - states r_t, where $x^*_{\ell rt}$ is the amount of output to be produced on capacity of type ℓ and $z^*_{\ell srt}$ is the quantity of capacity of type ℓ and age s to be held in time - state r_t. Now consider the following extremal representation:[1]

$$\text{Maximize} \sum_{r_{t+1}} \frac{\theta_{r_t r_{t+1}} p_{r_{t+1}} x_{r_t}}{(1+\rho_{r_t r_{t+1}})} + \sum_{\ell,s,r_{t+1}} \frac{\theta_{r_t r_{t+1}} v_{\ell s+1 r_{t+1}} z_{\ell s r_t}}{(1+\rho_{r_t r_{t+1}})}$$

$$- [\sum_{\ell} c_{\ell r_t} x_{\ell r_t} + \sum_{\ell,s} c_{\ell s r_t} z_{\ell s r_t} + \sum_{\ell} v^+_{\ell r_t} z^+_{\ell r_t} - \sum_{\ell,s} v^-_{\ell s r_t} z^-_{\ell s_t}]$$

$$- M \sum_{\ell} (x^+_{\ell r_t} + x^-_{\ell r_t}) - M_{\ell} \sum_{\ell,s} (\underline{z}^+_{\ell s r_t} + \underline{z}^-_{\ell s r_t})$$

subject to:

$$\varphi_{r_t} \qquad x_{r_t} = \sum_{\ell} x_{\ell r_t} \qquad (2.1)$$

$$\mu_{\ell r_t} \qquad x_{\ell r_t} \leq \sum_{s} q_{\ell s r_t} \qquad (2.2)$$

$$\xi_{\ell s r_t} \qquad z_{\ell s r_t} = z_{\ell s r_t} = z^*_{\ell s-1 r_{t-1}} - z^-_{\ell s r_t} \qquad s \geq 1 \qquad (2.3) \quad (I)$$

$$\xi_{\ell o r_t} \qquad z_{\ell o r_t} = z^+_{\ell r_t} \qquad (2.4)$$

$$\psi_{\ell r_t} \qquad x_{\ell r_t} + x^+_{\ell r_t} - x^-_{\ell r_t} = x^*_{\ell r_t} \qquad (2.5)$$

$$\psi_{\ell s r_t} \qquad \underline{z}_{\ell s r_t} + \underline{z}^+_{\ell s r_t} - \underline{z}^-_{\ell s r_t} = z^*_{\ell s r_t} \qquad (2.6)$$

All variables non-negative

Briefly, the constraints of this system relate total output x_{rt} potential outputs $x_{\ell rt}$ on various types of capacity ℓ (2.1) where, by condition (2.2), the latter magnitudes are constrained by available amounts $z_{\ell srt}$ and age related productivities $q_{\ell s}$ of capacities of type ℓ. Conditions (2.3) and (2.4) respectively equate retained capacity if any, to previously held capacity less relinquishments, and new capacity if any, to previously acquired and installed capacity. Finally, conditions (2.5), (2.6) incorporate elements of the optimal production and investment plan in the form of production and capacity goals $x^*_{\ell rt}$, $z^*_{\ell srt}$ together with potentials ($x^+_{\ell r}$, $x^-_{\ell r}$), ($\underline{z}^+_{\ell sr}$, $\underline{z}^-_{\ell sr}$) for deviations from them.

The objective of the system (I) is to maximize the expected (discounted) returns from anticipated revenue and retained or relinquished capacity *less* the sum of variable costs of production, maintenance costs of retained capacity, acquisition and installation costs of new capacity and preemptively weighted sums of deviations from the optimally determined goal levels $x^*_{\ell rt}$, $z^*_{\ell srt}$.

By inspection a feasible solution *always* exists for this problem. Further, if optimally $x^+_{\ell rt} = 0$, $x^-_{\ell rt} = 0$, $z^+_{\ell srt} = 0$, $z^-_{\ell srt} = 0$, then that optimal solution is consistent with an intertemporally optimal production plan $x^*_{\ell rt}$, $z^*_{\ell srt}$, *and conversely*.

From this a result to the effect that such optimal production plans may be both represented and determined as optimal solutions to appropriately specified goal programming problems is immediate. Going further, according to a definition of a linear programme as one composed from a linear objective and linear constraints it follows that such optimal plans may be both represented and found as optimal solutions to optimally specified linear programmes. More subtly, since these would be more restrictive specifications, such optimal plans are also consistent for example with specifications *as if* identically $z_{\ell sr} = z^*_{\ell srt}$ in (2.2) with the subsequent constraints (2.3)...(2.6) as if omitted as well as all but measures associated with x_{rt}, $x_{\ell rt}$ omitted from the objective.

It is important to notice that equivalences between intertemporally optimal plans and linear and goal programming specification and/or solution procedures here do not rely on any kind of assumption of linearity, or indeed of continuity or differentiability for individual production or pricing or valuation processes. This suggests that, even if attention is confined to a primal specification such as (I), linear and goal programming methods have a much wider theoretical and computational range and power than has yet been generally recognized.

Associating the indicated dual variables with the constraints of (I) yields the following dual relationships :

$$\text{Minimize} \sum_{\ell} \sum_{s} \xi_{\ell sr_t} z^*_{\ell s-1r_{t-1}} + \sum_{\ell} \psi_{\ell r_t} x^*_{\ell r_t} + \sum_{\ell,s} \psi_{\ell sr_t} z^*_{\ell sr_t}$$

subject to:

$$x_{r_t} \qquad \varphi_{r_t} \geqq \sum_{r_{t+1}} \frac{\theta_{r_t r_{t+1}} p_{r_{t+1}}}{(1+\rho_{r_t r_{t+1}})} \qquad (2.7)$$

$$x_{\ell r_t} \qquad \varphi_{r_t} \leqq \mu_{\ell r_t} + c_{\ell r_t} + \psi_{\ell r_t} \qquad (2.8)$$

$$z_{\ell sr_t} \qquad \mu_{\ell r_t} q_{\ell s} \geqq \xi_{\ell sr_t} - \sum_{r_{t+1}} \frac{\theta_{r_t r_{t+1}} v_{\ell s+1r_{t+1}}}{(1+\rho_{r_t r_{t+1}})} + c_{\ell sr_t} + \psi_{\ell sr_t} \qquad (2.9)$$

(II)

$$z_{\ell or_t} \qquad \xi_{\ell or_t} \geqq \sum_{r_{t+1}} \frac{\theta_{r_t r_{t+1}} v_{\ell r_{t+1}}}{(1+\rho_{r_t r_{t+1}})} \qquad (2.10)$$

$$z^+_{\ell r_t} \qquad \xi_{\ell or_t} \leqq v^+_{\ell r_t} \qquad (2.11)$$

$$z^-_{\ell sr_t} \qquad \xi_{\ell sr_t} \geqq v^-_{\ell sr_t} \qquad (2.12)$$

$$x^+_{\ell r_t},\ x^-_{\ell r_t} \qquad -M \leqq \psi_{\ell r_t} \leqq M \qquad (2.13)$$

$$\underline{z}^+_{\ell sr_t},\ \underline{z}^-_{\ell sr_t} \qquad -M \leqq \psi_{\ell sr_t} \leqq M \qquad (2.14)$$

$\mu_{\ell r_t} \geqq 0$. All other variables unrestricted in sign.

First consider the *constraints* of this system. Conditions (2.7) require that output (if any) be produced up to the point where the anticipated price equals production cost at the margin where, by condition (2.8), the cost minimizing set of capacities are used for production, with marginal production cost being constituted from capacity rental $\mu_{\ell rt}$ variable cost $c_{\ell rt}$, together with a goal compliance measure $\psi_{\ell rt}$ condition (2.9), in turn, the marginal capacity costs $\mu_{\ell rt}$ are optimally related to state contingent *changes* in capacity valuations together with maintenance costs and, again, relative goal compliance measures $\psi_{\ell srt}$. By conditions (2.11) and (2.10) new capacity of type ℓ is optimally acquired and installed only if its current valuation would be at least sufficient to recoup acquisition costs and, respectively, to be recouped by discounted anticipated future values. Finally, conditions (2.13) and (2.14) correspond to potential deviations in the primal problem and constrain the goal complaince measures $\psi_{\ell rt}$, $\psi_{\ell srt}$.

The *objective* of the system (II) corresponds to the minimization of the sum of : i) Alternative opportunity-based valuations for the initial physical capital stocks $z^*_{\ell s-1rt-1}$ and ; ii) penalties potentially evaluating deviations, if any, from the production and capacity goals $x^*_{\ell rt}$, $z^*_{\ell srt}$

Notice that, if the latter magnitudes correspond to a production and investment plan which is optimal in the sense that they are both feasible and intertemporally optimal, then the primal programming specification is consistent with feasible and optimal conditions as if identically $x^+_{\ell rt}$ = 0, $x^-_{\ell rt}$ = 0, $z^+_{\ell srt}$ = 0. And the dual programme (II) is apparently consistent with conditions as if feasibly and optimally $\psi_{\ell r}$ = 0, $\psi_{\ell sr}$ = 0 i.e. as if in such relatively completely specified systems the goal compliance measures $\psi_{\ell rt}$, $\psi_{\ell srt}$ associated with an intertemporally optimal plan, together with the goal compliance constraints (2.5), (2.6) appear as if optimally *redundant*.

Such a perspective might immediately suggest interpretations as if the measures $\psi_{\ell rt}$, $\psi_{\ell srt}$ may be explored as if potentially systematically corresponding to measures of relative specification and/ or measurement *determinacy/ certainty*. And from a clearly closely related perspective such relations might suggest wider and essentially more interesting classes of interpretations for these goal complaince measures in relation to relative price and/ or quantity specification and/ or measurement *indeterminacy/ uncertainty*. This point is developed further below.

9.3 Optimal finance and accounting

First, making the (weak) assumption that an optimal production plan is feasible, the equality of the objectives of the dual pair of programmes (I), (I)' accord with ex ante supernormal profit conditions for each time state r_t as follows:

$$v_{r_t} = \sum_{\ell} c_{\ell r_t} x^*_{\ell r_t} + \sum_{\ell s} c_{\ell sr_t} z^*_{\ell sr_t} + \sum_{\ell} v^+_{\ell r_t} z^+_{\ell r_t} - \sum_{\ell s} v^-_{\ell sr_t} z^{-*}_{\ell sr_t} + \xi^*_{\ell sr_t} z^*_{\ell s-1r_{t-1}} \quad (3.1)$$

Variable Inputs | Maintenance Inputs | Acquired Capacity | Relinquished Capacity | Initial Capacity

where the starred values are the optimal values of the variables and

$$v_{r_t} \equiv \sum_{r_{t+1}} \frac{\theta_{r_t r_{t+1}} p_{r_{t+1}} x^*_{r_t}}{1+\rho_{r_t r_{t+1}}} + \sum_{\ell s r_{t+1}} \frac{\theta_{r_t r_{t+1}} v_{\ell s+1 r_{t+1}} z^*_{\ell s r_t}}{(1+\rho_{r_t r_{t+1}})} \quad (3.1a)$$

Anticipated Output Valuation | Anticipated Capacity Valuation

Condition (3.1) shows that, under a regime in which futures markets were complete, the operations of firms could be financed by the exchange of claims to inputs for contingent claims on outputs, or production capacity, with output claims themselves being freely tradeable in such a way that individually optimal contingent consumption and investment plans are secured.

Alternatively, and still assuming a complete set of forward markets, once -and -for -all exchanges may be made at the beginning of the initial period between current input claims and contingently optimal future consumption claims.

Perhaps more interestingly, these relationships are consistent with finance by means of stocks and bonds, whether wholly owned by the managers of the firm or subscribed wholly or in part by outside investors.

With the assumptions of zero transactions costs and complete information, the degree of complexity of transactions intervening between property rights vested initially in inputs and finally exercised as optimally determined claims on future consumption will not affect the consumption outcome. In this sense the three regimes are equivalent.

Because the first two regimes closely identify physical and financial phenomena, they leave no substantive financial or accounting issues and will not be pursued further here. The third regime, however, not only has distinctive and more realistic financial and accounting implications but, when conjoined with limited or unlimited liability and no bankruptcy conditions in the following section, also has the strong qualitative implications that competitive firms will undertake merger takeover and diversi- fication activities on financial grounds. Such activities, while widely observed, would not be necessary under either of the first two regimes.

Assume then, for simplicity, that in each period firms are financed by means of one period shares and bonds in the ratio $1 - \gamma_{r_t} : \gamma_{r_t}$, their sum being both equal in value to (and secured against) the discounted expected value of the firm at the end of the period. Then equation (3.1) can be interpreted to yield an opening balance sheet for period r_t and an income statement contingent on the forthcoming state.

Considering the balance sheet first, the right hand side of the equation represents the assets of the firm at the beginning of period r_t, namely net capacity, variable inputs to production, and maintenance inputs. These together are equal to the firm's liabilities to the stock and bondholders who finance their utilization by the firm. So:

$$B_{r_t} + S_{r_t} = v_{r_t} = \sum_{\ell} c_{\ell r_t} x^*_{\ell r_t} + \sum_{\ell,s} c_{\ell s r_t} z^*_{\ell s r_t} + \sum_{\ell} v^+_{\ell r_t} z^+_{\ell r_t} - \sum_{\ell,s} v^-_{\ell s r_t} z^{-*}_{\ell s r_t} + \sum_{\ell,s} \xi^*_{\ell s r_t} z^*_{\ell s-1 r_{t-1}} \tag{3.2}$$

where
$$B_{r_t} = \gamma_{r_t} V_{r_t} \tag{3.3}$$
$$S_{r_t} = (1-\gamma_{r_t}) V_{r_t} \tag{3.4}$$

Now consider a contingent income statement in stages. Assume that state r_{t+1} is forthcoming at the end of period r_t and *define* $\Delta_{r_{t+1}}$, $\Delta_{\ell s r_{t+1}}$ as follows:

$$\frac{\Delta_{r_{t+1}}}{1+\rho_{r_t r_{t+1}}} = \frac{p_{r_{t+1}}}{1+\rho_{r_t r_{t+1}}} - \sum_{r_{t+1}} \frac{\theta_{r_t r_{t+1}} \, p_{r_{t+1}}}{1+\rho_{r_t r_{t+1}}} \tag{3.5}$$

$$\frac{\Delta_{\ell s r_{t+1}}}{1+\rho_{r_t r_{t+1}}} = \frac{v_{\ell s r_{t+1}}}{1+\rho_{r_t r_{t+1}}} - \sum_{r_{t+1}} \frac{\theta_{r_t r_{t+1}} \, v_{\ell s r_{t+1}}}{1+\rho_{r_t r_{t+1}}} \tag{3.6}$$

These definitions, together with equation (3.1), generate the following relationship:

$$p_{r_{t+1}} x_{r_t} + \sum_{\ell s} v_{\ell s+1 r_{t+1}} z_{\ell s+1 r_t} = \sum_{\ell s}(1+\rho_{r_t r_{t+1}})(c_{\ell r_t} x_{\ell r_t} + c_{\ell s r_t} z_{\ell s r_t})$$

$$+ \sum_{\ell}(1+\rho_{r_t r_{t+1}}) v^{+}_{\ell r_t} z^{+}_{\ell r_t} + (1+\rho_{r_t r_{t+1}}) \sum_{\ell s}(\xi_{\ell s r_t} z_{\ell s-1 r_{t-1}} - v^{-}_{\ell s r_t} z^{-}_{\ell s r_t})$$

$$+ \Delta_{r_{t+1}} x_{r_t} + \sum_{\ell s} \Delta_{\ell s r_{t+1}} z_{\ell s r_t} \quad (3.7)$$

That is, whatever the forthcoming state of the world, the value of sales, if any, and production capacity, if any, at the end of the period is optimally equal to the sum of the state contingent accumulate variable and maintenance costs, capacity acquisition costs, and accumulated opportunity cost of initial capacity net of relinquishments. The final terms in (3.7) are net revenue and net capacity valuation gains/ losses relative to a state contingent rate of return ρ_{rtrt+1}.

Notice that the relevant optimal decision rules will *always* ensure that, together, contingent revenues and asset valuations are exactly sufficient to merit contingent obligations to creditors since :

$$p_{r_{t+1}} x_{r_t} + \sum_{\ell, s} v_{\ell s+1 r_{t+1}} z_{\ell s r_t} = (1+\rho_{r_t r_{t+1}}) v_{r_t} + \Delta_{r_{t+1}} x_{r_t} + \sum_{\ell, s} \Delta_{\ell s r_{t+1}} z_{\ell s r_t} \quad (3.8)$$

$$= (1+\rho_{r_t})\gamma_{r_t} + (1-\gamma_{r_t}) v_{r_t} + (\rho_{r_t r_{t+1}} - \rho_{r_t}\gamma_{r_t}) v_{r_t} + \Delta_{r_{t+1}} x_{r_t} + \sum_{\ell, s} \Delta_{\ell s r_{t+1}} z_{\ell s r_t} \quad (3.9)$$

The first term represents obligations to bondholders, the second is the initial investment by shareholders and the third the contingent return to shareholders over and above their initial investment. The income of the enterprise net of variable inputs, capital appreciation or depreciation and obligations to bondholders can be straightforwardly represented as follows:

$$\pi_{r_{t+1}} = p_{r_{t-1}} x_{r_t} - \sum_{\ell} c_{\ell r_t} - \sum_{\ell s}(v_{\ell s r_t} + c_{\ell s r_t} - v_{\ell s+1 r_{t+1}} z_{\ell s r_t}) - \rho_{r_t}\gamma_{r_t} v_{r_t} \quad (3.10)$$

Observing that, from the constraints of (I)' at an optimum, the final three terms of (3.2) can be represented simply via the expression $\Sigma v_{\ell srt} z_{\ell srt}$ and defining:

$$\bar{v}_{r_{t+1}} = p_{r_{t+1}} x_{r_t} + \sum_{\ell s} v_{\ell s+1 r_{t+1}} z_{\ell s_t} \quad \text{in (3.10)}$$

that equation can be written equivalently as:

$$\pi_{r_{t+1}} = \bar{v}_{r_{t+1}} - v_{r_t} - \rho_{r_t}\gamma_{r_t} v_{r_t} \quad (3.11)$$

or

$$\pi_{r_{t+1}} = (\rho_{r_t} r_{t+1} - \gamma_{r_t} \rho_{r_t}) v_{r_t} + \Delta_{r_{t+1}} x_{r_t} + \sum_{\ell s} \Delta_{\ell s r_{t+1}} z_{\ell s r_t}$$

There is a distinction to be drawn here between the *depreciation* allowances in the income statement and the optimal ex post *amortization* allowances $\mu_{\ell s}(t) q_{\ell s}$. The former simply measure undiscounted differences in realized valuations after allowance for maintenance cost, if any, whereas conditions (2.11) show that the latter also generally include allowances for contingent interest and capital gains or losses.

In principle capacity may optimally appreciate, depreciate or remain constant in value with the passage of time and consequently depreciation allowances may be negative, positive or zero. Indeed in general *negative* values for production capacity may be consistent with the optimality of production plans (for example reflecting substantial closure/ cleanup costs).

It follows that in general the aggregate contingent valuation of the enterprise v_{rt+1} in equation (3.11) may be small compared to the other terms, or even negative, with the consequence that contingent profits may also be negative *whatever the leverage of the enterprise.* (A sufficient condition is that for at least one forthcoming state of the world, v_{rt+1} be negative when v_{rt} is positive.)[3] This being negative it follows that profits and hence (undiscounted) expected returns to shareholders may also be negative. Using equation (3.11) these relationships are:

$$E(\pi_{r_{t+1}}) = E(v_{r_{t+1}}) - v_{r_t} - \rho_{r_t} \gamma_{r_t} v_{r_t} = (1-\gamma_{r_t})\rho'_{r_t} v_{r_t} \qquad (3.12)$$

The expected rate of return to shareholders ρ_{rt}' is thus unrestricted in sign. In particular expected (undiscounted) profits may be negative even when the (aggregate) initial investment is positive.

Before proceeding to develop the implications of negative contingent profits further, it seems worth underlining the point that the preceding developments have no particular implications for risk as measured either by relative rates of return to stock and bondholders or by relative initial capitalized returns. Consider these points in turn.

Especially since the expected rate of return ρ'_{rt} is unrestricted in sign, it is evident that there is nothing in the preceding analysis which guarantees that this rate will exceed a (positive) contingent bond rate ρ_{rt}. More generally conditions which relate these rates of return to valuations stem from (3.12)' as follows :

$$\rho_{r_t} \lesseqgtr \rho'_{r_t} \iff \sum_{r_{t+1}} \frac{\theta_{r_t r_{t+1}} \bar{v}_{r_{t+1}}(\rho_{r_t})}{1+\rho_{r_t r_{t+1}}} \gtreqless 0 \iff (1+\rho_{r_t})v_{r_t} \lesseqgtr E(\bar{v}_{r_{t+1}}) \qquad (3.13)$$

That there is no guarantee that the discounted imputation to stockholders will exceed the value of their initial investment is apparent from the following equation :

$$v_{r_t} = E\,\frac{(1+\rho_{r_t})\gamma_{r_t} v_{r_t}}{(1+\rho_{r_t r_{t+1}})} + (1-\gamma_{r_t})v_{r_t} + E\,\frac{(\rho_{r_t r_{t+1}} - \rho_{r_t})\gamma_{r_t} v_{r_t}}{(1+\rho_{r_t r_{t+1}})} \qquad (3.14)$$

The last term of (3.14) may be interpreted as an ex ante risk premium attributable to stockholders. It is positive, negative or zero according as:

$$\sum_{r_{t+1}} \theta_{r_t r_{t+1}} \frac{(\rho_{r_t r_{t+1}} - \rho_{r_t})\gamma_{r_t} v_{r_t}}{(1+\rho_{r_t r_{t+1}})} \gtreqless 0 \qquad (3.15)$$

Conditions (3.13) clearly do not generally imply conditions (3.14) and vice versa. The expectation of realized "superprofit" $(E(\bar{v}_{rt+1}) - (1+\rho_{rtrt+1})v_{rt})$ may be *positive* when discounted "super-profit" $(E(\rho_{rtrt+1} - \rho_{r_t})v_{rt}\gamma_{rt}/(1+\rho_{rtr+1})$ is *negative* and vice versa,the difference coming about because the former condition (3.13) weights the discount factors by contingent valuations, whereas in the latter condition the same weight is common to each component of the summation.

9.4 Modigliani Miller, partnerships, proprietorships and limited liability

The preceding assumptions and developments are consistent with the well known Modigliani Miller thesis (10) which can be summarized using the present notation, by means of two of their fundamental propositions as follows:

Define $\bar{\rho}$ by:

$$E(\bar{v}_{r_{t+1}}) \equiv \bar{\rho} v_{r_t} = (1+\rho_{r_t})\gamma_{r_t}V_{r_t} + (1+\rho'_{r_t})(1-\gamma_{r_t})v_{r_t} \quad (4.1)$$

Recalling the definitions $B_{rt} \equiv \gamma_{rt}V_{rt}$ and $S_{rt} \equiv (1-\gamma_{rt})V_{rt}$ we have the following propositions:

Proposition I $$\bar{\rho} \equiv \frac{E(\bar{v}_{r_{t+1}})}{v_{r_t}} = \frac{E(\bar{v}_{r_{t+1}})}{B_t + S_t} \quad (4.2)$$

Or, the average cost of capital to the enterprise is independent of its leverage.

Proposition II $$\rho'_{r_t} = \frac{E(\bar{v}_{r_{t+1}}) - \rho_{r_t}D_{r_t}}{S_{r_t}} \quad (4.3)$$

Or, the expected rate of return on shares varies with leverage to support Proposition I.

The seminal implication which was drawn by Modigliani and Miller from these two propositions is that, although the expected rate of return on shares may vary with leverage, the average cost of capital to the firm is independent of its leverage.

The substantive issue here is that although this thesis is consistent with the essentially price taking, full information and zero *ex ante* superprofit assumptions which have thus far been made, it *no longer applies* generally when the additional (and more realistic) assumption is made that enterprises must operate either under conditions of limited liability or conditions of unlimited liability and no bankruptcy.

The following developments show that, while such additional conditions may also be consistent with the preceding "competitive" assumptions, they generally imply: *diversification* by enterprises to secure them *and*; that, once the conditions are secured, in any given period the leverage of any enterprise will generally be bounded above at significantly less than the 100% level, the magnitude of the relevant bound being determined by the market rate of interest on bonds and the lowest potential contingent valuation of the enterprise (and its owners in the unlimited liability case) at the end of the period.

It also follows that, at least in the limited liability case, considerations of managerial risk make it plausible to suppose that in each period the relevant upper bound may be enforced by the capital market, thus determining an *uniquely* optimal leverage for a given production plan and market rate of interest. This is in sharp contrast to the unrestricted domain ($0 \leq \gamma_{rt} \leq 1$) for leverage of the Modigliani Miller thesis.

In brief the salient points of the argument as it applies to limited liability enterprises are as follows.

A limited liability requirement is equivalent inter alia to the condition that in each period the minimal contingent profit (maximum contingent loss) attributable to stockholders is not greater than their initial investment. It implies that the stockholder's liability is restricted to the initial investment and that he/ she cannot then be called upon to subscribe further capital to cover contingent losses. The condition is:

$$-(1-\gamma_{r_t})v_{r_t} \leq \min \pi_{r_{t+1}} = \min_{r_{t+1}} (\bar{v}_{r_{t+1}} - v_{r_t} - \rho_{r_t}\gamma_{r_t}v_{r_t}) \qquad (4.4)$$

Equivalent limited liability conditions are:

$$\min [\rho_{r_t r_{t+1}} v_{r_t} + \Delta_{r_{t+1}} x_{r_t} + \sum_{\ell,s} \Delta_{\ell s r_t} z_{\ell s r_t} - (1+\rho_{r_t})\gamma_{r_t} v_{r_t}] \geq - v_{r_t} \qquad (4.5)$$

And, the one which will be used most in subsequent developments:

$$\gamma_{rt}(1+\rho_{rt})v_{rt} \leq \min \bar{v}_{rt+1} \qquad (4.6)$$

Clearly therefore a limited liability requirement places an upper bound on leverage. Conversely it constrains the firm's choice of optimal plans for each period to that subset of plans for which the limited liability condition can be met whatever the forthcoming state of nature. This is an important point because, as has been seen, in general min $\bar{v}_{rt+1}$ may be negative. In such cases the limited liability requirement has the consequence that firms must *necessarily* diversify their activities by merger, takeover or new operations to meet and sustain it.

Finally, if the limited liability condition is attainable and upper bounds on leverage can be enforced by the capital markets, then, clearly, given the optimal production plan, the leverage of the firm is fixed *uniquely* by the market interest rate on bonds.

To consider more general cases now divide enterprises into two classes namely partnerships/ proprietorships and limited liability companies. Assume that partners and proprietors raise all of their capital either by means of one period fixed interest bonds or from themselves, and that limited liability companies are wholly financed by equity capital and bonds.

In both cases, assume that production plans are required to be selected in such a way that the probability of bankruptcy is zero.

Consider first an unlimited liability enterprise. If γ_{rt} is the proportion of debt financed by means of bonds in period r_t, the conditions of internal finance of risk and no bankruptcy together put the following financial constraints on the production decisions of the firm for the following period:

$$0 \leq \gamma_{r_t}(1+\rho_{r_t})v_{r_t} \leq \min_{r_{t+1}} (\bar{v}_{r_{t+1}} + w_{r_{t+1}}) \qquad (4.7)$$

Where $\bar{v}_{rt+1}$, w_{rt+1} are respectively the (state contingent) values of the firm and of the residual wealth of its proprietors/ partners if state r_{t+1} is forthcoming in period t+1. Without further restrictions, *either or both* $\bar{v}_{rt+1}$ and w_{rt+1} are unrestricted in sign and hence may represent net liabilities.

Conditions (4.7) require that in the event that either quantity is negative the other must be sufficiently positive to ensure that whatever the forthcoming state of the world the bonds can be redeemed and the no bankruptcy condition met. The inclusion of the quantities w_{rt+1} in conditions (4.7) is the unlimited liability feature of partnerships and proprietorships. Given the no bankruptcy condition the liability of the owners extends to encompass their (state contingent) current wealth.

In the case of limited liability enterprises conditions (4.7) specialize to conditions (4.6) viz:

$$0 \leq \gamma_{r_t} (1+\rho_{r_t}) v_{r_t} \leq \min_{r_{t+1}} \bar{v}_{r_{t+1}}$$

Again, $\bar{v}_{rt+1}$ may be (or become) negative in general and hence the limited liability condition may be (or become) an active constraint on,the decisions of the enterprise.

In either the limited or the unlimited liability case the important point is that the leverage, γ_{rt} of the firm is not free to vary in the range $0 \leq \gamma_{rt} < 1$, for the value of γ will generally be bounded above by the relevant one of conditions (4.6), (4.7).

Only exceptionally will these bounds admit a value in the range $1 \geq \gamma_{rt} \geq 1 - \epsilon$. In the limited liability case this would require that $\bar{v}_{rt+1}$ be (almost) invariant with the forthcoming states of world and in the unlimited liability case, the (possibly weaker) conditions is that the sum of the owners' wealth and the realized value of the operations of the firm be (almost) sufficient to redeem their fixed interest obligations again regardless of the forthcoming state of the world.

Note that an unlimited liability enterprise may be able to sustain a higher leverage than a limited liability enterprise having identical capacity and prospects, the reason being that conditions (4.7) imply diversification, with owners' wealth partially invested in the firm and partially elsewhere.

If this state contingent residual wealth was (non-zero and) always sufficiently large, the owners would have the freedom always to fund their enterprise entirely via fixed interest bonds. In this case the interesting point emerges that any net return above bond interest might appear to be supernormal profit, while actually being a pure return to riskbearing (or entrepreneurship).

With reference to the Modigliani-Miller thesis then, in both the limited and the unlimited liability cases the bounds on leverage imposed by conditions (4.6) and (4.7) respectively will generally violate their unrestricted domain production for leverage.

A class of exceptions for the unlimited liability case appears in the preceding paragraph, but this carries with it a strong condition regarding the magnitude and contingent distribution of owners' residual wealth. In the limited liability case (almost) 100% debt would require that in each period the net contingent valuation of the activities of the firm be (almost) independent of the forthcoming state of nature. This, again, is a very strong condition.

Notice, too, that in either the limited or the unlimited liability case, the relevant bounds are determined by the worst potential outcome rather by risk considerations and will generally be independent of risk class as measured, for example, by the expected net return to the enterprise and their variance.

With this in mind it is perhaps not surprising that limited liability status does not itself imply an attitude to risk as measured either by relative rates of return or by current valuation. Limited liability status implies the following conditions:

$$0 \leq (1+\rho_{r_t})\gamma_{r_t} v_{r_t} \leq \min \bar{v}_{r_{t+1}} \leq \min [E(\bar{v}_{r_{t+1}}), (1+\rho_{r_t})v_{r_t}] \quad (4.8)$$

Of the two conditions on the right hand side of (4.8) the first is true by definition and the second by the assumption of perfect capital markets.

I have shown above (p.278) that the relative magnitude of the expected rates of return ρ'_{rt}, ρ_{rt} on risk capital and on bonds respectively are related by the conditions (3.13):

$$\rho_{r_t} \gtreqless \rho'_{r_t} \iff (1+\rho_{r_t})v_{r_t} \lesseqgtr E(\bar{v}_{r_{t+1}})$$

Clearly any of these cases is consistent with the limited liability conditions (4.8).

Similarly the signs of the terms which have been interpreted as ex ante risk premia in conditions (3.14) on p.278 remain unrestricted by conditions (4.8). In general, none of the three sets of conditions imply (or are implied by) any of the others.

Thus far it has been argued only that the leverage of firms, whether subject to limited or to unlimited liability conditions, is bounded above, these bounds being determined with reference to the worst (lowest valued) contingent outcome of the production plan in any period. It seems plausible to suppose, however, that, at least in the limited liability case, *iff this lowest valued outcome were known* to the capital markets, these bounds might be enforced as conditions of the finance of the activities of the firm. The owners of its capital would thereby secure a measure of ex ante control over management decisions, decisions which determine the outcome for *all* contingencies rather than simply the worst.

Expanding on this point, iff the upper bound on leverage is enforced for a given production plan, then:

$$\gamma_{r_t}(1+\rho_{r_t})v_{r_t} = \min_{r_{t+1}} \bar{v}_{r_{t+1}} \qquad (4.9)$$

and, if not, the condition is:

$$\gamma'_{r_t}(1+\rho_{r})v_{r_t} < \min_{r_{t+1}} \bar{v}_{r_{t+1}} \qquad (4.10)$$

Evidently enforcement of the bound controls min $\bar{v}_{rt+1}$ and consequently eliminates managerial discretion with respect to the efficiency with which the *entire* production plan is implemented. One measure of discretion is thus the (positive) difference $(\gamma_{rt} - \gamma'_{rt})$. Reinforcing this, if leverage is set *below* its maximum level the maximum loss which the firm can sustain without violating its limited liability status is *increased* by the (larger) difference $(\gamma_{rt} - \gamma_{rt})v_{rt}$.

If leverage bounds (when attainable) were always enforced then, not only are optimal leverages uniquely determined, but also shareholders' risks are confined to those associated with investments themselves, rather than being also associated with the managers who undertake them.

In the event that min $\bar{v}_{rt+1}$ is negative, limited liability status is *not* sustainable in period r_t and the managers of the enterprise must seek diversification, possibly through merger or takeover, or seek to dissolve the enterprise or be taken over in order that the resulting aggregate will conform to the limited liability condition even if the worst outcome is forthcoming.

In any of these cases they must be prepared to divulge information concerning the full range of their current and proposed operation and prospects both to their own investors and to other managers,and this is an additional incentive to their efficiency.

It has just been argued that in the limited liability case minimum contingent profit controls management discretion if limited liability status is sustainable, and merger and takeover considerations control it otherwise. The form of the goal programming specification (I) itself emphasizes that even in the essentially certainty equivalent and frictionless "competitive" environment on which developments have focused here, behavioural motivations relating to sales of output and acquisitions and sales of capacity must be imputed to managers in adddition to the (efficiency) objective of profit maximization, if they are to independently determine intertemporally optimal production plans.

Combining these two aspects of managerial decisionmaking, a framework emerges in which managers, when distinct from the owners of capital, are recognized as having objective functions whose arguments include sales and capacity variables and in which their decisions are constrained not just by technical and market relationships but by minimum contingent profit and takeover constraints.

Thus this framework, although primarily "competitively" oriented, nevertheless contains within it essential features of a variety of non-competitively oriented behavioural and managerial theories of the firm featuring (potential) management discretion both in the choice of optimal production plans and with respect to the efficiency with which they are implemented all in ways systematically related to one another.

In particular a clear motivation and magnitude is provided for minimum profit and takeover constraints. Sales and capacity objectives for managers are pre-conditions for profit maximization, efficient output and capacity relationships have been determined with reference to commodity and property markets, while minimum profit and takeover constraints have been related directly to capital market considerations through the limited and unlimited liability conditions.[4]

9.5 Diversification, merger and takeover

If the (weak) condition holds that the minimum aggregate contingent valuation of all enterprises in an economy is always positive whatever the forthcoming state of nature, it is easily demonstrated that either limited or unlimited liability status is always attainable by each enterprise, whatever their number. Given this assumption, a sufficient condition for limited liability status for all enterprises is that they be identical and that the following leverage condition be satisfied by each enterprise in each period:

$$0 \leqq \gamma_{r_t} (1+\rho_{r_t}) v_{r_t} \leqq \frac{1}{n_{r_t}} \min_{r_{t+1}} \bar{\bar{v}}_{r_{t+1}} \qquad (5.1)$$

where v_{rt} is the initial value of each of the n_{rt} firms in period r_t and $\bar{\bar{v}}_{rt+1}$ is their contingent aggregate value if state r_{t+1} is forthcoming.

Since the firms are identical by assumption of course $\bar{\bar{v}}_{rt+1} = \Sigma \min \bar{v}_{rt+1}$. The above notation has the advantage however that it emphasizes the point that, given a limited or unlimited liability assumption, aggregate as well as individual leverages will generally be bounded above at significantly less than the 100% level.

A sufficient condition for the attainability of unlimited liability status for all enterprises is again that they be identical, in which case, by assumption, the net realized value of the operation of each (diversified) enterprise will always be non-negative, which is the condition for unlimited liability status.[5]

It follows that a consistent mix of limited and unlimited liability enterprises is also always attainable. A sufficient condition is that the economy be partitioned into two disjoint sets of identical firms, one having limited liability and the other having unlimited liability status.

Apart from serving to demonstrate the attainability of limited and unlimited liability status for all enterprises under "competitive" assumptions, these extreme cases put the central role of diversification, merger and takeover activities into stark perspective.

The assumption that all enterprises are identical implies that the production, investment and (consequent) divestment[6] decisions of each must comprehend the full range of activities in the economy, including, for example, housing activities as well as the introduction of additional products and technologies. It implies that each enterprise must operate spatially in all areas with identical spectra of outputs and capital in each area. It implies further that in each category (Limited or Unlimited Liability) each firm must raise its capital in an identical manner.

This comprehensive identity implies comprehensive *diversity* of operations even for unlimited liability enterprises and, equally significantly, it implies either invariance of the number of enterprises in each category or comprehensive merger or takeover activity to accommodate changes in numbers of enterprises while preserving their identity.

The diversity of the activities of individual enterprises here is based solely on financial considerations.[7] Such diversity is easily comprehended by this analysis since in each period the optimal decision by each enterprise for each type of output may be represented and determined as the unique solution to a preemptive goal programme.

Since such solutions are inherently independent and optimal they would then together constitute an optimal production plan for the enterprise for that period. Although optimal production decisions would be independent, their financial implications would not. This is because, as has just been seen, the limited liability and unlimited liability bounds apply to the worst (lowest contingent valued) outcome for the enterprise as a whole and will thereby generally constrain its activities.

In the cases considered so far, enterprises have been identical and lowest contingent valuations have been non-negative by assumption. While the assumption of identical enterprises is unduly strong (and quite unrealistic) both in itself and in its implications, this assumption together with the non-negativity assumption has been shown to be sufficient to ensure conformity with the limited and unlimited liability conditions. For such cases negative minimum net contingent valuations for some types of output and associated elements of capacity are necessarily more than offset by positive valuations for the remainder.

As a move in the direction of realism now consider the other extreme case by making the assumption that individual enterprises are confined to at most one type and age of production capacity and its associated output (if any). The main consequence is that the limited and unlimited liability conditions become much stronger. With complete information such a structure is sustainable if the minimum contingent net valuation of each enterprise is never such as to violate the relevant one of the condition (4.6), (4.7) viz:

$$\gamma_{r_t}(1+\rho_{r_t})v_{r_t} \leq \min_{r_{t+1}} \bar{v}_{r_{t+1}}$$

$$\gamma_{r_t}(1+\rho_{r_t})v_{r_t} \leq \min_{r_{t+1}} (\bar{v}_{r_t} + w_{r_{t+1}})$$

In the limited liability case such conditions preclude investment by the enterprise in any type of capacity whose net contingent valuation may become negative. The non-negative minimum contingent valuation condition requires that the probability of total loss and net closure costs always be zero. It thereby prohibits investment by such specialized limited liability enterprises in capacity for which the probability of fire or other natural (?) disaster is positive, however small, and for which the associated contingent loss of assets and loss through claims to third parties and closure costs would violate the limited liability conditions. (Contemporary examples might be some classes of oil tanker loss and consequent damage).

As a further class of example the limited liability condition would also prohibit the existence of limited liability enterprises for which the forthcoming sequence of states of the world could become such that the realized magnitudes of actual and potential revenues from sales of output and valuations for elements of capacity would dictate the closure and sale of the enterprise, at a net loss, as a contingently optimal course of action. Such cases might include innovations failing ex post for market reasons whether macro or microeconomic in character).

Although, given complete and free information, enterprises could *insure* against violation of their limited or unlimited liability status, in the limited liability case, (even putting to one side consideration of moral hazard), such insurance would here violate the (temporary) working assumption that firms specialize through the ownership and management of a single type of production capacity. Insurance itself implies diversification both for the insurer and for the insured.

In the unlimited liability case a measure of *self* insurance is provided by the contingent wealth in conditions (4.7). It has already been seen that, as long as a weak aggregate non-negative minimum net contingent valuation condition holds, unlimited liability status can be assured through comprehensive diversification of investment by the owners of unlimited liability enterprises.

Such diversification remains possible here but, if it is attained, as above, by the fragmentation of ownership of unlimited liability companies, then to the extent that ownership is fragmented, the real distinctions between ownership and management is vitiated.

In practice a de facto distinction between owners, managers and investors (sleeping partners) would be likely to emerge and, unless the total number of partners in the enterprise was small, problems of internal accountability and control would be likely to become such that public accountability and limited liability status would be sought.

If, for control reasons, the number of partners is small, the unlimited liability condition may become an active constraint on the *scale*as well as the nature of the operation of the firm. These operations are in any case restricted to those for which the partners (or the proprietor) can both provide risk capital and ensure that their maximum contingent losses are always at least offset by their collective contingent residual wealth.

It has just been seen that this residual wealth may be invested in other unlimited liability enterprises but that considerations of control are in practice likely to preclude widely diffused investment, and consequent diversification by this means. Alternatively, residual wealth may be invested in limited liability enterprises via holdings of stocks or bonds but, again, as long as the number of owners is restricted, the nature and scale both of the enterprise itself and of this diversified investment is likely to become actively constrained by the unlimited liability condition (4.7).

In summary, assuming throughout that minimum contingent valuations are positive for the economy as a whole, if firms are identical, then either limited liability or unlimited liability status can be assured for all enterprises. But this implies comprehensive diversification and either comprehensive merger and takeover activity or invariance of the number of diversified enterprises in each period.

If, on the other hand, firms are required to specialize in a single type of production capacity and if, in the unlimited liability case, the number of partners in each is restricted by accountability and control considerations, then real restrictions are placed on the nature and scale of risks which may be undertaken by either type of enterprise. Also, given the specialization assumption, limited liability enterprises would be prohibited from owning and controlling capacity for which the lowest valued contingent outcome was negative and, in consequence, such capacity must necessarily be controlled by unlimited liability enterprises.

But the scale of unlimited liability enterprises, and hence of their undertaking of such risks, is constrained by the magnitude of the contingent wealth of their owners. Underlining this, when the specialization assumption applies, because net negative valuations are inconsistent with limited liability status, a limited liability company would necessarily relinquish its limited liability status and not simply its assets (in this case strictly its liabilities) in any period for which the set of potentially forthcoming states of the world include a state for which the contingent valuation of the enterprise would become negative.

This is a much stronger requirement than one pertaining only to states which are actually forthcoming. It prohibits limited liability enterprises from continuing to claim limited liability status when the worst potential forthcoming state would violate it, however small the probability of that state being forthcoming.

If the specialization assumption does not apply, then, such an enterprise could ensure continuous conformity to a limited liability condition by comprehensive merger, takeover and innovative activity (assuming that in the first two cases this is met with the consent of the other parties to the transaction and in any case with the consent of the suppliers of capital to the firm).

The important point here is that with the identity assumption, merger, takeover and diversification activities would be pandemic. With the specialization assumption, pressures towards such activities are implicit in the actual and potential existence of negative contingent valuations on the limited liability case, and in the wealth constraints and issues of control in the unlimited liability case.

In practice *either* of these sets of extreme conditions is unrealistically strong. One would generally expect (and does in practice observe) that an economy would be partitioned into changing sets of variously diversified and undiversified limited and unlimited liability enterprises (including government enterprises).

But such a mixed structure, too, is consistent with the essential arguments of the preceding analysis for, given the (weak) assumption that the minimum contingent valuation of enterprises in the aggregate is always non-negative, it will always be possible to partition the economy in this way, with firms always being able to secure conformity with the relevant one of the limited and unlimited liability conditions (4.6) and (4.7) respectively through appropriate merger, takeover and diversification activities and/or through transitions from limited to unlimited liability status, or conversely.

9.6 Some implications for theory and policy

The observation which concludes the preceding Section has a number of qualitative implications both with reference to enterprises at a given point in time and for the processes whereby they evolve through their life cycles as distinct corporate entities.

First, within this extended "competitive" regime, the managers of enterprises, whether or not they manage efficiently, must generally be aware of (and sometime necessarily engage in) merger, takeover and diversification activities, not only in order to ensure the limited or unlimited liability status of their own enterprise, but also as partners, or potential partners, to such activities by other firms. That is, such activities, whether actual or potential, constitute an integral part of the function even of efficient managers in this environment.

A second and closely related implication of this analysis is that the prominent role of merger, takeover and diversification activities implies the necessity for a current contingent valuation basis, both for accounting and for takeover purposes, common to *all* enterprises, rather than bases specific to particular firms or industries. In this context also, at least in the limited liability case, it seems desireable that the nature and magnitude of the worst potentially forthcoming prospect for an enterprise be required to be indicated in its Report in addition to information concerning more favourable prospects, since it is this (potential) event which ultimately governs the leverage of the enterprise.8

A third implication is that, under this extended "competitive" regime, broad classes of mergers, takeovers and other diversification activities have an essentially *co-ordinating* function. They may be undertaken to attain and sustain the limited or unlimited liability status of enterprises while at the same time being consistent with competitive conditions. Insofar as such a competitive regime is identified with the public interest, these activities may promote the public interest rather than conflict with it.

Hence in such an environment whenever antitrust legislation was applied to prevent such co-ordinating mergers, its application would itself be contrary to the public interest because it would then inhibit (or prevent) developments potentially associated with net negative contingent returns as their worst outcome.

In practice high risk developments are often undertaken, or at least in part underwritten, by the state, and backed by its resources. This remark serves to indicate a fourth and related implication for policy.

State activities are generally diversified in the aggregate but (at least in the British case), numbers of state enterprises have nevertheless been operated as statutory monopolies, or near monopolies, enjoined to adopt self sustaining policies (e.g. railways gas supply, electricity generation and supply).

It is well known that monopoly status confers powers which may be employed *against* the public interest as construed by government - this is one reason for bringing such enterprises within the public sector and for regulating those outside it. It is less obvious that the status of single product monopoly (statutory or otherwise), if legally required, also prevents diversifying merger, takeover or innovation activities which may *promote* the public interest.

Intra industry examples are the diversification by railways into other types of transportation or by energy industries into new and risky types of fuel technology. Such a requirement also prevents inter-industry diversification by such enterprises as one means of insuring against cyclical and other sources of variation in profitability. New and risky developments may be inhibited or prevented in consequence for, whereas in a diversified company large profits would be consolidated with losses, at least in the British case, such consolidation, as well as the common financial accounting and valuation, procedures which would necessarily underlie it, are both conspicuously absent.

It is emphatically not being argued here that monopoly, merger, and restrictive practices legislation and regulation necessarily operate contrary to the public interest.

One contribution of the present analysis is, however, the provision of a broader (analytical) foundation within which such activities may conform to the public interest and may then be both allowed and encouraged in the public interest. At least in the British case this has, of course, been the emphasis of legislation. Generally the onus has been placed by legislation on the relevant party (or parties) to demonstrate that their past or proposed future actions at least do not harm the public interest, but judgements in favour of mergers, etc., sit uneasily with a more conventional competitive analysis.

While for purposes of comparison with established literatures, the analysis here has retained the strong (competitive) assumptions that commodity and property markets as well as capital markets are competitive, and consequently act as controls on efficiency, latterly limited or unlimited liability conditions have also been explored and this is the extended "competitive" background against which monopoly mergers and takeovers and diversification activities which may promote the public interest have been analysed. Incidentally, these analyses allow the possibility that enterprises be monopolies as long as this term is interpreted narrowly to mean that an enterprise is the sole actual producer of an economic commodity and that here the property market serves as control among other things by ensuring free entry conditions.

If a proposed merger does conform to the public interest, then given these qualifications concerning competitive efficiency, the absolute sizes of enterprises both before and after any proposed merger are immaterial to the public interest, while their relative sizes and consequent relative contributions to minimum contingent returns may be crucial to their compatibility for mergers.

This is a fifth implication. Under competitive conditions firm size *per se* is a matter of social indifference, while relative size may not be so. Large firms may become larger and more or less diversified in their activities, or may be required to be broken up in order to ensure compatible mergers which promote the public interest.As an extreme case an enterprise may be able to grow by means of a sequence of compatible mergers and takeovers to the point where it controls the whole economy but, as has been seen, even this circumstance is not generally in conflict with competitive assumptions or with limited or unlimited liability requirements. The production economy would simply be moved from a more or less decentralized regime to a centralized one, assuming that at each stage, the other party (or parties) to mergers and takeovers acceded to them.

This potential for growth by some enterprises within such a modified competitive environment reinforces the links between this analysis and *behavioural* theories of the firm for it is consistent with explicit growth objectives for managers as long as these are consistent with the competitive conditions just cited.

Notice finally that a maximum leverage requirement is only one type of control on enterprises. As an extension, if, for example, a specific leverage requirement e.g. 50%, is a condition of the finance of the proposed activities of firms by the capital markets, then if it is attainable for the economy this requirement may itself promote merger takeover, innovation or other diversification activities at a greater level than would be necessitated by the simple limited or unlimited liability conditions, in order that it be sustained. The arguments closely parallel those given above and do not require elaboration.

Also of course, leverage controls constitute only one type of control which can be placed on the activities of enterprises by the capital markets. Indeed the preceding analysis, arguments and implications for diversification, could be extended generally to comprehend various kinds of agency and/or industrial policy related incentive and efficiency issues such as those considered respectively by Innes {6} and Ricketts {11} in separate contexts, or Littlechild {9} in a wider industrial policy context. More particularly they could be extended to comprehend the examination of other types of control including, for example, prospective dividend conditions as reflected by constraints on the variability of contingent profits.

An examination of other criteria focusing on distinctions between short and long term obligations and prospects (e.g. the current assets to current liabilities "acid test" ratio) would necessitate extensions of the analysis to comprehend multiperiod shares and bonds, thereby relaxing the simplifying assumption that financial capital is committed and redeemed on a period to period basis and introducing associated distinctions between distributed and retained earnings.[9]

Footnotes

1. For an introduction to goal programming in various contexts see {2} and {3} as well as earlier chapters in this book.

2. Leverage may be zero in which case, of course, interest expenses are also zero. For simplicity taxes are assumed to be zero.

3. Recall here that optimal contingent output (and hence sales revenue) may be zero. If profits are positive they may or may not be distributed as dividends to shareholders. The retention policies of firms with respect to profits will not concern us here. The focus here will be on the complementary case in which profits are (or may become) negative when, without further restrictions, riskbearers may be called upon to subscribe additional capital over and above their original investment to cover such contingent losses.

4. Consider comparisons and contrasts between the present essentially "competitive" analysis and non-competitive models stemming from the work of Cyert and March {5}, Simon {14} and others. Links between the present analysis and this behavioural and managerial literature can be developed in various ways. First, and as a prerequisite for such comparisons it has been argued that the objective functions of managers even in such "competitive" environments must comprehend other variables in addition to profit including at least sales and capacity variables. Second, the minimum profit conditions which are here specified by limited and unlimited liability requirements appear isomorphic with those essential to most behavioural analyses, but without their determinants being spelt out in detail. These analyses include O.E. Williamson's well known discretionary models {16} in which managers pursue non-profit maximizing objectives subject to a minimum profit condition dictated, in principle, by-takeover considerations. Minimum profit constraints determined, in principle, by shareholders play a prominent role in Baumol's well known (static) sales maximization model {1} and, again with reference to takeover considerations in J.Williamson's profit growth and sales maximization models {15}. Thirdly technical efficiency, which I have here assumed (as do the three preceding authors) is enforced in this analysis by the conjunctive operation of competitive commodity and property markets. And, too, through the enforcement by the capital markets of maximum leverage conditions and so of the associated minimum profit conditions and fortiori managerial and labour efficiency is enforced. Without these latter conditions, even if property and commodity markets were competitive, X-inefficiency, in the sense of Leibenstein {7}, {8} would be possible as long as capital was committed in advance of output and bankruptcy was permissable. Here the policing measures (in the sense of Crew, Jones-Lee and Rowley {4}) necessary to secure efficiency are included via the limited liability with maximum leverage and the unlimited liability cum no bankruptcy conditions respectively with dynamic accommodations via mergers, takeovers and other diversification measures being one means of securing these conditions. Finally, and significantly, recall that although the qualitative analyses here require the assumption of full information the search and solution procedure associated here with preemptive goal programming is applicable to the imperfect information case and indeed, following Simon, to satisticing approach of various kinds.

5. In a closed economy the aggregate contingent value of enterprises equals aggregate contingent income from sales output plus the contingent value of the capital of the enterprises. This observation underlines the mildness of the non-negativity assumption for $\overline{v}_{rt+1}$. At the same time it indicates a relationship between the microeconomic analysis which is the focus of this chapter and macroeconomic analysis.

6. In order that *any* enterprise increase *any* type of capacity at least one enterprise must logically decrease (sell or transfer) existing capacity for conversion. This is true a fortiori when such capacity has been acquired or retained in anticipation of such a (contingent) conversion.

7. This is because "competitive" conditions have been assumed and, for simplicity, no joint production on elements of production capacity.

8. Note that even failing such an indication, a limited liability enterprise whose minimum contingent valuation (net of it obligations to its bondholders) was negative would seek merger takeover, or diversification by other means, in advance of the possible realization of such a negative outcome in order to ensure its status, thus itself signalling the potential of such a negative outcome.

9. 100% distribution was espoused by Rubner {12} as one means of controlling the discretion of managers with respect to retained earnings. The working assumption of one period bonds and shares is equivalent to this in its implication when combined with the limited liability or unlimited liability cum no bankruptcy conditions.

References

{1} Baumol W.J.,(1959), *Business Behaviour, Value and Growth*, Macmillan, New York.

{2} Charnes,A. and W.W. Cooper, (1961), *Management Models and Industrial Applications of Linear Programming*, 2 volumes, Wiley, New York.

{3} Charnes, A.,R.W. Clower and K.O.Kortanek, (1967), *Effective Control Through Coherent Decentralization with Preemptive Goals*, Econometrica, 35, pp.294-320.

{4} Crew M.A., M.W.Jones-Lee and C.K.Rowley, (1971), *X-Theory vs. Management Discretion Theory*, Southern Economic Journal, 38, pp.173-184.

{5} Cyert R.M. and J.G.March, (1963), *A Behavioural Theory of the Firm*, Prentice Hall, Englewood Cliffs.

{6} Innes R.D., (1990),*Limited Liability and Incentive Contracting with Ex Ante Action Choices*, Journal of Economic Theory, 52, pp.45-68.

{7} Leibenstein H., (1966), *Allocative Efficiency versus X-Efficiency*, American Economic Review, 56, pp.392-415.

{8} Leibenstein H., (1979), *The Missing Link' - Micro-Micro Theory?* Journal of Economic Literature, 17, pp.477-502.

{9} Littlechild S.C., (1978), *The Fallacy of the Mixed Economy*, Hobart Paper 80, Institute of Economic Affairs, London.

{10}Modigliani F.and M.H.Miller, (1958), *The Cost of Capital, Corporation Finance and the Theory of Investment'*, American Economic Review, 48, pp.261-297.

{11}Ricketts M., (1987), *The Economics of Business Enterprise*, Wheatsheaf Press,London.

{12}Rubner A., (1965), *The Ensnared Shareholder*, Penguin, London.

{13}Ryan M.J., (1978), *Qualitative Interpretations of Urban Phenomena* Journal of Regional Science, 78, pp.383-395.

{14}Simon H.A., (1960), *The New Science of Management Decision*, Harper and Row, New York.

{15}Williamson J., (1966), *Profit, Growth and Sales Maximization*, Economica, 33, pp.1-16.

{16}Williamson O.E., (1964), *The Economics of Discretionary Behaviour: Managerial Objectives in a Theory of the Firm*, Prentice Hall, Englewood Cliffs.

10 Non-renewable resources, inflation and uncertainty

10.1 Introduction

The central result here is that whereas,given positive time preference, in a deterministic framework non-renewable resource price inflation might seem not just economically inevitable but arguably socially desireable, in relatively uncertain economic environments neither of these conditions necessarily applies.

The central inflationary results are not in themselves surprising. Similar results have been established for certainty cases using a deterministic framework and a continuous calculus by a variety of authors including Hotelling's pioneering work {4} and, more recently, Swallow {5} and Aarestad {1}. Other authors have considered extensions to uncertainty cases.For example Fishelson {3} in a recent paper considers an extension of the Hotelling model in which all of its parameters may be liable to random variations, with the result that under conditions of risk neutrality for mine owning firms, not only do precautionary motives apply to raw materials (as in Arrow and Chang's model {2}), but to all other parameters.But again these models employ a continuous calculus.

With the context of this non-renewable resource literature a distinctive feature of the present analyses and results is their emphasis on discontinuities,including those associated with the establishment and change of elements of extractive capacity,necessarily associated with principles and processes of change over time,both under conditions of certainty and *a fortiori* under conditions of uncertainty.

More generally, the form of the models which are employed here generalizes those used in the previous chapter by incorporating explicit non-renewable resource availability conditions. So it can be seen as directly linked to all of the preceding developments pertaining to individually and socially optimal choices of allocations and distributions of economic commodities in space, as well as over time.

10.2 A deterministic model

Consider first a deterministic model of an enterprise in an extractive industry which produces output x(t) in amounts $x_\ell(t)$ on various types of capacity ℓ, so that:

$$x(t) = \sum_\ell x_\ell(t) \tag{1.1}$$

where output of type ℓ may be produced on any or all of various ages of capacity specific to that output, or:

$$x_\ell(t) \leq \sum_s q_{\ell s} z_{\ell s}(t) \tag{1.2}$$

Here $q_{\ell s}$ is the potential productivity of capacity of type ℓ and age s.

Now recognize that capacity may be acquired or relinquished in any period. Conditions determining availability of acquired and/or converted capacity of type ℓ for period t are:

$$z_{\ell o}(t) = z_\ell^+(t) \tag{1.3}$$

and for the ages s of retained capacity of type ℓ in period t:

$$z_{\ell s}(t) = z_{\ell s-1}(t-1) - z_{\ell s}^-(t) \qquad s \geq 1 \tag{1.4}$$

Assuming, for simplicity, that each element of output requires a single unit of the non-renewable resource under consideration, if $x^\sim(T)$ is the non-renewable resource available at the beginning of the planning interval T, then:

$$\sum_{\ell,t} x_\ell(t) = \tilde{x}(T) \tag{1.5}$$

Notice immediately that, unless the planning interval is very long, (in which case the non-renewability of most kinds of "non- renewable" resources would come into question) this constraint would not in practice be the applicable one since, in general, it would not be either socially or economically optimal to exhaust all available endowments over that interval.Nor in general would future-oriented opportunity costs associated with such potential depletions be independent of quantities currently used - and thus effectively denied to the future.

Recognizing both of these points, the condition (1.5) can be extended to incorporate them by means of piecewise linear social regret relations such as are indicated schematically in Figure 1 as follows:

$$\sum_\ell x_\ell(t) = \tilde{x}(t)$$

Total non-renewable resource demand over the planning interval $\sum \tilde{x}(t)$ is supplied from the various available price ranges k, or:

$$\sum_t \tilde{x}(t) \leq \sum_k \tilde{x}_k(T) \tag{1.6}$$

where

$$\tilde{x}_o(T) + \tilde{\tilde{x}}_o(T) = R_o(T) \qquad (1.7)_o$$

$$\tilde{x}_k(T) + \tilde{\tilde{x}}_k(T) = R_k(T) \qquad k \geq 1 \qquad (1.7)_k$$

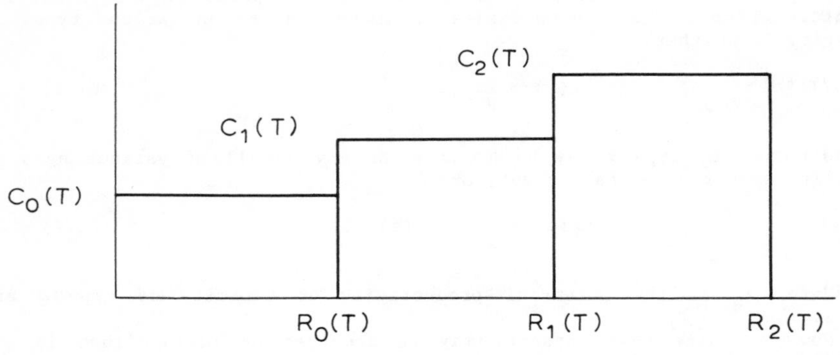

Figure 10.1

Here the magnitudes $c_k(T)$ correspond to potentially increasing opportunity costs associated with potentially increasing quantities which would be denied to relatively future periods by use in a period t.

Assuming now that the objective of the enterprise is to maximize a measure of social gain associated with any particular production, investment and resource utilization plan while, at the same time, minimizing social opportunity costs imputed to that plan, the overall problem for a particular planning interval can be represented as a multi period goal programming problem as follows (compare the model in Chapter 9 on p.273 above)

$$\text{Maximize} \sum_{\ell st} \frac{1}{(1+\rho)} \left[\frac{p(t+1)}{(1+\rho)} x(t) - c_\ell(t)x_\ell(t) - c_{\ell s}(t)z_{\ell s}(t) - v_\ell^+(t)z_\ell^+(t) + v_{\ell s}^- z_{\ell s}^-(t) \right]$$

$$+ \sum_{\ell s} \frac{1}{(1+\rho)^{T+1}} \left[v_{\ell s}(T+1)z_{\ell s}(T) + \sum_k \tilde{c}_k(T)\tilde{x}_k(T) \right]$$

$$- \sum_{\ell} \left[c_\ell^+ \underline{x}_\ell^+(t) + c_\ell^- \underline{x}_\ell^-(t) \right] - \sum_{\ell s} \left[c_{\ell s}^+(t)\underline{z}_{\ell s}^+(t) + c_{\ell s}^-(t)\underline{z}_{\ell s}^-(t) \right]$$

subject to:

$\theta(t)/(1+\rho)^t$ $\qquad x(t) = \sum_\ell x_\ell(t)$ (1.1)

$\mu_\ell(t)/(1+\rho)^t$ $\qquad x_\ell(t) \leq \sum_s q_{\ell_s} z_{\ell_s}(t)$ (1.2)

$\xi_{\ell_o}(t)/(1+\rho)t$ $\qquad z_{\ell_o}(t) = z_{\ell_{s-1}}(t-1) - z_{\ell_s}^-(t)$ (1.3)

$$\xi_{\ell_s}(t)/(1+\rho)^t \qquad z_{\ell_s}(t) = z_{\ell_{s-1}}(t-1) - z_{\ell_s}^-(t) \qquad (1.4)$$

$$\xi_{\ell_s}(0) \qquad z_{\ell_s}(-1) = z_{\ell_s}^*(-1) \qquad (1.4)'$$

$$\lambda(t)/(1+\rho)^t \qquad \sum_{\ell} x_{\ell}(t) = \tilde{x}(t) \qquad (1.5)' \qquad \text{(I)}$$

$$-\gamma(T) \qquad \sum_{t} \tilde{x}(t) \leq \sum_{k} \tilde{x}_k(T) \qquad (1.6)$$

$$\gamma_o(T) \qquad \tilde{x}_o(T) + \tilde{\tilde{x}}(T) = R_o(T) \qquad (1.7)_o$$

$$\gamma_k(T) \qquad \tilde{x}_k(T) + \tilde{\tilde{x}}_k(T) = R_k(T) \quad k \geq 1 \qquad (1.7)_k$$

$$\psi_{\ell}(t) \qquad x_{\ell}(t) + \underline{x}_{\ell}^+(t) - \underline{x}_{\ell}^-(t) = x_{\ell}^*(t) \qquad (1.8)$$

$$\psi_{\ell_s}(t) \qquad z_{\ell_s}(t) + \underline{z}_{\ell_s}^+(t) - \underline{z}_{\ell_s}^-(t) = z_{\ell_s}^*(t) \qquad (1.9)$$

All variables non-negative

Here physical production and investment/ disinvestment targets are represented respectively by the magnitudes $x_{\ell}^*(t)$ and $z_{\ell s}^*(t)$, with the non-negative quantities ($\underline{x}_{\ell s}^+(t)$, $\underline{x}_{\ell s}^-(t)$),($\underline{z}_{\ell s}^+(t)$, $\underline{z}_{\ell s}^-(t)$) being associated with potential deviations from these targets in the objective function.The remaining terms in the objective function have straightforward interpretations as follows: The first terms correspond to the discounted value of anticipated revenues to output. The second terms measure variable input costs of production and the third measure aniticipated maintenance costs of elements of production capacity. The next two terms respectively measure costs and returns associated with acquisitions and relinquishments of elements of capacity. These are followed by terms representing (discounted) horizon values for elements of capacity, quantity-dependent opportunity costs of non-renewable resources and, finally, the terms potentially imputing penalties to deviations from output and capacity goals.

Notice that, in principle, *any* intertemporally attainable production and investment/ disinvestment plan for such an enterprise might be both represented and found by means of such a goal programming formulation.In that sense any consideration of duality properties and dually related optimal decision rules is arguably redundant.But, whether or not they are explicitly acknowledged, such properties and decision rules are implicit in the structure of this programme and, if made explicit, can be used to generate enlightening information and interpretations which here include not just privately (corporately) intertemporally optimal production, investment and non-renewable resource-related decision rules, but also potentially include related, yet distinct,*socially* intertemporally optimal production, investment and non-renewable resource utilization rules.

To see these latter points associate the indicated dual variables with the constraints of the system (I) and use linear dependence arguments to generate its dual as follows:

$$\text{Minimize} \sum_{\ell s t} \xi_{\ell_s}(o) z_{\ell_s}(-1)^* + \sum_k \gamma_k(T) R_k(T) + \sum_\ell \psi_\ell(t) x_\ell^*(t) + \sum_\ell \psi_{\ell_s}(t) z_{\ell_s}^*(t)$$

subject to:

$$x(t)/(1+\rho)^t \qquad \theta(t) \geq \frac{p(t+1)}{1+\rho} \qquad (1.10)$$

$$x_\ell(t)/(1+\rho)^t \qquad \theta(t) \leq c_\ell(t) + \mu_\ell(t) + \lambda(t) + \psi_\ell(t) \qquad (1.11)$$

$$z_{\ell_s}(t)/(1+\rho)^t \qquad \mu_\ell(t) q_{\ell_s} \leq \xi_{\ell_s}(t) - \frac{\xi_{\ell_{s+1}}(t+1)}{(1+\rho)} - c_{\ell_s}(t) + \psi_{\ell_s}(t) \qquad (1.12)$$

$$z^-_{\ell_s}(t)/(1+\rho)^t \qquad \xi_{\ell_s}(t) \geq v_{\ell_s}(t) \qquad (1.13)$$

$$z_\ell^+(t)/(1+\rho)^t \qquad \xi_{\ell_o}(t) \leq v_\ell^+(t) \qquad (1.14)$$

$$z_{\ell_o}(t)/(1+\rho)^t \qquad \xi_{\ell_o}(t) \geq \frac{\xi_{\ell_1}(t+1)}{(1+\rho)} \qquad (1.15)$$

$$\tilde{x}(T) \qquad \frac{\lambda(t)}{(1+\rho)} \leq \gamma(T) \qquad (1.16)$$

(I)'

$$\tilde{x}_k(T) \qquad \gamma(T) + \gamma_k(T) \leq 0 \qquad (1.17)$$

$$\tilde{\tilde{x}}k(T) \qquad \gamma_k(T) \geq -c_k(T) \qquad (1.18)$$

$$\underline{x}_\ell^+(t),\ \underline{x}_\ell^-(t) \qquad -c_\ell^-(t) \leq \psi_\ell(t) \leq c_\ell^+(t) \qquad (1.19)$$

$$z_{\ell_s}^+(t),\ z_\ell^-(t) \qquad -c_{\ell_s}^-(t) \leq \psi_{\ell_s}(t) \leq c_{\ell_s}^+(t) \qquad (1.20)$$

It will be helpful to consider two kinds of solutions to (I)' by first considering special cases for which all goals are not only potentially attainable (i.e. feasible) solutions to that system, but are optimally attained via that system before considering more generally applicable classes of cases for which such conditions are not appropriate.

In the first class of cases conditions would obtain as if *optimally* $\underline{x}_\ell^+(t) = 0$ and $\underline{x}_\ell^-(t) = 0$ all ℓ, t if optimally $\underline{z}_\ell^+(t)$, $\underline{z}_\ell^-(t) = 0$ all ℓ,s,t in (I), and thence as if optimally then associated goal compliance measures $\psi_\ell(t)$, $\psi_{\ell s}$ (t) and the final two sets of inequalities (1.19), (1.20) were all redundant in the dually related system (I)'. In those circumstances the remaining conditions of that system would take on interpretations at the optimum of kinds which will be familiar to those familiar with private "competitive" market-based competitive models. In particular, in such circumstances the enterprise would produce in period t, if at all, then only up to the point where, via (1.10), the marginal supply cost would be recovered by the (anticipated) revenues with marginal supply cost being made up of a variable component $c_\ell(t)$, an optimally determined extraction and processing capacity component $\mu_\ell(t)$, and an optimally determined non- renewable raw material component $\lambda(t)$ as in (1.11).

In turn in any period t: i) each optimal capacity cost (rental) element

$\mu_\ell(t)$ is related to capital productivities $q_{\ell s}$ and capital appreciations/ depreciations net of maintenance costs $c_{\ell s}(t)$, via conditions (1.12), where inter alia values of retained capacity are not less than alternative market values (by condition (1.13)) and values of newly acquired and installed capacities optimally reflect anticipated internal opportunities and/or external market values (by conditions (1.14) and (1.15)). Also, according to conditions (1.16), non-renewable resources would optimally remain unused in period t *unless* the present value of returns to them were sufficient to recoup their opportunity costs $\gamma(T)$ where, via conditions (1.17) and (1.18) these latter magnitudes would reflect the marginal opportunity costs of such non-renewable resources at the beginning of the planning interval.

Notice that two related implications also follow from conditions (1.16). First non-renewable resources would be used in any given period t only if returns $\lambda(t)$ at the margin were sufficient to recoup *accumulated* opportunity costs $\gamma_t(1+\rho)^t$ at that margin. From this follows a second implication namely that, under the conditions considered thus far, the magnitudes $\lambda(t)$, interpreted as non-renewable resource prices, will optimally increase at the rate of inflation from period to period over the interval during which such resources are optimally retained, and that, in general, that optimally determined interval may lie inside the planning horizon.(Sufficient conditions for this are that, throughout some interval, T-r,...T, $\lambda(t) = 0$ all t).

But cases for which the goal compliance constraints and associated goal compliance measures $(\underline{x}_\ell^+(t), \underline{x}_\ell^-(t)), \underline{z}_{\ell s}{}^+(t), \underline{z}_{\ell s}{}^-(t))$ are as if optimally redundant correspond only to one particular class of solutions to the systems (I), (I)'.As might be expected from developments in Chapter 8 these models can also admit more general cases which in principle can embed such potential private market cases in wider social and regulatory frameworks according to interpretations as if measures $\psi_\ell(t)$, $\psi_{\ell s}(t)$ associated with potential conditions would potentially correspond to elements of socially determined regulatory taxes, subsidies and laws.

For example, with such a perspective, conditions (1.11) might now be interpreted as if potentially corresponding to optimal rules according to which production is undertaken in period t only if, at the margin, supply price is sufficient to recoup production costs where the latter is now made up not just of variable capacity and non-renewable resource cost components, but also of a goal compliance measures $\psi_\ell(t)$ with conditions as if optimally $\psi_\ell(t) = -c_\ell(t)$ corresponding to conditions of underproduction relative to a target and consequent relative subsidy, and conditions as if optimally $\psi_\ell(t) = c_\ell^+(t)$ corresponding to conditions of overproduction relative to a target, and consequent relative taxes.Similar remarks and associated social extensions and potential relative tax/ subsidy implications derive, too, from the measures $\psi_{\ell s}(t)$in the conditions (1.12) and (1.20).

In each case the forms of these various conditions and interpretations will also suggest extensions to the models themselves, for example to include multi-level regulatory structures, or goals relating to an overall level of output x(t) (rather than only to outputs $x_\ell(t)$ via particular processes ℓ as in (I), (I)').

More directly in the present context of non-renewable resource pricing, the form of relations in (I), (I)' will suggest extensions to include single or multi-level goals and associated regulatory structures relating to levels of utilization x(t) of non-renewable resources. From such extensions it would immediately follow among other things that even in deterministic cases non-renewable resource prices would *not* in general optimally increase at the rate of interest over time .... .

Rather than pursue these kinds of extension further within a deterministic framework, I now want to proceed in a different direction to pursue implications of uncertainty for intertemporally optimally determined non-renewable resource prices and utilization rates.

10.3 Extensions to uncertainty cases

Using an obvious notation the system (I) on p.294 can be extended to comprehend uncertainty for two period cases as follows (multi period extensions are also straightforward and would only introduce more complexity of notation):

$$\text{Maximize} \sum_{\ell st} \frac{\theta_{r_t r_{t+1}} p_r(t+1) x_r(t)}{1+\rho_{r_t r_{t+1}}} - \sum_{\ell} c_{\ell_r}(t) x_{\ell_r}(t) - \sum_{\ell s} c_{\ell s_r}(t) z_{\ell s_r}(t)$$

$$- \sum_{\ell s} v_{\ell_r}{}^{+}(t) z_{\ell}{}_r^{+}(t) - \sum_{\ell s} v_{\ell s_r^-}(t) z_{\ell s_r^-}(t) \;)$$

$$+ \sum_{\ell sr} \theta_{r_t r_{t+1}} \left[\frac{v_{\ell s+1r}(t+1) z_{\ell sr}(t)}{1+\rho_{r_t r_{t+1}}} + \tilde{c}_{kr}(t) \tilde{x}_{kr}(\tilde{t}) \right]$$

$$- \sum_{\ell r} [c_{\ell_r}{}^{+}(t) x_{\ell_r}{}^{+}(t) + c_{\ell_r}{}^{-}(t) x_{\ell_r}{}^{-}(t) \;]$$

$$- \sum_{\ell sr} [c_{\ell s_r}{}^{+}(t) z_{\ell s_r}{}^{+}(t) + c_{\ell s_r^-}(t) z_{\ell s_r}{}^{-}(t)]$$

subject to:

$\theta_1(t)$	$x_r(t) = \sum x_{\ell_r}(t)$	(2.1)	
$\mu_r(t)$	$x_{\ell r}(t) \leq q_{\ell s} z_{\ell r}(t)$	(2.2)	
$\xi_{\ell or}(t)$	$z_{\ell or}(t) = z_{\ell s}{}^{+}(t)$	(2.3)	(II)
$\xi_{\ell sr}(t)$	$z_{\ell s_r}(t) = z_{\ell s-1r}{}^{*}(t-1) - z_{\ell s_r}{}^{-}(t) \quad s \geq 1$	(2.4)	
$\lambda_r(t)$	$\sum_{\ell} x_{\ell r}(t) = \tilde{x}_r(t)$	(2.5)	
$-\gamma_r(t)$	$\tilde{x}_r(t) \leq \sum_k \tilde{x}_{kr}(t)$	(2.6)	
$\gamma_{kr}(t)$	$\tilde{x}_{kr}(t) + \tilde{\tilde{x}}_{kr}(t) = R_{kr}(t)$	(2.7)	
$\psi_{\ell r}(t)$	$x_{\ell r}(t) + x_{\ell r}{}^{+}(t) - x_{\ell r}{}^{-}(t) = x_{\ell r}{}^{*}(t)$	(2.8)	
$\psi_{\ell sr}(t)$	$z_{\ell s_r}(t) + z_{\ell s_r}{}^{+}(t) - z_{\ell s_r^-}(t) = z_{\ell s_r^*}(t)$	(2.9)	

All variables non-negative

The structure of this system is the same as that of (I) except that, by contrast with (I), the coefficients of the future oriented output price and production capacity valuation measures correspond to expected (state contingent) price and valuation measures respectively.Now associate the indicated dual variables with the system (II) and use linear dependence arguments to generate a system (II)' as follows:

$$\text{Minimize } \sum_{\ell sr} \xi_{\ell s_r}(t) z_{\ell s-1r}(t-1) + \sum_{\ell r} \psi_{\ell r}(t) x_{\ell r}{}^*(t) + \sum_{\ell sr} \psi_{\ell s_r}(t) z_{\ell s_r}{}^*(t) + \sum_{kr} \gamma_{kr}(t) R_{kr}(t)$$

subject to:

$x_r(t)$
$$\theta_1(t) \geqq \sum_{r_{t+1}} \frac{\theta_{r_t r_{t+1}} p_r(t+1)}{1+\rho_{r_t r_{t+1}}} \tag{2.10}$$

$x_{\ell r}(t)$
$$\theta_r(t) \leqq \mu_{\ell r}(t) + c_{\ell r}(t) + \lambda_r(t) + \psi_{\ell r}(t) \tag{2.11}$$

$z_{\ell s_r}(t)$
$$\mu_{\ell r}(t) q_{\ell s} \geqq \xi_{\ell s_r}(t) - \sum_{r_{t+1}} \frac{\theta_{r_t r_{t=1}} v_{\ell s+1r}(t+1)}{1+\rho_{r_t r_{t+1}}} + c_{\ell s_r}(t) + \psi_{\ell s_r}(t) \tag{2.12}$$

$z_{\ell s_r}{}^-(t)$
$$\xi_{\ell s_r}{}^-(t) \leqq v_{\ell s_r}(t) \tag{2.13}$$

$z_{\ell r}{}^+(t)$
$$\xi_{\ell o_r}(t) \geqq v_{\ell r}{}^+(t) \tag{2.14}$$

$z_{\ell o_r}(t)$
$$\xi_{\ell o_r}(t) \geqq \sum_{r_{t+1}} \frac{\theta_{r_t r_{t+1}} v_{\ell 1r}(t+1)}{1+\rho_{r_t r_{t+1}}} \tag{2.15}$$

$\tilde{x}_r(t)$
$$\lambda_r(t) \geqq \gamma_r(t) \tag{2.16}$$

(II)'

$\tilde{x}_{kr}(t)$
$$\gamma_r(t) + \gamma_{kr}(t) \leqq 0 \tag{2.17}$$

$\tilde{\tilde{x}}_{kr}(t)$
$$\gamma_{kr}(t) \geqq - \sum_{r_{t+1}} \frac{\theta_{r_t \tilde{r}_{t+1}} c_{kr}(t+1)}{1+\rho_{r_t r_{t+1}}} \tag{2.18}$$

$x_{\ell r}{}^+(t)$, $x_{\ell r}{}^-(t)$
$$-c_{\ell r}{}^-(t) \leqq \psi_{\ell r}(t) \leqq c_{\ell r}{}^+(t) \tag{2.19}$$

$z_{\ell sr}{}^+(t)$, $z_{\ell sr}{}^-(t)$
$$-c_{\ell s_r}^-(t) \leqq \psi_{\ell s_r}(t) \leqq c_{\ell s_r}^+(t) \tag{2.20}$$

By contrast with interpretations relating to (I)', relations of (II)' generate not just contingently optimal ex ante production,investment and disinvestment, pricing, valuation and accounting rules, but distinctively different ex post rules. In particular,in these contingently uncertain cases, ex post, relative profits or losses will accrue to realized translations to otherwise relatively uncertain outcomes.

To see this in more detail first consider ex ante cases as follows. From (2.10) and complementary slackness, if at an optimum $x_r(t) > 0$, then:

$$x_r(t) > 0 \Rightarrow \theta_r(t) = \sum_{r_{t+1}} \frac{\theta_{r_t r_{t+1}} p_r(t+1)}{1+\rho_{r_t r_{t+1}}}$$

Or, optimally produce positive amounts of output in time-state r_t only if the anticipated (discounted) price equates to marginal supply costs $\theta r(t)$. This in turn relates to an opportunity cost minimizing set of capacities Q in period t since $x_r(t) > 0$ implies $x_{\ell r}(t) > 0$ for some ℓ and, from conditions (2.11) and complementary slackness:

$$x_{\ell r}(t) > 0 \Rightarrow \theta_r(t) = \mu_{\ell r}(t) + c_{\ell r}(t) + \lambda_r(t) + \psi_{\ell r}(t)$$

This condition yields the ex ante rule: Optimally use capacity of type ℓ, if at all, then only up to the point where marginal capacity, variable input, raw material and control costs will be recovered.

Notice now that: i) if optimally $x_{\ell r}(t) > 0$ then optimally $z_{\ell sr}(t) > 0$ for some ages s of capacity of type ℓ, so that condition (2.12) optimally holds with equality for some ℓ, s, and that; ii) if optimally $x_r(t) > 0$ then non-renewable resources supplied $\tilde{x}_r(t)$ are optimally positive so that, at an optimum, condition (2.16) will hold with equality as well as conditions (2.17), (2.18) for some k. Together with (2.10) these conditions imply the following more comprehensive *ex ante* marginal income-expenditure conditions:

$$\sum_{r_{t+1}} \frac{\theta_{r_t r_{t+1}} p_r(t+1)}{1+\rho_{r_t r_{t+1}}} = \frac{1}{q_{\ell s}} [\xi_{\ell s_r}(t) - \sum_{r_{t+1}} \frac{\theta_{r_t r_{t+1}} v_{\ell s+1 r}(t+1)}{1+\rho_{r_t r_{t+1}}}] \qquad (2.12)$$

$$+ c_{\ell s_r}(t) + \psi_{\ell s_r}(t)\ ) - c_{\ell r}(t) + \sum_{r_{t+1}} \frac{\theta_{r_t r_{t+1}} \tilde{c}_{kr}(t+1)}{1+\rho_{r_t r_{t+1}}} + \psi_{\ell r}(t)$$

According to these conditions output is optimally scheduled to be positive in time-state r(t) only if for the optimally determined set of types and ages of capacity anticipated discounted marginal resources will be sufficient to recoup anticipated contingent capacity costs (including maintenance and depreciation costs), variable production costs, raw material costs and output and capacity related goal compliance costs.

Clearly the relations (2.12)' can suggest optimal *ex post* as well as optimal *ex ante* rules. Such ex post interpretations would be qualitatively different insofar as they would involve distinct and essentially state contingent elements of relative gain/ loss due to realized differences between anticipated and realized output prices, anticipated and realized capital valuations and, more interestingly in the present context, realized differences between anticipated and realized resource prices.

To make these distinctions explicit now consider translations/ transformations as follows (see also Chapter 9, p.276):

$$\frac{p_r(t+1)}{1+\rho_{r_t r_{t+1}}} = \sum_{r_{t+1}} \frac{\theta_{r_t r_{t+1}} p_r(t+1)}{1+\rho_{r_t r_{t+1}}} + \frac{\Delta_r(t+1)}{1+\rho_{r_t r_{t+1}}} \qquad (2.21)$$

$$\frac{v_{\ell s_r}(t+1}{1+\rho_{r_t r_{t+1}}} = \sum_{r_{t+1}} \frac{\theta_{r_t r_{t+1}} v_{\ell s_r}(t+1)}{1+\rho_{r_t r_{t+1}}} + \frac{\Delta_{\ell s_r}(t+1)}{1+\rho_{r_t r_{t+1}}} \qquad (2.22)$$

$$\frac{\tilde{c}_{k_r}(t+1)}{1+\rho_{r_t r_{t+1}}} = \sum_{r_{t+1}} \frac{\theta_{rtrt+1} \tilde{c}_{k_r}(t+1)}{1+\rho_{r_t r_{t+1}}} + \frac{\Delta_{k_r}(t+1)}{1+\rho_{r_t r_{t+1}}} \qquad (2.23)$$

Substituting these relations into (2.12)' yields:

$$\frac{p_r(t+1)}{1+\rho_{r_t r_{t+1}}} = \frac{1}{q_{\ell s}} \left(\xi_{\ell s}(t) - \frac{v_{\ell s+1r}(t+1)}{1+\rho_{r_t r_{t+1}}}\right) + c_{\ell s}(t) + \psi_{\ell s}(t)$$

$$+ c_{\ell r}(t) + \frac{c_{kr}(t+1)}{1+\rho_{r_t r_{t+1}}} + \psi_{\ell r}(t) + \frac{\Delta_r(t+1)}{1+\rho_{r_t r_{t+1}}} + \frac{\Delta_{\ell sr}(t+1)}{1+\rho_{r_t r_{t+1}}}$$

$$+ \frac{\Delta_{kr}(t+1)}{1+\rho_{r_t r_{t+1}}} \qquad (2.12)''$$

And this relation provides optimal ex post decision rules as follows : For any future time-state r(t+1) subsequent to a present time-state r(t) set the price of outputs such that they recoup the sum of: i) accumulated state contingent and productivity related capital amortization and maintenance costs net of goal compliance measures $\psi_{\ell sr}(t)$ if any, *plus* : ii) accumulated (and again state contingent) working capital costs of variable inputs and raw materials, again net of goal compliance measures $\psi_{\ell r}(t)$, if any, *plus*; iii) the net magnitude of realized and state contingent measures of, respectively, price related, capital related and resource opportunity cost related gains/ losses $\Delta_r(t+1)$, $\Delta_{\ell sr}(t+1)$, $\Delta_{kr}(t+1)$...

Each of these latter measures may be positive, negative or zero in magnitude. In principle, therefore, their net total may amount to a net positive, negative or zero return over and above accumulated imputations to factors at a rate equivalent to their cost in period r(t) plus a state contingent rate of return ρ_{rtrt+1}

Notice, too, that there is not any principle here according to which one kind of relative uncertainty/ indeterminacy induced gain or loss may offset or be offset by another, or others.That said, the condition (2.12)'' is consistent with outcomes according to which for example state contingent output price and/ or capital gains to production capacity may reflect realized resource cost increases. More subtly, according to conditions (2.10) of (II)', output price $p_r(t+1)$ might increase, decrease or remain constant relative to current opportunity costs $\theta_r(t)$, though there is a bias here, as elsewhere, to relative price *increases* via the measure $(1+\rho_{rtrt+1})$. Thus, while in particular cases,*axiomatically* inflationary[1] produced output price increases in (II), (II)' appear consistent with prior raw material price increases, they are also (contingently) consistent with previously relatively reduced, or unchanged, raw material prices.

Further, while in the essentially deterministic systems (I), (I)', via conditions (1.10), (1.18), apparently output and raw material prices *optimally increase* over opportunity cost $\theta_r(t)$ and over raw material prices $c_k(T)$ respectively, in the arguably empirically more realistic and relatively indeterminate systems (II), (II)',via conditions (2.10), (2.15), apparently output and raw material prices do *not* necessarily increase over prior production costs and raw material costs. A fortiori, while in (I), (I)' essentially inflationary raw material and output prices may appear to be arguably logically correlated, in the relatively indeterminate systems (II), (II)' output price increases do *not* necessarily connote prior raw material cost increases, and vice versa.

10.4 Summary and conclusions

In this final chapter I have focussed directly on topical issues pertaining to intertemporally optimal resource utilization policies and results to the effect that, while in conditions of certainty, intertemporally optimal resource utilization policies will generally imply intertemporally optimal price inflation policies, in more realistic and plausible conditions of relative uncertainty, intertemporally optimal resource utilization policies may or may not imply, or be implied by, output and non-renewable resource price inflation.

It has been shown, too, that in uncertain cases optimal resource utilization policies will imply the generation of ex post magnitudes $\Delta_r(t+1)$, $\Delta_{\ell sr}(t+1)$, $\Delta_{kr}(t+1)$ connoting relative gains or losses to relatively unanticipated output price changes, production capacity valuations and optimally determined non-renewable resource prices respectively. These various measures have been introduced in such a way that direct contact can be made with related issues and developments pertaining to corporate finance and accounting in general, and to partnerships, proprietorships and limited liability in contexts of potentially financially induced mergers, takeovers and/ or bankruptcies in Chapter 9.

More directly, a focus here on non-renewable resource pricing and depletion policies and potentially associated production technologies all in goal programming frameworks of analysis, has been used to broaden developments in the preceding chapter to comprehend taxes, subsidies, and other regulatory issues and instruments by means of appropriately broadened definitions of the measures associated with potential deviations from social production, investment and resource utilization goals.

Finally, and more technically, it is possible to use elements of the analysis in this Chapter to show that in general, other things being equal, relative as well as absolute increases in raw material prices are consistent with efficient raw material utilization. This point recognizes that, even though raw material prices *may* optimally increase with time - and would necessarily do so in certainty cases with positive time preference - prices of outputs and/ or other inputs to production will not necessarily do so. For example, if capacity of type ℓ is optimally not fully utilized in any given period t its rental $\mu_{\ell r}(t)$ will optimally fall to zero in conditions (2.11), (2.12). Or, it follows from conditions (2.11)...(2.15) that elements of capacity will be retained for optimally determined *intervals* according to which ex ante (discounted) expected rentals, terminal values and/ or sales of relinquished capacity are sufficient to recoup anticipated conversion, maintenance and capacity-related goal compliance costs, and according to which, ex post, elements of capacity are retained only as long as internal evaluations $\xi_{\ell sr}(t)$ equal or exceed externally related opportunity values $v_{\ell s}(t)$. Or, going further, conditions (2.10)...(2.15) are together consistent with optimal decision rules according to which elements of capacity may be optimally augmented optimally augmented or displaced, e.g. by capacity of relatively higher productivity $q_{\ell s}$ and/ or relatively lower maintenance cost $c_{\ell s}(t)$ only if: i) that other type of capacity is optimally to be used for production with costs $\mu_{\ell r}(t) + c_{\ell r}(t) + \lambda_r(t) + \psi_{\ell r}(t)$ potentially equal to or lower than the lowest currently attainable and/ or, if: ii) the discounted sum of expected rentals and terminal values is sufficient to recoup its initial acquisition and conversion cost and its anticipated maintenance cost over an optimally determined retention interval .... .

Footnote

1. With a single produced output, as here, if one output price increases, all output prices increase.

References

{1} Aarestad, J.,(1990) *Simultaneous Use of Renewable and Non-Renewable Natural Resources*, Resources and Energy 12, pp.253-262.

{2} Arrow, K.J. and Chang, S. (1982), *Optimal Pricing, Use and Exploration of Uncertain Natural Resource Stocks*, Journal of Environmental Economics and Management 9, pp.1-10.

{3} Fishelson, G. (1990), *The Hotelling Model Under Uncertainty: A Note*, Resources and Energy 12, pp.353-359.

{4} Hotelling, H. (1931), *The Economics of Exhaustible Resources*, Journal of Political Economy 39, pp.137-175.

{5} Swallow, S.K. (1990), *Depletion of the Environmental Basis for Renewable and Non-Renewable Resources*, Journal of Environmental Economics and Management 19, pp.281-296.